Islamic Thought in China

Islamic Thought in China
Sino-Muslim Intellectual Evolution
from the 17th to the 21st Century

Edited by Jonathan Lipman

EDINBURGH
University Press

We dedicate this book to the memory of
Elisabeth Allès (1953–2012)
Scholar, colleague, activist, friend

Edinburgh University Press is one of the leading university presses in the UK. We publish academic books and journals in our selected subject areas across the humanities and social sciences, combining cutting-edge scholarship with high editorial and production values to produce academic works of lasting importance. For more information visit our website: www.edinburghuniversitypress.com

© editorial matter and organisation Jonathan Lipman, 2016
© the chapters their several authors, 2016

Edinburgh University Press Ltd
The Tun – Holyrood Road
12 (2f) Jackson's Entry
Edinburgh EH8 8PJ

Typeset in 11/15 Adobe Garamond by
Servis Filmsetting Ltd, Stockport, Cheshire

A CIP record for this book is available from the British Library

ISBN 978 1 4744 0227 9 (hardback)
ISBN 978 1 4744 0228 6 (webready PDF)
ISBN 978 1 4744 1493 7 (epub)

The right of the contributors to be identified as authors of this work has been asserted in accordance with the Copyright, Designs and Patents Act 1988 and the Copyright and Related Rights Regulations 2003 (SI No. 2498).

Contents

Glossary of East Asian Names	vii
Glossary of East Asian Terms	xi
List of the Contributors	xix
Editor's Introduction: Four Centuries of Islamic Thought in Chinese *Jonathan Lipman*	1

PART I   THE QING EMPIRE (1636–1912)

1. A Proper Place for God: Ma Zhu's Chinese Islamic
   Cosmogenesis   15
   Jonathan Lipman

2. Liu Zhi: The Great Integrator of Chinese Islamic Thought   34
   James D. Frankel

3. *Tianfang Sanzijing*: Exchanges and Changes in China's
   Reception of Islamic Law   55
   Roberta Tontini

4. The Multiple Meanings of Pilgrimage in Sino-Islamic Thought   81
   Kristian Petersen

PART II MODERN CHINA

5. Ethnicity or Religion? Republican-Era Chinese Debates on Islam and Muslims 107
Wlodzimierz Cieciura

6. Selective Learning from the Middle East: The Case of Sino-Muslim Students at al-Azhar University 147
Yufeng Mao

7. Secularisation and Modernisation of Islam in China: Educational Reform, Japanese Occupation and the Disappearance of Persian Learning 171
Masumi Matsumoto

8. Between 'Abd al-Wahhab and Liu Zhi: Chinese Muslim Intellectuals at the Turn of the Twenty-first Century 197
Leila Chérif-Chebbi

Bibliography 233

Index 260

Glossary of East Asian Names

Bai Shouyi 白壽彝
Bao Tingliang 保廷樑
Cai Dayu 蔡大愚
Chen Guangyuan 陳廣元
Chen Keli 陳克禮
Chen Si 陳思
Da Pusheng 達浦生
Ding Baochen 丁寶臣
Ding Shiren 丁士仁
Ding Zhuyuan 丁竹園
Du Wenxiu 杜文秀
Fei Xiaotong 費孝通
Feng Zenglie 馮增烈
Ha Decheng 哈德成
Hai Weiliang 海維諒
Han Haichao 韓海朝
He Yaozu 賀耀祖
Hong Lu 洪爐
Hu Dengzhou 胡登洲
Hu Fangquan 胡枋權
Hu Songshan 虎嵩山

Huang Wanjun 黃万均
Huang Zhenpan 黃鎮磐
Jiang Jieshi (Chiang Kai-shek) 蔣介石
Jin Diangui 金殿桂
Jin Jitang 金吉堂
Jing Rizhen 景日眕
Kang Youxi 康有璽
Kawamura Kyōdō 川村狂堂
Li Xizhen 李希真
Li Zhenzhong 李振中
Liang Qichao 梁啓超
Liang Yijun 梁以浚
Lin Changxing 林昌興
Lin Song 林松
Lin Xinghua 林興華
Lin Zhongming 林仲明
Liu Mengyang 劉孟揚
Liu Sanjie 劉三杰
Liu Zhi 劉智
Lu Jiuyuan (Xiangshan) 陸九淵 (象山)
Lu You 鹿祐
Ma Anli 馬安禮
Ma Anliang 馬安良
Ma Dexin (Fuchu) 馬德新 (復初)
Ma Enxin 馬恩信
Ma Fuxiang 馬福祥
Ma Jian 馬堅
Ma Lianyuan 馬聯元
Ma Linyi 馬鄰翼
Ma Mingliang 馬明良
Ma Qiang 馬強
Ma Qixi 馬啟西
Ma Songting 馬松亭
Ma Tong 馬通
Ma Wanfu 馬萬福

Ma Xian 馬賢
Ma Xingzhou 馬興周
Ma Xiulan 馬秀蘭
Ma Yuming (pseud. Xiao Ma A-ge) 馬玉明 (小馬 阿哥)
Ma Zhixin (Baha Ahong) 馬志信
Ma Zhu 馬注
Min Shengguang 敏生光
Na Zhong 納忠
Pang Shiqian 龐士謙
Qi Xueyi 祁學義
Sai Dianchi (Sayyid Ajall Shams al-Din) 賽典赤
Sakuma Teijirō 佐久間貞次郎
Sha Shanyu (Shouyu) 沙善余 (守愚)
Shan Guoqing 山國慶
Shi Zizhou 時子周
Shou Jin 壽金
Sun Yat-sen (Sun Yixian, Sun Zhongshan) 孫逸仙，孫中山
Tanaka Ippei 田中逸平
Tang Yichen 唐易塵
Tong Jili 童基立
Wang Daiyu 王岱輿
Wang Enrong 王恩榮
Wang Jingzhai 王靜齋
Wang Jixian 王繼賢
Wang Kuan 王寬
Wang Mengyang 王夢揚
Wang Ruilan 王瑞蘭
Wang Shiming 王世明
Wang Yingqi 王英麒
Wang Yousan 王友三
Wu Sangui 吳三桂
Wu Zixian 伍子先
Wuhuaguo (pseud.) 無花果
Xu Yuanzheng 徐元正
Xue Wenbo 薛文波

Yang Du 楊度
Yang Feilu 楊斐菉
Yang Huaizhong 楊懷中
Yang Sishi 仰思室
Yin Boqing 尹伯清
Yu Ke 愚克
Yu Zhengui 余振貴
Yuan Guozuo 袁國做
Yuan Ruqi 袁汝琦
Yuan Shikai 袁世凱
Zhang Bingduo 張秉鐸
Zhang Chengqian 張承遷
Zhang Weizhen 張維真
Zhang Zai 張載
Zhao Zhongqi 趙鍾奇
Zhou Dunyi 周敦頤
Zhou Lianggong 周亮工

Glossary of East Asian Terms

ahong 阿訇 or 阿洪, Muslim cleric, from Per. *akhūnd*
ahong zaixian 阿訇在線, online *ahong*s
Ajiashugisha アジア主義者, Japanese Pan-Asianists
bai 拜, worship, Ar. *salāt*
baihua 白話, vernacular Chinese
Beijing Huijiao Hui 北京回教會, Islamic Association of Beijing
Beiping Huimin Gonghui 北平回民公會, Beiping Muslims Association
Beiping Yisilan Xueyouhui 北平伊斯蘭學友會, Beiping Islamic Students Association
benran 本然, Root Suchness
benti 本體, original substance
bentuhua 本土化, indigenisation
bu 部, the 'cultural spheres' of the Qing empire
buzhengguo, zhengjiao 不爭國、爭教, defend Islamic belief (lit., 'do not contend over the state, rather contend over religion')
chaojin 朝規, pilgrimage, Ar. *hajj*
Chaojin tuji 朝覲途記, *Record of the Pilgrimage Journey*, Ma Dexin
Cheng-Zhu lixue 程朱理學, orthodox Neo-Confucianism
Chengda Shifan Xuexiao 成達師範學校, Chengda Normal School
chuan 傳, a tradition
chuanyi 穿衣, 'don the cloak', to be ordained as an *ahong*

ci'en 慈恩, mercy
dan 石, a dry measure for grain, sometimes called 'picul' or 'bushel' and officially equivalent to 60 kg
dao 道, the Way, also 'universal law', Ch. translation of Ar. *sharī'a*
dao da quan 道大全, the *dao* was fully revealed
daocheng 道乘, vehicle of the Way, Ch. translation of *ṭarīqa*
daotong 道統, filiative transmission of the Way
daoxue 道學, study of the Way, in some contexts meaning Persian studies
daxian 大賢, great worthy
diting 帝庭, divine court
enci 恩慈, bestowal
erlin 爾林, Ch. transliteration of Ar. *'ālim*, scholar or cleric
fa 法, human jurisprudence, Ch. translation of Ar. *fiqh*
fan Jing yi su 反經異俗, 'opposing the *Qur'ān* and diverging from correct customs'
fangmin 坊民, mosque congregations
fengsu xiguan 風俗習慣, customs and habits
ge 合, a dry measure for grain, 1/10 of a *sheng*
gedimu 格底目, from Ar. *qadīm*, 'the old way' or 'tradition', indicating the mosque-centred non-Sufi communities of Chinese Muslims
gewu 格物, investigation of things
gong 功, meritorious acts
Gongguo ge 功過格, ledgers of merits and demerits
Guerbang 古而邦, Ch. transliteration of Ar. *Qurbān*
Guomindang 國民黨, the Guomindang/Kuomintang (GMD), the Nationalist Party
Han kitāb 漢克塔布, seventeenth–nineteenth-century Islamic translations and writings in classical Chinese
hange Musilin 罕戈穆斯林, sincere Muslims, from Ar. *ḥaqq*, 'true'
hanhua 漢化, Hanification, sinification/sinicisation
Hanxuepai 漢學派, 'the Han learning solidarity', indicating the Xidaotang
Hanzu 漢族, 'the Han *minzu*', the Han Chinese
hege de Musilin 合格的穆斯林, sincere Muslims (see *hange Musilin*, above)
houren 後人, later generations
huang 皇, the August One (God)

Huihe 回紇 or *Huihu* 回鶻, originally 'Uyghurs', later became *Huihui* 回回 and referred to Sino-Muslims
Huijiang 回疆, the Muslim frontier, Xinjiang
Huijiao 回教, Islam (lit., 'the Hui teaching')
Huijiao minzu guojia 回教民族國家, countries of the Muslim 'nation' (*minzu*)
Huilong Gongsi (J. *Kairyū Konsu*) 回隆公司, the Huilong Company
Huimin 回民, Hui people, Muslims
Huiru 回儒, Muslim Confucians
Huizu 回族, 'the Hui nationality', the officially approved ethnic term for Sino-Muslims, post-1950s
Huizu Qingnian 回族青年, *Huizu Youth*, a journal published by Xue Wenbo
Huizu Yanjiu 回族研究, *Journal of Hui Muslim [Huizu] Minority Studies*, published in Ningxia
Huizuhui 回族會, the Huizu Association
hukou 户口, household registration
hunhe paibie 混合派別, 'mixed factions'
jiangjing 講經, 'discussing/disputing the Scriptures'
jiaopai 教派, a religious group or faction
jidacheng 集大成, 'assembles great achievement'
jie 戒, fasting, Ar. ṣawm, or prohibitions
jiejing 解經, 'explaining the Scriptures'
jiliesheng zhi dacheng 集列聖至大成, 'the great culmination of all the sages'
jingtang jiaoyu 經堂教育, mosque (lit. 'scripture hall') education
jinshi 進士, the highest degree in the civil service examination system
jiyale 擠呀勒, visitation, Ch. transliteration of Ar. *ziyāra*
ju 聚, gathering together, Ar. *hajj*
kaozheng 考證, Confucian textual studies movement
ke'erbai 克而白, Ch. transliteration of Ka'aba
kewen 客問, question and answer (literary format)
Laifuming 來復銘, a 1528 Islamic stone inscription from Shandong
laojiao 老教, Old Teaching, originally referring to *Gedimu* but later including many other types of Islamic solidarity

laopai bu lao, xinpai bu xin 老派不老新派不新, 'old faction no longer old, new faction no longer new', factions are mingled, 'traditional' and 'modern' change

laorenjia 老人家, Sufi master (lit., 'venerable one')

laoshi 老師, teacher

li 理, principle or pattern

li 禮, ritual, propriety, etiquette

licheng 理乘, vehicle of principle, Ch. translation of *sharīʿa*

Lifa Qi'ai 禮法啟愛, *Opening Love for Ritual and Law*, Ma Anli

Liudong Qingzhen Jiaoyuhui 留東清真教育會, Muslim Educational Association of Students in Tokyo

Manla 滿拉, from Ar. *mawla*, religious students (in a Qurʾānic school)

Meng-Zang weiyuanhui 蒙藏委員會, Mongolian and Tibetan Affairs Commission of the Nationalist government

menhuan 門宦, a Sufi sub-order, usually characterised by father-to-son transmission of the *shaykh*'s charisma

minban xuexiao 民辦學校, a popular (private) school

ming 命, mandate

mingde 明德, (inherent) luminous or bright virtue

Mingde jing 明德經, *Scripture of Bright Virtue*, Ma Dexin

Mingde zhongxue 明德中学, Mingde High School

minzu 民族, generic term for an ethnic group, minority nationality, or 'nation'

minzuhua 民族化, ethnicisation

Moke 墨克, Mecca

Muhanmode Erli 母罕默德爾里, Muḥammad ʿAlī Pāshā of Egypt

Mumin 穆民, Muslims, Ch. transliteration of Ar. *muʾmin*

Neidi shenghuo xiguan teshu zhi guomin 內地生活習慣特殊之國民, citizens of the inner provinces with characteristic life habits

nian 念, remembrance, Ar. *shahāda*

nü ahong 女阿訇, a woman cleric

qian–kun 乾坤, male and female or Heaven and Earth, the first two hexagrams in the *Book of Changes*

Qingzhen shuju 清真書局, Islamic Bookstore, a website

Qingzhenhui 清真會, Islamic Association

Qingzhenjiao 清真教, the pure and true religion, Islam
ren 仁, humaneness/benevolence
Sailaifeiye 塞莱菲耶, Salafiyya
sanjiao heyi 三教合一, Three Teachings (Confucianism, Daoism, Buddhism) united as one
Santai 三台, 'three elevations', a Chinese nickname for the Salafiyya
Shanghai Yisilan shifan xuexiao 上海伊斯蘭師範學校, Shanghai Islamic Normal School
shaoshu minzu 少数民族, generic term for minority nationality
shehui zhi zhongzu 社會之種族, 'a social race'
sheng 聖, sage(s)
sheng 升, a dry measure for grain, 1/10 of a *dou*
shengmen 聖門, disciples of holy people
Shengren 聖人, sage, Ch. translation of 'prophet'
Shengxun 聖训, Hadith
shi 施, almsgiving, Ar. *zakāt*
shibie 識別, differentiation or distinction
Shigekawa kikan 茂川機関, the Shigekawa Agency
Shisan-ben jing 十三本經, the Thirteen Classics of Sino-Muslim education, in Arabic and Persian
Sidian Yaohui 四典要會, *Essence of the Four Canons*, Ma Dexin
taiji 太極, the Great Ultimate
Taijitu 太極圖, diagram of the Great Ultimate
tian 天, Heaven (God)
tianfang 天房, Heavenly House, the Ka'aba
tianfang 天方, Heavenly Square, the Ka'aba
Tianfang dianli 天方典禮, *Norms and Rituals of Islam*, Liu Zhi
tianxian 天仙, heavenly beings, angels
Tianzhu 天主, Lord of Heaven, Ch. translation of Lat. *deus*
tiren 體認, to know something by cognition
tonghua 同化, assimilation
Tongmenghui 同盟會, the United League, an anti-Qing organisation established in Tokyo in 1905 by Sun Yat-sen and his associates
wanwu 萬物, phenomenal reality (lit. 'the myriad things')
wei 位, administrative office or authority

wu paibie 無派別, denying, or without, factions
wudian 五典, the five social norms, or five relationships, of Confucianism
wugong 五功, 'Five Meritorious Acts', the Five Pillars of Islam, sometimes translated as 'ritual endeavours'
wuji 無極, the Beyond Ultimate
wujiao'an 侮教案, cases of offence against religion
wuju 武舉, military examination
wuru Huizu'an 侮辱回族案, cases of offence (or insult) against the *Huizu*
wuxing 五行, the Five Phases
wuzu gonghe 五族共和, republic of five nations/peoples
Wuzu Guomin Hejinhui 五族國民合進會, Association for Common Progress of the Citizens of the Five *Zu*
xianglao 鄉老, the elders of a Sino-Muslim community
xianren 先人, forefather(s)
xiansheng 先聖, former sages
xianxian 先賢, former worthy
xiaoerjing (xiaoerjin) 小兒經 or 小兒錦, phonetic transliteration of Chinese into the Arabic alphabet
xiaosheng 小生, young student
xiaozi 小子, young fellow, junior pupil
Xibei Gongxue 西北公學, Northwest Academy
Xibei Xingye Yinhang (J. *Seihoku Kogyo Ginkō*) 西北興業銀行, Northwest Commercial Bank
Xidaotang 西道堂, a Muslim solidarity based in southern Gansu
xiejiao 邪教, heterodoxy
xifang 西方, 'the West'
xin paibie 新派別, new factions
xin 信, integrity/faithfulness
xing 性, nature
Xing Fengsu 性風俗, *Sexual Customs*, a 1989 book widely regarded as insulting to Islam and Muslims
Xinghuipian 醒回篇, 'Awakening the Muslims', a 1908 Chinese Muslim journal published by overseas students in Tokyo
xinglixue 性理學, study of nature and principle

xingshi 行事, 'conducting matters', administering the community
xinjiao ziyou 信教自由, freedom of religious belief
xiucai 秀才, first-level examination degree
xiyang shu 西洋書, Occidental books
xiyuzhe 西域者, those from the western regions
xuetong 血統, 'common blood'
xuezhe 學者, scholars
xunmeng 訓蒙, educating children, educating the ignorant
yi 義, righteousness/morality
yi Ru quan Jing 以儒詮經, using Confucianism to comment on the scriptures, a common description of the *Han kitāb* texts
yi Ru shi Yi 以儒释伊, using Confucianism to explain Islam, a common description of the *Han kitāb* texts
Yiguang 伊光, 'Light of Islam', a Republican period Chinese Muslim journal
Yihewani 伊赫瓦尼, Ch. abbreviation for Ar. *Ikhwan*, the Brothers, a solidarity of Wahhabi inspiration, founded in northwest China in the late nineteenth century
yin–yang 陰陽, *yin* and *yang*, the complementary forces that provide the cosmos with dynamic energy through their constant interaction
Yisilan 伊斯蘭, Ch. transliteration of 'Islam'
Yisilan Xueshu Cheng 伊斯蘭學術城, Chinese Islamic Study City, a website
Yisilan xuexiao 伊斯蘭學校, Islamic School
Yisilanzu 伊斯蘭族, 'the Islamic nation/people'
Yisiliamu 伊斯倆穆, Ch. transliteration of 'Islam'
yue 約, covenant
zaowu 造物, the Creator
zhen 真, True/Real
zhencheng 真乘, vehicle of truth, Ch. translation of *haqīqa*
zhenci 真慈, true compassion
Zhengjiao zhenquan 正教真詮, *True Explanation of the Orthodox Teaching*, Wang Daiyu (1642)
zhengming 正名, rectification of names
zhengzhi ahong 政治阿訇, political ahongs
zhenzai 真宰, True Lord, God
Zhenzhu 真主, True Lord, *Allāh*, God

zhi 智, wisdom/knowledge
zhizhi 致知, extension of knowledge
Zhong-A xuexiao 中阿學校, Sino-Arabic school
Zhongguo Huijiao jiaoyu 中國回教教育, Chinese Islamic education
Zhongguo Huijiao Jujinhui 中國回教俱進會, Chinese Islamic Progressive Association (CIPA)
Zhongguo Huijiao xiehui 中國回教協會, Chinese Islamic Association
Zhongguo Huijiao Zonglian Hehui 中國回教総聯合會, All-China Islamic Union
Zhongguo Huizu Qingnianhui 中國回族青年會, Chinese Huizu Youth Association
Zhongguo Yisilanjiao Xiehui 中国伊斯蘭教協會, Islamic Association of China, also *Yixie*
zhu 主, lord, master
Zhuzai 主宰, the Lord Ruler, God
ziran 自然, Self-So nature; in modern times, nature itself
ziyou 自有, exist in-and-of-themselves
zunzhe 尊者, the revered one

The Contributors

Leila Chérif-Chebbi graduated from the Political Science Institute, Paris, in Chinese and Arabic languages and international relations, specialising on the Arab and Muslim world. She is presently an associate member of the Centre for Turkish, Ottoman, Balkan and Central Asian Studies (CETOBAC) at the École des hautes études en sciences sociales, Paris, publishing as an independent scholar on Islam in China, especially fundamentalist movements.

Wlodzimierz Cieciura, PhD, University of Lodz, is Assistant Professor in the Department of Sinology, University of Warsaw. His historical monograph, *Muzulmanie Chinscy* (*Muslims of China*), was published in 2014.

James D. Frankel, PhD, Columbia University, is Associate Professor of Religion at the University of Hawai'i at Mānoa, and of Cultural and Religious Studies at the Chinese University of Hong Kong, where he also serves as Associate Director of the Centre for the Study of Islamic Culture. He is the author of *Rectifying God's Name: Liu Zhi's Translation of Monotheism and Islamic Ritual Law in Neo-Confucian China* (2011).

Jonathan Lipman, PhD, Stanford University, is Felicia Gressitt Bock Professor Emeritus of Asian Studies and Professor Emeritus of History at Mount Holyoke College. His books include *Familiar Strangers: A History of*

Muslims in Northwest China (1997) and, with Barbara Molony and Michael Robinson, *Modern East Asia: An Integrated History* (2011).

Yufeng Mao, PhD, George Washington University, is Assistant Professor of History and East Asian Studies at Widener University. Her current research focuses on Sino-Muslim activism during the Republican era.

Masumi Matsumoto, PhD, Niigata University, is Professor in the College of Liberal Arts at Muroran Institute of Technology, Hokkaido, Japan. She has written numerous papers and books – in Japanese, Chinese and English – on China's national integration, Sino-Muslim affairs, gender and Muslim women's empowerment, migration and ethnic representation in graphic journals.

Kristian Petersen, PhD, University of Washington, is Assistant Professor of Religious Studies at the University of Nebraska Omaha. His research and teaching interests include theory and methodology in the study of religion, Islamic Studies, Chinese religions and Media Studies.

Roberta Tontini, PhD, University of Heidelberg, is a post-doctoral research fellow at the Sinology Department and the cluster Asia and Europe in a Global Context, University of Heidelberg. She recently completed the monograph, *Muslim Sanzijing: Shifts and Continuities in the Definition of Islam in China* (forthcoming).

Editor's Introduction: Four Centuries of Islamic Thought in Chinese

Jonathan Lipman

A Brief History of Sino-Muslim Studies

Muslims have lived in the Chinese culture area since the seventh or eighth century – the mid-Tang dynasty – and have acculturated, as all immigrants do, in order to live comfortably in what began as an alien environment. Over a millennium, through ordinary social processes, including intermarriage with local women, they ceased being utterly foreign and became local but different, Sinophone but not entirely Chinese. Though they spoke the Chinese of their home districts, many of them nonetheless retained female endogamy (males could marry non-Muslim women who converted to Islam), pork avoidance, unfamiliar rituals, mosque-centred community solidarity, and outlandish vocabulary, rendering them unconventional, somewhat distant, sometimes defensively hostile towards their non-Muslim neighbours, who saw them as 'familiar strangers'.[1]

Some of the Chinese Muslim elites also wrote about themselves, especially as their differences from their neighbours grew less obvious. Conservatives among them worried lest their acculturation should reach assimilation, at which point they would no longer be Muslims in any meaningful religious sense.[2] Intellectual leaders among them worried that they would seem alien and antagonistic to the culture of their homeland and the orthodoxy mandated by their Qing overlords. So they wrote treatises, apologia, and genealogies

– familial, intellectual, spiritual – to keep their co-religionists faithful to some version of Islamic tradition. Oral traditions evolved explaining how Muslims came to live in China, extolling their Arabian heritage as civilised, cultured and valuable. Their internal narratives had Chinese emperors eagerly seeking knowledge of Islam, welcoming high-ranking Muslim dignitaries as honoured guests, and even converting.[3] However unlikely these stories may seem, in the twenty-first century they continue to function as justifications for both the Muslim presence in China and their desire to remain different. From Mongol-period inscriptions to the seventeenth-century *Genealogy of the Transmission and Lineage of Classical Learning (Jingxue xichuan pu)*, from early twentieth-century arguments about whether Sino-Muslims constitute a 'nation', or an 'ethnic group' or a 'religious group' (see Cieciura, Chapter 5, this volume) to contemporary Internet debates (see Chérif-Chebbi, Chapter 8, this volume), Sino-Muslim insiders have described and argued in Chinese about their origins, their history and their collective nature.

Outsiders have written about them as well. Some non-Muslim Chinese penned scurrilous anti-Muslim prose and poetry, while others praised the Muslims' courage, scientific skill and business acumen. A fourteenth-century inscription composed by a non-Muslim from southeastern China narrated Islamic history and the renovation of a local mosque.[4] Early non-Chinese notices of the Sino-Muslims include Ibn Battuta, Marco Polo, Rashid al-Din and Matteo Ricci. Since the nineteenth century, a still-growing scholarly literature in several European languages has undertaken to explain their presence and historical evolutions.[5] Japanese scholars, including spies and military functionaries as well as academics, have also produced an extensive secondary literature (see Matsumoto, Chapter 7, this volume).[6]

As the bibliography demonstrates, colleagues all over the world have contributed to this strong foundation for modern scholarship on the Sino-Muslims.[7] For intellectual history, we should acknowledge the senior scholars Sachiko Murata, Zvi Ben-Dor Benite, Donald D. Leslie, Matsumoto Akirō, Tazaka Kōdō, Françoise Aubin, Yang Huaizhong and Jin Yijiu, whose writings variously inform the chapters in this volume. General historians of the Sino-Muslims have also helped us by creating contexts for intellectuals' lives, including Fu Tongxian, Jin Jitang, Bai Shouyi, Yu Zhengui, Nakada Yoshinobu and Saguchi Tōru, among many others.

Despite this large scholarly literature, the Sino-Muslims – most of whom would now be called 'members of the Hui minority (*Huizu*) in the People's Republic of China – remain nearly unnoticed in Islamic Studies and are visible only at the margins of Chinese Studies. Scholars still write as if they were too Chinese to be of Islamic interest or too Muslim to be of Sinological interest. We are persuaded that neither of these descriptions is true. Indeed, the Sino-Muslims present the Islamic Studies field with a large and fascinating case study of acculturation and adaptation, in many ways as valuable as analysis of the accommodations of Muslims in India, Europe or North America. For Sinologists, the Sino-Muslims offer a view from the edge, some of them having resisted over a millennium of pressure to assimilate completely to their cultural milieu. Others, of course, have done so and disappeared into the mainstream. This book deals with the evolution of intellectual resources to avoid complete assimilation, while simultaneously proving Islam to be a civilised *dao*, a long-term balancing act of great interest.

Sino-Muslim Intellectual History

Though Muslims have been writing about their religion in Chinese since no later than the sixteenth century, the Chinese language – unlike Persian, Turkish, Urdu or Malay – has not become an 'Islamic language', but it was the only civilised written medium available in the Chinese culture area. So in the historical process of rendering Islam compatible with Chinese civilisation, Chinese-speaking Muslims created a large and relatively unexplored body of texts collectively known, since the nineteenth century, as *Han kitāb* (Ch. *Han ketabu*), the subject of this volume's first four chapters, and intellectual ancestor of the others. This bilingual term – *Han* a Chinese word meaning in this case 'Chinese' and *kitāb* the Arabic for 'book' or 'text' – captures the dual, simultaneous nature not only of the texts, but also of their authors. The *Han kitāb* texts describe, explain, justify and provide tools for understanding Islam in written Chinese, the classical language used for all serious non-fiction writing in China before the twentieth century. However well they might have known Arabic and Persian, their authors thought about Islam in Chinese, their native language, and they expressed themselves productively in its written form.[8]

We have epigraphic evidence that Muslims wrote about their religion in Chinese before the mid-seventeenth century, but the earliest extant book is the *True Commentary on the Orthodox Teaching* (*Zhengjiao zhenquan*) of Wang Daiyu, dated 1642. For the next two centuries, authors calling themselves Sino-Muslim literati (*Huiru*) used the literary language of their Chinese cultural homeland to explain the religion of their other, mostly theoretical, homeland in Arabia. All of them engaged deeply, sometimes critically but usually conventionally, with the Three Teachings (*sanjiao*) of their day – Confucianism, Buddhism and Daoism – but their aims varied. Some wrote primers of Arabic, others created introductions to religion in the genre of the Confucian *Three Character Classic* (*Sanzijing*) (see Tontini, Chapter 3, this volume) or translated Islamic works from Arabic and Persian. Most important for our purposes, they created explanations of Islam as a civilised *dao*, a Way compatible with the norms of civilisation as articulated and lived in China. In conventional Chinese prose, they also attempted to demonstrate that in some areas, such as cosmogony and eschatology, Islam actually surpassed Chinese teachings (see Lipman, Chapter 1, and Frankel, Chapter 2, this volume).

These apologetic texts served two audiences. They intended to guide Muslims literate only in Chinese away from assimilation and non-belief by correct understanding of their ancestral *dao* – Islam – in the context and vocabulary of their Chinese culture. In addition, they wanted to persuade non-Muslim Chinese literates that Islam, far from being an outlandish or barbaric teaching, fulfilled the same civilising functions as the principles elucidated in the Chinese canon. Both of these audiences required that Islam be *translated* into Chinese language and culture, in the same way that Buddhism, Christianity, Judaism and other exogenous religions had been. Unlike 'Islamic' languages, however, written Chinese could not easily absorb Arabic or Persian vocabulary as transliterations. Phonetic transliteration emphasised the foreignness and thus uncivilised nature of Islam, antithetical to the purposes of the *Han kitāb*. Instead, the authors had to create a new or reinterpreted Chinese lexicon to elucidate Islamic monotheism in a language that lacked many of its basic concepts. Though they did sometimes transliterate, from the seventeenth century onward they generally preferred translation.[9]

Adherents of Judaism and Roman Catholic Christianity were trying to solve this problem at roughly the same time. Like the Muslim literati, culturally Chinese Jews and culturally alien Catholic priests with their local converts wrestled with the dilemmas of rendering their foreign religions as civilised, even superior *dao*s. Some Muslims read the tracts of Matteo Ricci (1552–1610) and his colleagues, and Ricci had access to some of the Chinese Jewish texts. We may thus observe in the seventeenth century three loosely connected attempts to render the Mediterranean monotheisms familiar, civilised and compelling in Chinese. These intellectual efforts reveal translation as a mediating process, for the core ideas of those religions – in Hebrew, Greek, Latin, Arabic and Persian – had to be rendered into the alien idiom of Chinese to fulfil their desired functions.

That translation process lies at the heart of the Sino-Muslim intellectual history elucidated in this book. The four chapters in Part I (Lipman, Frankel, Tontini, Petersen) deal with the evolution of the *Han kitāb* texts themselves, their theology, genres, scope and bicultural simultaneity. They involve detailed textual analysis of terms, ideas, arguments and genres, and careful biographical–contextual understanding of the authors and their times. Focusing on five important figures and moments generally regarded as central to Sino-Muslim thought – Wang Daiyu (mid-seventeenth century), Ma Zhu (fl. late seventeenth century), Liu Zhi (fl. early eighteenth century), Yuan Guozuo (fl. late eighteenth century) and Ma Dexin (fl. mid-nineteenth century) – these chapters trace the scholarly work of Muslims writing in Chinese through the course of the Qing dynasty (1636–1912). We thus continue the pioneering work of Zvi Ben-Dor Benite, who elucidated the Qing period Sino-Muslim scholarly networks,[10] and Sachiko Murata, who with her colleagues has introduced and translated core *Han kitāb* texts.[11]

Intrepid Sufis from northwestern China made the long and perilous journey to (or towards) the Islamic heartlands in the eighteenth century, and their return to Gansu sparked crucial religious and social conflicts in that region. But they did not write about their experiences in Chinese, and their stories do not connect with the *Han kitāb* until the late nineteenth century. By then, some late Qing Sino-Muslim thinkers, exemplified by Ma Dexin (see Petersen, Chapter 4, this volume), had built a new relationship between their local traditions and the Muslim heartlands. These scholars ended centuries of relatively isolated Sino-Muslim intellectual evolution. Emphasising Arabic language training and the pilgrimage to Mecca (Ar. *hajj*), taking advantage of modern steamship transportation, they began a new era of inter-regional communication that reached a high point in the careers of dozens of Chinese Muslim intellectuals who studied in the Middle East (see Mao, Chapter 6, this volume).

Modernity clearly played a powerful role in transforming not only the thoughts and writings, but also the identities of Sino-Muslim intellectuals. Though some imams in northwestern China continued with traditional theological debates, conflicts among competing Sufi orders, and articulation of Islamic ideas in *xiaoerjin* Arabic-script transliteration (see Matsumoto, Chapter 7, this volume), Sino-Muslim intellectuals in China proper joined in the same sort of struggles as their non-Muslim colleagues. They learned a new vocabulary, minted in Japan in Chinese characters and thus available to both Chinese and Korean literates, to cope with the wealth of new concepts entering East Asia, including the nation, ideology, science and dozens of isms.[12] They learned that Confucianism was outmoded – the Qing abolished the civil service examination curriculum in 1905 – and that Europe, North America and Japan possessed new knowledge that enabled them to conquer the world.

China thus entered the twentieth century with its foundations and self-conceptions under apparently irresistible attack from the outside. In order to be both Chinese and Muslim, Sino-Muslims then developed complex and innovative intellectual relationships with Chinese nationalism and the sociopolitical processes that created a modern nation-state, China, out of the declining then defunct Qing Empire. After the de-canonisation of Neo-Confucian orthodoxy, twentieth-century Sino-Muslims had to adapt to the new potential orthodoxies of modernity: nationalism, liberalism, socialism and more. Like their non-Muslim compatriots, they accessed these ideas through China's contacts with Japan, Europe and North America.

But Muslim intellectuals also utilised Islamic channels of communication, including the pilgrimage and study in centres such as al Azhar University in Cairo. As the Nationalist and Communist Parties vied for national power, Muslims debated 'who we are' in a rapidly changing, often dangerous new world. Wlodzimierz Cieciura's chapter (Chapter 5) makes that debate concrete and personal, recreating the contending voices of Yin Boqing and Jin Jitang, co-workers of the great *imam* Wang Jingzhai,[13] in the 1930s. Their argument over whether Sino-Muslims are 'Han Chinese who believe in Islam' or 'the Hui people', a separate bloodline and national solidarity, defined a crucial division within the Sino-Muslim intellectual world.

The victory of the Chinese Communist Party ensured the triumph of the latter theory, at least on the mainland, and it has dominated Chinese thinking about the Sino-Muslims since 1949. The Maoist decades (1949–78) dealt heavy blows to all the religious traditions of China, branding Islam as 'feudal superstition', sometimes punishing believers for following even the most basic tenets of their faith such as pork avoidance and communal prayer. Defining (and dividing) China's Muslim population as members of ten different 'national minorities' (*shaoshu minzu*),[14] the People's Republic of China also established centralised institutions such as the Islamic Association of China (*Zhongguo Yisilanjiao Xiehui*) as well as official Religious Affairs Offices (*Zongjiao Ju*) at many levels of government. These Party-dominated bodies both legitimise and control Islamic belief and practice, creating a procrustean template for religious life. While recognising Islam as one of China's legal religions, the state has also defined some forms of Islamic activity, such as teaching children to pray, as criminal.

Since 1978, the tide has turned back towards somewhat more lenient acceptance of Islamic activity, especially among Sino-Muslims.[15] Larger numbers of pilgrims have been permitted to travel to Saudi Arabia; Sino-Muslim scholars, students and merchants have again sojourned in the Middle East, including an expanding exchange with Iran; and a spate of mosque building has created numerous new religious centres. At the same time, the government has exercised greater control over the content and form of Islamic religious education, training imams in state-operated seminaries with a centrally designed curriculum and mandating 'patriotic education' for all religious professionals.

Outside the homogenising, state-controlled madrasas, however, new debates have flourished among Sino-Muslims in officially and privately published books and journals (especially in the 1980s and 1990s) and on the Internet. Chérif-Chebbi's chapter (Chapter 8) analyses profound disagreements over the issue of acculturation: should contemporary Sino-Muslims be more like the *Han kitāb* author Liu Zhi – writing and thinking about Islam in Chinese – or 'Abd al-Wahhab, the iconic Arabian anti-accretionist who gave his name to a crucial variant of Islamic fundamentalism? To what extent and in what realms may Sino-Muslims be part of the transnational Islamic congregation (*umma*) while participating fully in Chinese political and cultural life as patriotic citizens?

The four chapters in Part II, dealing with modern China, thus elucidate a far more politicised, sociological 'intellectual history' than those focused on the *Han kitāb* of the Qing period. Some Muslims continued to wrestle with apologetics and the literary problems of translation, including translations of the *Qur'ān* into Chinese, but most had to contend with more immediate and pressing issues: how shall we describe and define ourselves as Muslims in modern China (see Cieciura, Chapter 5, this volume)? What must we learn and teach in order to remain Muslims in this rapidly changing, often dangerous, China (see Matsumoto, Chapter 7, this volume)? What should be our relationship with the Muslim heartlands (see Mao, Chapter 6, this volume)? And, most recently, in the post-1978 atmosphere of 'reform and opening', how can we use both conventional publications and 'new media' such as the Internet to define and advance our individual and collective purposes, as both Muslims and Chinese (see Chérif-Chebbi, Chapter 8, this volume)?

As we will discuss below, those purposes themselves have become more diverse, more diffuse and, in some cases, locally and nationally contentious in the past century. The reader will thus note a shift in focus from the first four chapters on the Qing period to the last four on the twentieth century, a shift from Islamic ideas and how to express them in Chinese towards Chinese Muslims and their conceptions of who they are or should be. This makes good sense, for during that period the world of Chinese thought, writ large, moved from the serene self-confidence of the universal imperium that ruled All-Under-Heaven to the dangers of rough-and-tumble interactions among competing states and ideologies, in which 'China' – newly emerging as a modernising nation-state – occupied a lower-tier position.[16] The thinkers' contexts thus determined the focus of our studies, and the thinkers could not avoid politics.

This book will examine an important facet of Islam in China – its intellectual heritage – over the *longue durée*, each chapter based on careful reading of primary sources as well as contemporary scholarship in history, religious studies, anthropology and other disciplines. Going beyond the pioneering work of Ben-Dor Benite and Murata, it will clarify important issues in the translation of exogenous traditions into Chinese, opening new possibilities for comparison with Christianity, Judaism, Marxism, liberalism and more. Neither a comprehensive history nor a systematic historiography, our work rather focuses on specific thinkers and moments to narrate the evolution of a rich and innovative intellectual tradition.

Conventions

We have not included non-Latin orthographies in the text or bibliography. The glossaries provide traditional Chinese characters (*fantizi*) for East Asian names and terms mentioned in the book. We presume that readers interested in our East Asian and Middle Eastern sources will be able to convert from romanisation to the original orthographies. Transliterations from Chinese are mostly in *pinyin* and unmarked; words from other languages are indicated by Ar. (Arabic), Per. (Persian), J. (Japanese) or Lat. (Latin). Some names from Taiwan are given in Wade-Giles romanisation. All dates are Common Era (CE).

Except as a subject of analysis (see Cieciura and Chérif-Chebbi), we have avoided the discourse of 'minority nationalities' or 'ethnic groups' as it has been practiced in the People's Republic of China since the 1950s. The term *Huizu*, universally used in the People's Republic of China (and often in Taiwan) to refer to the Sino-Muslims, thus appears only when one of the contributors needs to consider words people use, not as a natural descriptor. The conflict over 'who we are' described by Cieciura, the argument over *Huijiaotu* versus *Huizu*, has not been 'solved' by the PRC victory, for no answer can be 'the correct one', except through application of political power.

Evolution of this Volume

A glance at our List of Contributors will demonstrate the transnational character of our field. The eight of us come from six countries – China, Japan, the United States, France, Italy and Poland – and were educated in their languages and conventions (plus one PhD from Germany). Though we share English and Chinese in common, we think very differently about our subject, strongly influenced by the national cultures in which we were raised. This produces a broad diversity of topics, styles, modes of analysis, even fundamental assumptions, and that diversity has enabled very productive conversations.

This collection began as a panel, 'Evolution of the Sino-Islamic Intellectual Tradition', at the annual meeting of the Association for Asian Studies (AAS) in Honolulu, in the spring of 2011. At that session, five of us – Chérif-Chebbi, Cieciura, Frankel, Lipman and Petersen – presented early versions of the chapters in this volume. Since then, we have met at four more AAS meetings and other venues, debating our sources, improving our arguments, and adding Tontini, Mao and Matsumoto as contributors to fill crucial gaps in coverage. We hope that this book will stimulate scholars in Islamic Studies to take more interest in China as a site of Islamic thought, and those in Chinese Studies to consider the Muslims of China as both legitimately Chinese and different in instructive ways. We are persuaded that both fields will be enriched by study of this conjunction.

Notes

1. See Lipman, *Familiar Strangers*, ch. 2, and Benite, 'Follow the white camel'.
2. This evolution towards complete assimilation occurred most dramatically in Fujian and Taiwan, in southeastern China, after the Ming state (1368–1644) drastically limited overseas trade and communication. See Pillsbury, 'No pigs for the ancestors', and Abt, 'Muslim Ancestry'.
3. In his scholarly writings, the Sino-Muslim jade merchant Hajji Yusuf Chang (Zhang Zhaoli) argued, with circumstantial but (to him) persuasive evidence, that Zhu Yuanzhang, the first emperor of the Ming dynasty, had become a Muslim. See Benite, 'The Marrano emperor'. The *Han kitāb* text entitled *Huihui yuanlai*, 'Origins of the Chinese Muslims', written 1,000 years after Muslims arrived in the Chinese culture area, includes some of the legends of early Chinese-Muslim contact, invented in many different contexts and embellished through oral transmission. For a recent review, see Garnaut, 'Hui legends'.
4. Park, *Mapping the Chinese and Islamic Worlds*, pp. 123–5.
5. For a masterful summary of some of that literature, see Aubin, 'Reflections' (with an introduction in Chinese). Major items of the European-language literature have been gathered by Israeli, *Islam in China*.
6. Hammond, 'The conundrum of collaboration'.
7. None of the contributors to this volume has studied the Russian literature on the

Sino-Muslims, and that leaves a conspicuous gap in our coverage of the secondary literature.
8. For a detailed listing of *Han kitāb* authors and texts, see Leslie, *Islamic Literature*.
9. Among themselves, Sino-Muslims did and do use a great deal of transliterated spoken Arabic and Persian vocabulary – the creole-like 'lexicon of authenticity' called *Huihuihua* – but that would not do when presenting Islam to outsiders in prose. See Yang Zhanwu, *Huihui yuyan wenhua*.
10. Benite, *The Dao of Muhammad*.
11. Murata, *Chinese Gleams*; Murata, Chittick and Tu, *The Sage Learning of Liu Zhi*.
12. See Liu, *Translingual Practice*, especially the appendices.
13. See Kurzman, *Modernist Islam*, ch. 52.
14. This term has also been translated as 'minority nationalities' and in recent years as 'ethnic groups'. Since it has no obvious English equivalent, for the most part we will use *minzu* in this collection.
15. This apparently liberal acceptance has not generally applied to other Muslim *minzu*, especially not to the Uyghurs of Xinjiang, whose Islamic practice has been much more severely circumscribed by state surveillance and regulation.
16. Schwarcz, *The Chinese Enlightenment*, brilliantly narrates this transformation through six generations of non-Muslim Chinese intellectuals, from the late nineteenth century to the 1980s, elucidating the context in which the Sino-Muslim thinkers also worked.

PART I
THE QING EMPIRE (1636–1912)

1

A Proper Place for God: Ma Zhu's Chinese-Islamic Cosmogenesis

Jonathan Lipman

The Seventeenth-Century Context

In the Ming period (1368–1644), Chinese Muslim writers began to explain their ancestral religion of Islam in the language and conceptual schema of their contemporary Chinese culture.[1] That is, they participated fully in two literate, self-confident and, at least potentially, exclusive cultures, so they had to produce a textual justification that allowed them to be legitimate insiders in both. This will be a constant theme in this book, for the same impulse has continued to motivate Chinese Muslim intellectuals to think and write for the past 400 years. As Zvi Ben-Dor Benite put it, these early scholars engaged in 'the foundation and distribution of a specifically Chinese form of Islamic knowledge, one that claimed to be compatible with – indeed, a subset of – Confucian knowledge and learning'.[2] They thus created the first coherent body of Chinese texts articulating a Sino-Islamic intellectual history, embodying both the simultaneity and inherent tensions of their dual identities.[3]

This evolution blossomed in the tumultuous seventeenth century, as the Ming state weakened and collapsed under the pressure of domestic rebellion and foreign invasion. In an atmosphere of widespread anti-foreign, especially anti-Manchu, hostility and action, the authors of these 'Chinese [Islamic] books' (Ch. *Han* Ar. *kitāb*)[4] walked a fine line between, on the one hand, avoiding an uncomfortable and potentially dangerous alterity, and, on the other hand, preserving their Islamic commitments from excessive or distorting accretions from Chinese culture. From the earliest extant *Han kitāb* text, Wang Daiyu's *Zhengjiao zhenquan* (1642),[5] to the translations of Wu Zixian a few decades later,[6] the first published books in this genre probed the possibilities of expressing accurate Islamic meaning in the conventional language of learned Chinese discourse. Ma Zhu (1640–after 1710), the subject of this chapter, followed in the footsteps of these early writers, both translating selected passages from Arabic and Persian sources and using literary Chinese to formulate his own systematic understanding of Islam, maximally compatible with the norms of his Chinese culture.

One of the most intractable translation problems for Chinese Muslim intellectuals lay in the Mediterranean conviction, shared by Jews, Christians and Muslims alike, that God had created the physical cosmos from nothing (Lat. *creatio ex nihilo*), and that God remained in a position *outside* that cosmos, filling it with divine presence, but nonetheless utterly different from visible physical reality. This explanation of cosmogenesis, repeated in both the Old Testament's narratives (Genesis 1–2) and in scattered verses of the *Qur'ān* (e.g., 11:9 and 41:9-12), had no equivalent in early Chinese thought. Texts of the Zhou dynasty (thirteenth–third centuries BCE) and their later commentarial traditions held that everything that exists must be located within the cosmos and follow its rules, and thus that the cosmos emerged more or less on its own, and was not created by an external power.[7] This difference constituted an important obstacle to both the expression and the acceptance of these foreign religions in Chinese culture. This chapter does not attempt a survey of Sino-Muslim efforts to create a persuasive translation of Islamic cosmogenesis into Chinese, but rather focuses on one text – Ma Zhu's *Qingzhen zhinan* – as a well-known and popular exemplar of those efforts, written at an important juncture in the written expression of Chinese Muslim thought.

The roots of Ma Zhu's Sino-Islamic analysis lay at least several centuries before his lifetime, as Muslim and non-Muslim literati undertook the arduous process of cultural translation, of rendering into the Chinese language Islamic truths originally expressed in Arabic and Persian. The earliest known attempts depended primarily on the vocabulary and ideas of Song dynasty

Neo-Confucian texts in a process reminiscent of early Chinese Buddhist translation and its reliance on Daoist vocabulary.[8] Lacking appropriate Chinese terminology for the expression of Islamic ideas, they used terms such as *huang*, the August One, and *tian*, Heaven, to identify the Islamic God (Ar. *Allāh*), and they translated Islamic sources only indirectly.

One of the earliest Sino-Islamic texts, the *Laifu* stone inscription, located in the courtyard of the South Great Mosque of Ji'nan (Shandong), cited not the *Qur'ān* or the *Hadith*, but rather the works of Neo-Confucian scholars Zhang Zai (1020–1077) and Zhou Dunyi (1017–1073) to prove the truth of Islamic doctrine. Written in 1528 by Chen Si (dates unknown), a religious leader (*ahong* from Per. *akhūnd*) of that mosque, the *Laifu* inscription presented a very short version of God's creation of the cosmos *ex nihilo*, a process unlike virtually all previous Chinese cosmogonies, but nonetheless couched in conventional vocabulary:

> The Beyond Ultimate (*wuji*) and the Great Ultimate (*taiji*), *yin* and *yang* and the Five Phases (*wuxing*) all originated in the Soundless and began with the Formless.[9]

The 'Soundless' and 'Formless' represented an early attempt to capture Arabic *Allāh* in the recalcitrant vocabulary of Chinese, which lacked any obvious or natural appellations for a monotheistic deity. More than a century and a half later, Ma Zhu elaborated this simple progression into a more detailed cosmogony uniting Islamic and Confucian theories.

Ma Zhu and the *Qingzhen Zhinan*

Born in 1640, Ma Zhu came from Baoshan in western Yunnan, a frontier region known for Islamic learning as well as conventional Neo-Confucian studies. Xu Xiake, the famous late Ming geographer and writer, observed the area about the time Ma Zhu was born. Xu concluded that the Baoshan/Tengyue district was 'the edge of the empire, a Chinese political and cultural frontier', where numerous highland peoples lived at the intersection of three potentially influential states: the Ming, based in distant Beijing; Burma, its king in somewhat nearer Toungoo; and the local Tai statelets collectively called *Sipsongpanna* (Ch. *Xishuangbanna*).[10] Baoshan/Tengyue was the most important Chinese district in that part of the Salween watershed, and its population included a substantial Chinese Muslim community made up of merchants, soldiers, miners and caravaneers.¹¹ Ma Zhu's hometown could thus be an allegory for his identity: both domestic and alien, thoroughly Chinese but positioned between China and non-China.¹²

Ma Zhu's father, a Muslim teacher of the Chinese classics, chose the secular civil service examination path for his son before dying young, with Ma Zhu proving to be a prodigy and earning his first-level (*xiucai*) degree in the late 1650s while still in his teens. He inherited his father's profession as a Confucian teacher, served briefly in one of the rump Ming courts, and published two collections of essays, neither now extant. In the late 1660s, he fled to Beijing as the Qing court intensified its conflict with Yunnan's ruler, Wu Sangui, and his allies, the dynasty's southern feudatories.¹³ Though he had been educated primarily in the Confucian curriculum, Ma Zhu then spent ten years in Islamic study in Beijing's madrasas, reading Arabic and Persian texts.

Ma Zhu found Chinese Muslims' understanding of their faith to be shallow and riddled with error – no surprise after centuries of reduced contact with the Islamic heartlands – and Chinese non-Muslims to be ignorant of or even hostile towards his ancestral religion. So he undertook to produce a complete explanation and justification, *Qingzhen zhinan*, the compass (or guide) to Islam, in the Chinese literary language. Writing with grammar and vocabulary appropriate to his station as an official degree-holder, he addressed his book primarily to insiders, other Chinese-literate Muslims, but also to non-Muslims and even to the Qing court. During his ten-year residence in Beijing, Ma Zhu attempted to persuade the Kangxi emperor (r. 1662–1722) that the descendants of the Prophet Muhammad – a status Ma Zhu himself claimed through his ancestor, the Mongol period soldier-governor Sayyid Ajjal Shams al-Din (Sai Dianchi) – ought to occupy a place of honour in China equal to that of the descendants of Confucius, the Kong family, originally of Qufu in Shandong.¹⁴

After his decade in Beijing, during which he completed the bulk of his book, Ma Zhu made his way back to Yunnan with his family, stopping along the way at major Muslim centres, from Shandong and Henan to Jiangnan and Xi'an, to share his eight-chapter manuscript and collect encomiums. In addition to Ma Zhu's brief autobiography, the first chapter of the *Qingzhen zhinan* contains numerous prefaces and poems praising the book and its author, including one by Liu Sanjie, Liu Zhi's father (see Frankel, Tontini and Petersen, Chapters 2–4, this volume). After he arrived in Yunnan, he spent the next fifteen years editing and re-editing the book, adding two new chapters to reflect the problems he and the Muslim community faced in his home province.[15]

By the seventeenth century, mainstream Islam around the world had been profoundly affected by Sufism (from Ar. *sūf*, a coarse woollen garment favoured by ascetics), a widespread and diffuse movement advocating that Muslim individuals and the solidarities they formed should attempt direct approaches to, even unity with, God through repetitive prayer, austerities and meditation. To that end, leading Sufi adepts (Ar. sing. *shaykh* or *murshid*) developed techniques to heighten their engagement with the divine and more effectively lead their followers (Ar. sing. *murīd*) to entranced, sometimes ecstatic religious experiences. Philosophers, too, analysed the mystical relationship between the created and the Creator, theorising stages of progress towards the deepest understanding. An enormous textual tradition evolved, attempting to balance the quotidian requirements of Islamic law (Ar. *sharī'a*) with the austerities and goals of the Sufi path (Ar. *tarīqa*), which advanced beyond simple obedience to God's law in the direction of mystical unity with the divine. Some of these texts found their way to China and influenced the *Han kitāb* writers.

Though the Islam he described in his book was infused with mystical ideas, with the search for perfect relationship between quotidian and spiritual religious practice,[16] Ma Zhu had no patience with Sufis if they broke the conventional mould of Sino-Muslim life.[17] When Qalandars, 'wild Sufis',[18] from India built a following among Muslims in Yunnan, Ma Zhu stood firmly on the side of conservative morality and the conventional elite, accusing the outsiders of heterodoxy (*xiejiao*), under both Qing statute law and Islamic law.[19] In his continuing intellectual work, he focused on philosophical and ritual problems appropriate to an Islamic–Confucian simultaneity, solutions to which would make living as a Chinese Muslim comfortable, even compelling. Ma Zhu had to position himself between two orthodoxies, both of which he defended from heterodoxy without and from ignorance within.

Non-Muslims might have found Ma Zhu's textual conventions odd, perhaps even criminal, for he elevated God's name (*Zhenzhu*) one space above his text and placed the Prophet Muhammad's name at the top of a new vertical line, one space below God's. He used this Chinese style, parallel to the elevation of the emperor's titles, as a substitute for the conventional Arabic epithets, such as 'Upon Whom Be Peace'. But non-Muslim readers would not be accustomed to treating a foreign, Islamic deity or sage (*shengren*, which Ma Zhu used to translate Ar. *nabī*, 'prophet') on a par with the emperor.

We may thus surmise that Ma Zhu intended the audience of the *Qingzhen zhinan* to be mainly other Muslims, literate in Chinese but not in Arabic or Persian, people like the literati who read his book as he travelled home to Yunnan. In his personal introduction, he created an extended metaphor of human life as commerce, a despised activity in Neo-Confucian ideology but much respected in the Islamic world:

> Islam's highest principle holds that human beings are sojourning merchants, that the material world is the marketplace, that human nature and the heavenly decree are the capital, that exchanges with friends are the transactions, that personal intentions are the measuring scale, that good and evil are the goods for sale, that death is returning home, that God's rewards in Heaven are riches, and that God's punishments in Hell are poverty. The sojourning merchant always returns home, and the goods on loan in the end return to their original Master. Whatever business you may be in – it comes and then it goes, flying by in no time at all. Fame and fortune have their seasons, as does conjugal love. Death cannot be predicted.[20]

Could this passage have been aimed primarily at a non-Muslim Chinese audience? Neither heaven-as-reward nor hell-as-punishment would have been unfamiliar to literate Chinese who had read Buddhist texts or illiterates who knew Buddhist iconography, but no Buddhist 'Master' or 'Lord' controlled the process or produced the 'goods on loan' from God to humankind. Nor would a non-Muslim audience know that Muhammad, the Seal of the Prophets, Messenger of God and exemplary personality of Islam, had been a merchant himself. The passage nonetheless appears to be original with Ma Zhu, not a translation or paraphrase of an existing Islamic text. We cannot know what a non-Muslim reader would have made of this passage and many others in the *Qingzhen zhinan*. However, we can examine Ma Zhu's explication of God's creation of the cosmos *ex nihilo* to discover how he handled the delicate problem of fitting Abrahamic monotheism into Neo-Confucian culture and language.[21]

Unlike Wu Zixian, who translated Rāzī's *Mirsād al-Ibād* directly from Arabic, Ma Zhu created his Chinese text from scratch, rendering Arabic and Persian material into Chinese as he needed it rather than translating an entire Islamic treatise. He was, after all, an accomplished writer of Chinese prose, a successful candidate in the civil service examinations, and a proud protégé of the Yunnanese Chinese literary establishment. He was also an important member of the Sino-Muslim literary elite described by Benite, the writers of the *Han kitāb*. That is, Ma Zhu was a dual insider, a Confucian literatus and an advanced Islamic scholar; he defined and elaborated the *dao* of Islam in the vocabulary of Ming–Qing Neo-Confucian orthodoxy, with its customary sprinkling of Buddhist and Daoist vocabulary and ideas.[22] Like American *imams* disavowing polygyny[23] or Matteo Ricci eliding original sin, the crucifixion and the resurrection from his Chinese account of Roman Catholicism,[24] Ma Zhu had to present a legitimate Islam as being entirely compatible with the culture in which he lived and with the norms of late Ming and early Qing Neo-Confucian civilisation.[25]

Translating Creation into Chinese

Though myriads of Chinese thinkers had pondered ultimate reality, China had not been fertile ground for systematic theology, study of the nature of God. Focusing on abstractions such as Principle or Pattern (*li*), the Way (*dao*), Great Ultimate (*taiji*), and Root Suchness (*benran*), Chinese thinkers did not attempt to describe an Omnipotent, Omniscient, Omnipresent, Ineffable yet Personal Creator – for Chinese culture had not generated that kind of deity and had no self-evident words to describe it. Chinese Muslim authors, however, had no choice but to do so, for the Islamic tradition demanded, in James Frankel's words, 'affirmations of [God's] personality and conscious will as the creator'."[26] Only by correct understanding of God's work of cosmogenesis could Muslims comprehend God's nature and his relationship to phenomenal reality, including humankind, so Ma Zhu's prose built upon earlier attempts to articulate that understanding in written Chinese.

Facing this task, like all the *Han kitāb* authors, Ma Zhu had to utilise a lexicon that threatened to deny the nature of Islam's generative Deity, either by abstracting God into impersonality or by eliding God's ultimate reality as Creator. In Islamic cosmology, all human beings already possess inherent knowledge of God because they were made in God's form. But Ma Zhu also had to write within the Neo-Confucian intellectual tradition, which had for centuries presented its participants with a cosmos entirely lacking a conscious, wilful Creator and thus gave them few tools and no obvious vocabulary to recognise (in Murata's sense) or comprehend Islamic conceptions of God's nature and God's work.[27]

Ma Zhu's predecessor Wang Daiyu, in his chapter on 'Origins', utilised a metaphor from Rāzī's *Mirṣād al-ibād*, later translated into Chinese by Wu Zixian, of God as a confectioner creating sugar in many grades of purity, from the most refined (the Prophet Muhammad) to the darkest and coarsest (the beasts, fish and birds).[28] This did not satisfy the more deeply Confucian Ma Zhu.[29] Remaining faithful to both his cultural matrices, Ma Zhu followed the *Laifu* inscription in moving Chinese Muslim readers towards an intellectual recognition of a creating God consistent with the cosmological theories of Neo-Confucianism. This process reached its culmination in the writings of Liu Zhi, a member of the next generation of *Han kitāb* writers. We may thus see Ma Zhu as a crucial intermediate stage in the production of a sophisticated Sino-Muslim intellectual capacity, expressing Islamic religious ideas in Chinese as accurately as that language and its cultural context allowed.

Orthodox Neo-Confucianism – in Chinese, *Cheng-Zhu lixue*[30] – recognised the *Taijitu*, the 'diagram of the Great Ultimate', and its commentary by Zhou Dunyi as accurately explaining the origins of the cosmos. The *Laifu* inscription cited above followed Zhou's diagram in claiming that the cosmos originated from the Beyond Ultimate, an uncreated chaos.[31] The *Taijitu*, well known to all Neo-Confucian literati, including some Muslims, portrayed the Beyond Ultimate, alone in uncreated void, without conscious effort or consciousness bringing forth the Great Ultimate, which then equally unconsciously and without volition generated *yin* and *yang*. The still unintentional interaction of those paired complementary qualities provided the dynamic energy for the remaining stages of cosmogenesis, first, by the differentiation of the cycle of Five Phases (*wuxing*), followed by the separation into male and female (*qian–kun*, which may also be translated as 'Heaven and Earth'),[32] from which emerged phenomenal reality (*wanwu*, literally 'the myriad things').

This chain of transformation did not require or even hypothesise a conscious, wilful creating God like that of the Mediterranean monotheisms. Chinese cosmologists had not theorised such a God, since pre-Song texts followed by Zhou Dunyi and subsequent commentators told them that the material universe arose spontaneously from the sequence of Beyond Ultimate, Great Ultimate, *yin–yang*, Five Phases, and *qian–kun*. In the generation before Ma Zhu, Liang Yijun, one of Wang Daiyu's Muslim disciples, had written that though Confucianism perfectly explicates the Middle Way, its teachers could not explain the beginning or the end.[33] That is, to grasp the nature and significance of Creation and the afterlife, two key expressions of God's omnipotence and thus essential articles of Islamic faith, all must turn to Islam for correct understanding. Ma Zhu, therefore, *did* need to explain the irreplaceable creator God of the *Qur'ān*, so like Liang Yijun he argued that Neo-Confucian cosmogony, though correct as far as it went, did not suffice.

In the 'True Benevolence' (*zhenci*) chapter of his guide, Ma Zhu solved this dilemma by placing God, whom he called *Zhenzhu* or just *Zhu*, the 'True (or Real) Lord', as a conscious actor prior to Beyond Ultimate in the chain of changes that led to the existence of the cosmos. He did so without defensiveness, confident that only Islam could provide the solution to the problem of the cosmos's apparently Self-So nature (*ziran*):

> The various schools of [Chinese] thinkers have not understood the original Mover of Creation. They say that *wuji* gave birth to the *taiji*, which could not but transform and generate *yin* and *yang*. *Yin* and *yang* could not but transform and give birth to phenomenal reality. Pushing back before the *wuji* [in their theory], there is no Master to rely on, and they take Heaven and Earth as existing in-and-of-themselves [*ziran*].[34] [In their eyes,] sageliness and stupidity derive from the quality of vital essence (*qi*),[35] death and life from the rotation of *karma*,[36] intelligence and talent as belonging [entirely] to personal ability. No wonder that ignorant men and stupid women mistake the created thing for the creating God and the formed thing for the Ancestor of the Formless.[37] Thus do they invert the root and

branch and are incapable of fathoming the surface and the core. They live like drunkards and die in a dream, drifting [passively] along without ideas of their own.[38]

For Ma Zhu, Neo-Confucianism defined moral human relations, but God the Creator must be given his proper place as the *causa causans*. Without God, Ma argued, the cosmos makes no sense, and thus Zhou Dunyi's incomplete diagram contradicts inherent human knowledge. In this passage, Ma used many of the same arguments that Roman Catholics were using at the same historical moment to centre *Deus* (the Lord of Heaven, *Tianzhu*) as creator of a Chinese-reading Christian cosmos.[39]

Ma Zhu accepted Chinese claims about ancient cultural innovation: Fuxi drew the Eight Trigrams; Cangjie created written characters; Rongcheng designed the calendar; Suiren discovered fire; and so on. But he also argued a first cause that no non-Muslim Chinese philosopher had adduced, with the exception of some early Chinese Roman Catholics, that without God's direct guidance, even these great men could not have done these things: 'The myriad activities come from the [human] heart-mind but not from human beings' own volition.' To argue otherwise would be like arguing that water and earth, of their own accord, can produce the grains, flowers, and fruits.[40]

In one of his 'question and answer' (*kewen*) sections, Ma Zhu repeated his cosmogony with a more substantial argument for God's unique and essential place as First Cause:

> The guest asked: Not worshipping Heaven and Earth and [only] worshipping God [the True or Real Lord] is like that [it makes sense]. May I ask, from where did Heaven and Earth, humankind, and phenomenal reality originate? I answered: It is just like planting the five staples – rice, millet, sorghum, wheat, and beans. This year plant a seed and next year harvest a *ge*, the following year harvest a *sheng*, and the year after that a *dan*.[41] In light of this, we may deduce that starting from planting a single grain seed, all grains are produced from it. Ten thousand people, traced back a hundred years, were only a thousand. Traced back a thousand years, they were fewer than a hundred. Before a hundred, they were but a few, and before a few, only one. If you start to go back before that one, all humankind was produced from here. Sun, moon, stars, and celestial bodies, fire, wind, water,

and earth all originally were born from the *taiji*. The *taiji* was originally produced from the *wuji*. But if you start to go back before the *wuji*, Heaven and Earth were all produced from this.

Thus, Heaven and Earth had a point of origin, so we know that they did not exist in-and-of-themselves (*ziyou*). If they do not exist in-and-of-themselves, they certainly cannot eternally be preserved without decay or everlastingly rest without motion; not rely on heavenly beings (*tianxian*) to move themselves; not borrow the sun and moon to illuminate themselves; not capitalize on [the bounty of] rain and dew to moisten themselves; not rely on the various seeds to germinate themselves. Day could become night, spring could become autumn – all these belong to processes that absolutely cannot govern themselves, and they cannot be outside God's total power to bestow things. If heaven and earth are like that, then people and things cannot be outside heaven and earth – how much less can they be said to exist in-and-of themselves? . . . Therefore Beginning-less-ness and End-less-ness can only be properties of God the Unique One; having a Beginning but no End can only be properties of heavenly beings, men, and spirits; while having a Beginning and an End are properties of flying and walking [creatures] on sea and land, grasses, trees, metals and rocks. Plants, trees, metals, and rocks are not the same as flying and walking [creatures] on sea and land, which are not the same as heavenly beings, men, and spirits, which are not the same as God-the-Creator.

In this Islamic–Confucian synthesis, human virtue derived not only from humankind's Neo-Confucian social roles such as 'ruler' or 'father', but also, directly and originally, from God's generative perfection. The discovery and cultivation of the self, the 'I', remained humankind's highest responsibility, and for Ma Zhu, the existence of that 'I' proved the existence of God. In the *tiren*[42] chapter, we find:

A smelter of gold, silver, copper, and iron [can create] a life-like man. But can he smelt its seeing, hearing, speaking and moving? A sculptor in wood, stone, plaster or conglomerate [can create] a life-like man. But can he mould its thoughts of eating when hungry, or thoughts of drinking when thirsty? If my body did not have a smelter or sculptor to create it, how then could it see, hear, speak or move in a lively and exquisite fashion? [How could I] meet family and know filiality, meet elders and know respect, meet my liege lord and know loyalty, meet a friend and know modesty?[43]

That is, for Ma Zhu the existence and human consciousness of the Confucian virtues – filiality, respect, loyalty, modesty – actually demonstrate the inescapable reality of the Islamic God's existence and cosmogenetic power.

In the 'True Benevolence' chapter, Ma similarly argued the analogy between God's love for humankind, which engenders religious faith (Ar. *imān*), and parental love for their children, which engenders filial piety. Parents create children as God created all phenomenal reality, inculcating inherent luminous virtue (*mingde*), expressed as filial piety, within them: 'If it were not for the parents' concern and attachment preceding the children's, whence would come pure filiality?'[44]

Since the dominant Neo-Confucian culture of China professed no creed, no fundamental statement of faith, Ma Zhu found that it lacked consciousness of the basic and (for a Muslim) natural, inherent relationship between the individual self and God. For Ma Zhu, recognition of the self, certainly characteristic of Neo-Confucianism, demands recognition of God: 'Only uncover that one character, "I", and God's totality and action will be entirely discerned in the mind.'[45] Writing about Liu Zhi, thirty years Ma Zhu's junior, Sachiko Murata affiliates this Islamic idea with Mencius: '"He who fully realises his heart knows his nature. He who knows his nature knows Heaven." (7.A.1.1) To the Huiru [Sino-Muslim Confucians], this must have seemed a Chinese version of the *hadith*, "He who recognises himself recognizes his Lord."'[46]

Preceding Liu Zhi, Ma Zhu tried to convince his readers that reality simply does not make sense without faith in a creating God. He called upon both Chinese and Islamic texts to make his arguments, which included the conventional argument that only a Great Craftsman could create so vast and complex a universe as we see around us:

> Dragons can soar, tigers can bite, bulls can gore, horses can kick, cocks can rouse, dogs can guard, apes can climb, rats can burrow, silkworms can spin, spiders can make a web, ants can form ranks, bees can make honey – their forms are different, so too their special abilities; their diets vary, as do their voices. These are analogous to artisans making tools. Though their forms

and collection are dissimilar – the square and round, horizontal and vertical, small and large, long and short – each is appropriate to its function. We can see the subtle working of their use and know the craftsman's remarkable skill. No one, gazing on the craftsman's uncanny skill, could possibly call it the thing's own inherent nature. Why do bells not give birth to bells? Why do drums not give birth to drums? Can a wooden horse whinny, or a stone cow low?[47]

Our senses, too, give evidence of God's power, for our sense organs are merely pathways for sensory stimuli that only God could create:

> Without bodies we cannot prove the profound and subtle mysteries of Heaven and Earth. Without heart–mind, we cannot prove the brightness of Highest Heaven. Without intelligence, we cannot prove God's eternal being. That which is proved by Heaven and Earth is the inclusiveness of their totality. That which is proved by Highest Heaven is the brightness of its scope. That which is proved by God is the totality of His action [lit. 'movement/stillness'].[48]

Another line of argument lay in the relationship between the human capacity to know and God's infinite generative power. At the beginning of the *Zhinan*'s third chapter, Ma Zhu dealt with the relationship between Confucian epistemology and Islamic faith. The Confucian classics hold 'investigation of things' (*gewu*) to be humankind's most fundamental responsibility, undertaken in order to set the cosmos in order through individual self-cultivation. For a Muslim thinker like Ma Zhu, every step in that 'investigation of things' must necessarily lead to a deeper and more accurate perception of God as creator of all. 'I cannot see a single thing without more deeply recognizing the Lord.'[49] So the *gewu* process mandated in the Confucian classic *Great Learning* (*Daxue*) must lead inevitably to faith, which constitutes God's 'real solicitude' for humankind and God's irreplaceable role as Creator.[50] For Ma Zhu and other *Han kitāb* writers, the *dao*, which Neo-Confucians held to be the pattern for all existence and all human morality, did not possess God's *a priori* nature. The *dao* cannot be the original Lord of Creation, but only an expression of the order and perfection of God's generative power.

Conclusion

The writers of the *Han kitāb* saw being Muslim and being Chinese – that is, participating wholeheartedly in the cultural enterprise of their homeland while remaining 'different' – as perfectly compatible, and they justified the combination through philosophical and religious argumentation. Ma Zhu sought a satisfying resolution to the dilemma of a foreign religion in a self-confident civilisation: how can we both belong here and maintain our differences without being judged heterodox or barbarous? How can we be true to our ancestral faith and remain within the pale of a Sinocentric orthodoxy? How can we merge the knowledge we have gained of two disparate, sometimes conflicting *dao*s into a coherent, correct, and satisfying whole?

Contemporary Sino-Muslim philosophers have attempted to make sense of what they call *Huizu* – that is, ethnic Chinese Muslim – cosmogony.[51] Yang Guiping, for example, explains the *Han kitāb* approach to Creation thus:

> The beginning of Heaven and Earth came solely out of the Root Suchness (*benran*) of the Lord. Truly, the Lord is the fundamental source of heaven, earth, humankind, and things. All principle and living essence come out of this Root Suchness.[52]

This argument originated with Ma Zhu, and Liu Zhi utilised it later. Without specifying any chain of creation or divine acts, this abstracted Root Suchness constituted God as the precursor of 'all principle and living essence', so even principle, the patterns of existence – Neo-Confucian *li*, analogous to Platonic forms – must stem solely from God. Impossible in a non-Muslim Neo-Confucian cosmology, God's creation of the cosmos from nothing makes sense to Chinese Muslims, expressed in their native language.

Twentieth- and twenty-first-century Chinese scholars describe Ma Zhu and his colleagues as articulating what they conceived as the superiority of Islamic cosmology over that of Confucians, Buddhists and Daoists. Their failure to generate any large-scale agreement with their arguments illustrates both the deep-seated, conservative biases of Qing Neo-Confucianism – Confucians were satisfied that their ideology was universally correct – and also the Chinese elite's fundamental mistrust of anything foreign. Despite their appropriation of Neo-Confucian vocabulary and their clear belonging to Chinese culture, Muslim authors like Ma Zhu could not persuade their non-Muslim intellectual neighbours of Islam's most cherished truths.

But that was only one of the *Qingzhen Zhinan*'s purposes, and perhaps not the most important. Rarely have Sino-Muslims advocated widespread proselytisation of their non-Muslim neighbours. (See Cieciura, Chapter 5, and Chérif-Chebbi, Chapter 8, this volume, for modern exceptions.) Rather, Ma Zhu aimed to educate Muslims literate only in Chinese about their religion and to induce them to remain Muslims, not to acculturate entirely to Chinese ways. In that task he succeeded to some extent. Beginning with those poetic prefaces gathered during Ma's return journey to Yunnan in the late seventeenth century, Chinese Muslims have studied and praised his work. His book persists as a standard source for Chinese-language understanding of Islam. It remains in print today, over 300 years after it was written, its story of God's Creation expressed clearly and forcefully at one intersection of Chinese and Islamic civilisations

Notes

1. A Yuan period (1348) stele commemorating the reconstruction of a mosque in Dingzhou does deal with Islamic doctrine, but it was written by a non-Muslim official, Yang Shouyi.
2. Benite, *Dao of Muhammad*, p. 6.
3. The same impulse endures to the present, as many twenty-first-century Sino-Muslim intellectuals attempt to define an Islamic religious ideology compatible with the procrustean demands of Chinese socialism, with its powerful nationalist and potentially xenophobic elements.
4. Benite, *Dao of Muhammad*, p. 5.
5. Introduced by Sachiko Murata, *Chinese Gleams*, pp. 19–24.
6. Leslie, *Islam in Traditional China*, p. 117, and Murata et al., *Sage Learning*, p. 4, note that Wu's translation of the *Mirsād al-ibād min al-mabda 'ila 'l-ma'ād* of Najm al-Din Rāzī appeared in 1670 as *Guizhen yaodao*.
7. Mote, *Intellectual Foundations of China*, pp. 13–14.
8. The process called *geyi*, 'concept matching', involved pairing a Buddhist term in Sanskrit or Pali with a Daoist term in Chinese, thus incorporating the entirely foreign Indian vocabulary into a familiar linguistic-conceptual framework. Needless to say, this type of translation could not capture the subtle differences

between cultures and their systems of thought, but it did make the texts' foreignness less off-putting and more approachable.

9. Matsumoto Akirō, *Chūgoku Isurāmu shisō*, p. 2.
10. The relationship of the Tais of Sipsongpanna to their more powerful and unified neighbours was summed up in a local proverb, 'The Chinese as father, the Burmese as mother' (Giersch, *Asian Borderlands*, p. 36).
11. Giersch, *Asian Borderlands*, p. 25.
12. Many scholars have noted the tendency among Chinese-speaking Muslims to build communities along cultural frontiers, where China meets non-China. Centres such as Baoshan/Tengyue in Yunnan, Hezhou (now Linxia) and Taozhou (now Lintan) in Gansu, and Baotou in Inner Mongolia all share this location, and many of their Muslim residents worked as commercial middlemen or brokers.
13. In his autobiographical chapter, Ma Zhu claimed that numerous omens persuaded him that Yunnan was about to be overtaken by disaster: the appearance of a stone lion; the collapse of Taihua Mountain; and a comet blocking the sun (Ma Zhu, *Qingzhen zhinan* 1.61b). All citations from the *Qingzhen zhinan* are taken from the reprint edition in *Huizu he Zhongguo Yisilanjiao guji ziliao huibian*, Collection 1, box 7, and all translations are mine. This collection, published by Ningxia People's Publishing Company, reproduces an 1868 woodblock edition.
14. See his memorial in Ma Zhu, *Qingzhen zhinan* 1.55a–59a. In this effort he failed entirely.
15. These are the final chapters of the *Qingzhen Zhinan*, Nos 9 and 10.
16. Aubin, 'Quels Naqshbandis?'
17. Ma Zhu rendered the three stages of Sufi progress – *sharī'a, tarīqa, haqīqa* – into Chinese as the 'Three Vehicles of Teaching, Dao and Perfection', using the same term for 'vehicle' as Buddhist translators had. Other Sino-Muslim authors coined different translations.
18. For a comprehensive account of Qalandars in Central Asia, see Papas, *Mystiques et vagabonds*, especially the Introduction.
19. In this Ma Zhu resembled – or may have been consciously following – the great Indian renewer of Islam, Ahmad Sirhindi (1564–1624), who wrote: 'The *tariqah* and the *haqiqah* [the second and third stages of the Sufi approach to God] for which the Sufis are known, are subservient to the Shari'ah' (Ansari, *Sufism and Shariah*, p. 221). Though he does not mention reading Sirhindi, Ma's Yunnan homeland lay on well-travelled trade routes to the South Asian subcontinent

via Burma, and we have some evidence that Sirhindi's writings circulated in the province.
20. Ma Zhu, *Qingzhen zhinan* 1.26a–b, 'Zishu'.
21. Murata, Frankel and Jin Yijiu, among others, have already done this, focusing on Liu Zhi. Here we are concerned with an earlier contributor to the *Han kitāb* discourse, an intermediary between Wang Daiyu's direct appropriation of Islamic meanings and Liu Zhi's more sophisticated syncretism.
22. Liu Zhi, Ma's even more famous successor, did precisely the same. See Frankel, Chapter 2, this volume.
23. Available at: http://www.slate.com/articles/life/faithbased/2007/07/what_to_expect_when_youre_expecting_a_cowife.2.html, last accessed 19 July 2013.
24. Ricci, *Tianzhu shiyi*, cited in Hsia, *A Jesuit in the Forbidden City*, p. 224. Hsia's summary of Ricci's text includes a number of arguments and elements that appear in Ma Zhu's work and later in Liu Zhi's. Roman Catholic tracts and translations would have been easy for Liu Zhi to obtain in Nanjing, but Ma Zhu makes no mention of reading such books either in Yunnan or Beijing. Nonetheless, Ma's defence of the claim that the True (or Real) Lord (*Zhenzhu*, Ar. *Allāh*) created the cosmos follows many of the same lines as Ricci's somewhat earlier assertion regarding the Heavenly Lord (*Tianzhu*, Lat. *Deus*).
25. Jin Zhong, a fifteenth-century Chinese Jewish writer, followed the same pattern by creating a syncretic 'first human being', combining the Chinese (originally Indian) Pangu with the Old Testament's Adam (Lipman, 'Living Judaism', p. 272), a device also used by some *Han kitāb* writers. Jin Zhong also demonstrated Judaism's civilised nature by stating that Jews behave just like all other Chinese: 'all the [Jewish] people observe and preserve the established laws, know how to honour Heaven and venerate the ancestors, and show themselves loyal to their lord and filial to their parents'. To justify such peculiar and obviously foreign religious dictates as the Sabbath and the Day of Atonement, Jin quoted the *Book of Changes* (*Yijing*), not the Hebrew Scriptures.
26. Frankel, *Rectifying God's Name*, p. 128.
27. Murata et al., argue from the axiom of innate understanding (Ar. *irfān* or *ma'rifa*) – which Murata calls 'intellectual knowledge' – to Liu Zhi's Islamic–Confucian synthesis in the Introduction to *Sage Learning*, pp. 22ff.
28. Wu Zixian, *Guizhen yaodao* (1891 edition), 1.16a–17b.
29. Unlike Ma Zhu, Wang Daiyu had never studied for or passed the civil service examinations, and, by his own admission, he had never become deeply familiar with the Neo-Confucian curriculum. See Lipman, *Familiar Strangers*, p. 76.

30. That is, 'the Cheng brothers' and Zhu Xi's study of principle'.
31. See Joseph Adler's translation and explanation of Zhou's brief work, and the importance given to it by Zhu Xi, in DeBary and Bloom, *Sources of Chinese Tradition*, ch. 20.
32. These are the names of the first two hexagrams in the *Book of Changes* (*Yijing*), the former made up of six unbroken (*yang*, male) lines, the latter of six broken (*yin*, female) lines.
33. Liang Yijun, '*Zhengjiao zhenquan xu*', pp. 4–5.
34. Ma Zhu used the term *ziran*, which means 'nature' or 'natural' in modern Chinese, but in the seventeenth century had a more abstract implication.
35. Here we see that Ma Zhu was knowledgeable in the Three Teachings (Confucian–Buddhist–Daoist) synthesis characteristic of late imperial China, and he refuted their various views of the human place in the cosmos, beginning with the Neo-Confucian notion of clear and turbid *qi*. See Frankel, Chapter 2, this volume.
36. This phrase indicates Ma Zhu's desire to confound Buddhist as well as Neo-Confucian theories by demonstrating the superiority of Islamic cosmology.
37. Here Ma Zhu refers to and revises the vocabulary used much earlier by the *Laifu* inscription.
38. Ma Zhu, *Qingzhen zhinan* 2.25a–b. Here Ma Zhu's argumentation, its final simile derived directly from Cheng Hao as cited by Zhu Xi, resonates with a standard Muslim philosophical position, that non-believers are blind and deaf or like drunkards in their senseless ignorance. In his Confucian discourse, Cheng Hao had not intended to describe non-believers in Islam, but rather men of his own time who, despite their talents, did not focus on their own self-cultivation. See Tillman, 'Chen Liang on Statecraft', for Chen Liang's interpretation of the simile.
39. Frankel, *Rectifying God's Name*, p. 80, among others.
40. Ma Zhu, *Qingzhen zhinan* 2.24a.
41. These are dry measures for grain. Ten *ge* made a *sheng*, ten *sheng* a *dou* ('bushel'), and ten *dou* a *dan* ('picul').
42. *Tiren*, a term used by Zhang Zai (eleventh century) and Zhou Lianggong (who became a *jinshi* the year Ma Zhu was born), meant something like 'viscerally (physically) recognise', or 'know something by cognition'. As Zhou Lianggong wrote, 'Every day you can viscerally recognize (*tiren*) the good and evil you have done.'
43. Ma Zhu, *Qingzhen zhinan* 2.39a–b.
44. *Ibid.*, 2.28a.

45. *Ibid.*, 2.39a.
46. Murata et al., *Sage Learning*, 65.
47. Ma Zhu, *Qingzhen Zhinan*, *zhenci* chapter. This imagery, arguing for the existence of God from the complexity and wondrous qualities of phenomenal reality, is reminiscent of Sufi articulations of love of God.
48. Ma Zhu, *Qingzhen Zhinan*, *tiren* chapter.
49. Wu Yandong, *Zhongguo Huizu*, ch. 5, Pt 3.
50. Murata, *Chinese Gleams*, p. 67.
51. For the early twentieth-century debate regarding Sino-Muslims' nature – as a religious group or an ethnic people – see Cieciura, Chapter 5, this volume.
52. Yang, 'Ming-Qing shiqi', p. 35.

2

Liu Zhi:
The Great Integrator of Chinese Islamic Thought

James D. Frankel

History is replete with stories of visionaries whose genius was unappreciated in their own time and place. Many luminaries have been criticised, some even persecuted, by the governing authority under which they lived, or by their public or by both. Some have found acceptance abroad or have been vindicated posthumously. In the words of Jesus, 'A prophet is not without honour except in his own town and in his own home.'[1] The Prophet Muḥammad followed in the footsteps of the prophets who preceded him. He was jeered at, reviled and struggled for decades against members of his own clan and tribe before overcoming his enemies and uniting Arabia under the banner of Islam. The message of Islam thence spread in all directions, claiming followers over a massive swath of Afro-Eurasia. Those who tread the prophetic path, trammelled by adversity, must be willing to sacrifice everything for the sake of delivering their message. The followers of the prophets similarly have faced initial hardships before enjoying success, their triumphs sometimes becoming clear only after their deaths. According to the *ḥadīth*, 'Scholars are the heirs of the prophets.'[2] For some 1,400 years, Islamic scholars have carried the legacy of the prophets, earning thereby obloquy and acclaim, or some measure of each.

Within a century of the Prophet's death in 632 CE, Islam's eastward expansion had brought Muslims to China, but it would take almost a millennium before the legacy of Islamic scholarship reached its Chinese apogee in the person and the writings of Liu Zhi (*c.* 1660–*c.* 1730), the most prolific and celebrated of the *Han kitāb* writers. Liu Zhi embodied Chinese Muslim simultaneity, reflected in his ability to participate in both the Islamic and Chinese intellectual worlds as an insider. Calling upon his literary talents and linguistic finesse, he seamlessly integrated Islamic and Confucian values and tenets into his worldview, which enabled him to harmonise the two traditions in his writings. As reflected in his work, Liu Zhi understood himself truly to be the heir of both the Islamic prophets and the Chinese sages, whom he conflated into a single class under the Chinese term *sheng*, thereby integrating Chinese and Islamic concepts of the ideal person, 'a human being endowed with special qualifications that make him a suitable mediator between the divine and mundane realms'.[3] Liu Zhi thus harked back to Confucius and Mencius, who had expressed the notion that righteousness was not an exclusively Chinese virtue.

This Confucian idea reached its culmination in the universalistic teachings of the Song dynasty (960–1279) philosopher Lu Jiuyuan (Xiangshan) (1139–92), whom Liu Zhi invoked. Lu wrote compellingly of sages coming from both the East and the West. The Islamic tradition likewise affirmed that God had sent prophets to all nations,[4] and that distinctions such as East and West are meaningless in the face of God's omnipresence.[5] By integrating Confucius and Muḥammad into a single brotherhood, Liu Zhi could substantiate the claim that their respective teachings derived from a single source of moral authority, a universal Truth transcending temporal, geographic, linguistic or cultural differences:

> The sage of the West, Muḥammad, lived in Arabia long after Confucius, so far removed in time and space from the Chinese sage that we do not know exactly by how much. Their respective languages are mutually unintelligible. So how is it that their *dao* is in full accord? They were of one mind. Therefore, the *dao* is the same.[6]

Like the prophets, scholars achieve transcendence through their words and deeds. But they are nevertheless also products of their particular time and place. In the case of Liu Zhi, this was Nanjing of the early Qing dynasty (1644–1911), under the reign of the Kangxi emperor (r. 1662–1722). As Chinese society, and particularly its literate elite, recovered from the traumatic fall of the Ming (1368–1644), the Qing attempted to transform their conquest regime into a legitimate imperial dynasty. The new imperium sought to establish hegemony and, despite its own foreign origins, to project an image of legitimate rule over an ethnically and culturally diverse realm.

The Manchus' own identity reconstruction created an opportunity for various other cultures to promote positive self-definitions in their pursuit of validation and security. Chinese Muslims were among these ethnocultural communities that, despite putative non-Chinese ancestry centuries earlier, had become a naturalised segment of Chinese society.[7] In many ways, Liu Zhi epitomised a community in the process of defining itself after a millennium-long evolution accelerated by dramatic changes in the Ming period and the turbulence of the Ming–Qing transition.

Liu Zhi was not 'without honour' in his hometown during his lifetime. Born into a gentrified Nanjing Chinese Muslim family with a scholarly pedigree, later in life he travelled in elite non-Muslim literati circles as well. During his lifetime, Liu Zhi was already acknowledged as an important member of the Chinese Muslim scholarly establishment, as the finest product of the 'scripture hall education' (*jingtang jiaoyu*).

Beginning his studies with his father, Liu Sanjie – a noted *Han kitāb* author in his own right – and then, starting around the age of twelve, under the tutelage of Yuan Ruqi (b. *c.* 1640), Liu Zhi would have cut his teeth on the basic *jingtang jiaoyu* curriculum, which likely included reading and recitation of the *Qur'ān* and elementary Arabic and Persian instruction. Liu Zhi's early education at the mosque at Nanjing's Wuxueyuan (Garden of Military Studies) also included the basic ritual practices of Sunni Islam.

Liu Zhi's primary education certainly taught him to read and write Chinese, enabling him to begin studying the Confucian canon at the age of fifteen. Given the fact that between the sixteenth and eighteenth centuries a large number of Arabic and Persian texts had been translated or explicated in Chinese within the *Han kitāb* network, Liu Zhi's early training in classical Chinese also allowed him to study these Chinese Islamic texts as well.

Following eight years reading the Confucian classics, according to his own account Liu Zhi spent six years with Arabic and Persian books about Islam, then three years on the Buddhist canon, and one year on Daoist texts. He also claimed to have read over a hundred 'Occidental books' (*xiyang shu*), which most scholars suppose to be the translations and compositions of the Jesuits, active in Nanjing during the preceding century. Thus, after eighteen years of preparation, around the age of thirty-three, Liu Zhi had acquired the knowledge and honed the formidable linguistic and intellectual skills required for his career as an Islamic scholar and a professional writer of Chinese.

By the time he finished writing, the prolific Liu Zhi had produced no fewer than a dozen distinct titles. Unlike his predecessor Ma Zhu (1640–1711), for example, rather than writing one monumental volume covering the spectrum of Islamic knowledge (see Lipman, Chapter 1, this volume), Liu Zhi wrote numerous books, each focusing in detail on a particular facet of Islam. He did not specialise in a single field of knowledge, but rather worked 'horizontally' across a variety of literary genres. His body of works thus represents a cross-section of the canon as a whole, many of them in categories corresponding directly to the *jingtang jiaoyu* curriculum. For example, Liu Zhi wrote a book of Arabic letters and philology, the *Tianfang zimu jieyi* (*Explaining the Meaning of Arabic Letters*). He also wrote Islamic history, including the *Huihui shuo* (*Explaining Huihui*), about the historical origins of Islam in China and the ethnonym 'Huihui', and the *Tianfang chunqiu* (*Islamic Spring and Autumn Annals*), which dealt with Arabian and early Islamic history. Of his overtly didactic works, the best known is his *Tianfang sanzijing* (*The Islamic Three-Character Classic*), a rhyming primer of Islamic belief and practice following the Confucian genre.[8] His corpus also includes at least one direct translation of a Persian text into Chinese, the *Zhenjing zhaowei* (*The Subtleties of Illumination in the True Classic*) (see below).

His most famous books by far constitute his '*Tianfang* Trilogy': the *Tianfang xingli* (*Metaphysics of Islam*), *Tianfang dianli* (*Norms and Rituals of Islam*), and *Tianfang zhisheng shilu* (*True Record of the Ultimate Sage of Islam*). Each of these books is devoted to a single main theme, but together they represent the systematic exposition of the author's comprehensive view of Islamic knowledge. Liu Zhi articulated his grand vision of the interconnections among these three books: 'As far as these books are concerned, they are three yet actually constitute one whole. They were published in incremental steps as I attained mastery [over their subject matter] to some extent.'[9]

Describing how the three texts combined to present a single, comprehensive vision of Islam, Liu Zhi wrote:

> The *dianli* is a book that explains the teaching (*jiao*). The *xingli* is a book that explains the way (*dao*). This edition, the *Zhisheng [shi]lu*, is intended to explain the profound origins of the teaching and the way.[10]

Well respected as a scholar and as a person of character both within his community and beyond it, he did, however, also receive criticism from various quarters. Conservative voices within the Chinese Muslim community regarded his methods and ideas, and the *Han kitāb* in general, as overly conciliatory to Chinese traditions and therefore a dilution or bastardisation of Islam. Some non-Muslim critics, despite acknowledging Liu Zhi's erudition and literary skill, could not be persuaded that Islam was anything but an absurd, foreign religious teaching.

Liu Zhi was sensitive to the criticism. Although his genius was recognised by many of his contemporaries, he still yearned for approval and understanding. He expressed these sentiments in a deeply personal and reflective essay appended to his last major work, *The True Record of the Ultimate Sage of Islam*. In it he wrote about the trials and hardships he faced as a semi-reclusive scholar, and about his strong motivation for writing:

> Particularly difficult was the fact that I had no companions or colleagues. Even kith and kin considered that I could not make a living, which is unfortunate. But I did not rest from pursuing my ambition, and with firm determination continued to expound Islamic learning in order to disseminate it among the people.[11]

Ensconced in his studies, Liu Zhi felt isolated and misunderstood. Moreover, he worried that amid all the criticism, or even the adulation, his work received, his underlying message and overarching purpose might be lost to his readers. Significantly, he also worried about his legacy, about how future generations would regard his work:

> I respectfully hope that the gentlemen of this world will remember my humble self not as one whose perceptions were extensive, nor whose expressions were ingenious, but whose single ambition was to propound and

elucidate orthodox learning, correct any errors in it, and fill whatever was lacking or omitted from it. If my embellishments generally lack grace, it is so that I could achieve a grand vision. And if I am able to bequeath my lesson to eternity, then this is the good fortune of the *dao*.[12]

Liu Zhi was conscious of his place in history and in the *Han kitāb* lineage. His reverence for the Chinese sages and the prophets of Islam demonstrates his devotion to the ancestors and antiquity. As one of Liu Zhi's non-Muslim colleagues, Xu Yuanzheng,[13] remarked in a preface to the *Tianfang xingli*: 'How could we have known that the breadth of Master Liu's mind was so extensive, or that his work would stretch so far back into the past?'[14]

This retrospection, combined with concern for his posterity, reveals Liu Zhi's sense of his own importance as a link between the past and future. Yuan Guozuo (b. 1712), the grandson of Liu Zhi's teacher, Yuan Ruqi, captured this role perfectly as he looked back at his venerable predecessor: 'Not only did he perform meritorious service to the sages of the past, but he has also brought profound benefit to the generations that came after him.'[15] Similarly, Liu Zhi was convinced of the magnitude of his own literary enterprise. As noted above, he regarded his work as a 'grand vision'. Describing the purport, and acknowledging the import, of his undertaking he expressed his ambition to make known the splendour of Islam, lest it 'be relegated to one (small) corner, and . . . not be the universal learning of the world'.[16]

Did Liu Zhi achieve his grand vision? The answer depends on our measurements of success. He did not succeed in making Islam the 'universal learning of the world', but he did help to gain it a place at the table, so to speak, and he did so through a combination of his scholarship and his personality. He and his work were admired within his own scholarly community and, as we shall see, beyond it during his lifetime. Predictably, Liu Zhi's co-religionists honoured his work most effusively. Muslim friends and associates, in addition to praising his extensive learning and literary accomplishments, also spoke in superlatives of his character. For example, his teacher, Yuan Ruqi, wrote:

> What sort of a man is Jielian? Is he not a great man? He is not great in terms of worldly affairs, but rather in . . . the virtue of the *dao*. He is not

only great in terms of human ability, but moreover in terms of what people are unable to do.[17]

Liu Zhi would undoubtedly have been gratified by such praise from his teacher and other elders among the Muslim community. Indeed, he solicited such testimonials. After completing the *Tianfang dianli*, Liu Zhi travelled to Beijing with the manuscript, perhaps intending to present it at court. He did not receive an audience with the emperor, but while in the capital he did meet and develop collegial, even friendly, relations with several high-ranking non-Muslim Confucian officials. These gentlemen and other literati provided the feedback Liu Zhi sought regarding his book. Like Ma Zhu before him, Liu Zhi adorned his books with as many laudatory prefaces as he could obtain (see Lipman, Chapter 1, this volume). Demonstrating a cosmopolitanism that surpassed his Yunnanese predecessor, Liu Zhi also included prefaces from prominent non-Muslim scholars alongside those written by fellow Muslims.

Generally, non-Muslim commentators articulated a twofold assessment. On the one hand, they were pleased to discover that Islam was so compatible with their own Confucian tradition; on the other hand, they uniformly praised Liu Zhi's work ethic, erudition and literary skill. Some readers were also moved to praise Liu Zhi's universalistic worldview as evidenced in his ability to harmonise Islamic and Confucian principles. This harmonisation was intended to persuade a non-Muslim audience that Islam was no threat to Chinese political and social norms. Consequently, of the entire *Han kitāb* corpus, Liu Zhi's writings were most warmly received by non-Muslim elites. His commitment to the teachings of Confucius and the ancient Chinese sages garnered enthusiastic approval from non-Muslim literati like Xu Yuanzheng, who saw in Liu Zhi a fellow Confucian:

> Master Liu's translation into Chinese also teaches about China and that which China holds dear. This book brings back into view the *dao* of the ancient Sages: Yao and Shun, Yu and Tang, King Wen, King Wu, the Duke of Zhou, and Confucius. Thus, although this book was written to explain Islam, it actually glorifies and magnifies our own Confucianism.[18]

One preface writer after another extolled Liu Zhi and his writing, echoing each other's praises of two qualities in particular: universalism and erudition.

The following passage from a preface to the *Tianfang xingli* by Lu You, a Vice-Minister of the Board of War,[19] addresses the inter-relation of these qualities:

> I am delighted by Master Liu's broad knowledge and rare talent for expression. His mind is on the infinite and universal; he is not only proficient in the Islamic canon, but also has a thorough understanding of the Chinese classics, and he has blended them harmoniously and woven them together to write a book in order to clarify these teachings.[20]

Lu You depicts a scholar driven to erudition by his desire for universal knowledge and understanding, who also endeavoured (or was gifted with the ability) to express his ideas to a diverse audience. Jing Rizhen, an imperial censor of the Shaanxi Circuit, further commented on Liu Zhi's erudition with a detailed account of how well read he was:

> The gentleman Liu, who goes by the style name of Jielian, is mild-mannered and restrained, studious and fond of books. Drawing from a variety of scriptures and classics, histories, novels, romances, fiction, fictitious histories, law books, books of divination, as well as the writings of the Two Schools,[21] there is nothing he did not peruse or research. Furthermore, he was also able to reconcile all of the above with the Six Classics. He researched into the totality of Neo-Confucian metaphysics, and deeply fathomed the essential subtleties of the Confucian literati tradition.[22]

It would not be exaggerating to say Liu Zhi was among the best-read men in China at the time. It appears he read just about anything on which he could lay his hands, and his extremely rare set of language skills (Chinese, Arabic and Persian) permitted him access to literary genres and canons that most of his countrymen did not have. In a preface to the *Tianfang dianli*, Yang Feilu, a fellow Muslim scholar, similarly extolled the breadth of Liu Zhi's learning: 'Indeed, there is nothing that he has not grown familiar with, but through painstaking and exhaustive research.'[23]

These many accolades highlight the acceptance of Liu Zhi and his work during his lifetime by colleagues on both sides of his dual audience. Yet, while he was proud of the recognition (he published the prefaces in his books), it was likely more important to him that the people of the world should understand the grandeur of his vision. Unfortunately for Liu Zhi, he did not live to see the far-reaching effect his writings would have in the promotion of Islamic learning in China. Some of his most notable achievements were actually posthumous honours and distinctions.

It would be impossible to estimate how many Chinese Muslims were affected, directly or indirectly, by Liu Zhi's work and his enduring legacy. From followers of succeeding generations who shared his worldview he received the highest degree of veneration. Posthumously, he has been virtually canonised within the Chinese Muslim community. His epitaph writers took the association of Liu Zhi with the 'sages of the past' to superlatives – the inscription on his tombstone in Nanjing memorialises him as a 'former worthy' (*xianxian*), the worthies being the disciples and followers of the sages according to Confucian tradition.[24] The maintenance of his grave down to the present day shows the extent to which later generations of Chinese Muslims have continued to revere him.

Liu Zhi came to be remembered as a 'great integrator', literally one who 'assembles great achievement' (*jidacheng*), an epithet first used by Mencius in praise of Confucius.[25] Liu Zhi used a similar expression to describe the Prophet Muḥammad, describing him as 'the great culmination of all the sages' (*jiliesheng zhi dacheng*).[26] Yuan Guozuo later used the term *jidacheng* in reference to Muḥammad, yet another instance of associating the Prophet with the sages of ancient China.[27] It seems only fitting, perhaps, that Liu Zhi, who endeavoured so diligently to harmonise the teachings of Confucius and Muḥammad, would eventually inherit the same title as the luminaries he revered. Had he lived to hear this praise, his customary humility probably would have compelled him to decline it, though it certainly vindicated his claim to a 'grand vision'.

Confucius thought of himself as a collator and editor of the wisdom of the ancient sages, humbly insisting, 'I have transmitted what was taught to me without making up anything of my own.'[28] The Prophet Muḥammad was instructed by the *Qur'ān* to say, 'I am not an innovator among the messengers ... I follow only what is revealed to me.'[29] Both men became fulcra of their respective traditions, serving as links in the transmission of the most profound knowledge from past to present and future generations.

Similarly, Liu Zhi wrote, 'I only transmit what I have learned' from the generations who preceded him.[30] In this way, he assembled and integrated that which he inherited from both sides of his ethnic, cultural, religious and intellectual background. Liu Zhi was historically situated to serve as the fulcrum of the Chinese Islamic intellectual tradition embodied in the *Han kitāb*. He merged philosophy and theology, forging a way to reconcile the theology of Islamic monotheism with a Neo-Confucian metaphysics devoid of a creator God (see Lipman, Chapter 1, this volume). Thus, he persuasively harmonised ideas from traditions that were geographically and chronologically distant from one another: 'The teachings of the sages are the same in the East and West, and in the present as in the past.'[31] With its crucial theory of the rectification of names (*zhengming*), Confucianism takes the use of names and epithets seriously. Later generations of Chinese Muslims referred to Liu Zhi as a 'former worthy' and a 'great integrator', demonstrating both the extent of their belonging in China as well as their profound respect and admiration.

In terms of influence on future generations, later *Han kitāb* scholars looked up to Liu Zhi and wrote laudatory prefaces and commentaries for editions of his books published after his death. The fact that Liu Zhi's books continued to be printed and reprinted in multiple editions long after he died – some are still in print – is solid evidence of his lasting influence. Completing a full circle, some of Liu Zhi's writings, including parts of the *Tianfang xingli*, were translated into Arabic in Yunnan in the late nineteenth century to be used as instructional texts in local mosque education (see Petersen, Chapter 4, this volume).

Probably the most widely circulated of all of Liu Zhi's writings, the *True Record of the Ultimate Sage of Islam* (a biography of the Prophet), was not published by Yuan Guozuo until 1785, many years after Liu Zhi's death. Liu Zhi's writings strongly influenced Yuan Guozuo (see Tontini, Chapter 3, this volume), who helped to propagate them among subsequent generations, editing, publishing and re-publishing several titles. Yuan Guozuo printed the *True Record* complete with his own preface and postscript in which he praised Liu Zhi in strongly Confucian terms, writing, 'Master Liu's loyalty, filiality, benevolence and kindness truly were inconceivable'.[32] He also appreciated Liu Zhi's pivotal role in the lineage of Islamic scholarship:

If Master Liu had not continued his father's will, endlessly magnifying the benevolent favour of the Teaching of the Sage, how could there have been such dazzling brilliance as this?[33]

Liu Zhi explicitly acknowledged his debt to previous generations of scholars, especially his own father:

My late father thought that ritual law was not understood clearly. As I am but his son and not clever, how shall I ever dare here to aspire to such ambition and say that I shall continue his undertaking? Therefore, I only transmit what I have learned.[34]

Albeit under the strong influence of his intellectual forebears, Liu Zhi was also highly original in his use of sources and the integration of ideas coming from disparate traditions. His sources included not only the 'orthodox' Islamic and Confucian canons, but also texts that might have been deemed heterodox by some critics; that is, he liberally cited Sufi books and frequently alluded to Daoist and Buddhist writings. With regard to the Three Teachings (Confucianism, Daoism and Buddhism), he seems to have subscribed to the syncretic trend prevalent among the literati elite in late Ming and early Qing China (sixteenth–seventeenth centuries), many of whom embraced such universalistic slogans as 'The Three Teachings united as one' (*sanjiao heyi*). Liu Zhi explicitly stated that he wrote the *Norms and Rituals of Islam* for 'the reader who thoroughly understands and practices the Three Teachings but needs to learn about Islam'.[35] Previous *Han kitāb* authors had mentioned the Three Teachings, but none in so positive a tone nor so willing to harmonise Islam with Chinese traditions.[36]

This is not to say that he fully approved of either Daoism or Buddhism. Actually, in the manner of the Confucian establishment, he referred to the 'Two Schools' as heterodoxies and decried their mistaken theories of 'emptiness' and 'non-action', respectively.[37] Nevertheless, since Daoist and Buddhist concepts and terms had been assimilated into the religio-philosophical discourse of the age, Liu Zhi showed no compunction whatsoever about reaching across scholastic lines in order to make his case for Islam.

His willingness to borrow from a wide range of teachings notwithstanding, Liu Zhi's inspiration came first and foremost from the Islamic and

Confucian canons, which he regarded as co-orthodoxies: 'Although the principle (*li*) is expressed in Islamic books, it is no different from what is found in the Confucian canon.'[38] As Lu You had indicated, Liu Zhi was 'not only proficient in the Islamic canon, but also [had] a thorough understanding of the Chinese classics, and he has blended them harmoniously'. After the *Qur'ān*, *Ḥadīth*, Four Books and Five Classics, he explored the vast commentarial and philosophical traditions of both Islamic and Chinese literature. But perhaps the strongest and most direct sources for his own work of integration came from *Han kitāb* authors of the generations before him, especially Wang Daiyu (*c.* 1570– *c.* 1660) and Ma Zhu.

The influence of these earlier *Han kitāb* scholars appears most obviously in Liu Zhi's metaphysics, cosmology and theology. Wang Daiyu had received a traditional Chinese Islamic education before realising its limitations and starting 'to read books on metaphysics and history'.[39] These more advanced studies likely introduced him to the Neo-Confucian and Sufi ideas of the underlying oneness of ultimate reality that suffuse his writings. Liu Zhi similarly focused on theories of metaphysical oneness, which he conflated with the Islamic principle of divine unity (Ar. *tawḥīd*). By extension, he emphasised the monistic idea that everything originates in unity and ultimately returns to unity. He expressed this in Neo-Confucian terms as the 'complete union of Heaven and Man', in turn evocative of the Sufi spiritual concepts of annihilation (Ar. *fanā'*) of the limited ego and subsistence (Ar. *baqā'*) in union with God.

Wang Daiyu's worldview undoubtedly influenced Liu Zhi's, though the latter surpassed the former in his conciliatory stance with regard to Chinese tradition. Wang Daiyu had employed Confucian ideas and terminology, but 'maintained the fundamental truths and superiority of Islam', whereas Liu Zhi tended to place 'Islam and Confucianism on an equal footing'.[40]

Liu Zhi expressed his debt to Ma Zhu in evoking similar cosmological constructions, attempting to reconcile Qur'ānic creationism with the Chinese paradigm of a self-generating cosmos:

> much like Ma Zhu before him, Liu Zhi simply glossed over this essential metaphysical incongruity and, as we shall see, grafted the creator, Allah,

atop the Chinese cosmological scheme as a prime mover existing before and beyond the vicissitudes of 'creation and transformation'.[41]

We may also observe Liu Zhi's simultaneous faith in God and commitment to Confucian ethics in his epistemological reasoning about theology. Just as he and Ma Zhu had modified the traditional Chinese cosmology by introducing the creator God, Liu Zhi also inserted the Islamic theistic principle into basic Confucian epistemology:

> If someone . . . does not know who the Lord and Master is, then how could he be one who 'extends knowledge and apprehends the principle in things', penetrating the mysteries of Heaven and Earth?[42]

Any literate Chinese reader would have easily recognised the phrase 'extending knowledge and apprehending the principle in things' as an allusion to the *Daxue* (Great Learning). That Confucian text describes how to achieve world peace based on cultivation of the individual self, the entire process beginning with the extension of knowledge (*zhizhi*) through the investigation of things (*gewu*).[43] Following this classical thought closely, Liu Zhi advocated 'enlightening one's mind and seeing into one's own nature', then 'following nature and cultivating the way'.[44] Where Liu Zhi differed from the traditional Confucian programme was in his integration of the theistic component: all is predicated upon first acknowledging the Islamic God as Lord and Creator.

Both Wang Daiyu and Liu Zhi were natives of Nanjing, the most cosmopolitan city of late imperial China and an intellectual nexus for many schools of thought. They could not help but be influenced by the ideas that circulated in the city. And there was no shortage of reading materials in Nanjing's unparalleled libraries and bookshops. Wang Daiyu famously participated in animated interfaith discussions with members of Nanjing's literary and religious elite. Yet Liu Zhi's open-mindedness surpassed Wang Daiyu's, as reflected in his reading lists, which went beyond the canons and secondary literature of Islam and the Three Teachings of China. Liu Zhi was the first *Han kitāb* writer explicitly to claim Christian writings among his sources: 'one hundred thirty-seven types of Occidental books'.[45] Jesuit literature in Chinese was readily available in Nanjing at the time, and Liu

Zhi availed himself of it. Yang Feilu confirmed this as he briefly described the sum of Liu Zhi's curriculum:

> He studied the Islamic classics in his youth, and tackled Confucian studies when he grew older. He subsequently amassed besides a broad knowledge of the Two Schools and European literature.[46]

Traces of Liu Zhi's borrowing from Christian, and possibly even Jewish, sources may be detected in his theological discussions, especially his quest for appropriate nomenclature for God.[47]

Liu Zhi read Islamic sources without discrimination. The distance of Chinese Muslims from the heart of the Islamic world removed Liu Zhi and other *Han kitāb* scholars from deep prejudices and burning debates among rival schools of thought that affected the West and South Asian Muslim literary elites. Liu and his colleagues could treat any Arabic or Persian text, whether Sunni, Shiʿi, or Sufi, as genuinely Islamic and orthodox. Liu Zhi's bibliographies feature Sufi texts with particular frequency, for by the time Liu Zhi began writing in the late seventeenth century, Sufi ideology had diffused throughout the world of Islamic thought. Chinese Muslim teachers, too, had already assimilated Sufism into their curriculum, and even the early *Han kitāb* authors had incorporated Sufi ideas into their writings.

In the bibliography to the *Tianfang xingli*, Liu Zhi identified four Sufi sources as foundational: (1) al-Rāzī's *Mirṣād al-ʿIbād min al-mabdā ilā'l-maʿād*[48]; (2) al-Nasafī's *Maqṣad-e Aqṣā*[49]; (3) Jāmī's *Ashiʿʿāt al-lamaʿāt*[50]; and (4) *Lawāʾiḥ fī bayān maʿānī ʿirfāniyya*.[51] The first three of these books had already been translated into Chinese and circulated within the Chinese Muslim educational network when Liu Zhi was a student; he translated the fourth himself. Like his *Han kitāb* predecessors, by translating Liu Zhi also contributed to the curriculum of the *jingtang jiaoyu*, continuing a tradition begun by Hu Dengzhou (1522–1597), the great pioneer of Islamic educational reform in China.

Liu Zhi's use of Sufi ideas and writings was nothing new in China, but his systematic documentation of these sources was innovative among the *Han kitāb* authors. In this regard, Liu Zhi followed in the footsteps of contemporary Neo-Confucian scholarship, which recognised bibliographies as a mark of erudition. During this period bibliographies grew increasingly important as a feature of the Confucian textual studies (*kaozheng*) movement.⁵² Once again, we see Liu Zhi borrowing a Chinese literati practice systematically to enhance Islamic scholarship, while bequeathing to posterity a grasp of his own sources of inspiration.

Liu Zhi's erudition and affirmation of Confucian values made him acceptable, even welcome, in non-Muslim literati circles. These qualities probably also contributed to the unique distinction of the *Norms and Rituals of Islam* within the entire *Han kitāb* canon, namely, its inclusion in the *Siku quanshu* (Compendium of the Four Treasuries). The *Siku quanshu* was compiled under imperial commission between 1773 and 1782, making inclusion of his work in it yet another posthumous honour for Liu Zhi. When the Qianlong (r. 1736–96) court called for books and manuscripts from all over the empire, Yuan Guozuo responded by submitting a bibliography of existing *Han kitāb* texts,⁵³ the *Norms and Rituals of Islam* prominent among them. Yuan Guozuo may also have presented a copy of Liu Zhi's book, along with its companion volumes, the *Metaphysics of Islam* and *True Record of the Ultimate Sage of Islam*, to the emperor in 1782.⁵⁴

When one considers how many Neo-Confucian and non-Confucian texts did not appear in the *Siku*, the status of the *Norms and Rituals of Islam* as the lone representative *Han kitāb* book appears momentous. In actuality, while this was a great honour celebrated by Chinese Muslims and helped to solidify Liu Zhi's pre-eminent (posthumous) status within his own community, it did not guarantee universal approval. The selection process used by the *Siku quanshu* Commission extended far beyond simple inclusion or exclusion. The Commission evaluated thousands of texts, many of which they rejected as politically or ideologically objectionable. Of these, some were not only excluded, but also actually burned, making the *Siku* not only imperial China's largest literary compendium, but also a sweeping censorship initiative, often called a 'literary inquisition'.

Nor did every book that avoided the Commission's pyres achieve the unequivocal approval of the imperium. Some, such as the *Norms and Rituals of Islam*, gained mention in the *Annotated Catalogue*, a somewhat more ambiguous category part way between the perfectly acceptable and the utterly reprehensible. Rather than a complete reprinted text, granted to the most orthodox and approved works, the *Catalogue* included the title, author and a review of those books judged to contain mostly virtuous material, but also some things outside the norms of Confucian propriety. The *Siku* commissioner who read the *Norms and Rituals of Islam* wrote a review that objectively described Liu Zhi's personal history and scholarly accomplishments as well as a summary of the book's contents. At the end of the blurb, however, he offered these editorial remarks:

> Everything is explained in detail, with great respect for his own religion's teaching. Islam is fundamentally far-fetched and absurd. However, [Liu] Zhi has extensively studied Confucian texts, so he intermingled various ideas from the Classics in order to embellish his discourse. His literary style is actually rather elegant. However, the premise is at its root untrue and so the clever literary ornamentation does him no good.[55]

That is, the reviewer paid Liu Zhi a compliment so backhanded that he scarcely veiled its prejudicial and negative conclusion. Had Liu Zhi been alive to read the review, he likely would have been mortified by the opinion that his writing was stylish but insubstantial. Judging from what he had written about his motivation for studying and writing, indeed, his whole raison d'être as a person, he would have been most disappointed by his failure to persuade such a highly placed and cultured reader of Islam's universal appeal. But it is doubtful that any degree of erudition or eloquence on Liu Zhi's part would have changed that. He faced the same insurmountable ideological wall that any non-Confucian teaching – Christianity, for example – would have faced in late imperial China.

Perhaps the gravest misunderstanding to emerge from this entry, however, is the reviewer's assessment that Liu Zhi's 'intermingling' of Confucian and Islamic concepts constituted mere literary embellishment. This evaluation indicts Liu Zhi for disingenuousness, concluding that his connection to the Confucian tradition was superficial or false. The preponderance of evidence presented above indicates that what the *Siku quanshu* Commission dismissed as mere ornamental intermingling ran deeply and consistently in Liu Zhi's identity and his writings. Contrary to the evaluation, Liu Zhi aimed at a genuine and coherent Chinese Islamic simultaneity, a deliberate effort at complete integration, or at least harmonisation, of two intellectual worlds. This integration took place within the minds of Liu Zhi and his colleagues on an existential level. It was anything but superficial and certainly not disingenuous.

Despite the subordinate placement and ambivalent review of the *Norms and Rituals of Islam* in the *Annotated Catalogue* of the *Siku quanshu*, the fact that it appeared at all was of immense importance to the Chinese Muslim community, for whom Liu Zhi's posthumous achievement was, and continues to be, a great source of pride. This recognition sealed the perception of the author as the pre-eminent Chinese Muslim scholar, both within and outside his own community. It also conferred upon the *Han kitāb* canon and the scholars who produced it a status of authority and legitimacy that has endured for several centuries.

The apogee of this aspect of Liu Zhi's legacy appeared in the early twentieth century, far removed from the highly Sinicised Muslim communities of Nanjing and other cities in eastern China. Liu Zhi's books and other *Han kitāb* texts became the core curriculum for the Xidaotang (lit. 'Hall of the Western Way'), a home-grown Islamic movement founded by Ma Qixi (1857–1914) in Gansu province.[56] The Xidaotang looked up to Liu Zhi as one of the founding fathers of their philosophy and worldview, which celebrated Chinese Muslim simultaneity and regarded the future for Muslims in China as being inextricable from that of a rapidly modernising Chinese nation. This new movement thus reified an intellectual heritage for Sino-Muslim people, who came to be called the *Huizu*, that allowed them to participate as citizens in both the Republic and later the People's Republic of China (see Cieciura, Chapter 5, and Chérif-Chebbi, Chapter 8, this volume).

As an integrator and synthesiser, Liu Zhi preserved and transmitted the traditions he had received from his predecessors, created new theories and methodologies, and inspired those who came after him. As an embodiment of a thousand-year encounter between Islam and China, he honoured the past, created significant advances during his lifetime, and served as a bridge to future generations of Chinese Muslims, who saw in his person and thought a model for cultural, religious and intellectual simultaneity. Thus, beyond the 'innate metaphysical and philosophical value' of his writings, Liu Zhi:

crossed religious and civilizational frontiers and created harmony between two intellectual worlds through an appeal to the underlying unity that constitutes the basis of the perennial philosophy.[57]

Identifying a core of ultimate truth (equally Islamic and Confucian), Liu Zhi may be counted as a 'perennialist' thinker. Yet Liu Zhi's grand vision and ability to see beyond the boundaries of time and space, to envision a universal and ubiquitous truth, allowed him fully to claim the intellectual legacies of both sides of his dual heritage, thereby showing himself to be an heir of both the Confucian sages and the Islamic prophets.

According to a famous *ḥadīth*, the Prophet Muḥammad exhorted his followers to 'seek knowledge even though it be in China'.[58] At the advent of Islam, who could have supposed that China would one day be a creative centre for its own form of Islamic scholarship, in the Chinese language, epitomised by the work of Liu Zhi? Blending within himself the ideals of the Confucian literati and Islamic ʿ*ulamāʾ*, Liu Zhi lived according to another *ḥadīth*: 'The word of wisdom is the lost treasure of the believer, and so he has the truest claim to it wherever he finds it.'[59] Gathering scattered treasures from his dual traditions, he integrated them into a coherent, sophisticated body of work, and in so doing he earned honour in his own town and his own home, an honour he hoped to bequeath to his brethren throughout China.

Notes

1. Matthew 13:57.
2. This *ḥadīth* has been related by Tirmidhī, Abu Dawūd, Nasāʾī, Ibn Mājah, Aḥmad ibn Ḥanbal, Ibn Ḥibbān and others. Ibn al-Mulaqqin, Zaylaʿī, Ibn Ḥajar, and others deemed it acceptable (*ḥasan*) or authentic (*saḥīḥ*).
3. Frankel, *Rectifying God's Name*, p. 83.
4. 'for every nation there is a messenger in every era' (*Qurʾān* 10:47); 'And verily, We have sent among every nation a Messenger' (*Qurʾān* 16:36).
5. 'To God belong the East and the West, so wherever you turn, there is the face of God' (*Qurʾān* 2:115).
6. Liu Zhi, 'Yuanjiao pian', in *Tianfang dianli*, p. 11.
7. The extent to which this assertion reflects genetic history has been disputed. Certainly, many Sino-Muslims *claimed* descent from foreign Muslims, but intermarriage between Muslim men and local women (permitted by Islamic

law) created obvious connections between Muslims in China and their non-Muslim neighbours. Patrilineal calculation may be partly responsible for this contradiction, since some scholars did (and do) not recognise women's contribution to bloodline (*xuetong*).

8. See Tontini, Chapter 3, this volume. This work is related to an earlier *Han kitāb* text, the *Sipian yaodao* (*Essential Way of the Four Chapters*), a 1653 translation by Zhang Junshi of a Persian catechistic text, the *Chahār Faṣl* (*Four Chapters*).
9. Liu Zhi, 'Zhushu Shu', in Bai Shouyi (ed.), *Huizhu renwu zhi* (*Qingdai*), p. 357.
10. Ibid., p. 357.
11. Ibid., pp. 357–8.
12. Ibid., p. 360.
13. Xu Yuanzheng held the highest civil service examination degree (*jinshi*) and served as Vice-Minister of the Board of Rites like his father Xu Zhuo, writer of a preface to the *Norms and Rituals of Islam* cited above. See Leslie, *Islamic Literature*, p. 119.
14. Xu Yuanzheng, 'Xu Xu (ii)', in Liu Zhi, *Tianfang xingli*, p. 4a.
15. Yuan Guozuo, 'Xu', in Bai Shouyi (ed.), *Huizu renwu zhi* (*Qingdai*), p. 226. See Tontini, Chapter 3, this volume.
16. Liu Zhi, 'Zi xu', in *Tianfang xingli*, p. 1a.
17. Yuan Ruqi, 'Xu', in Bai Shouyi (ed.), *Huizu renwu zhi* (*Qingdai*), p. 372.
18. Xu Yuanzheng, 'Xu Xu (ii)', in Liu Zhi, *Tianfang xingli*, p. 4a.
19. See Leslie, *Islamic Literature*, p. 119.
20. Lu You, 'Lu xu', in Liu Zhi, *Tianfang dianli*, p. 2a.
21. That is, Daoism and Buddhism.
22. Jing Rizhen, 'Yizhai xu', in Liu Zhi, *Tianfang dianli*, p. 5a.
23. Yang Feilu, 'Yang xu', in Liu Zhi, *Tianfang dianli*, p. 7a.
24. See Jin Ding, 'Liu Jielian Xiansheng Mubei'; see a photograph of the tombstone in Lipman, *Familiar Strangers*, fig. 12.
25. Mencius, *Wan Zhang*, Book II, verse 1. See also Benite, *Dao of Muhammad*, pp. 174–7.
26. Liu Zhi, 'Liyan', in *Tianfang dianli*, p. 2.
27. The term *jidacheng*, as applied to Muḥammad, occurs in Yuan Guozuo's preface to the 1785 edition of Liu Zhi's biography of the Prophet Muḥammad, *True Record of the Ultimate Sage of Islam*. See Yuan Guozuo, 'Xu', in Bai Shouyi (ed.), *Huizu renwu zhi* (*Qingdai*), p. 226.
28. Waley, *The Analects of Confucius*, p. 123, VII:1. Alternatively, 'Following the

proper way, I do not forge new paths; with confidence I cherish the ancients' (Ames and Rosemont, *The Analects of Confucius*, p. 111, 7.1)
29. Qur'ān 46:9.
30. Liu Zhi, 'Zi xu', in *Tianfang dianli*, p. 12a.
31. Ibid., p. 12a.
32. Yuan Guozuo, 'Xu' in Bai Shouyi (ed.), *Huizu renwu zhi* (*Qingdai*), p. 226.
33. Ibid., p. 226.
34. Liu Zhi, 'Zi xu', in *Tianfang dianli*, p. 12a.
35. Liu Zhi, 'Liyan', in *Tianfang dianli*, p. 3b.
36. Ma Zhu, for example, wrote of the Three Teachings and the movement to syncretise them as an 'affliction' (Ma Zhu, *Qingzhen zhinan*, p. 109).
37. Liu Zhi, 'Renshi pian', in *Tianfang dianli*, pp. 23–4.
38. Ibid., p. 12a.
39. Wang Daiyu, *Zhengjiao zhenquan*, p. 16.
40. Lipman, *Familiar Strangers*, p. 77.
41. Frankel, *Rectifying God's Name*, p. 124. See Lipman, Chapter 1, this volume.
42. Frankel, *Rectifying God's Name*, p. 124.
43. The *locus classicus* for this Confucian maxim is *Daxue* I.4. The fifth chapter of the *Daxue*, now lost, explained the meaning of 'apprehending the principle in things and extending knowledge' in detail. Modern editions contain, in its place, a reconstruction of that ancient commentary, based on the views of one of the Cheng brothers, according to Zhu Xi (see Legge (trans.), *Confucius*, p. 365).
44. Liu Zhi, 'Renshi pian', in *Tianfang dianli*, p. 23.
45. Liu Zhi, 'Zhushu Shu', in Bai Shouyi (ed.), *Huizhu renwu zhi* (*Qingdai*), pp. 357–8.
46. Yang Feilu, 'Yang xu', in Liu Zhi, *Tianfang dianli*, p. 7a.
47. See Frankel, *Rectifying God's Name*, ch. 6.
48. This title, by Abū Bakr ʿAbdullāh bin Muḥammad Najm al-Dīn al-Rāzī (1177–1265), may be translated as *The Servants' Progress from Origin to Return*.
49. This title, by ʿAzīz bin Muḥammad al-Nasafī (d. 1263), may be translated as *The Highest Aim*.
50. This title, by Nūr al-Dīn ʿAbd al-Raḥmān Jāmī (1414–92), may be translated as *Rays of Brilliance*.
51. This title, also by Jāmī, may be translated as *Signs in the Elucidation of the Meanings of Perception*. In addition to these four books, among his sources, Liu Zhi also listed several other well-known (mostly Persian) Sufi works, including: *Kashf al-Maḥjūb* ('Revealing the Concealed') by Hujwīrī; *Kashf al-Asrār*

('Revealing the Secrets') by Maybudī; and *Tadhkirat al-Awliyāʾ* ('Remembrance of the Saints') by ʿAttār (Murata, *Chinese Gleams*, p. 214 n. 32).
52. Elman, *Philosophy to Philology*, p. 160.
53. Benite, *Dao of Muhammad*, pp. 156–7.
54. Leslie, *Islamic Literature*, p. 92.
55. Ji Yun, *Siku quanshu zongmu*, p. 240.
56. Lipman, *Familiar Strangers*, p. 188.
57. Murata, Chittick and Tu, *The Sage Learning*, p. ix.
58. This *ḥadīth*, narrated by Anas, is cited by al-Bayhāqi in *Shuʿab al-Imān* and *al-Madkhāl*, Ibn ʿAbd al-Barr in *Jāmiʿ Bayān al-ʿIlm*, and al-Khāṭib through three chains of transmission in *al-Riḥla fī Ṭalāb al-Ḥadīth*, though it was later deemed 'weak' (Ar. *daʿīf*) by some scholars.
59. *al-Tirmidhī*, No. s2611

3

Tianfang Sanzijing: Exchanges and Changes in China's Reception of Islamic Law

Roberta Tontini[1]

Introduction

While scholars have investigated the impact of Arabic and Persian sources on the development of Chinese textual scholarship on Islam, we still lack scholarly analysis of Chinese Muslims' reaction to norms developed outside the Chinese legal framework. This chapter attempts to fill this void by exploring the commitment of Chinese Muslim scholars to the task of articulating and legitimising their own interpretation of Islamic law. Their efforts had the potential to separate Chinese Muslim legal thought from its Arabic and Persian matrix of origin. Thus, our core question will be, how did Chinese scholars justify and legitimate their own interpretation of Islamic law vis-à-vis the legal thinking of other areas of the Muslim world?

This chapter thus examines the implications of the legal discourse set forth in a Chinese primer for Muslims, the *Tianfang sanzijing* (*Three Character Classic of Islam*),[2] regarding local notions of Islamic 'legitimacy' and 'orthodoxy'. Credited to the author of the *Norms and Rituals of Islam* (*Tianfang dianli*), Liu Zhi (1662–c. 1736) (see Frankel, Chapter 2, and Petersen, Chapter 4, this volume),[3] and animated by that book's purpose of reconciling Islamic law with the legal culture of the Qing,[4] Liu's concise primer on the main tenets of Islam spoke to a broader audience than its textual antecedent. As argued below, the Muslim *Sanzijing* laid the ground for an independent development of Islamic law in the Chinese context, one that had the power to detach China from conventional Islamic jurisprudence outside its frontiers, while remaining consistent with the overarching legal principles of Sunni Islam.

The Muslim *Sanzijing* and its Audience

> Cloistered in retreat in the *Qingliang* mountain for several winters and summers, [Liu Zhi] not only [undertook] numerous readings and researches, but also a great number of writings. By seeing that the people from China and Arabia (*Tianfang*) were meeting each other without being able to communicate, he generously exclaimed: 'Translating their writings and exposing their meaning, enabling people from within and without China [to coexist] harmoniously [by virtue of] their common customs: perhaps this is my responsibility.' Thereupon, he picked the norms and rites of our [Qing] dynasty and translated them into the language of Arabia, in order to let people coming from afar learn about their refinement, elegance and brilliance, and lead them to feel anxious and happy to comply. He also took the rites of Arabia and translated them into Chinese. [Although] pages piled up thickly, [he] could not cover but a part of the [whole] matter.[5]

The above statement by Yang Feilu, in his preface to the 1710 edition of Liu Zhi's *Norms and Rituals of Islam*,[6] provides a sense of the normative dilemma experienced by Liu Zhi prior to his endorsement of a scholarly enterprise aimed at reconciling Islam with the legal culture and the core values of Chinese culture and the Qing state. Yang's preface suggests that people from China and the Muslim world[7] eventually shared the same geographical space (China) without being able to 'communicate' and 'coexist harmoniously' with one another. The communication gulf was not simply linguistic in nature; its roots were ultimately normative, inferred from the author's allusion to each encounter's peculiar baggage of 'norms and rites'.[8] In his argument, different normative cultures and incongruent patterns of social order might challenge each group's understanding of the legal tradition of the other.

On the whole, Yang's preface illuminates Liu Zhi's sensitivity to potential normative conflicts between the legal culture of Islam, on the one hand, and of the Qing state, on the other. Islamic law in its Arabic and Persian guise was not directly translatable into the political context of Manchu-ruled China. Hence, Liu Zhi attempted adjustments at what proved to be an opportune time for a well-read Chinese scholar to translate meanings between these two normative traditions, thus aligning Islam with the school of Confucian learning to which the recently established dynasty subscribed.[9] Both Liu Zhi and Yang Feilu seemed convinced by an inherent compatibility of Islam and Confucianism. However, far from being self-evident, this compatibility remained to be demonstrated, a task presented by Yang Feilu as the ultimate direction of Liu Zhi's scholarly endeavour. In his description, Liu Zhi was driven by a deep commitment to the responsibility of 'enabling people from within and without China [to coexist] harmoniously [by virtue of] their common customs'.

Yang's preface thus approached the *Norms and Rituals of Islam* as an outgrowth of Liu Zhi's systematic attempt to reconcile Islamic law with the normative Neo-Confucian culture.[10] The text intended to show that Islam and Confucianism were ultimately based on identical principles, and were thus mutually consistent despite possible divergences in their formal articulation.

> Although [the Muslim norms are] recorded in the books of Islam, they are not different from the norms of the Confucians. Indeed, abiding by the rites of Islam is [a mode of] compliance with the teachings of the former sages and kings. The teachings of the sages are the same in the East and the West and are one today as in the past. Subsequently, later generations refrained from cultivating them, and they gradually became lost.[11]

A crucial challenge was that most Chinese Muslims were not sufficiently literate in Chinese to understand and appreciate the refined nature of Liu Zhi's legal synthesis. In his own preface to the *Norms and Rituals of Islam*, Liu Zhi lamented the complexity of the task he undertook, which compelled him to rewrite his legal work multiple times before advancing a digested version of its original content.[12] Moreover, despite his efforts at reducing the complexities of the work, he still perceived the text as being beyond the intellectual scope of the uneducated classes. Indeed, even his selection required a high degree of literacy in the classical heritage of Chinese literature and philosophy:

This book is not intended for uncultivated people. Uncultivated people can be instructed by their teachers according to the scriptures. They don't need this book. Those who need this book are rather those people who are by necessity familiar with the Three Teachings [Confucianism, Buddhism, and Daoism], but who lack knowledge of the rites of our teaching [Islam]. By reading its content and mastering its meaning, they will naturally gain some benefit.[13]

Given this premise, one might wonder, if the *Norms and Rituals of Islam* sought to introduce Islamic law to a literate audience, how should 'uncultivated' Muslims learn? Were they consciously excluded from the scholarly enterprise endorsed by the author of the text? The historiography on Liu Zhi depicts him as a member of the Muslim intelligentsia who eschewed social work, let alone interaction, in order fully to devote himself to textual scholarship and intellectual pursuits.[14] His entire reliance on written materials could well have compromised his intellectual access to the lower classes, who lacked the training to read and write in Chinese. Nonetheless, this chapter advances an alternative view, seeing Liu Zhi in communication with a broad segment of his contemporary Muslim society. As I demonstrate below, the scholarship credited to this author engaged even the average Muslim with the attempt to reconcile Islamic law with the normative culture of imperial China.

Liu Zhi's *Tianfang sanzijing*[15] appeared in Nanjing after the publication of the *Norms and Rituals of Islam*.[16] Its title, translated into English as *Three Character Classic of Islam*, carries the attributive term *Tianfang* ('Islam' or Arabia), linking this piece of Liu Zhi's writing to the theological realm as represented in his so-called *Tianfang* 'trilogy'[17] (see Frankel, Chapter 2, this volume). At the same time, the second section of the title resonates with the name of a widely used Chinese primer, the *Three Character Classic* (*Sanzijing*). Presumably authored during the Song, this booklet on the main tenets of Confucian learning enjoyed considerable circulation in the context of Qing primary education.[18]

Although both texts shared a similar architecture, being organised in clusters of rhymed triplets, we may observe key differences between them. While small children approaching education for the first time are generally identified as the main audience of the Confucian version, this does not apply to the Muslim *Sanzijing*. Below, I problematise this issue in order to highlight the universalistic ambition of the Muslim version and the targeting of a comparatively large segment of contemporary Muslim society in its author's pedagogy. Indeed, both the Confucian and the Muslim version of the *Sanzijing* provide direct evidence concerning their intended audiences, for both texts address their readers with particular terms. While the Confucian primer employs the expression *xiaosheng*, a term which in English roughly translates as 'young student', the Muslim version uses the expression *xiaozi*, a term with a broader nuance, approximating to 'young fellow' or 'junior pupil'. As explained below, this seemingly minor difference in the vocative choice of each primer reflects a difference in their intended audiences. For example:

> And you, young fellow! When knowledge approaches, learning is plain and simple, it does not [require] deep reflection.[19]

At times, both expressions — *xiaosheng* and *xiaozi* —referred to students approaching the teachings of earlier scholars. 'Young' is thus used with respect to knowledge, not necessarily to age. However, Liu Zhi generally avoided referring to his audience with expressions replicating too precisely the vocabulary of the Confucian version. The possibility that this formal option entailed an actual difference in the expected audience of the Muslim version gains additional resonance if combined with another stance contained in the text, one that conveys a better sense of the author's opinion about age and gender requirements for a *xiaozi* about to approach learning:

> And you, young fellow, should carefully listen: undertaking the practice of learning is a mandate of God! Any human being should commit completely [to this], no [matter whether] man or woman, no [matter whether] old or young.[20]

While these triplets suggest that the author had a broader audience in mind than just the young male pupils addressed by the Confucian *Sanzijing*, we can use a more rigorous standard to measure the educational aims of the Muslim primer, which addressed issues of concern for Muslim elders, including the proper place of women. The ritual section of the work presents multiple references to post-pubescent changes and even marital relations. For example, the excerpt below refers explicitly to sexual intercourse, wet dreams and other sensitive issues meant for a more mature audience:

> When the essence of pleasure emerges; when husband and wife are together; when [one] sleeps, and wet dreams occur; after menses; when delivery ends. Those five forms [of *yu* ablutions] are mandates of God.[21]

Furthermore, we find allusions in the text to physical features not found in children. For example, this passage contains directions for the process of *mu* ablutions, specifically guiding worshipers to cleanse their beards:

> You need to know that *mu* [ablutions] consist of four norms: the first is washing the face, from the hairline to the jaw, including the lobe of the ears. Those [who have] dense beards will need to dig into [the thick hair].[22]

Other passages indicate that the primer also attended to issues for females. Unlike its Confucian counterpart, which mentioned women only sporadically and mainly for the purpose of educating men,[23] multiple triplets contained in the Muslim version speak directly to an audience of mature female Muslims. For example, the passage below draws attention to taboos of direct concern for women, such as the suspension of ordinary ritual duties during pregnancy and menstruation:

> During menses and gestation one should suspend seven things. Do not pray and do not fast, do not engage in [marital] intercourse,[24] do not undertake the pilgrimage, do not enter the mosque, do not touch the *Qur'ān* and do not recite its norms. Apart from these, others are not restricted.[25]

With this argument in mind, a caveat is in order: it is possible that the text was written in conformity with a Chinese theory on education that encouraged pupils to memorise as children what they would have to internalise at a later stage in life. In this sense, one could argue that any *Sanzijing* ultimately sought to educate 'prospective' adults. This view acknowledges the possibility that the actual comprehension of the meaning of the triplets was expected to occur long after their initial memorisation. This interpretation could be derived from the primer's conclusion, which contains a short sentence describing the *Sanzijing* as the initial stage of a longer learning path awaiting Muslim 'beginners':

And you, young fellow, know well all this. For people beginning to learn, [what has been said] can already suffice.²⁶

Clues as to the actual reception of Liu Zhi's primer by Muslim adults can be found in a commentary to the text authored by Yuan Guozuo (1712–?)²⁷ that appeared at the beginning of the nineteenth century (1809)²⁸ – the *Tianfang sanzijing zhujie qianshuo* or 'Commentarial introduction to the *Three Character Classic of Islam*',²⁹ and a postscript to the commentary added decades after its composition (1870). It contains a description of local transactions surrounding the primer after the end of the Taiping rebellion ('Since the bandits of Guangxi rebelled'), describing an ahong (Wang Jixian) and a scholar (Tong Jili) confronted with the difficult task of keeping Islam alive despite the unavailability of sources. The preface contains insights into the way Muslims actually used the text during this chaotic and unstable phase of Qing rule, the mid-nineteenth century, when the scarcity of books and reference materials was such that people's knowledge of Islam could not rely on written sources. In a climate of 'great anxiety with regards to bodies of instruction', the Muslim *Sanzijing* became a crucial reference on Islamic matters, thanks especially to Tong Jili, who saved and shared his own copy of the text:

> Since the bandits of Guangxi rebelled, unseen disasters and great calamities [occurred, after which] books became completely lost. Now that warfare has come to an end and culture and education are gradually rising, Wang ahong [Jixian] came fortunately to preside over learning and Master Tong Daosheng [Jili] came to assist him in teaching and exploring the *dao*. Therefore, [he] took out his hidden *Sanzijing* to display it in these times of great anxiety with regards to bodies of instruction, [when] the search did not [lead to] any reliable source. Thereupon, [the book] was circulated [for people] to see, and it was suggested that [its] original text be reprinted. Within a month the printing was accomplished to benefit later [generations of] students. With this done [they could] master this [text] and access quickly the realm of wisdom.³⁰

The commentator, Yuan Guozuo, was a native of Nanjing bound by kinship ties to Liu Zhi's teacher, Yuan Ruqi. An editor by profession, this scholar was extraordinarily active in reprinting and popularising Liu Zhi's works. His preface to the commentary contains useful indications of the expected audience and functions of Liu Zhi's *Sanzijing*. Family background and professional commitment gave Yuan Guozuo a singular understanding of Liu Zhi's philosophical thought, along with the powerful legacy of his theological writings. This acquaintance persuaded Yuan that the *Tianfang sanzijing* was Liu Zhi's only work inspired by a didactic purpose:

> Master Yizhai [Liu Zhi] authored several books based on the Muslim classics and histories, [which were] handed down for generations and became known to every household. [Among those,] only the *Tianfang sanzijing* [was intended as] a book to educate the ignorant. Furthermore, he selected words [which were] seemingly plain and simple to [encompass] the whole essence of the *Qurʾān*, the Sunna, principle (*li*), and the *dao*.³¹

The compound expression *xunmeng* recurs twice in Yuan Guozuo's preface and could be translated as 'educating children' or as 'educating the ignorant'. A reader inclined to approach the *Sanzijing* as a primer for children might be confounded by the dramatic level of difficulty recalled by an adult scholar like Yuan Guozuo during his own reading of the text:

> I have spent several years in explaining [it], thinking hard and pondering persistently, [until I] slightly mastered it, and I am now [adding] explicatory notes – by referring only to the actual meaning of the forefather [in my attempt] to stop the hard labour of later scholars, without daring to put myself at [Liu Zhi's] level by presumptuously adding [new] meanings [to his work]. Whenever it comes to educating ignorant people and seeking guidance, directions must be provided one by one. This is an excellent [way] to manage the people and order the world.³²

At this point, one might legitimately wonder what made Liu Zhi's *Sanzijing* so difficult to interpret. Yuan Guozuo himself admits that Liu Zhi 'selected words [which were] seemingly plain and simple' to compose his only educational primer. Nonetheless, this small booklet was demanding to the point of causing hard labour to later scholars, including well-read intellectuals like Yuan. What was so challenging about this text that it compelled him to devote several years to its interpretation, forcing him to think hard and ponder so persistently? A reply can be deduced from Yuan Guozuo's preface to the commentary:

> The languages of East and West were different. After reading them it was not [possible] to understand their meaning, and those who inquired were not [able] to capture their principles. Generally speaking, the forefather (*xianren*) set up a theory easy in words but dense in meaning, which awaited the interpretation of later generations (*houren*) in [order to achieve] additional clarity and fluency, so that the rest of its content [could be] grasped by [means of] deep reflection.[33]

Yuan Guozuo implies that the inherent challenge of the *Tianfang sanzijing* was not to be found in the surface meaning of its words – which by his own admission were 'seemingly plain and simple' – but rather in the comprehensive theory the text set forth, 'easy in words' and yet very 'dense in meaning'. This theory awaited the interpretation of later readers able to grasp its content, hidden behind its plain words.

Continuity as a Premise for Change: A Localist View of Islamic Legal History

Reading Liu Zhi's *Tianfang* writings, a multitude of meanings can be derived from their overarching architecture rather than a literalist interpretation. The *Tianfang sanzijing* text starts with a proposition responding to the first statements of its Confucian, non-Muslim predecessor. While the latter claims that in the beginning 'there was the man' – opening with a straightforward discussion on human nature – the Muslim version takes a few steps back and argues that in the beginning 'there was one God'. Human beings and their nature came only subsequently, as the ultimate conclusion of a creation process that, through the division of *yin* and *yang*, brought about the existence of phenomenal reality, the 'ten thousand things':[34]

> At the origin of heaven and earth, at the beginning of the ten thousand things, there was a supreme majesty called the Real God. God wove creation, moved principle and vital energy, divided *yin* and *yang*, evolved heaven and earth, settled mountains and rivers, aroused grasses and shrubs, defined disaster and blessing [and] displayed the sun and the moon. Once God had

animated the birds and the beasts, infused life to the fishes and shaped the ten thousand species, only then did God create humankind.[35]

Liu placed this clarification strategically at the beginning of the text, suggesting an essential difference between the mind-set of a Muslim and that of other Confucian Chinese. Subsequently, the text realigns itself with the core agenda of the Confucian version by briefly illustrating the importance of education and learning. The following section stresses the importance of cultivating Confucian virtues, such as humanity and tolerance, with particular emphasis on filial piety, crucial to one's development of a sense of authority through a correct performance of ceremonies and rites, and a pious acceptance of the pre-eminence of parents, teachers and rulers. In other words, the reader is encouraged to master Confucian learning prior to approaching Islam, a sequence that replicates Liu Zhi's own intellectual itinerary.[36]

Liu assigns priority to Confucian ethics in order to avoid the dangers of delving into Islam's complexity before gaining a sound acquaintance with the socio-political principles of China. Liu places this subtle warning against a de-contextualised approach to Islamic learning in the transition between the triplets on God's Creation and the main body of the primer, which deals with the main tenets of Islam:

> Learn filial obedience, serve rulers and teachers, be clear about [the hierarchy of] seniors and juniors [and] distinguish noble and vulgar. Know humanity and tolerance, practice rites and ceremonies, be careful with words and conduct [and] beware of improper behaviour. When some progress occurs you will be told about the *dao*.[37]

With this proviso in place, the subsequent section of the Muslim *Sanzijing* explores Islamic law in its twofold realms of *mu'amalat* and *'ibadat* prescriptions.[38] These two aspects of Islamic legal reasoning had already been reconfigured, in the narrative of the *Norms and Rituals of Islam*, respectively, within the social and the ritual space of the five social norms (*wudian*), that is, the five relationships of Confucianism, and the five ritual endeavours (*wugong*), that is, the five pillars of Islam (see Petersen, Chapter 4, this volume).[39] Liu encouraged the reader of the *Sanzijing* to conform to the five relationships while meticulously adhering to strict performance of the Muslim rites.[40] The next section of the Muslim *Sanzijing* is devoted to the latter issue, with a remarkable stress on guiding the process of prayer and ritual ablution, while its final section contains a concise reconstruction of Islamic political and intellectual history. Its importance lies in the fact that these triplets entail a crucial aspect of Liu's theory 'simple in words but dense in meanings', which caused so much hard labour[41] to later scholars and interpreters like Yuan Guozuo.

The section starts with a few lines on the transmission of the *dao* of Islam over time through several sages. Following Muḥammad's prophecy, the *dao* was fully revealed (*dao da quan*) and its transmission narrowed to people close to him. The initial inheritors of the *dao* were his companions, the caliphs who guided the Muslim community after his death, transmitting the *dao* to each other and the generations to come:

> The sages of old and recent times [numbered] one hundred and twenty four thousand [and only] explicated half of the *dao*. As our sage Muhammad completed fully the *dao* there were continuity and change. When our sage passed away, his companions continued [its transmission]: Abu Bakr, Umar, Uthman and Ali. These four companions transmitted the office [to each other] across the generations.[42]

At this point this semi-historical narrative incorporates more explicit legal nuances by probing the formation of the early schools of Sunni jurisprudence:

> After the four companions, four worthy [scholars] took over [the *dao*, and] the head of our scholarship is Abu Hanifa. Those four worthy [scholars] are respectively obeyed by the people. By preventing their mutual blending, purity can be achieved. All that the four worthies had taught [pertains to] the *dao* of the sage. [Their expression] is superficial or deep [or different in the] details. [In any case,] the transmission of the worthies descends from the sage, and the transmission of the sage derives from the four companions.[43]

As we shall see, the final section of the text gradually delves into an issue of crucial importance for a Muslim minority under non-Muslim rule, the process of localisation of Islamic law, paired with its fragmentation into branches of jurisprudence following the expansion of Islam beyond the initial territorial unit of Medina. Muḥammad, the sage who received from God a complete version of the *dao*,⁴⁴ was also the first one to employ its principles to administer a political jurisdiction, initially enclosed within Medina's walls. After his death, the administrative office (*wei*) was handed down to Abu Bakr, Omar and finally to Ali, also entrusted with the task of expanding the territory under Islam.⁴⁵ By the end of this early caliphate, the political geography of Islam had stretched to include increasingly diverse peoples and places.

Precisely at this point in the text the concept of *dao* begins to overlap with the notion of Islamic universal law, or *shari'a*,⁴⁶ along with the challenge of its human interpretation and jurisprudence. The administration of the new territories could not be entrusted to a single interpretation of the *dao*, that is, the law revealed by God to Muḥammad. Muslims were increasingly diverse, and so were their histories, customs and geographies. Under such circumstances, normative uniformity could not be a workable option. As a consequence of political expansion, the interpretation of the *dao* had to cope with problems and diversity that ultimately led to its fragmentation into four juridical branches. Their number symbolically matched the basic spatial directions of geography. Yuan Guozuo provided additional hints about the meaning of these triplets:

> The four companions passed away one after the other. Afterwards, four imams came to act for [them], all [of whom] affirmed the *dao* of the ultimate sage. Its [expression] shared the same overarching principle, although in conducting a matter [a procedure] was [judged as] fitting a given [context while] not fitting another, or there were deep or superficial [expressive] subtleties. Consequently, the religious law was divided into four branches. Since the four directions had different environmental features, they were established on the basis of people's characters and local customs.⁴⁷

The metaphor of the four directions speaks to an important legal development that occurred after the death of Muḥammad, when no single geographical centre could any longer sustain univocal interpretation of the *dao*.⁴⁸ The political heartlands of Islam now included four spatial directions, surrounding territories with social features of their own, and increasingly diverse in terms of culture and political requirements.⁴⁹ The text illustrates how each direction eventually produced a legal scholar of its own, who ultimately became the regional adjudicator of Islamic jurisprudence *in loco*.⁵⁰

Moreover, given the heterogeneity and the customary diversity of the territories under Islamic control, the *dao* could no longer be entrusted to military leaders but rather to scholars, a statement subsequently paraphrased by Yuan Guozuo, who reiterated that 'afterwards, four imams came to act for [them], all [of whom] affirmed the *dao* of the ultimate sage'. The Muslim *umma*, an increasingly composite community of co-religionaries, now required leadership equipped with the intellectual skills to produce consistent interpretations of the *dao*, ever mindful of the specific territories to be administered.[51] As a result, the transmission of the *dao* experienced a new turn, from the level of substantive politics and military expansion undertaken by the four caliphs to that of legal scholarship embodied by four imams, the founders of the four schools of Sunni jurisprudence. The *Sanzijing* thus assigned to an intellectual elite of Muslims the inheritance of an office originally assigned to political–military leaders. The imams governed the Muslim community by virtue of their intellectual access to the *dao* and its legal implementation in different contexts.

By designating legal scholars as legitimate successors of the caliphs, text and commentary generated an implicit statement in favour of a regional or local implementation of the *dao*, an approach that bound the interpretation of the law to the normative experience of the regions hosting Islam. This argument for regionalism is reinforced by subsequent lines, which assign each scholar to a different native place. Yuan Guozuo cites the individual names of Abu Hanifa, Shafi, Malik and Ibn Hanbal in association with their legal schools, whose establishment set the basis for a regional development of Islamic jurisprudence in response to the different environmental features marking the vast breadth of the territory under Islam.[52]

The acknowledgement that eventually the 'religious law was divided into four branches'[53] did not imply that a split occurred within the universal law of Islam itself. Rather, the authors argue that the *dao* never ceased to be an undivided and consistent whole. The split occurred merely at the level of substantive jurisprudence, not at that of its universal principles. The branches split because of the interpretations of the universal *dao* produced regionally by the various schools. Although the commentary did not distinguish between universal law (Ar. *shari'a*, Ch. *dao*) and human jurisprudence (Ar. *fiqh*, Ch. *fa*) of Islam, the expression 'conducting matters' (*xingshi*) in order to identify patterns 'fitting a given [context while] not fitting another'⁵⁴ certainly refers to Islamic jurisprudence in its disciplinary nuance.

Thus, before drawing out the implications of this regionalist argument for the Muslims of China, the text clarified that the judgements of each school were equally legitimate from an Islamic legal perspective, as each scholar equally 'affirmed the *dao* of the ultimate sage', Muḥammad.⁵⁵ Differences concerned substantive jurisprudence, affected by context or analytical angle of approach to the final judgement, informed by 'deep or superficial [expressive] subtleties'.⁵⁶

To put it simply, the text prepared the reader to accept the principle that *context matters* when it comes to norms. While the law of Islam remains essentially one, its interpretation may vary according to time and place. Indeed, because of contextual differences, the Muslim way of 'conducting matters' fragmented into branches of jurisprudence in view of the geographical expansion of Islam. The commentator's use of terms such as four directions, environmental features, people's character, local customs and native places shapes his argument that context matters enough to impact the local interpretations of the universal law of Islam. These premises ultimately enabled the four schools to be simultaneously correct in their different readings of the law, for they all represented legitimate developments of the universal *dao*, sharing the same overarching principle despite reacting to distinct contexts.

After acknowledging the simultaneous legitimacy of the legal schools, the text warns against the fallacy of confusing them:

> If people comply with one [school's] books without mixing them up, they can be defined as pure Muslims (*Mumin*). Therefore [Liu Zhi] especially stressed this [point].⁵⁷

Once the value of context had been made clear, the necessity to refrain from mixing up the teachings of different schools became self-evident. That would be equivalent to mixing up their contexts. For instance, implementing in China interpretations of the *dao* informed by the environmental features and customs of other Muslim settings would naturally result in a de-contextualised implementation of Islamic law that, in the long run, might translate into a challenge to social order. Hence, once the teachings of a particular school embedded themselves in a particular context, local Muslims should make sure to stick to the sources of that school and to the legal statements developed by its scholars over time. This purist approach set the ground for the sustainable development of that community in its particular context, granting its people the honourable title of Muslims, *Mumin*. With this said, the authors approached more closely the implications of this legal reasoning for the Muslims of China, both text and commentary clarifying exactly where Chinese Muslims stand vis-à-vis the teachings of the schools:

> The head of our scholarship is Abu Hanifa, and 'Arzham' is the title of a grandly respected imam, who completely handed down the equitable *dao* of the ultimate sage.[58]

This line provides a straightforward claim for Chinese Muslims' membership in the Hanafi school of Sunni jurisprudence. As for what led Chinese Muslims to prefer the teaching of this school over the others, a credible answer can be inferred from this sentence:

> By observing that each imam entirely adhered to his native place, [one] can know that only Arzham harmonised the most correct [interpretation of the] *dao*, [which he made] worthy of compliance across ten thousand generations.[59]

Abu Hanifa, identified elsewhere in the commentary as the earliest legal scholar of Islam, ultimately received credit for having 'harmonised the most correct [interpretation of the] *dao*'.[60] Features of his teaching enabled his school to travel through space and time, crossing the borders of its founder's native place and gaining credibility across 10,000 generations. Clearly, the text assigned to the Hanafi mind-set a degree of universality and flexibility unparalleled by other schools, highlighting its extraordinary capacity to survive in diverse contexts, reaching people located great distances and centuries away from the historical heartland of Hanafi legal thought.

While the authors ultimately left the reader to speculate about these features, we must note that the Hanafi school of Sunni jurisprudence advanced an especially developed notion of territoriality that distinguished its approach to regional contexts from that advocated by other schools of jurisprudence. This attitude often translated into a comparatively flexible stance regarding the implementation of Islamic legal norms beyond the jurisdiction of a Muslim state.[61] In addition, it displayed a remarkable capacity to appropriate and rework local meanings in order to reconcile them with the normative reasoning of Islamic law. This facility made the Hanafi school especially appealing to Muslims in East Asia, as it could supply them with the necessary theoretical leverage to cope with the norms and the values of non-Islamic states. Thus, the Hanafi mind-set was well equipped to fit the specific demands of Muslims in China,[62] as they responded to the authority of a non-Islamic state with a legal culture of its own and substantive legal codes of non-Islamic origin.[63]

In short, Chinese Muslims' adherence to the Hanafi school corresponded with the regionalist approach captured and supported by the Muslim *Sanzijing*. Chinese Muslim writings inclined towards theoretical approaches to Islamic law that respected, rather than challenged, the normative culture of the Qing state. Indeed, the Hanafi school seemed capable of offering this balance by its ability to make room for space and time in its particular interpretation of the *dao*. This premise enabled it to find credibility among Chinese scholars like Yuan Guozuo, who defined the Hanafi approach as the most correct one, acknowledging its founder as the head of Islamic legal scholarship in China.

Nonetheless, questions surrounding the legal legitimacy of the regionalist stand called for deeper thinking. For instance, if space and time mattered so much in determining the simultaneous legitimacy of multiple interpretations of the *dao* – as demonstrated by the existence of four equally trustworthy schools of Islamic law – what standard should be applied to judge the orthodoxy of a given interpretation vis-à-vis the universal law revealed in the *Qur'ān*? How should one distinguish between correct and incorrect interpretations of the *dao*, not taking as correct any interpretation that happened to fit the demands of a particular place and time? To put it simply, if the interpretation of Islamic law varied with the context, where should one draw the borders of its flexibility, given what was revealed to Muḥammad in the *Qur'ān*? The excerpt below carries an answer to these questions. Once the designation of Abu Hanifa as the 'grandly respected Imam, who completely handed down the equitable *dao* of the ultimate sage' was set, Yuan Guozuo clarified Liu Zhi's own criterion of Islamic orthodoxy:[64]

[The notion of] *daotong* relies on the exploration of the [transmission] flow [backwards] in search of the source. If there is even a minor mistake, the *dao* is not correct.⁶⁵

Here, we must introduce the notion of *daotong* as necessary to an understanding of the particular approach to Islamic orthodoxy and legitimacy set forth by the primer. The concept of *daotong* had the power of evoking simultaneously legal principles with strong resonance and credibility for both Muslim and Confucian thinkers.⁶⁶

From a Neo-Confucian perspective, the term *daotong* indicates the 'filiative transmission of the way', a concept developed by the Dao school of Confucian thought.⁶⁷ Dao scholars appropriated it to argue for the legitimacy of their interpretation of the meaning of the Confucian classics. In their view, the *dao* had been travelling across space and time since its completion by the ultimate sage, Confucius. Sages received and delivered it in a filiative genealogy of intellectual transmitters with the Dao scholars as its ultimate heirs. Eventually, this linear pattern of intellectual genealogy, captured within the concept of *daotong*, became the Dao scholars' essential measure of orthodoxy, which they exploited to argue in favour of their particular interpretation of the *dao*. Subsequently, sectarian groups opposed to the Dao school appropriated the same concept of *daotong* to demonstrate the orthodoxy of their own interpretive stands.⁶⁸ During the Ming–Qing transition the credibility of this pattern of ancestral reasoning reached its highest peak, in a political climate of increased attention to issues of ancestry and genealogy.⁶⁹ The passages that follow highlight how this sectarian approach to the intellectual past and to orthodoxy, shared by competing factions within Confucianism, also could make sense from a Muslim perspective.⁷⁰

Intellectual lineages had played a significant role in Islam since the early centuries after the death of Muḥammad, when the proliferation of traditions (Ar. *ḥadīth*) of doubtful origin and credibility propelled the intellectual community to create analytical tools to test the orthodoxy of their claims. An authentication device known in Arabic as *isnad* indicated the chain of transmission by which a given *ḥadīth* had travelled over time sustained by a filiative line of intellectual authorities. The *isnad* method required dynamics similar to those informing the transmission principle of *daotong*. In both cases, the orthodoxy of a given message was ultimately measured by judgement of the filiative line of transmission tracing its content to a reliable human source (Confucius or Muḥammad). The credibility of the message was diminished by blanks in its transmission line. This broad overview of Islamic and Confucian patterns of intellectual transmission illustrates how shared concerns for issues of doctrinal orthodoxy converged in the narrative of the Muslim *Sanzijing*, producing a synthesis of common modes of ancestral reasoning aptly captured by the term *daotong*.

With this in mind, we turn back to the question of the legal legitimacy of the *Sanzijing*'s regionalist stance. If the interpretation of Islamic law varies with the context, where should one draw the borders of its legitimacy in relation to God's revelation to Muḥammad in the *Qurʾān*? Yuan Guozuo replied by advocating the concept of *daotong*, using a Neo-Confucian authentication approach whose logic closely replicates that of the Arabic *isnad*. In Yuan Guozuo's reconstruction of Liu Zhi's original argument, the orthodoxy of a regional interpretation of Islamic law could not be measured against its formal conformity with the narrow letter of the revelation. Instead, orthodoxy must be defined by continuity in the transmission line.[71]

Following this reasoning, Islamic orthodoxy can be claimed as long as a filiative line of intellectual transmission runs between the divine revelation and its ultimate regional interpretations, regardless of how far the latter had travelled in space and time since that epoch-making event. On the other hand, any regional interpretation of Islamic law necessarily fails to meet the standard of Islamic orthodoxy if mistakes are discovered in its filiative transmission line. To reinforce his point, Yuan Guozuo clarified that if the transmission flow presents even 'a minor mistake, the *dao* is not correct'.[72] Since orthodoxy 'relies on the exploration of the [transmission] flow [backwards] in search of the source', any interpretation of the *dao* devoid of a linkage to the ultimate source of the transmission flow, which is eventually God,[73] should be regarded as heterodox and fallacious.

Clearly, Muslim and non-Muslim scholars at the time spoke essentially the same language, qualifying doctrinal orthodoxy in terms of intellectual ancestry. However, the *Sanzijing* clarifies the existence of a substantial difference in the line of transmission of the Muslim *dao*, whose sages were not always the same as those advocated by other Confucian sects. Starting from the very identity of the 'ultimate sage' who reformed the transmission – no longer Confucius, but rather Muḥammad – the Muslim 'sect' had a distinct understanding of how the *dao* was revealed and transmitted over time through a chain of worthies and sages of its own whose ultimate source was eventually God:

> Therefore, starting from the end and moving upwards, with worthies transmitting to worthies and sages transmitting to sages until God is [retroactively] pursued, four attendants [are] necessary in between. These are four heavenly immortals serving in proximity to the honourable God.[74] In their midst God has a latent secret that people cannot know, [and] only God can know.[75]

The Muslim *Sanzijing* thus identifies the main personalities involved in the critical junctures of the transmission line preceding and following God's revelation to Muḥammad and prior to the translation of Islam in China. Its description of the transmission process sees God revealing the *dao* to various sages (*sheng*) in multiple epochs, aided by angels. Muḥammad's prophecy completed and sealed this revelation process. Afterwards, the *dao* was first transmitted to Muḥammad's four companions (the righteously guided caliphs), and then to four imams, who divided it into branches of jurisprudence. These intellectuals eventually took over the guidance of the Muslim community, transmitting the *dao* to diverse sets of people in awareness of regional variation and character.

Ultimately, the customs of China were such that the school of Abu Hanifa fit better in this context. Linking China's Islamic legal scholarship to the Hanafi school of Islamic jurisprudence, and the Hanafi school of Islamic jurisprudence to the transmission of four worthy scholars and companions, the text clarifies that the transmission of those worthies descends from the sage, and the transmission of the sage derives from the four attendants, who serve 'in proximity to the honourable God'.[76] Liu Zhi thus eventually identifies God as the ultimate retroactive source of the transmission of Islamic law in China. In a theoretical approach to Islamic legal thought that identifies *continuity* as an essential measure of orthodoxy, the legal culture of Muslims in China thus could claim consistency vis-à-vis the revealed law of Islam, at least as far as it kept developing within the overarching frame of the Hanafi school.

This narrative strategy claims the existence of a filiative relationship between God's initial revelation in Mecca and its ultimate reception and reinterpretation in China. The text implies that scholarly principles set down by the Hanafi school travelled and kept developing in China on a regional basis. The Muslim *Sanzijing* summarises those principles. Since the text aims to demonstrate the legitimacy and the continuity of its own legal views descending from the revelation of Islam in Mecca, its concluding section only sketches the main turns of the transmission of the *dao*. The authors do not concern themselves with spelling out the identity of subsequent links in the transmission chain,[77] but rather with situating the *Sanzijing* itself in the transmission flow:

> According to [what was said] before, the origin of heaven and earth were incited by only one God, [and] it can be seen that the *Sanzijing* comes from it. If not for the mercy (*ci'en*) of God, people could have not explained it, [as its] posterior return is shrouded in mystery, but it is nevertheless a return to that initial origin. If not for a bestowal (*enci*) of God, people could have not transmitted it.[78]

The Muslim *Sanzijing* thus completes its narrative circle. After affirming God's responsibility for the origin of heaven and earth and preparing the reader to accept the legitimacy (and the necessity) of regional developments of Islam's law in different contexts, the text concludes by re-establishing a connection between the Muslim *Sanzijing* and the God who 'incited' the origin of heaven and earth. The text represents a regional development of Islamic law, both narrating and justifying its gradual transmission and late reception by Muslims in China.[79]

The overarching legal legacy of the Muslim *Sanzijing* may be summarised as follows. At the root of everything lies one single God, a premise spelled out by the *Sanzijing* in its initial triplets. God's *dao* was revealed to the Prophet Muḥammad, who transmitted it to posterity. Following the geographical expansion of Islam, the interpretation of the *dao* split into four main branches of jurisprudence, assuming different legal guises in different contexts in which Muslims lived. The environmental features and customs of China were such that the legal premises of the Hanafi school had a better fit to this area. Chinese Muslims eventually embraced this particular pattern of

Islamic jurisprudence, which they developed by identifying and articulating congruencies with China's normative culture.

After the *dao* was revealed to Muḥammad, its interpretation flowed across space and time through transmission chains. The text does not identify the individual, intermediate links of the transmission within China. However, the *Sanzijing* displays confidence in its self-presentation as an orthodox regional outgrowth of Hanafi legal thought in the Chinese context. This confidence is rooted in its embeddedness in a continuous line of transmission of the *dao* that retroactively developed from the one God who incited the 'origin of heaven and earth'. Since 'the *Sanzijing* comes from it',[80] the legitimacy of its approach to Islamic law is ensured.

This final argument reassures the reader that the Muslim *Sanzijing* is ultimately orthodox from a Muslim legal perspective and squarely consistent with the law of Islam as it was initially revealed by God in the *Qurʾān*. Indeed, the *Sanzijing* represents a posterior development of that original law. As a consequence, formal asymmetries between the letter of the *Qurʾān* and the legal narrative of the Muslim *Sanzijing* should not lead beginners to question the direct linkage between the two. With this reassurance in mind, beginners may confidently approach the text as a reliable guide to the main tenets of Islamic law:

> If beginners are capable of reading it repeatedly, examining it deeply, comprehending it clearly, and practicing it solicitously, reflection will lead to understanding, and its usage will never exhaust itself throughout [their] lives.[81]

Conclusion

While attention has been directed to the relationship between Chinese Muslims' scholarly production in Chinese and Islamic theological sources in Arabic and Persian, Chinese Muslim scholars' ability to separate their legal thought from theological experiences outside the Chinese matrix remains largely unexplored. This study attempts to approach this particular aspect of Chinese Muslim textual scholarship by addressing the contours and the implications of the regionalist theory set forth by a primer for Sinophone Muslims.

In order to legitimise its Chinese (re)interpretation of Islamic law, the text needed to prove its legitimacy in relation to the revealed sources. The goal was achieved by interpreting Islamic history as a gradual process of regionalisation of the law, in which orthodoxy was maintained by means of continuity in the transmission. Through its resonance with legal principles of the Sunni tradition, the primer appropriated the analogous Chinese notion of *daotong* to allow the legal reasoning of Sunni Islam to find congruence in China, never colliding with the normative culture of the Qing state.

Thus, the *Tianfang sanzijing* primed an approach to orthodoxy that could detach Chinese Muslim interpretation of Islamic law from legal constructions formulated outside China, while acknowledging the relevance of local Muslims' intellectual past.[82] Its regionalist discourse averted the possible emergence of unreflective appropriations of juridical stances produced in other contexts, of patterns of orthodoxy that overlooked the importance of continuity in the transmission, and of literalist interpretations of the revealed scriptures of Islam. In Liu Zhi's view, the revealed scriptures could not be final statements of the legal contours of the *dao*, but rather initial steps of an evolving legal path open to transformation and supportive of regionalism, though in constant conversation with the historical heritage of Sunni Islam.

The Muslim *Sanzijing* attempted to pave the way for a sustainable development of Islamic law in the Chinese context. Its message, designed to spread among heterogeneous layers of contemporary Chinese Muslim society and to reach a unprecedented number of teachers and learners, was intended to mediate their understanding of the foreign sources of their *dao*. As the text implicitly delegitimised the appropriation of juridical stances frozen in spaces and times other than Manchu-ruled China, the text set the premises for Islamic law to follow a normative course of its own, grounded in the revealed scriptures and yet in constant dialogue with the norms and values informing the non-Muslim state and culture.

Notes

1. My sincere thanks to Chen Bo, Jonathan Lipman, Gotelind Mueller-Saini, Sergio Mukherjee, Rudolf Wagner and Zhao Xinhua for their helpful comments and suggestions. Any imperfections in the chapter are of my own making.

2. The present study deals with the earliest version of the *Tianfang sanzijing*, ascribed to Liu Zhi and analysed through the narrative lens of a later commentary by Yuan Guozuo. Other versions are explored in Tontini, *Muslim Sanzijing*.
3. Liu Zhi's lifespan is a source of debate. For additional perspectives, see Sun Zhenyu, *Wang Daiyu, Liu Zhi*, pp. 209–11.
4. Tontini, '*Tianfang dianli*', pp. 513–23.
5. 'Yang [Feilu] xu', in Liu, *Tianfang dianli*, pp. 36–7.
6. The complete name of the text was *Tianfang dianli zeyao jie* (*Selective Explanation of the Norms and Rituals of Islam*). According to Bai Shouyi, *Huizu renwu zhi*, p. 55, 'the *Tianfang dianli* (*Norms and Rituals of Islam*) was originally a comprehensive text on the rites and the laws of Islam (*tianfang lifa*). Due to its extensive length, its fundamentals were selected and [the text was] called *Tianfang dianli zeyao*. Subsequently, out of fear that beginners could fail to comprehend it, explanations were added [and the text was ultimately] called *Tianfang dianli zeyao jie* (*Selective Explanation of the Norms and Rituals of Islam*).' Bai Shouyi's interpretation resonates with the first paragraph of the 'Author's Preface' ('Zixu', in Liu, *Tianfang dianli*, pp. 44–5).
7. That is, people affiliated to China's mainstream culture (*Zhonghua*) and to Islam (*Tianfang zhiren*). Liu, *Tianfang dianli*, pp. 36–7.
8. Yang Feilu refers to these, respectively, as 'rites of *Tianfang*' (*Tianfang zhi li*, hence 'rites of Islam') and 'norms and rites of our dynasty' (*wo chao dianli*, the 'norms and rites' promoted by the Qing's central authority).
9. Frankel, 'Liu Zhi's journey', p. 47.
10. Tontini, '*Tianfang dianli*', pp. 519–23.
11. 'Zixu', in Liu, *Tianfang dianli*, p. 45.
12. Ibid.
13. Liu, *Tianfang dianli*, pp. 52–3.
14. For a reconstruction of Liu Zhi's image in contemporary Chinese historiography, see also Ma Jing, 'Qingdai guanfang'.
15. References to the earliest version of the *Tianfang sanzijing* may be found in Israeli, 'The Muslim revival', p. 129; Bai Shouyi, *Huizu renwu zhi*, p. 69; Stoecker-Parnian, *Jingtang jiaoyu*, p. 197; Na Guochang, 'Qimeng duwu'; and Benite, *The Dao of Muhammad*, p. 152. A partial translation of the primer can be consulted in Cotter and Reichelt, 'The Three Character Classic'.
16. Yuan Guozuo's preface to his own commentary on Liu Zhi's text is dated 1809. The present study is based mainly on a reprinted version published in 1870.
17. The so-called *Tianfang* 'trilogy' included *Tianfang dianli* (*Norms and Rituals of*

Islam), *Tianfang xingli* (*Metaphysics of Islam*) and *Tianfang zhisheng shilu* (*True Record of the Ultimate Sage of Islam*). See Bai Shouyi, *Huizu renwu zhi*, p. 357. For monographs on *Tianfang dianli* and *Tianfang xingli*, see Frankel, *Rectifying God's Name*, and Murata, Chittick and Tu, *The Sage Learning*.

18. Bai Limin, *Shaping the Ideal Child*; Leung, 'Elementary education', p. 93.
19. Yuan Guozuo, *Tianfang sanzijing*, p. 5. It is worth comparing these triplets to the Confucian version: 'It is wrong for children not to study [from an early age]. If they do not learn in childhood, what will they do [as they grow] old?' Chinese text from Giles, *Elementary Chinese*, pp. 13–14; the translation is mine.
20. Yuan Guozuo, pp. 11–12.
21. Ibid., p. 27.
22. Ibid., p. 25.
23. Giles, *Elementary Chinese*, pp. 136–9.
24. A distinction between *yu* and *mu* ablutions is offered in Liu, *Tianfang dianli*, p. 297.
25. Yuan Guozuo, *Tianfang sanzijing*, pp. 27–8.
26. Ibid., p. 31.
27. Bai Shouyi, *Huizu renwu zhi*, p. 68.
28. Ibid., pp. 68–71
29. The *Tianfang sanzijing* is listed among the texts gifted by Yuan Guozuo to Hai Furun prior to Hai's arrest during the Qing literary inquisition. See Bai Shouyi, *Huizu renwu zhi*, p. 69, and Lipman, 'A fierce and brutal people', pp. 101–2.
30. Yuan Guozuo, *Tianfang sanzijing*, p. 32.
31. Ibid., *Xu*.
32. Ibid., *Xu*.
33. Ibid., *Xu*.
34. 'Human beings by origin are of good nature. Natures are close, [but] customs diverge', in Giles, *Elementary Chinese*, pp. 3–4. On Sino-Muslim cosmogony, see Lipman, Chapter 1, this volume.
35. Yuan Guozuo, *Tianfang sanzijing*, p. 1.
36. For Liu Zhi's intellectual itinerary, see Liu Zhi, *Zhushu shu* (*On Authoring Books*) in Bai Shouyi, *Huizu renwu zhi*, p. 357. However, Yang Feilu disagreed, arguing that Liu Zhi studied the Muslim classics before approaching the Confucian curriculum. Liu, *Tianfang dianli*, p. 36.
37. Yuan Guozuo, *Tianfang sanzijing*, p. 5.
38. Yuan Guozuo, *Tianfang sanzijing*, p. 17. For the Chinese reconfiguration of

Islamic legal patterns within Chinese social ethics, see Tontini, 'Tianfang dianli', pp. 513–19.
39. Liu, *Tianfang dianli*, pp. 78–9.
40. Yuan Guozuo, *Tianfang sanzijing*, p. 17.
41. Ibid., *Xu*.
42. Ibid., p. 29.
43. Yuan Guozuo, *Tianfang sanzijing*, p. 31.
44. Ibid., p. 29.
45. Ibid., p. 30.
46. For the convergence of *dao* and *sharī'a*, see Tontini, 'Tianfang dianli', pp. 513–19.
47. Yuan Guozuo, *Tianfang sanzijing*, p. 30.
48. Ibid., p. 30.
49. Ibid.
50. Ibid., p. 29.
51. Ibid.
52. Ibid.
53. Ibid.
54. Ibid.
55. Ibid.
56. Ibid.
57. Ibid., p. 31.
58. Ibid.
59. Ibid., pp. 30–1.
60. Ibid., p. 30.
61. El Fadl, 'Islamic law and Muslim minorities', pp. 173–4.
62. See also Israeli, *Muslims in China*; Khadduri, *The Law of War*.
63. Dicks, 'New lamps for old', p. 357.
64. For the problem of 'orthodoxy' in Islam, see Calder, 'The limits of Islamic orthodoxy'.
65. Yuan Guozuo, *Tianfang sanzijing*, p. 31.
66. More specifically, the study refers to Chinese scholars affiliated to Sunni Islam and to Neo-Confucianism.
67. 'An important organizing category in Neo-Confucian genealogy is *daotong*, conventionally translated as "tradition of the Way". But this translation is misleading since *daotong* does not signify a tradition as such, but rather a filiative lineage of sages regarded as the sole transmitters of the true Confucian Way.' See Wilson, 'Genealogy and history', p. 9.

68. Ibid., pp. 25–6.
69. As reflected by the lineage policies of the Qing, for which see Rowe, 'Ancestral rites and political authority'.
70. For the usage of genealogical narrative patterns in Islamic legal literature, see Calder, 'The limits of Islamic orthodoxy', and Tsafrir, *The History of an Islamic School*. For their usage in the context of Chinese Muslim literature, see Benite, *The Dao of Muhammad*, and Zhou Chuanbin, *Xinhuo xiangchuan*.
71. In Islam, as in Confucianism, the intellectual 'authority' of a transmitter is also considered of crucial importance for assessing the reliability of a given transmission chain.
72. Yuan Guozuo, *Tianfang sanzijing*, p. 31.
73. As God had revealed the *dao* to Muḥammad in the first place.
74. The text refers to the angels, presented as mediators between God and humankind.
75. Yuan Guozuo, *Tianfang sanzijing*, p. 31. See also Wilson, 'Genealogy and history', p. 13.
76. Yuan Guozuo, *Tianfang sanzijing*, p. 31.
77. It is worth noting that Zhao Can's *Jingxue xichuan pu* (*Genealogy of the Transmission and Lineage of Classical Learning*) (1677) dealt extensively with subsequent 'links' of the transmission chain of Islam in the context of China. See Benite, *The Dao of Muhammad*.
78. Yuan Guozuo, *Tianfang sanzijing*, p. 31.
79. Ibid.
80. Ibid.
81. Ibid.
82. While it is beyond the scope of this study to delve into the legal discourses motivating the 'call for orthodoxy' endorsed by the *Tianfang sanzijing*, it is worth keeping in mind the contemporary existence of competing factions within Chinese Islam. See Lipman, *Familiar Strangers*, pp. 58–72.

4

The Multiple Meanings of Pilgrimage in Sino-Islamic Thought

Kristian Petersen

During the pre-modern period, pilgrimage constituted one feature of Islamic religiosity that formulated a sense of belonging and authenticity for Muslims. For the Sino-Muslim community, the *hajj* embodied several central elements of religious substance. Most broadly, the pilgrimage conveyed a sense of communal identification, which intensified Muslims' collective memory of cultural heritage, brought with it religious and social authority, and united all Muslims under the banner of Islam as a single transcultural congregation (Ar. *umma*). Praising or participating in the pilgrimage allowed Muslims at the geographic periphery of the Islamicate world to move to the *umma*'s centre. Their physical distance from the sacred heart of Islamic geography did not prevent them from connecting with their co-religionists through their perceptions, beliefs or practices.

This chapter focuses on religious pilgrimage and sacred space as a universal category of Islamicate societies and of religious traditions more generally. Through an analysis of Sino-Muslims' attitudes towards pilgrimage, as they have been expressed in Sino-Islamic intellectual production, we may view their thoughts as part of the broader Muslim world, presaging future comparative inquiry.

All three authors studied here – Wang Daiyu (1590–1658), Liu Zhi (1670–1724?) and Ma Dexin (also called Ma Fuchu) (1794–1874) – cherished the pilgrimage as a religious duty, but authors in successive generations gave it greater weight. As Sino-Muslims entered the global context in the eighteenth and nineteenth centuries, their writings increasingly underlined the *hajj* as an indispensable and obligatory Islamic practice. Other authors also considered the *hajj*, and a number of Sino-Muslims actually performed the pilgrimage (Wang and Liu did not), but these three represent attitudes reflected in Sino-Islamic scholarship in general and the *Han kitāb* specifically.

Overall, the perception of the *hajj* changed from a symbol of true belief to a potentially critical practice, and in the late nineteenth century it finally became an essential observance and religious duty. Wang Daiyu described the theological foundations of the pilgrimage, its role as a link to the time of Creation and union with God. Liu Zhi underlined the physical practice of pilgrims, stressing the ceremonial and experiential aspects of the pilgrimage by detailing the practices associated with it. Ma Dexin emphasised the performative aspect of the journey itself, while arguing for its power to rectify and renew religious understanding and asserting its doctrinal necessity.

Wang Daiyu and the *Hajj*

Wang Daiyu addressed the *hajj* pilgrimage as a religious duty and a rewarding spiritual exercise in a concise and modestly detailed discussion. He argued for faith in the benefits of the pilgrimage and the sacred geography it established, delineating the theological implications of the *hajj* and connecting it to the establishment of God's house, the Ka'aba, at the time of creation. While never personally having gone on the *hajj*, he stressed the direct harm that neglecting it can bring and the transformative experience it can provide for a believer.

The Pillars of Virtue in Chinese culture

Wang directly explored the *hajj* in a chapter entitled the 'Five Meritorious Acts' (*wugong*) in the first chapter of the second half of his *True Explanation of the Orthodox Teaching* (*Zhengjiao zhenquan*), which deals with religious praxis. Here Wang assigned a recognisable and esteemed status to the Five Pillars of Islamic religion within the Chinese context, laying the five meritorious acts of Islam in parallel with the Five Constant Virtues, conventional Confucian ethical values: humaneness/benevolence (*ren*), righteousness/

morality (*yi*), ritual/propriety (*li*), wisdom/knowledge (*zhi*) and integrity/faithfulness (*xin*).

These cardinal principles of the Confucian philosophical tradition, correctly followed, would cause the world to operate as a unified moral whole. Confucius and Mencius initially laid out the foundation for this perspective, replicated and augmented by generations of later authors and commentators.[1] Wang masterfully linked the primary actions of Islamic religious commitment with the moral dispositions of traditional Chinese thought. This method both accentuated the importance of the Five Pillars from the Islamic perspective and appropriated the authority of Confucian ideology within this specific semiotic framework. This earliest *Han kitāb* text thus established a methodology for Islamic–Confucian simultaneity.

Wang began his discussion by delineating the five principles within their Islamic context. 'The five meritorious acts of the orthodox teaching are God's clear commands. Namely, the five meritorious acts are remembrance (*nian*),[2] almsgiving (*shi*), fasting (*jie*),[3] worship (*bai*),[4] and gathering together (*ju*).'[5] The remainder of this chapter of the *Zhengjiao zhenquan* outlined the Five Pillars and sketched their theological foundations and import. Regarding the *hajj*, Wang explained that 'The last constant virtue is called gathering. Gathering together is called a covenant (*yue*). A complete covenant is called faith (*xin*).' Here, Wang demonstrated that through performing the *hajj*, each pilgrim completes an individual covenant with God and reaffirms personal faith. The *hajj* typically consummates a life of religious observance, and Wang stressed its capacity for demonstrating the faith of a believer.

The covenant and cosmography

For Muslims, God's covenant (Ar. *mīthāq* and *'ahd*) is both personal and communal (*Qur'ān* 2:40, 3:81, 3:112, 5:7, 33:7).[6] Individual, personal commitment to obey God's commands confirms that God's acts are not capricious or arbitrary (*Qur'ān* 6:164, 17:15). Wang connected a believer's personal covenant and commitment to faith with the communal covenant established through the relationship between God and creation through Adam.

> When the beginning itself began to open up, the human ancestor descended to the Heavenly Square. The Heavenly Square lies precisely at the centre of

the four poles, just as a state has a ruler and the body has a heart. How the shadows cast by the sun can confirm this! Afterwards, the human ancestor, Adam, obeyed the True Lord's clear command and then possessed the orthodox teaching.[7]

Wang thus established Adam's pivotal role as the bearer of God's trust (Ar. *amāna*) (*Qur'ān* 33:72) and the establishment of the Ka'aba as the centre of God's sacred geography. The Ka'aba thus constitutes both the terrestrial nucleus of the cosmos and its most crucial organ, its leader. By returning to this central axis on the *hajj*, the faithful proclaim their fidelity to God and fulfil the obligation of the covenant.

In Wang's explanation, the obligation to return to the Ka'aba to perform the *hajj* was established during Creation, and Adam disseminated this duty.

> The imperial command of the human ancestor, Adam, expounded and propagated to the masses that one time in each life they should go on pilgrimage to the Heavenly Square. One should part with what one loves and leave home. Continuously, in the past and present, we mutually inherit the traces of the orthodox teaching because we do not forget the experience of the foundation.[8]

In Wang Daiyu's vision, the movement from the profane world to the sacred centre reinforces the principles of the religion. The pilgrim inherits the legacy of those believers who previously returned, and the pilgrim will continue to fortify faith for future pilgrims. He explained that during the *hajj* the pilgrim would also be inwardly transformed.

> Arriving at this space one travels to His courtyard building and does not see the former person. During the pilgrimage experience of the Heavenly Square one returns to consider the original Lord, and the self opens up and begins to awaken. What is this that creates and transforms heaven and earth?[9]

This spiritual change positions the pilgrim within the communal and cosmographical environments by generating a feeling of belonging to both a community of believers and to a sacred cosmos imbued with purpose and meaning. Wang demonstrated that the theological motivations for the process of returning established within the *hajj* verify the foundations of Islam and locate the intersection of God's interaction with humankind at the Ka'aba. In sum, the pilgrimage re-establishes individual and communal elements of the covenant between God and creation and confirms the sacred centre of the cosmos.

Embodying the Five Pillars

Finally, Wang presented the *hajj* as the quintessence of the Five Pillars and asserted its crucial importance for Islamic praxis. He declared, 'This orthodox teaching of gathering is the faith of the congregation; it covers the five meritorious acts of the orthodox teaching.'[10] For Wang, performing the pilgrimage demonstrated the believer's commitment and dedication to fulfil the duties of a Muslim, and encompassed the deeds actualised through the declaration of faith (Ar. *shahāda*), giving of alms (Ar. *zakāt*), daily prayer (Ar. *salāt*), and fasting during Ramaḍān (Ar. *ṣawm*). He also argued for the importance of completing the *hajj* and not regarding it as a supplementary requirement. He viewed pilgrimage as an essential aspect of Islam, the foundation of the Islamic path (*dao*). He explained:

> In general, when one knows this path but does not observe and adhere to it, transgressions are doubled, and the heart is even more confused. That is, it resembles being able to eat yet not digesting. Surely they are stagnant and not comfortable. Not only do they lack benefit but they also turn back to transferring harm. Are they not able to stop and reflect?[11]

Wang condemned those who did not observe this duty because of its difficulty or the abundance of resources it required. He understood pilgrimage to be an integral, primary practice of Islam and that not performing it would be a grave detriment to personal salvation and communal fellowship.

Wang thus situated the pilgrimage as a paramount obligation, embodying the qualities of the other pillars of faith and personally transforming the believer. He greatly valued the *hajj* because it enabled Muslims to actualise their covenant with God and return to the heart of their sacred geography. He also linked the Five Pillars to the Five Meritorious Acts of the Confucian tradition, bringing authenticity and authority to Islamic practices in a Chinese setting. Ironically, Wang never performed the pilgrimage himself. He did not discuss his own failure to go to Mecca, but we know that he remained in Nanjing, moving to Beijing only towards the end of his life.

Observing Wang's intellectual treatment of the pilgrimage, his clear criticism of those who did not undertake it and his personal immobility, we may conclude that he saw the *hajj* as essential to religious observance and personal redemption, but difficult to realise. This may be why Wang stressed the theological underpinnings of the pilgrimage and the symbolic dimensions of the Ka'aba's cosmography and connection to Creation and Adam. He discussed the pilgrimage from the perspective of faith because for him, and the Sino-Muslim community he addressed, the most essential feature of their Muslim identity lay in belief in the principles of the religion. He wanted to define clearly what he interpreted as the religion's traditional features, even if its ideals could not be achieved in practice.

He thus described Islam as a set of beliefs that situated the adherent as an observant Muslim, indicating that for this Nanjing Sino-Muslim in the mid-seventeenth century, the pilgrimage constituted a foundational belief, rather than a critical religious practice. In this regard, the *concept* of the pilgrimage generated a sacred geography that instilled purpose into a community that understood the signs of God. The believer would reflect on the desire to return to the Ka'aba and understand the *hajj* as a symbol of future union with God and fulfilment of God's covenant.

Liu Zhi and the *Hajj*

Liu Zhi also viewed the *hajj* as both a personally transformative experience and as a religious responsibility of the utmost importance. He discussed the pilgrimage at length in his *Norms and Rituals of Islam* (*Tianfang dianli*) and outlined each phase of the rites performed during the *hajj*. Liu clarified the theological and liturgical aspects of the *hajj* in order to bolster a strong faith in its benefits, established the Ka'aba's sacred geographical centrality, and urged all believers to perform it. However, he simultaneously set forth acceptable reasons for not performing the pilgrimage and methods for gaining equivalent merit. Therefore, like Wang, he emphasised the doctrinal foundations and transformative rewards of the *hajj*, but did not belabour its necessity. He creatively demonstrated Sino-Muslims' ability to perform obligatory observances and identify with the larger Muslim community while remaining geographically isolated from the *umma*.

Meritorious acts and Chinese culture

Like Wang, Liu analysed the pilgrimage within a broader discussion of the Five Pillars of Islam, also calling them the Five Meritorious Acts (*wugong*) and emphasising their somatic quality. He declared, 'To reverently admire the five meritorious acts is the completion of the way of Heaven.'[12] Here, too, Liu bonded Islamic practices with admirable and exemplary behaviour within the Chinese context. The concept of *gong*, or meritorious acts, developed from medieval Daoist ethical injunctions and Buddhist social practices, was popularised in late imperial China, when Liu was writing, through *Ledgers of Merits and Demerits* (*Gongguo ge*).[13] These defined and measured meritorious acts in order to help individuals determine what behaviours should be performed to accumulate positive merit and direct their fate to an advantageous end.[14] Liu skilfully tied the five compulsory observances of Islam with the moral ethics of Confucianism, the Buddhist concept of *karma*, and social norms of accumulating good and removing evil. This method captured the authority of these traditions on behalf of Islamic practices by associating them with recognisable and admirable actions within the Chinese setting.

His discussion of the pilgrimage reflected his overall view of the Five Pillars as the means to achieve union with God:

> How is the body to be rectified? The five affairs of the Sage's teaching are these: remembrance, by which one knows the place of coming home; propriety, by which one practices on the path of coming home; setting aside, by which one releases oneself from loves; fasting, by which one cuts oneself off from things; and assembly, by which one goes home to the Real [God].[15]

These actions enable the believer to enact individual religiosity through embodied practices. The pilgrimage completes that commitment, as Liu declared, 'Once in a lifetime, one makes pilgrimage to the Heavenly Tower in order to realise the true aspiration towards which one is sincerely inclined.'[16] Through pilgrimage the participant can join in the communal establishment of meaning with spiritual, social and political significance. In this regard, like Wang's, Liu's analysis outlined the transformative power of the *hajj* for individual pilgrims:

> As for the pilgrimage, one goes from distant to near and from outer to inner, returning to the position of knowing the original substance (*benti*). The external aspect of the pilgrimage maintains the traces of swiftly moving one's feet, but the internal aspect makes the pilgrim one with the substance of the True Lord (*zhenzai*) without leaving a trace. How could there be anything that surpasses these meritorious works of cultivating the way?[17]

Liu regarded the physical movement from one's mundane setting to the sacred centre as a symbol for the internal change that occurred as one approached God through the cosmographical hub positioned at the Ka'aba. Pilgrimage held the utmost theological import for Liu because, of the Five Pillars, it most clearly demonstrated the internal progress of the believer through the completion of each ritual action performed during the *hajj*, each ingrained with specific religious meanings.

Sacred cosmos

Liu also echoed Wang's discussion of the Ka'aba as the centre of a sacred geography. At the beginning of the *Tianfang dianli* Liu declared, 'A western proverb says, "The earth is like a millstone. The heavenly square is the navel of the millstone. As for its shape, the four sides are all below because this land is the axis of Heaven and Earth. Therefore, all places are drawn to it".'[18] This situated the Ka'aba as the nucleus of creation, from which all life is sustained. The Ka'aba thus links humankind to the origin of Creation and allows the return to the source. As Liu began his direct examination of the pilgrimage, he again asserted the Ka'aba's centrality in the universe as the origin of creation.

> The Heavenly Tower is none other than the hall of pilgrimage, also called the Heavenly House [*Tianfang*, Heavenly Square, or the homophonous *Tianfang*, Heavenly House, Ar. *Ka'aba* (*ke'erbai*)]. The Creator (*zaowu*)[19] constructed it as a place to which people in all places would make pilgrimage. It is located in Mecca (*Moke*) in Arabia. Mecca is really the ancestral land for everything under Heaven. The Heavenly Square is exactly at the

correct position of Heaven and Earth. Located at the centre of the whole earth, Mecca is also located at the centre of Arabia. Thus, the pilgrimage hall also resides in the centre of Mecca. Therefore, it is the direction of pilgrimage from all places. It is as if it is the heart of the four limbs of pilgrimage. It is the place that people must accept a personal investigation as pilgrims, returning to the place of the beginning of human life.[20]

Here Liu described a material environment pierced at a point of divine creation. Returning to the Ka'aba allowed pilgrims to reconnect with the power underlying Creation. Throughout his discussion, Liu reiterated many of the arguments that Wang had previously laid out, clearly outlining the theological conditions for understanding the role of the *hajj*, situating the Ka'aba as a physical access point to the sacred, and demonstrating that it internally transforms the individual.

Practice and ritual

Liu also included other details of the *hajj*. Here he diverged most from Wang Daiyu in his methods, providing a concrete explanation of the practices associated with the pilgrimage. This part of the *Tianfang dianli* focused on the order and performance of the pilgrimage rituals. That is, in addition to belief in the efficacy of the pilgrimage, Liu thought that knowledge of the ritual practices would reinforce the believers' efforts to perform the *hajj* themselves. Therefore, he explicated the details of *hajj* performance, their religious meaning and importance for spiritual growth.

Liu's analysis listed the significant moments of the pilgrimage in chronological order, with a few lines to several paragraphs explaining the logic behind each act. He began with preparations that should be made by the pilgrim before travelling. He warned, 'The journey's route extends a far distance and preparations must be made in advance. The journey is more than one to two years. Possessing the ability, they must go there.'[21] Immediately before entering the sacred precinct, he wrote, the pilgrim must undertake the following actions:

> Thus, upon reaching the gate, one adopts prohibitions.
> One first cleans oneself and bathes.
> One changes one's clothing and wears fragrance.

Pray and convey a declaration.
One should recite the confession of faith (Ar. *shahāda*).
Upon entering the state of the prohibitions (*jie*), one reveals the top of one's head; exposes one's feet; does not wear yellow or purple clothing; does not wear anything containing an odour; does not smell fragrant fruit; does not wash the head; does not cut or shave one's hair; does not trim one's moustache; does not clip one's fingernails; does not wear any decorations; and does not kill any living spirit.
One wears the clothing of the consecrated state of the prohibitions.[22]

In explaining each of these items, Liu went into great detail describing the way one should act and think, how things should look, and the minutiae of each necessary object or action. Thus, he took the reader through each step of the pilgrimage journey, outlining the meanings behind the acts. He described the various circumambulations, preparation of sacrificial animals, the activities at Arafat and Mina, the stonings, ritual sacrifice and visiting Muhammad's tomb. This comprehensive description would give the pilgrim a firm foundation in understanding the *hajj* and could be used as a manual for those undertaking it.

Substitution of pilgrimage

Despite this detailed description and compelling recommendation in favour of performing the pilgrimage, Liu Zhi himself never went on the *hajj*. He did travel widely in China, but was never able to pass its frontiers, and he did not explain why he failed in this religious duty. This made his passionate endorsement of the *hajj* more mysterious. How could he reconcile this disparity and mitigate his personal negligence? In a section titled 'Through pilgrimage, one restores the mandate and returns to the truth', he explained:

If a person's remembrance of their longing for home is deep, then their remembrance of their devotion to the way is shallow. The command to perform the pilgrimage causes one to commence a journey to an outermost frontier, leaving passions and desires, in order to approach the original source. Therefore, the pilgrims must part with what they love and leave home on a rugged trek after which they visit this realm. Then, those who cultivate the way must also overcome and depart from selfishness.

Thereafter, one may return to the truth by diligently cultivating ascetic practices. In this manner, one borrows the palpability of the pilgrimage in order to open up to the meaning of pilgrimage's impalpability.[23]

This argument demanded that even in dire circumstances one should perform the pilgrimage. Neither distance nor attachment to family or wealth should impede this key observance. However, at the conclusion of his pilgrimage chapter, Liu discussed at length the reasons why Muslims do not have to go on the *hajj*. One section set forth, 'The Scripture says, "Believers must perform the pilgrimage. If the road is arduous it is permissible to wait."[24] A tradition (*chuan*) says, "When one is blocked, or is in hardship, has no kin or friends, or is disabled, then they are permitted not to go on pilgrimage."'[25] This is a commonly held position in Muslim societies, and Liu's justification is not unusual:

> In general, all believers should go on the pilgrimage in order to complete the five meritorious acts commanded by the True Lord. However, if the journey is too difficult or obstructed, or one does not possess travelling expenses, or father and mother are living, or one is crippled by illness, then it is permitted not to go on the pilgrimage.[26]

We do not know Liu's own reasons for not going, but we can assume that he was bound by at least some of these constraints.

However, Liu did not leave the discussion at that. He employed a creative rhetorical interpretation in his treatment of the duty to perform the *hajj*, particularly stressing the importance of ritual practice. Through ritual performance Sino-Muslims could participate in the community of Muslims despite their position far from the sacred centre. Ritual activity enabled this community to be in contact with the *umma* and with God through the powerful sense of belonging created by rituals. Those unable to return to the Ka'aba could rely on other rituals to substitute for the observance. In this regard, Liu asserted that:

> *Qurbān* (*guerbang*) and pilgrimage have the same meaning. Altogether, they are intended to seek closeness to the Lord. However, while the pilgrimage is the ceremony of personally visiting the Heavenly House, *Qurbān* is for people from a great distance, who cannot reach the Heavenly House, and it

is a ceremony that is practiced everywhere. Therefore, their ceremonial rules are more or less the same.[27]

Qurbān is celebrated at the end of the *hajj* during *'Eīd al-'Aḍḥā* to commemorate Ibrāhīm's willingness to sacrifice his son 'Ismā'īl. Through the celebration of *Qurbān* and the sacrificing of a sheep, Sino-Muslims could demonstrate their desire to participate in the *hajj* even if they were constrained by circumstances. Liu's justification for this ritual substitution derived from the *Qur'ān*, which says, 'Complete the pilgrimages, major and minor, for the sake of God. If you are prevented [from doing so], then [send] whatever offering for sacrifice you can afford' (2:196). Liu highlighted this point as compensation for Sino-Muslims who were generally too distant to perform the *hajj*. By making the *Qurbān* sacrifice equivalent in merit with the pilgrimage, Liu presented his readers with a means to understand their relationship to God and the *umma* without culpability for contravening one of the pillars.

Liu also likened the pilgrimage ritual to more common activities that a much broader population of Sino-Muslims could undertake, extending moral and ethical merit to include familiar relationships and deeds:

> Father and mother are the origin of one's birth. Morning and evening one should visit one's parents. This is the pilgrimage of residing at home. Worthies and erudite individuals are the origin of thoroughly understanding the teachings. Morning and evening one should be intimate with them. This is the pilgrimage of residing at a natural position. The heart is the origin of a hundred affairs. Examine and investigate it while in motion and at rest. This is the pilgrimage of oneself. The Lord Ruler (*zhuzai*) is the root origin of the myriad transformations. Within the mouth silently invoke God, within the heart praise and extol God. This is the pilgrimage of the most earnest. Generally, most people are unable to go on pilgrimage to the Heavenly Square; but they can observe these several things and thus may have the merits and achievements of personally going on pilgrimage to the Heavenly Square.[28]

Here, Liu reveals his unique perspective. While participation in the pilgrimage would be most desirable, and knowledge and belief in its benefits are essential to spiritual development, sincere intentions produce equal merit from quotidian behaviour. Liu derived this perspective from a reading of Qur'anic passages that elevate sincerity (7:29, 40:14, 98:5) and *ḥadīth* such as the opening passage of the *Ṣaḥīḥ al-Bukhārī*, which reads, 'I heard God's Apostle saying, "The reward of deeds depends upon the intentions, and every person will get the reward according to what he has intended."'[29] Liu extrapolated this concept to his local community, most of whom could not easily perform the pilgrimage, but who could feel connected to the *umma* through ritual participation. Their sincere deeds would be judged based on their intention and not on the fact that they were not able to perform one of the Five Pillars. This enabled Sino-Muslims to feel secure about both their personal redemption and their communal belonging.

Overall, Liu Zhi emphasised both the theological and practical aspects of the *hajj*, simultaneously advocating participation and alleviating regret for not being able to do so. He outlined a cosmic geography revolving around the Ka'aba and demonstrated how believers could participate in returning to that sacred centre. He also established how those unable to go to Mecca could gain equal merit for their intentions to go on *hajj* while performing alternative rituals. This ritual exchange reveals that for Liu the meaning ingrained in the *hajj* could be attained without performing it. Other meaningful religious activities that could be performed at any time and in any location constituted authentic and authorised expressions of faith. This enabled Sino-Muslims to feel that they belonged to the broader *umma* despite their inability to return to the Ka'aba.

Ma Dexin and the *Hajj* Pilgrimage

Even more than Wang Daiyu or Liu Zhi, Ma Dexin most clearly advocated the importance of performing the pilgrimage and its status as a foundational religious observance. He viewed the *hajj* as both personally transformational and religiously obligatory, like his predecessors, but he also believed it was individually attainable and doctrinally rectifying. He discussed the pilgrimage directly in his *Scripture of Bright Virtue* (*Mingde jing*) and his *Record of the Pilgrimage Journey* (*Chaojin tuji*) and intermittently in the rest of his writings.

In the *Scripture of Bright Virtue*, Ma described the liturgical aspects of the pilgrimage, echoing Liu's treatment of the *hajj* in the *Tianfang dianli*, laying out the physical geography of the Meccan religious environment and the stages of passing through it. While he reiterated the importance of the *hajj*, he did not distinguish it from the other pillars in its performative flexibility, allowing it to be possibly ignored, as Liu had clearly asserted. In contrast to Liu's justifications for ignoring the *hajj*, Ma urged all believers to go and described the conditions for being required to journey. This discursive shift promoted the notion that all Muslims should perform the *hajj* rather than identifying acceptable reasons for not doing so. In *Record of the Pilgrimage Journey*, Ma mapped out the physical realities of the entire journey from China to the Middle East, intending to demystify the *hajj* for Sino-Muslims while simultaneously asserting its importance as an essential Islamic observance. Overall, he understood the pilgrimage as means for engaging the broader Muslim world and as a vehicle for gaining what he perceived as a traditional interpretation of Islam. By detailing the particulars of the voyage he gave Sino-Muslims both logistical knowledge and the determination and resolve for undertaking the pilgrimage.

Hajj and Islamic practice

Ma addressed the *hajj* directly in a chapter entitled 'Pilgrimage' (*chaojin*) in his *Scripture of Bright Virtue*, a text transmitted to us through one of Ma's foremost disciples, Ma Anli (d. 1899), as a chapter in the second part of *Opening Love for Ritual and Law* (*Lifa Qi'ai*). The short section reflected the earlier discussions by Wang and Liu in that it addressed the legal and theological dicta requiring the *hajj*. Overall, the discussion was prosaic in style and pragmatic in tone. For foreign names, the transliterated Chinese version appears next to the Arabic original.

Nonetheless, Ma situated his treatment of the pilgrimage in the *Mingde jing* differently from those of Wang and Liu, discussing it in the broader context of Islamic ritual activity. Therefore, he treated the *hajj* in parallel with wedding ceremonies, burial rituals, divorce, ablution and other acts of observance. The shift in discursive procedures indicated that by the time Ma was writing most Muslims who would be reading his texts understood the importance of the *hajj*, both as a necessary observance that was ethically compelling and one that would produce beneficial merit. Placing this discussion within a broader context of ritual practices shows that Ma presented the *hajj* as one of many social practices that was expected and established, even for Sino-Muslims.

Obligation and observance

The content of Ma's *Mingde jing* recalled Liu Zhi's *Tianfang dianli*, dealing primarily with the legal conditions of the pilgrimage and the traditional actions associated with the various stages of the ritual. He described ritual preparations for the *hajj*, appropriate clothing, and permissible and prohibited activities and items. Ma's narrative outlined the geographical routes within the Meccan sanctuary and referred to several specific locations. For example, he declared, 'Taking the oath (*shoujie*)[30] of the pilgrimage ceremony, one stays at 'Arafāt (*erleifate*) . . . Arriving at Muzdalifah (*muzideleifa*) one halts.'[31]

This specificity gave his explanation authority for understanding the journey, and his personal experience authenticated his outline of ritual observances. Concluding his account, he described, 'At Mina (*mile* [misspelled in Ma's Arabic]) one exits from the right point. Together they [pilgrims] recite the words of praise. The pilgrimage is completed with a measure of hair and the breaking of prohibitions.'[32] The physicality of the description in the *Mingde jing* enabled Muslims to imagine themselves in the Meccan surroundings, and Ma highlighted the importance of the religious journey as an essential component of faith and practice. He explained that, 'Visitation (*jiyale*, Ar. *ziyāra*) is the travel of the orthodox pilgrimage. It all belongs to the Lord's regulations.'[33] The *hajj*, the most essential but also the most difficult of the pillars, was extraordinary but still compulsory. 'In all of one's life one only has to go one time.'[34] Knowledge of each facet and feature of the *hajj* equipped the believer to enact and actualise the religious journey.

The *Scripture of Bright Virtue* clearly asserted that the pilgrimage was not a peripheral activity of secondary importance, but rather one of the cardinal observances of the Islamic tradition. Ma's opening passage specified who was required to perform the pilgrimage:

> As for the ceremony of pilgrimage, it is for good believers (*mumin*) who are twelve years old or above, in good health and lacking illness, who have travelling expenses, sufficient strength, have a steed, and who have practical

miscellaneous things, or who are rich and have much to spare, or whose household expenses are sufficient.³⁵

Ma clearly asserted that Sino-Muslims should not be remiss when considering the pilgrimage. Unlike Wang and Liu, he directly defined who was obliged to perform the pilgrimage rather than simply stating, 'If one is able, he must go there.' The contrast between Ma's and Liu's respective arguments on requirement of the *hajj*, or who might refrain from going, marked their distinctive perspectives. The explicit contrast between these cataphatic and apophatic approaches to religious duty revealed Ma Dexin as the most forthright in stipulating the observance of the pilgrimage. Liu articulated several justifications for overlooking this duty, while Ma outlined measures that would oblige a much larger portion of the Sino-Muslim population, arguing that more Sino-Muslims could fulfil this duty. For that reason, he found that it should be as binding as the other pillars of Islam and actualised by faithful believers.

A pilgrimage journey

Ma Dexin was the first Chinese pilgrim to record his *hajj* journey. His pilgrimage was extensive in its geographical exploration and extended in duration, beginning in 1841 and including eight years of travel throughout the Middle East, South Asia and South East Asia. Upon his return in 1849, he became a prominent scholar in southern China and produced his travel journal, *Record of the Pilgrimage Journey*. The Arabic original has been lost, but Ma Anli translated the text into Chinese in 1861, making it accessible to a broad Sino-Muslim audience.³⁶ In the *Chaojin tuji*, longer than many of Ma's theological works, Ma rarely reflected on his personal emotions or spiritual progress, but chose instead to describe in detail the characteristics of the pilgrimage journey itself. The formal, laconic, impersonal narrative outlined each stage of the journey and detailed the practical and advantageous features of travel. Throughout, Ma catalogued people he met, places he visited, and noted the date of each phase of his trip in both the Islamic calendar and in the Daoguang reign period of the Qing dynasty.

The choice to focus on the travel itself and the places he visited rather than the sentiments he felt along the way is revealing in several ways. By removing himself from the experience, Ma demonstrated what every pilgrim might encounter, enabling any Sino-Muslim to imagine how a personal pilgrimage might unfold. While Ma Dexin was an exceptional figure, this text downplayed his unparalleled knowledge and remarkable achievements in favour of the ordinary stages of a *hajj* journey. These details provided the quotidian logistical knowledge for pilgrims to embark on their own *hajj*, including the timing of each stage, lodgings and detailed descriptions of the holy sites and the Sacred Mosque.

Further, by withholding his personal feelings, Ma Dexin could encourage others to renew or sustain their determination to undertake their own pilgrimages. Certainly, Ma had troubled times and doubts during his travels, but we remain entirely unaware of them while reading of *Record of the Pilgrimage Journey*. Omitting these elements from Ma's text, which would have made it more a personal diary than a travel guide, effectively underlined his goal of encouraging other Sino-Muslims to make the pilgrimage.

Travelling in Muslim lands

Ma set off for the pilgrimage by travelling overland to Yangon, Myanmar, where spent five months waiting for a ship to the Middle East. His record described the features of the local Muslim communities, including the abundance of believers in the Hanafi *madhhab* and a few from the Shāfi'ī. After an arduous sea journey he reached Calcutta, where he resided for four months. At the time, Calcutta was both a cultural and a commercial hub, and Ma noted a religious landscape largely made up of Muslims, some of whom he labelled 'rejecters' (Ar. *rāfida*, most likely Shi'ites). He also observed a number of Wahhabi Muslims there. Ma appreciated the Muslim community of Calcutta and their dedication to preserving their religion through textual reproduction. He made specific note of the high level of publishing of sacred scriptures and religious texts. After a long journey Ma eventually arrived in Yemen, before heading to Jeddah shortly thereafter to begin the final phase before approaching Mecca.[37]

Ma went into great detail, describing the Ka'aba and its environs, even sketching the mosque in detail. But Ma's travels did not end in Mecca. He explored the celebrated sites of the area – the birthplace of the Prophet and the battlegrounds of Badr, among others – before heading to Medina. Most completely he detailed Muḥammad's tomb in the Mosque of the Prophet, the architecture, the religious institutions, and the positions and practices of people paying respect to the Prophet.[38]

The precision in his description of the Ka'aba, the Sacred Mosque and the Prophet's tomb was essential to his overall mission of making the *hajj* accessible and familiar for Sino-Muslims. Through his thorough mapping of the *hajj* geography, Sino-Muslims could become as familiar with it as they were with their local mosque. The intersubjectivity between Ma Dexin and his reader facilitated the domestication of the spiritual axis of the cosmos centred in Mecca, thus making it simultaneously native and foreign – both home and abroad – for the reader. This catalysed the diminution of Sino-Muslim alienation from the broader Muslim world and facilitated the elimination of any perceived social, financial and geographic obstructions and limitations. Ma's *Record of the Pilgrimage Journey* also helped to remove anxieties and fortify the hopes of Muslims as they planned to return to their religious homeland.

After the formal pilgrimage, Ma Dexin continued to travel widely through the Middle East. In Egypt, the vast number of Muslims and their religious enthusiasm impressed him. He noted the majestic beauty and grandeur of al-Azhar Mosque and the many disciples of holy people (*shengmen*). He visited the tombs of such notable Muslims as 'the great worthy (*daxian*)' [Imam] al-Shāfi'ī (767–820), 'the great worthy' Abu'l-'Abbas al-Mursī (d. 1288) and 'the revered (*zunzhe*)' Muḥammad al-Būṣīrī (1211–94). Before returning to China, Ma visited the Ottoman sultan, spent some time in Damascus, returned to Egypt, lived in Jerusalem for half a year, and studied astronomy and geography in South East Asia.[39]

The *Record of the Pilgrimage Journey* asserted the significance of the pilgrimage as a necessary and accessible Islamic observance. Ma also countered the uncertainty and anxiety about the *hajj* by mapping the physical terrain and delineating the logistical details for Chinese pilgrims. This text, more than any other, offered a new inspiration for Sino-Muslims to embark on the *hajj*.

Ideological reformation

For many Muslims, the pilgrimage could be a monumental event both spiritually and socially, an occasion of both inner and outer transformation of the pilgrims' perception of the world and their position within it. One of the long-term effects of Ma's pilgrimage experience was a shift in his interpretive viewpoint, for both his doctrinal beliefs and his interpretation of Islam changed as a result of his encounters with Middle Eastern Muslims. While *Record of the Pilgrimage Journey* primarily concentrated on the details of travel rather than autobiography, elsewhere in his writings Ma reveals his individual metamorphosis and allows us to glimpse his feelings towards the personal change that occurred as a result of performing the *hajj*.

Through his Middle Eastern experiences, Ma rectified his religious opinions and gained a new understanding of Islam's foundational observances. He explained his transition in one of his major works, the *Essence of the Four Canons* (*Sidian Yaohui*):

> Arriving in Arabia, I asked a scholar named Isma'il (*yisimoenlai*) 'In this land is there one who transmits the true way (*dao*), shining (light upon it) by means of investigation?'
> He answered: 'Do you consider the five meritorious acts (*wugong*), which everyone performs, as a falsehood? That which the Prophet gave to his disciples to perform is the five meritorious acts. That which the four famous worthies (*xian*) and the millions of learned worthies (*xian*) observe is the five meritorious acts. That which a thousand scriptures and myriad canons publish is also the five meritorious acts. How can this not be the true way (*dao*)? Contemporary scholars and many thousands of this land invariably regard them as an effort. Is it only you who consider them to be petty?'
> I said: 'I do not dare to look at them as petty. But I hear each scripture speak of the three paths of the vehicle of principle (*licheng*), the vehicle of the way (*daocheng*) and the vehicle of truth (*zhencheng*). I gaze at the Truth and rise to enter it.'[40]
> He said: 'Yes, but shallow people make the truth shallow; deep people make the truth deep. If small people do it, then it is small; if great people do it, then it is great. Generally, there is nothing beyond the five meritorious acts. Moreover, as for shining (light upon it) by means of investigation, even if there is the brightness of the sun, what is its benefit for blind eyes?'
> I heard these words and felt deeply ashamed, knowing that my views on this were not enough. I requested that he add to the lesson.

He said: 'Among that which is commanded, in the end, they must be obtained. Among that which is not commanded, excise what lacks an imperative. If other things seek you then it is easy, but if you seek other things then it is difficult. Furthermore, the five meritorious acts are considered that which the True Lord commanded, and I distinguish them as that which should be observed. The vehicle of the way and the vehicle of truth are not what the Lord commanded. Therefore, they are acts that I add myself and they are supplementary acts.'[41]

This clearly established that Ma had determined to cultivate a stronger adherence to the Five Pillars, including the *hajj*, among Sino-Muslims and that the Chinese texts he had read were infused with the vocabulary of Sufism, which his interlocutor regarded as supplementary, not essential, to Islamic practice.

In general, Ma's work is characterised by a strong literary connection between Chinese and Islamic sources, for he often relied on and deferred to traditional Islamic sources for his explanations of Islam. In particular, his student, Ma Anli, wrote that the knowledge Ma Dexin gained on the pilgrimage journey enabled him to explicate the tenets of Islam:

He made pilgrimage to the divine court (*diting*), submitting to the traditional customs and good governance of the former sages (*xiansheng*). He studied directly with famous worthies (*xian*) and erudite scholars. In a period covering over eight years, his knowledge of the study of human life (*xingming*) deepened. Upon returning, he closed his doors in order to examine and rectify [his understanding of Islam]. He joined together that which he obtained in Arabia and that which was possessed in the ancient collected canons of the eastern lands. He uncovered the essence [of Islam] by drawing out and gathering. This constitutes what is bound in the chapters of this book and serves as a kindness to my companions.[42]

From this passage we see that Ma's pre-pilgrimage convictions and practices needed to be re-examined after his exposure to Islamic thought and ritual in the Middle East. The experiential knowledge he gained from his trip, combined with his intellectual training, produced the fruits of his literary output. Therefore, Ma was directly influenced by the pilgrimage and it shaped how he understood the Islamic tradition and transformed his theological grounding.

Ma Dexin created a complete picture of the *hajj* for his Sino-Muslim audience. He delineated the details involved in orchestrating and executing a pilgrimage journey, provided the ritual requirements from a legal and geographical standpoint, and demonstrated the transformative power of the pilgrimage from his own experience. The *Scripture of Bright Virtue* outlined the individual observances of the pilgrimage, enabling believers to enact their faith in embodied practice. It also established that numerous Sino-Muslims should be qualified to undertake the *hajj*, opposing the notion that Sino-Muslims could forgo their pilgrimage duty because of their great distance from the heartlands. *Record of the Pilgrimage Journey* alleviated the anxieties and concerns of Muslims and stressed the importance of greater engagement with the broader Muslim world. Finally, in *Essence of the Four Canons* he remarked that the experiences gained during the journey reshaped his personal understanding of Islam. His *hajj* set a precedent for others to follow, and his description provided a valuable tool for Sino-Muslims who would undertake the journey for themselves.

Conclusions

All three authors treated the *hajj* as a religious act that embodied deep theological meaning and brought with it rich communal and individual results. The pilgrimage connected Sino-Muslims to the larger Muslim world, both physically in the Meccan setting and symbolically as part of the *umma*. It also represented the origins of the cosmos and stimulated the collective memory of the Muslim community, thus strengthening their sense of transcultural identification. Finally, it produced religious and social authority and authenticity for individuals and their interpretation of Islam, either by elevation of status as a teacher or a renewal of personal commitment through sincere action.

For Wang Daiyu, the pilgrimage was a principle of faith and a symbolic ritual for understanding one's place in the cosmos. However, he did not insist that Sino-Muslims should embark on the actual journey to the Ka'aba and never went himself. Liu Zhi reiterated these cosmographical notions, but also delineated the bodily manifestations of these theological ideals. His description added a layer of meaning by detailing each specific action undertaken during the *hajj* ritual. However, he too never went to Mecca, and his arguments emphasised that Sino-Muslims, so far from Arabia, lived in unique circumstances justifying omission of the actual journey.

Ma Dexin, in contrast, not only promoted the pilgrimage as an Islamic principle with theological and spiritual meaning, but also described it as an obligatory religious duty to be performed by all Muslims. His own pilgrimage substantiated his promotion of the *hajj*, its benefits not merely theoretical but embodied and experienced personally. His narrative of his religious journey evoked a longing for Mecca-centred devotion, promoting unity among Muslims and pan-Islamic sentiments connecting Sino-Muslims directly to the broader *umma*. The scholarly treatment of the *hajj* by these authors moved from an internal religious commitment to an external physical movement through time and space. As Sino-Muslims became more engaged with the globalising world of the nineteenth century, their capacity to perform the *hajj* increased, creating new patterns of religious exchange and interaction.

Notes

1. For further discussion on the Five Constant Virtues in the Confucian context, see Slingerland, *Confucius Analects*; Ivanhoe, *Confucian Moral Self Cultivation*; Shun, 'Ren 仁 and Li 禮 in the *Analects*', pp. 53–72; Li Chenyang, '*Li* as cultural grammar', pp. 311–29; Gardner, *Zhu Xi's Reading of the Analects*; and Makeham, *Transmitters and Creators*.
2. *Nian* can mean both 'to remember or meditate' and to 'recite or invoke aloud'. Wang's employment of this term allowed him to convey the dual sense of the *shahāda* as a vocal articulation of one's belief in God and the Prophet and as a constant reminder of one's faith in God. In Buddhist texts, the word translates as *mantra*.
3. Wang employed an interesting term here to evoke the notion of fasting. *Jie* means 'to guard against'. In the *Analects* Confucius said (16:7): 'The gentleman guards against three things: when he is young, and his blood and vital essence are still unstable, he guards against the temptation of female beauty; when he reaches his prime, and his blood and vital essence have become unyielding, he guards against being contentious; when he reaches old age, and his blood and vital essence have begun to decline, he guards against being acquisitive' (Slingerland, *Confucius Analects*, p. 195). This term is also used to denote a regulation in Buddhism. The five precepts (*wujie*) are the foundation of Buddhist lay

practice undertaken by all followers: do not take life, do not steal, do not engage in sexual misconduct, do not lie and do not take intoxicants.
4. *Bai* means bowing or making obeisance in a Confucian context.
5. Wang Daiyu, *Zhengjiao zhenquan*, p. 82.
6. For further discussion on the concept of a covenant, see Bowering, 'Covenant', pp. 464–7; Gwynne, *Logic, Rhetoric and Legal Reasoning in the Qur'an*, pp. 1–24.
7. Wang, *Zhengjiao zhenquan*, p. 87. Compare Wang's narrative with Ma Zhu's found in Lipman, Chapter 1, this volume.
8. Wang, *Zhengjiao zhenquan*, p. 87.
9. Ibid.
10. Ibid.
11. This final passage is reminiscent of the constant guidance given in the *Qur'ān* for humankind to reflect (3:190–1; 10:24; 30:21; 34:46; 35:28; 39:27–8; 39:42; 45:13), and the concern for those who do not reflect (7:184; 30:8). Wang, *Zhengjiao zhenquan*, p. 87.
12. Liu, *Tianfang dianli, Qingzhen Dadian*, p. 63; Liu, *Tianfang dianli*, p. 5.
13. For a further discussion, see Brokaw, *The Ledgers of Merit and Demerit*.
14. These ledgers were catalogues of moral actions, to be filled in after daily self-examination. The earliest type of ledgers functioned in a religious context, used by Daoist priests marking positive and negative actions after self-reflection. These were adopted by Buddhists and closely related to the belief in supernatural retribution for good and evil. Later *gongguo ge* promoted morality in political, social and intellectual contexts, and was practiced by many scholars and officials in tandem with Neo-Confucian methods of self-cultivation.
15. Murata Chittick and Tu, *Sage Learning*, p. 484.
16. Liu, *Tianfang dianli, Qingzhen Dadian*, p. 63; Liu, *Tianfang dianli*, p. 5.
17. Liu, ibid., p. 84; Liu, ibid., p. 77.
18. Liu, ibid., p. 60; Liu, ibid., p. 2.
19. Throughout his writings, the early philosophical Daoist prosateur, Zhuangzi (369–286 BC) outlined the relationship between humans and a creator (*zaowu*). Compare with Lipman, Chapter 1, this volume.
20. Liu, *Tianfang dianli, Qingzhen Dadian*, p. 104; Liu, *Tianfang dianli*, p. 141.
21. Liu, ibid.; Liu, ibid.
22. Liu, ibid., pp. 104–5; Liu, ibid., pp. 141–2.
23. Liu, ibid., p. 84; Liu, ibid., p. 77.
24. This is a paraphrase of *Qur'ān* 2:196.

25. Liu, *Tianfang dianli, Qingzhen Dadian*, p. 109; Liu, *Tianfang dianli*, p. 158.
26. Liu, ibid.; Liu, ibid., p. 159.
27. Liu, ibid., p. 111; Liu, ibid., p. 161.
28. Liu, ibid., p. 109; Liu, ibid., p. 159.
29. There is also an *ḥadīth qudsī* that was repeated often: 'If My servant intends good deed, then I count it for him as a good deed, even if he does not carry it out. And if he does carry it out, then I count it for him as ten like unto it.' This is included in Hammām b. Munabbih's *Ṣaḥīfah*, Muslim b. al-Hajjāj's *Saḥīḥ Muslim*, al-Nawawī's *Arbaʿūn*, Ibn ʿArabi's *Mishkāt al-anwār*, and al-Madanī's *al-Itḥāfāt al-sanīyah fī al-aḥādīth al-qudsīyah*.
30. In a Buddhist context, *shoujie* means to take the precepts and be initiated into monkhood.
31. Ma, *Mingde jing*, p. 484.
32. Ibid.
33. Ibid.
34. Ibid., p 483.
35. Ibid.
36. Wood blocks of Ma Anli's translation were produced in the same year. Ding Rong, 'Ma Dexin *Chaojin tuji* yanjiu', p. 60.
37. Ma, *Chaojin tuji*, pp. 348–9.
38. Ibid., pp. 349–50.
39. Ibid., pp. 350–7.
40. These three terms, among others, translate the 'three stages' of mystical approach to God in Sufi thought and practice: *sharīʿa, tarīqa, haqīqa*.
41. Ma Dexin, *Sidian yaohui*, p. 83.
42. Ma Anli, 'Xu', p. 14.

PART II
MODERN CHINA

5

Ethnicity or Religion? Republican-Era Chinese Debates on Islam and Muslims

Wlodzimierz Cieciura

Few in the People's Republic of China (PRC) question the legitimacy of identifying the Chinese-speaking Muslims as the *Huizu* ethnic minority. This status has been enshrined in the policies of the Chinese Communist Party (CCP) since it started to formulate its nationality discourse in the 1930s. The officially produced scholarship on *Huizu* history, culture, sociology and so on hardly ever omits the *Huizu* paradigm, and scholars in China discuss the Sino-Muslims outside it only with difficulty.[1] The *minzu* definitions produced in the PRC have proved to be so alluring that even foreign scholars have employed them as handy tools to describe the ethno-cultural landscape of the country, though most of them have noted their Procrustean rigidity.[2] The ethnic status of the *Huizu* is particularly problematic, however, even from the orthodox Marxist–Leninist point of view, as they do not meet the so-called Stalinist criteria of defining a nationality (*minzu*).[3]

Yet the CCP was not the first political force in Chinese history to find the Muslim question hard to approach. The omnipresence of Muslims in the Chinese culture area has created difficulties of perception and policy for most regimes since the Ming dynasty.[4] Before the advent of the PRC's *minzu* paradigm many scholars, both Chinese and foreign, found the Sinophone Muslims perplexing and ambiguous. Chinese Muslims have been a vexing cognitive problem especially for Euro-Americans, since they tested the boundaries of understanding of both China and Islam, often treated in their 'pure' forms in the Orientalist tradition. The central question was whether the Muslims inhabiting the Chinese culture area were a foreign element, both culturally and racially; a culturally distinct yet racially local population; or a special form of ethno-religious community, formed through the assimilation of outside ethnic elements into Chinese people. Many modern foreign observers have tended to favour the last option: seeing the Sino-Muslims as a somewhat transitional phase between being fully non-Chinese and fully Chinese, exhibiting traits of both local genes and foreign admixtures. Writing in 1936, the Swedish explorer Sven Hedin judged the Chinese-speaking Muslims, called Dungans in Xinjiang, to be 'Chinese who have embraced Islam and are probably also separated from the Chinese by certain racial differences'.[5]

J. H. Effenberg, an American Methodist missionary writing five years later, depicted the Muslims in China as 'in general foreign to this country. They are strangers in a strange land. They have come from far off and they were compelled by force or circumstance to settle among people of different race, different speech, different mentality, customs and religion. Chinese literature and history refers to them as Huichao [sic].' Effenberg also described how the Republic, established in 1912, ascertained that China was composed of 'five races all living within the Middle Kingdom', among them the Muslims, represented on the new national flag by the white stripe symbolising Muslim racial distinctiveness from the Chinese. After recounting different ethnic subdivisions of the Muslims in China, he stated that, 'we have to distinguish clearly between "Moslems in China" and "Chinese Moslems"', the latter being children of unions between Muslim fathers and Chinese mothers 'carefully brought up in the Moslem faith'.[6]

Whereas the cognitive problems of external observers can be understood within the context of traditional Western perceptions of non-Western cultures and communities, the internal Sino-Muslim debates on the correct understanding of their own status within China await a deeper analysis. Confronted since the late nineteenth century with the deepening racialist and nationalist discourses in their homeland, Chinese Muslim intellectuals undertook to reformulate their self-understanding and position vis-à-vis non-Muslim Chinese culture and the Chinese state. Using both traditional and modern Chinese vocabularies concerning Islam, Muslims and ethnicity, these elites produced a rich reservoir of arguments and polemics. Reacting to the spreading discourses of 'nation', 'ethnicity' and *minzu*, they articulated their own creative responses, drawing on multiple inspirations, both domestic and foreign, including Euro-American, Middle Eastern, Japanese and others. Being just one of several Muslim communities in the lands of the Qing empire, inherited by the Republic, Chinese-speaking Muslims had to find an answer to the question of whether they were closer to their Turkic co-religionists in the Xinjiang borderlands or to their non-Muslim Chinese neighbours, with whom they shared centuries of co-existence and conflict. Did they share *minzu* identity with the former or with the latter, as there seemed to be no escape from this new concept? Perhaps they were a *minzu* separate from both and could position themselves between the Han Chinese and the Turkic Muslims of Xinjiang.

This chapter narrates the development of modern Sino-Muslim discourse on the relationship between ethnicity and religion, which produced three main theories of Hui ethnic status. First, the 'Han believers in Islam theory' (*Hanren Huijiao shuo*), a late nineteenth-century idea, claimed the Sino-Muslims to be a religious community within the larger Han ethnos.[7] This idea, promoted by numerous Hui intellectuals in the Republican era, was employed by the Nanjing government in the 1930s in support of its unitary vision of the Chinese nation, the *Zhonghua minzu*.[8] Second, the 'Islamic nationality theory' (*Huijiao minzu shuo*) defined the Chinese Muslims as part of a larger Islamic ethnicity encompassing all Muslim groups in China, all belonging to a larger pan-Islamic nationality. Third, the 'Hui ethnicity theory' (*Huihui minzu shuo* or *Huizu shuo*), historically the last to appear but official in the PRC since the 1950s, proclaimed the Chinese-speaking Muslims to be an ethnicity unto themselves. The names of the last two theories can be misleading, as the main theoretical article of the Sino-Muslim scholar Jin Jitang, '*Huijiao minzu shuo*', actually favoured the *Huizu* theory and was used by the CCP in its rationalisation of the *Huizu* as (mostly) the Sinophone Muslims.[9] This confusion resulted from a context of terminological flux, which caused many authors to understand the same terms in different ways or to use them inconsistently.

PRC ideologues commonly assume that the first two theories resulted from political oppression of the *Huizu* under the Republic and the political opportunism of some *Huizu* intellectual elites, but this does not seem justified. In fact, it is likely that the first theory, that the Sino-Muslims differ from the Han only in religion, dominated the early years of the Republic. Its talented promoters among the Muslim intellectual elites of eastern China spared no effort in denying any primordialist understanding of their community. The concept of the Sino-Muslims as a religious community within the larger Chinese culture had a long history and was deeply rooted in the sentiments of many Sino-Muslim elites.

However, this chapter cannot pretend to reach any firm conclusions about Sino-Muslim positions on the ethnicity versus religion controversy. My evidence comes from a very limited geographical environment, the north China areas of Beijing and Tianjin and their orbits, close to the political centres of modern China, where the Muslim community was necessarily vulnerable to governmental and non-Muslim inspirations and pressures. All my sources were written by lay Muslims, representatives of secular modernist circles, in organisational cooperation with religious professionals with a very distinct understanding of Islam and its social dimensions. The influence of these northern intellectuals on their co-religionists in other parts of China requires further study, but it is possible that it was considerable, given the wide circulation of their periodicals.

A Brief History of the *Huizu* Controversy

It is difficult to pinpoint an exact moment when the term *Huizu* appeared for the first time. David Atwill identified one of its earliest usages in the 'Shuaifu bugao', a declaration of the Yunnanese rebel leader Du Wenxiu, issued by his Pingnanguo regime in Dali in 1876. Atwill, who translates the term in this context as 'fellow Hui', speculates that the appearance of the term at this time in Yunnan 'can perhaps be traced to links between the Pingnan regime and that of the Taipings', who used similar neologisms for other ethnicities in their documents.[10] Even though these ethnonyms with the suffix *zu* appeared well before the advent of *minzu* terminology in the last years of the nineteenth century, and though they had much less rigid and reified meanings, Atwill believes that they offered 'a distinct impression of an awareness that "Hui" are an ethnic category'.[11] *Huizu* also appears in other documents from Yunnan, both rebel and Qing, which strengthens the argument that the term was indeed born in that province.

Still, we may observe in the very same document a strong relationship between the Yunnanese Muslims, who might have developed some sense of pre-modern ethnic consciousness by this time, and the wider non-Muslim Chinese community. Explaining his army's offensive against the Qing forces, Du Wenxiu listed a number of justifications, among them not only the 'extermination of my fellow Muslims' (in Atwill's translation) by the Manchu Qing, but foremost the fact that the Manchus (*Manren*) have 'captured the central power of *our* China (*wo Zhongxia*) ... treated the people [here Du uses another neologism – *renmin*] like cattle and horses ... and hurt my compatriots (*shang wo tongbao*)'.[12] The usage of terms like *renmin* and especially *tongbao*, normally translated as 'compatriots' but literally meaning 'of the same womb', demonstrates that Du did not understand the term *Huizu* as denying Hui inclusion in Chinese culture and community and perhaps even consanguinity with non-Muslims. The contradictions visible in Du's manifesto haunted Muslim writers in the coming decades, causing confusion and interpretive problems.

Whatever Du Wenxiu meant by *Huizu*, the term came to be understood as a designation of separate ethnicity, or nationality, in the last decades of the Qing, especially after *minzu* terminology gained currency in the wake of the Sino-Japanese War and the wave of Chinese students studying in Japan. Though the definition of the *Huizu* was not clearly delineated until decades later, its usage became popular enough in the last years of the Qing for some Sino-Muslim elites to undertake a critique.

One of the early critical voices appeared in the first modern Chinese Muslim periodical, *Muslim Awakening* (*Xinghuipian*), which published one issue in 1908 in Tokyo. The magazine was part of a wider effort by a group of thirty-six Chinese Muslim students in Japan, including one woman and one imam, to mobilise their co-religionists in China culturally and politically. They aimed to reform Muslim education by expanding its curriculum to include patriotic and political instruction. The students, who formed the Muslim Educational Association of Students in Tokyo (*Liudong Qingzhen Jiaoyuhui*) in the summer of 1907, were inspired by the creation of the Revolutionary Alliance (*Tongmenghui*) in July 1905 under the leadership of Sun Yat-sen.[13] The leader of the Muslim Educational Association, the Yunnanese Bao Tingliang, and three colleagues participated in the founding congress of the Alliance, whose goals included rejuvenation of China, building a republic and political elimination of the Manchu dynasty.[14] The radical programme of the Revolutionary Alliance inspired the Muslim activists, but its xenophobic, even racialist, components alerted them to the dangers of the exclusivist, 'Han-centred' discourse of the revolutionary movement. Coming from all over China, from Yunnan to Beijing and Shaanxi to Guangdong, the students had to rethink their identity as Chinese Muslims studying in the only modernised nation-state in East Asia. They came to see the ethnic theory of their community, the *Huizu* theory, as a potential threat and reacted strongly against it.

Huang Zhenpan (1873–1942), the Association's secretary, a native of Zhili (now Hebei) province and student of political economy at Waseda University, provided the fullest criticism of the identification of the Chinese Muslims as an ethno-racial group. In his article 'On the *Hui* people' (*Lun Huimin*), Huang stressed that, '*Hui* is not the name of a race but of a religion'. He traced the Chinese name of the religion to the *Huihe* people of what later became Xinjiang, who had accepted Islam as their religion. The Chinese Muslims, however, shared with them only religion but not common descent. Huang repeated some of the stories found in the *Huihui yuanlai*, stating that the Muslims in China proper, to the east of Xinjiang, descended from Muslim traders and the 3,000 Muslim warriors sent to China by the Prophet Muḥammad during the Tang dynasty and their Chinese wives. Huang also argued that much of the Muslim community in China descended from local converts to Islam:

> In the year 628 [CE] messengers were sent to China to propagate the religion. At the same time many people in Gansu and Shaanxi converted to the religion, and the famous Huaishengsi mosque was built in Guangzhou. Up until today masses of people have entered the religion. Therefore it is clear that the religion does not come from the *Huihe* and that the believers are not from the *Huibu* lands [Xinjiang]. Instead they are descended from various groups of settlers during the Tang dynasty who were known by different names. They had five surnames – Ha, Ma, Da, Sha and Ding – and they all followed the religion [Islam]. In addition, three thousand *Hui* soldiers were received during the Tang who defended China and took wives.

> After more than one thousand years they multiplied and, as demonstrated by Hong Jun, were melted in this big oven and have become of the same kind (*tongzhong*) [as other inhabitants of China] – therefore how can they be called a different race (*zu*)?[15]

Huang went on to analyse examples of conscious racial and ethnic mixing in history, pointing to Alexander the Great ordering his soldiers to marry local women in Asia in order to create a racially homogeneous population, and asserted his belief that this should also be a goal for Chinese reformers. He rejected categorising different groups within China under racial and ethnic (*zu*) labels, as all the people of China suffered the same fate at the hands of foreign invaders. Furthermore, he found erroneous the names used in China to classify the different groups. Instead of setting the *Hanzu* against all others, Huang offered a more historically nuanced vision of the Han:

> Looking at the sources of the term *Han*, it originates from the times of the four ancient barbarian peoples. When the Emperor Han Wu[di] took control over all of them, his Han dynasty became the most glorious empire, awing Europe in the west and Japan in the east. Its script was named the Han script, and its people were named the *Hanzu*. If the people of our country have been created during four thousand years of history, is it possible that there is only one type of Han? Those called the Han must be almost identical to those outside of this group.

Clearly alarmed by the growing discourse of China being composed of various nationalities – Huang mentions Han, Mongols, Tibetans, Miao, Manchus and *Hui* – who might treat each other as enemies, he criticised the idea of the *Hui* being a separate *zu*:

> Leaving aside the Tibetans, Mongols and Miao, only the Han, Manchu and *Hui* inhabit the sacred inner lands of our great country in separate households. The so-called *Hui* (*suowei Huizhe*) live in harmony with others. Amongst their elderly there are some who claim that they only care about the religion and not about the country. This is perhaps because the *Huihui* entered China with the goal of preaching their religion. Our contemporaries do not realise the abovementioned facts, and they regard the Muslim people (*Huimin*) as a separate race – the *Huizu*. Therefore next to the Han

and the Manchus another hostile ethnicity has been established. I am afraid that in the next few hundred years the people of the yellow race will destroy one another and not even a trace of the yellow people will be left.

Thus, in Huang's assessment, the concept of *Huizu* – a 'Chinese Muslim ethnicity' – was a dangerous development, one that might eventually not only hurt the interests of China, but even lead to the extinction of the whole Chinese race.

These concerns became ever more burning when the Qing dynasty collapsed in 1912, and the Republic was established, as planned by the Revolutionary Alliance and its associates. China could become a nation-state, but elucidating the inner meaning of the nation involved fierce disputes. For Muslims in China, the revolution's success made the question of their nature and position all the more critical. In the wake of the 1911 revolution, a very new concept of the Chinese 'political nation' began to be promoted: that of the 'unity of five *zu*' or 'republic of five *zu*' (*wuzu gonghe*), the harmonious cohabitation of five officially recognised communities in China. The republican state reified five great *zu*, nationalities or ethnicities, namely Han, Manchu, Mongol, Tibetan and Muslim, attaching a *zu* suffix to the five Chinese characters used by the Qing for these cultures.

This idea of China can be traced to the Qianlong era conceptualisation of the Qing empire as comprising five cultural spheres (*bu*, namely, Manchuria, China proper, Mongolia, Tibet and Xinjiang) inhabited by distinct peoples (*zu*), each possessing unique cultural traits, among which a separate script was considered especially important.[16] Within the context of the Qing political system, the house of Aisin Gioro ruled over these five constituencies as supreme overlords and recognised the subordinate lords within each of them: Manchu banner chiefs, Turkic *begs* of Xinjiang, Han literati and so on.

This Qing concept was reformulated in constitutionalist and nationalist terms and introduced into the reformist discourse in the 1906/7 writings of Yang Du (1874–1932), a late Qing Confucian scholar and advocate of constitutional monarchy.[17] Yang subsequently became a monarchist political adviser to Yuan Shikai only to end his life as a secret member of the Communist Party. In his voluminous 1907 work entitled *Jintie zhuyi shuo* (*On the Doctrine of Gold and Iron*), he elaborated that China as a modern state includes twenty-one Han provinces (which subsume Manchuria), Mongolia, the *Hui* or Muslim lands (*Huibu*) and Tibet. Thus, its nation comprises the five *minzu* native to these regions, the *Hui* being one of them.[18] This definition categorised the *Huizu* as those Muslims who lived in the *Huibu*, a territory identical with the southern part of Xinjiang, inhabited mostly by Turkic Muslims and a much smaller group of their Sinophone co-religionists. This confusion over the nature of China's fourth *minzu* haunted policymakers and Chinese Muslim intellectuals in the coming decades, as various political forces employed Yang's conceptualisation in their struggles for political legitimacy after 1912.

The 'five *zu* concept', including the *Huizu*, triumphed as a powerful political slogan during the 1911 revolution.[19] From its leaders Sun Yat-sen derived the idea of a multi-ethnic China and included it in his political programme. Sun, a staunch anti-Manchu racialist radical, knew Yang Du as a political opponent from the early 1900s in Japan, but nonetheless found his concept to be a workable formula to safeguard the former Qing empire's territorial integrity for New China. The Republic's provisional constitution in 1912 included the *wuzu*, so the *Huizu* became a legal concept. However, unlike Yang's enumeration, the constitution did not refer to any specifically Muslim region and included Xinjiang among the twenty-two provinces. The *Hui* were no longer to be understood as a strictly geographically defined community in the definition of the Chinese nation.

The spread of the *wuzu* discourse did not go unnoticed by Muslim intellectuals, and some of them exerted themselves in criticism. On 8 April 1912, a Beijing Muslim paper, *Zhengzong Aiguobao* (*The [Orthodox] Patriotic Daily*), voiced the most eloquent argument against the idea of Muslims being one of China's five *zu*. Established six years earlier by a well-known activist, Ding Baochen (1875–1914), this vernacular daily catered to the working classes and promoted the democratic equality of all China's inhabitants in 'down-to-earth Beijing colloquialisms'.[20] The *Patriotic Daily* addressed a wide audience, not limited to Muslims, and its goals included, 'the awakening of people with yellow faces and black hair who share the same misery and who love China as they love their lives and inspiring them to support each other in the struggle for the happiness of our common kind and in their sacrifice for the country.'[21]

As post-revolutionary enthusiasm grew and Muslim elites in China prepared to organise themselves vis-à-vis the new republic, *Zhengzong Aiguobao* published a cautionary article criticising the intent of some elites to act as representatives of the fourth *minzu*, the *Huizu*. Signed by an author using the penname *Gongheguomin*, 'Citizen of the Republic', most probably Ding himself or his elder brother Ding Zhuyuan (1869–1935), an important publisher of Muslim periodicals in Tianjin, the article was entitled, 'Differentiation of the *Huijiao* and *Huizu*' (*Huijiao Huizu bian*).

The article opens with a vivid depiction of the new republican discourse creating confusion and hesitation among Muslim intellectuals as to what stance they should take in their dealings with republican ideals and the new state:

> Since last September [1911], talk of the unity of the five nationalities has spread to all provinces of the country ... Enthusiastic supporters of the Republic have attempted to establish unity among the Muslims of all the inner provinces. Intending to join the organisations [that promote] the idea of the unity of five nationalities, some Muslims have [also] begun to recognise themselves as *Huizu*. Still others have hesitated and paced back and forth, waiting to see [further developments].[22]

Admitting that he had been very cautious in articulating his arguments against the new trend among Muslim elites to identify as *Huizu*, the author went on to state that, 'Since the matter is of grave importance, this writer took his time to ponder [the issue] carefully. Since he has got some unpleasant things to say to both sides of the argument, he withheld his opinions for several months.'[23] However, when 'various friends of the author and other gentlemen have recently joined all sorts of associations [which promote the] unity of five *minzu* as representatives of the *Huizu*', he decided to speak out, worrying that 'if this issue is not criticised thoroughly today, I greatly fear that there might be more grave mistakes made [in the future].'[24] Ding's article clarifies the novelty of the term *Huizu*. He wrote, 'This writer has wanted to elaborate on the issue since the term *Huizu* appeared in September last year.'[25] As late as 1912, a well-read and experienced man of letters found the term *Huizu* novel and appalling, several decades after it had first appeared in Du Wenxiu's Pingnanguo. In Ding's account the term derived from the revolutionary discourse of the Wuchang uprising and its consequent political use by Sun Yat-sen and other republican revolutionaries. This perhaps allows us to map the spread of the *Huizu* concept from Yunnan to the revolutionary middle Yangzi and then to Beijing. Certainly, Ding must have also been familiar with the use of the term within the Japanese discourse of nationality, especially through his reading of the *Xinghuipian*.[26] It is worth noting here that Ding's newspaper played a key role in propagating the writings of the Tokyo students in China and establishing their position in Sino-Muslim history.[27]

Ding believed that the root of the '*Hui* problem' lay in the vocabulary employed in China to refer to Islam and its followers. He undertook a criticism of the term *Hui* as meaning both Islam and Muslims, not differentiating among various cultural and ethnic groups. To avoid confusion, he proposed to standardise the other traditional, and in his view more neutral, Chinese name for Islam: 'The mistaken appellation of *Huijiao* is prevalent in China nowadays. However, the correct name of this religion is *Qingzhenjiao* (the pure and true religion).'[28] For him the word *Hui* was too historically entangled and ambiguous to have place in the new political reality of China. It offered no nuances of the ethnic situation of Muslims in China and derived from the age-old inaccuracy of the Chinese people, who confused the ancient *Huihe* with all other Muslims:

> During Tang times the *Huihe* [Uyghurs] appeared in the western borderlands, and at the time the Tang-era people referred to this type of people as *Huijiao*. However, in fact the religion of the *Huihe* and the religion of Arabia were not the same. Our fellow countrymen did not examine this issue carefully enough and began to apply the term *Huijiao* to all the followers of *Qingzhenjiao* in the inner provinces. This mistake has been transmitted into our age and therefore the name *Huijiao* is still in use, repeated erroneously time after time, which has eventually led to the [appearance of the] word *Huizu*.[29]

In Ding's view, the term *Huizu* itself should not be rejected, as long as it clearly referred to the 'various Muslims of Xinjiang and the western borderlands'.[30] They were indeed the *Huizu* of official discourse. Meanwhile, the Sinophone Muslims in eastern China should not be treated either as an extension of the Xinjiang Islamic peoples in the inner provinces or as a separate ethnicity, as they were in fact thoroughly acculturated into local society:

> It [Islam, the *Qingzhenjiao*] originated in Arabia, and during the Sui and Tang dynasties it entered China. Beginning from Guangdong, it continued to Henan, Shaanxi, and other provinces. The believers' numbers grew every day, but they were not all Chinese. Even if at the beginning they were of the Arabian race, after hundreds of years there is no longer any difference between them and other people of the inner provinces. Moreover, after a thousand and three or four hundred years how nonsensical it is to claim that because of their religion they constitute a different race![31]

Ding warned that the government policy of including the Sinophone Muslims of the inner provinces in the *Huizu* category might lead to serious problems in communal relations.

Ding's article portrays the Chinese Muslims as Chinese people with Islamic belief, perhaps only partially and very distantly descended from outsiders, possibly Arab missionaries and warriors, but certainly not the inner Asian peoples of Xinjiang. That some Chinese Muslims called themselves *Xiyuzhe*, 'those from the western regions' (Xinjiang), he called 'a serious mistake', surpassed in its falsity only by even more incorrect terms such as *Huimin* and, above all, *Huizu*:

> *Qingzhenjiao* was originally called Islam (*Yisiliamu*), which has been translated [into Chinese] as *Qingzhenjiao* but now is called *Huijiao*, which might be a result of confusion with the *Huibu* (i.e., formerly *Huihe* areas), and hence the name *Huimin*. But, if I may ask, does this mean that the *Huimin* people are not people of China? Do we indeed have to call people by their religion? Why then we do not call the followers of Protestantism (*Yesujiao*) the *Yemin*? Why we do not call the followers of Catholicism (*Tianzhujiao*) the *Tianmin*? And those who profess Buddhism or Daoism the *Fomin* or *Daomin*? What would be the logic of this?[32]

If the Chinese Muslims were to have a safe future in China, they would have to be treated as citizens, differing from their compatriots only in religion. Ding closed his article:

Regardless of whether they are a race or not, today they should be viewed as citizens of the Republic, and they should enjoy the happiness of religious freedom (*xinjiao ziyou*). They should have the same obligations as other citizens of the Republic and should abide by the law of the state. I hope that false appellations will not be spread and will be recognised as wrong.[33]

Other authors in the Ding paper supported Gongheguomin's strong opposition to the concept of *Huizu*. Shortly after, another author, using the name Shou Jin, attempted to explain the difference between *Huijiao* and *Huizu*:

In modern times a Republic has been created, and five *minzu* have been united, the *Huizu* among them. The ignorant masses, however, continue hastily to associate those who believe in Islam (*Huijiao*) with *Huizu* or *Huimin*. This is absolutely and deeply scarring. By examining the historical records, and tracing the sources of numerous Chinese *minzu*, one can see that the so-called *Huizu* of today refers to the people of Xinjiang and not to the people who believe in Islam (*Huijiao*) in the inner provinces.[34]

Shou Jin repeated Ding's arguments that if the *Huizu* existed, it must refer to Muslims in Xinjiang, a place with 'rugged mountain chains and severely hot climate', whose 'population could not be compared with that of the inner provinces'.[35] He explained the popular confusion of Xinjiang's *Huizu* with Muslims in the inner provinces as a result of the confusing terminology: '*Huijiao* came to China from the West, [and since] in that time the art of geography was not refined, anything that came from the West was often named after those lands.'[36]

By the time Shou's article appeared, the issue of the term *Huizu* had become an intensely debated institutional question. In the following issue, Shou narrated recent disputes within the Muslim community. As the new republican government attempted to establish an official association for the promotion of *wuzu gonghe*, many local Muslim elites refused to act as representatives of the *Huizu*. When the offices of the Parliament moved to Beijing, the controversy entered the local Muslim stage. Fearful that the question could tear the community apart, the most senior Beijing Muslim leader, Wang Kuan (1848–1919), called a special meeting in the city's New

Mosque. Shou Jin, present at the meeting, proposed to form different associations for two different 'types' of Muslims: one for those from the inner provinces, to be named the Islamic Association (*Qingzhenhui*); and the other one for those from Xinjiang, to be called the *Huizu* Association (*Huizuhui*).[37] Sidike, a '*Huihe* duke' and former member of the Qing advisory parliament, was invited by letter to represent the 'local organisations' in preparation for the establishment of the *Huizuhui*. Until that happened, the *Qingzhenhui* was supposed to represent the Muslims in Xinjiang in all formalities vis-à-vis the state. Eventually, however, two associations, although acting as a united front, were to deal separately with these two parts of the Muslim population of the Republic of China.[38]

The vision of dual representation championed by *Zhengzong Aiguobao* did not materialise. In July 1912, Muslim activists in Beijing formed the Chinese Islamic Progressive Association (*Zhongguo Huijiao Jujinhui*, hereafter CIPA), headed by the modernist educator Ma Linyi (1864–1938), an early member of the Revolutionary Alliance.[39] Imams Wang Kuan and Wang Yousan served as deputy chairmen. In its charter the Association proclaimed the main goal of 'uniting Islamic people in the country to assist the Republic and support unity'.[40] Controversy still surrounded the Association, as evidenced in yet another *Zhengzong Aiguobao* article, this time written by Ding Baochen's brother Ding Zhuyuan, also an outspoken opponent of the *Huizu* concept. Writing of the CIPA's establishment, he stated:

> Concerning the first point [of the charter], it would be best and advisable to change the CIPA's name. Our religion is called Islam (*Yisiliamu*), which can be translated as *Qingzhenjiao*. The term *Huijiao* is erroneous, for this [Islam] is not a sect of the *Huihe*. From now on, it should be called the *Qingzhenjiao* on every occasion. As for the Progressive Association, how could it name itself with the two characters *Huijiao* in the first place?[41]

Despite the opposition of the Ding brothers and their circle, the CIPA continued to operate under its original name through most of the Republican era, with branches in many provinces and larger cities of the country. The leaders of the organisation did not seem to find the terminological problems to be of great importance. They employed a variety of lexical devices to differentiate between non-Sinophone Muslims of the frontier regions and

Chinese speakers in the inner provinces, as shown in their letter to the Turkic Muslim nobility of Xinjiang (including the traditional rulers of Hami, Kucha, Yarkand, Turpan and Khotan), calling on them to set up their own branches of the organisation:

> Since the establishment of the Republic, a unity of five *minzu* has been created, authoritarian rule has been wiped out, and freedom of belief has been secured. People of our Islam (*wo Huijiao renmin*) who inhabit the borderlands of China are one of those *minzu*.[42]

This ambiguous formulation left a lot of space for interpretation, for in the most literal reading the letter suggested that the eastern Chinese Muslim intellectuals acknowledged that they were of the *Huijiao* religion, but not of its *minzu*, understood as including only the Turkic-speakers of the borderlands.

One of the most emotional protests against the equating of Sinophone Muslims with *Huizu* appeared in the paper in May 1912, just after the founding of the Association for Common Progress of the Five *Zu* (*Wuzu Guomin Hejinhui*) under the political auspices of Yuan Shikai on 12 May. The Association elected its five vice-chairmen from among the representatives of the five *minzu*, with Wang Kuan representing the *Huizu*. This caused Liu Mengyang (1877–1943), a Muslim journalist from Tianjin[43] and CIPA activist, who participated in establishing the Association, to publish an angry open letter to the Association in the *Zhengzong Aiguobao*. He called Wang Kuan's morals into question and accused him of 'just passing as a *Huizu*' and 'going as far as to take the place of the *Huizu* in the organization',[44] which should be occupied by a proper *Huizu* from Xinjiang. Liu adamantly asserted that, 'Mr Wang is a *Hanzu* who believes in *Qingzhenjiao*, traditionally known as *Huijiao*, and [he] is not a *Huizu*.'[45] Arguing that the Association should not allow a non-*Huizu* to deceive the public by acting as a *Huizu* representative, he publicly resigned from the Association: 'I have been an initiator [of this Association] but I have never represented the *Huizu*. I am extremely opposed to the practice of identifying incorrectly the so-called people of *Huijiao* in China as *Huizu* . . . I request that my name be removed from the list of founding members of the Association.'[46] Interestingly, he signed his letter, 'a member of the Chinese Islamic people'.

Yuan Shikai's henchmen murdered Ding Baochen in July 1913 for his outspoken criticism of Yuan's policies. With the subsequent cessation of his paper, those opposed to the ambiguous *Huizu* terminology lost an important platform for their opinions,[47] but this did not stop them from campaigning against the Muslim ethnicity theory. Liu Mengyang remained on his guard, and new critics found ways to express their disagreement.

Systematisation and 'Scientification' in the Later Republican Era

In the 1920s, Yin Boqing (1888–1962) became one of the most outspoken proponents of a more systematic 'Han believers theory'. Born into a religious family in the Oxen Street Muslim district of Beijing, Yin worked as a close collaborator of the famous imam, translator and promoter of Islamic revival, Wang Jingzhai. He also cooperated with Chengda Teachers' College (*Chengda Shifan Xuexiao*), wrote for its *Yuehua* magazine and taught at its middle school, the *Xibei Gongxue*. In 1926, the Shanghai-based 'Muslim Scholarly Association Monthly' (*Zhongguo Huijiao Xuehui Yuekan*) published his article, again with the title, 'Differentiation between *Huijiao* and *Huizu*' (*Huijiao yu Huizu bian*).[48] One of the most coherent defences of the 'Han believers in Islam theory' (*Hanren Huijiao shuo*), the essay was recommended to the editorial board by another Beijing modernist, Wang Mengyang, and published with a foreword by the monthly's editor Sha Shanyu (writing under the pen name Shou Yu). Sha stated that, 'the ideas expressed herein are entirely in accordance with those previously published in our magazine and further clarify and criticise our Muslim compatriots' common mistake of applying the misleading name *Huizu* to themselves'.

Yin articulated a thorough critique of the ethnic concept of the *Hui* community (called here the *Huijiao minzu shuo*), using arguments based on what he saw as modern scientific knowledge, religious doctrine, ethics, logic and patriotism. To put Yin's text and its endorsement by the Shanghai editorial board into its historical context, at the time of its publication in 1926, China was on the eve of great changes brought about by the Nationalist Party's Northern Expedition and the subsequent domination of the Republic by the Chiang Kai-shek faction. With its assimilationist vision of the Chinese nation, the *Zhonghua minzu*, as an ethnically homogeneous whole dominated by Han culture, the Chiang government officially adopted a policy towards its Muslim citizens congruent with Yin's convictions. With the formalisation of this policy, which denied Muslims any special position within the Republic, the ethnic concept of the *Hui* community began to be treated in a highly politicised manner. As a result the 'Han believers' theory was promoted later in the 1930s by some of the leading Sino-Muslim intellectuals in the same scholarly and activist circles as Yin's, centred at Chengda Teachers' College, Shanghai's Islamic School and other modernist institutions.

In the mid-1920s, with China being torn apart by feuding warlords, to advocate *Hui* ethnic separateness sounded like supporting further division of the country. Yin could easily dismiss this idea as unpatriotic, endangering the very survival of the Chinese people. He began his article with humankind's genealogy, starting from Adam. While obviously within the Islamic tradition, this also subtly refuted the nationalist and racialist dogma of the common descent of all Chinese from the Yellow Emperor. Yin was probably attempting a sly refutation of the exclusivist arguments of some Chinese nationalists, who wished to exclude all those who did not consider themselves the Yellow Emperor's offspring from the *Zhonghua minzu*. Yin's arguments can be summarised as follows.

Logical arguments

Yin rejected the view that religious differences can breed racial and ethnic differences. He held that these two categories should not be used interchangeably: 'Religion is religion and nation is nation, and the two should not be confused.'[49] In his view, religious differences result from different spiritual beliefs, while racial differences stem from different physical constitutions. The common confusion of these two starkly different categories shocked Yin, who considered 'absurdly applying a religious name to an ethnic group [to be] a huge mistake'.[50] In Yin's view, the reckless and long-term conflation of the terms *Huijiao* and *Huizu* made it very difficult to specify the differences between the two words.

> *Huijiao* and *Huizu* – if there is no difference between these two terms . . . then the establishment of their respective meanings becomes very difficult. If, however, there is a difference, then it should be equally difficult to use them in the same meaning. So who are the Muslims of our country?

It should be stated that they are in fact Han in ethnicity and Muslim in religion.⁵¹

Religious and moral arguments

Hui customs that distinguish them from non-Muslims – visible in clothing, calendrical calculations, dietary proscriptions, the obligatory Ramadan fast and the Arabic script of the holy books – by no means prove ethnic distinctiveness from the Han. All those differences in ways of life are simply part of Islam, a universal religion that stands above all petty ethnic and national divisions, and is followed in numerous countries. Treating the Muslims as an ethnically different people results from Chinese ignorance of Islamic laws and traditions. This lack of knowledge appears even in the history of the term *Huihui* and its later evolution. Yin explains that in Arabia the religion is called Islam (*Yisilan*) and its followers Muslims (*Mushilin* or *Muwomin*). Arabic terminology clearly distinguishes between the religion and its believers, who constitute a community of convictions and faith. The use of the term *Huihui* should not be condemned, but rather reserved for the religion only, as it was used in that sense by the great Sino-Muslim writers Wang Daiyu, Liu Zhi and others.

Applying this name to Muslim people and applying ethnic sense to it aroused Yin's anger and high condemnation. He pointed out that according to some 'scientific books on geography', the inhabitants of China are divided into five ethnic groups or *minzu*: *Hanzu*, *Zangzu* (*Tubote* or Tibetans), *Mengzu* (Mongols), *Manzu* (Manchus) and Turks (*Tujue* or *Tu'erqi*), the latter also called the *Huizu*. The term *Huizu* could thus be accepted as an ethnic marker only for the Turkic Muslims of Xinjiang, not those of the inner provinces. Yin opted for ethnic and religious pluralism: 'In this world there are many religions and many races. In one nation there can exist many religions, in one religion many nations. Ethnicity should not be treated as being the same as religion. It is only natural.'⁵²

Like Huang Zhenpan, Yin illustrated his argument with a telling comparison:

> Let us take the example of our country. Here we have the Manchus, the Mongols and the Tibetans – they are all separated by their ethnicity, and

yet they all profess the Buddhist religion. Why then are they not called collectively the Buddhist nation?[53]

Similarly, Yin continued, the multi-religious character of the Han proves the absurdity of ethno-religious neologisms:

Among those inhabiting the inner provinces one finds almost exclusively the Han, who profess Confucianism, Buddhism, Daoism, Christianity and Islam. Why then are they not called respectively the Confucian nation, the Buddhist nation, the Daoist nation or the Christian nation?[54]

Yin found the ethnic separation of only the Muslims to be not only illogical, but also unjust.

Political arguments

The transfer of the ethnic name of the Xinjiang Muslims to the Chinese-speaking Muslims resulted from errors of the Chinese elites, made because of 'their love of the past that became an addiction'.[55] After the 1911 Revolution, the expulsion of the Manchu dynasty and the creation of an independent Mongolia, the revolution had transformed from a racial to a political process. In Yin's view, the fiction of the ethnic unity of all China's Muslims under the *Huizu* name also derived partially from Yuan Shikai's policies. After Yuan's agreement with Sun Yat-sen, he usurped total power and used Beijing's Muslims as false representatives of Xinjiang's *Huizu* in his government so that he could claim legitimate control over that region. Those political careerists 'have not spoken a single word against the veracity of this term or the treatment of the Chinese Muslims as part of the *Huizu*',[56] while the common Muslim people, 'by putting trust in their elites have accepted it and considered themselves as *Huizu*'.[57]

The strongly critical tone of Yin's assessment of the Beijing Muslim elites further reveals political conflict among religious and communal leaders, visible previously in Shou Jin's condemnation of Wang Kuan. The divisions ran not along religious lines, but reflected differing attitudes towards political and ethnic problems, cutting the community vertically. According to Yin, by supporting Yuan Shikai, some Muslim elites betrayed the revolution and its ideals. While Yin did not specify exactly the object of his criticism, it is easy to imagine that it was the activists, or at least some activists, of the CIPA. In addition to his religious, moral, historical and scientific arguments against the *Huizu* concept, Yin added an accusation of political disloyalty to the Republic and its founding principles. According to Yin, those Muslim leaders who supported the *Huizu* theory were not only political opportunists, but also violated religious law and harmed religion itself.

Here Yin pointed to one of the most controversial issues in Sino-Muslim historiography. He claimed that by equating being Muslim with being ethnic, they denied Chinese Muslims any right to proselytise among non-Muslim Chinese and thus negated any possibility of Islam's further growth in China. In a world of rival religions, none can afford to relinquish its right to gain new followers. Yin regretfully pointed out that Islam may not be 'as energetic as other faiths, but by its discrete influence it still has managed to convert wide masses'.[58] If being Hui stems from some innate national and ethnic traits, how could one join the community by one's own will? Furthermore, by positioning the *Hui* outside the Han, the proponents of the *minzu* theory added to the unnecessary hostility between the two groups.

Yin thus argued the need to educate Chinese Muslims about the universal, transnational and trans-ethnic nature of Islam. The dissemination of the *Huizu* concept proved that past efforts at propagating 'true Islam' had failed, for the Sino-Muslims' 'racial identity is deep, and their religious identity is shallow'.[59] To reify the ethnic dimension of Hui identity allows neglect of religious duties: 'they think that it is fine to do away with the religious prohibitions, that it is fine to eat whatever one likes. They treat the religious law as some pedantry, as superstition.'[60]

To complete his dramatic repudiation of the *Huizu* concept, Yin appealed to his fellow Muslims' patriotism, claiming that the Japanese utilise the *Huizu* theory to divide the Chinese nation and take over its riches. Thus, Yin hoped that the *Huizu* theory would be rejected and true understanding of Islam restored.

The *Huizu* as a Pan-Muslim Ethnicity

Two years after Yin's article, the Northern Expedition established Chiang Kai-shek's political domination over a considerable portion of China. The new Nanjing regime began gradually to move away from Sun Yat-sen's concept of a multi-ethnic China and to favour a more unitary vision, a China composed not of various *minzu*, but rather of cultural blocs within one ethnic group, the *Zhonghua minzu*. This conceptualisation of the nation described visible differences in culture as deriving from differing geographical conditions, not contradictory with the nation's political and ethnic unity. In the case of the Sinophone Muslims, Chiang's government sympathised with the Han believers theory. Only in its last years on the Chinese mainland did the GMD include Muslims in the category of 'citizens with particular life habits'.[61] This, however, caused tensions with some of the Sino-Muslim elites who believed that Muslims should be eligible for some special representation in the state structure, only possible with official state recognition of the *Hui* as a *minzu*. Disappointed with the Nationalist government's indifference to their calls for political privilege, some Muslim intellectuals moved towards a more ethnic definition of their community.

It is difficult to determine when the ethnic concept of the *Hui* became popular among the Muslim intellectuals and shifted the balance between the proponents of the two theories. This could have happened after the Japanese invasion of Manchuria (1931). In addition to the Japanese threat, growing disillusionment with Chiang and his policies and the rise of academic studies of *Hui* history added to the increasing popularity of the *Huizu* concept. Perhaps Japanese propaganda also played a part in the process, for the Japanese actively promoted the idea of *Hui* ethnicity, as bewailed by Yin, and ironically Japan became the first power in the region to address the *Hui* as a nationality.[62]

The activism of *Huizu* theory supporters received a major boost from the wave of Muslim protests over the publication in 1931 and 1932 of prejudiced articles on Islam and Muslim customs in several Chinese periodicals. Muslim activists and educators, especially in Beiping and Shanghai, outraged by insulting depictions of their religion, organised demonstrations and petitioned both local and national governments to prohibit future publication of insulting texts and introduce laws protecting Islam from slander. These initiatives were mostly successful, as the authorities confiscated some of the printed materials and punished the publishers and authors. On the wave of popular Muslim indignation, some Muslim magazines published special issues devoted to these scandals, allowing the younger members of the community to voice their opinion. Among them, the most vocal was 24-year-old Xue Wenbo (1909–84), a native of Beijing's Madian Muslim village, a law student at Chaoyang University, and co-founder of the 'Beiping Islamic Students' Association' (*Beiping Yisilan Xueyouhui*).

The editorial board of *Yuehua* invited Xue to contribute an article to the magazine's September 1932 special issue on the insulting publications. Unlike many other authors, who referred to cases of 'offence against religion' (*wujiao'an*), Xue chose to describe 'offences against the *Huizu*' (*wuru Huizu'an*). The *Hui*, Xue wrote, were 'historically the most oppressed and persecuted *minzu*', but have always been faithful to their country and remain a guarantee of its security.[63] Xue's text expressed a deep disappointment in the Republic, arguing that despite political persecution under the Qing, only in the Republican era have the Hui experienced true bitterness:

> What scares one most is the fact that such things happen nowadays – not in the era of Qing tyranny but after the national revolution, which was supposed to take care of the small and weak *minzu* inside the country, in an era of awakening of self-consciousness and self-government; not in the era of Qing lawlessness but now, during the renaissance of law; not in the era of bygone ignorance, but in the situation of today's knowledge . . . Even worse, such things did not happen when the country was at peace, but only now when the Japanese bandits tear the country apart, the Communist Party intensifies its aggression, and the death of the state might come any day.[64]

Xue called on the Nationalist (Guomindang, GMD) government to treat the tens of millions of *Huizu* as an indispensable component of the nation-state, to engage in a dialogue with Muslim elites and to respect their views on these problems.[65]

Xue's indignation against the social injustices still suffered by the *Hui* under the Republic made him radicalise his stance on the question of ethnicity and religion. He changed the name of his organisation to the 'Chinese *Huizu* Youth Association' (*Zhongguo Huizu Qingnianhui*) and established his own magazine, *Huizu Youth* (*Huizu qingnian*), published first in January 1933, probably the earliest use of the term in a periodical title. In the first issue's opening note, he stressed that 'even though this Association has very limited membership', it will strive to 'inspire *Huizu* youth to reinvigorate religion and save the country according to Sun Yat-sen's spirit of support for the reawakening and self rule of the weak *minzu*'.[66]

The first issue of *Huizu Youth* gave Xue a chance to articulate his political and ideological programme in an article titled, 'The Chinese *Huizu* Movement'. Despite his previous condemnation of 'Communist aggression', his text, published under the religious name Da'ud (*Dawude*), employed some vocabulary clearly derived from left-wing discourse.[67] Acknowledging that religion and *minzu* are two different things, he nevertheless stressed the uniqueness of Islam: 'Not only [is it] a propagation of completeness, of total equality of all *minzu*, of great unity of all mankind', but it is also 'a genuine socialism because it does not know the difference between the poor and rich and between the *minzu*.'[68]

Xue went even further with Leninist rhetoric, writing:

> The countries of the Muslim nations (*Huijiao minzu guojia*) were the first objects of oppression and exploitation by the Euro-American powers. Therefore those ruled and oppressed in the world are *Huizu*, the proletarians [of the world] are *Huizu*, and now the *Huizu* are already awakened, and most of them want to unite under the banner of Islam (*Huijiao*).[69]

Here Xue advocated pan-Muslim nationalism, defining the *Huizu* as encompassing all the Muslims in the world, not only in China. He claimed that the desire to become ethnic is universal in the Islamic world, driven not primarily by religion, but rather by the desire to utilise the Islamic banner to resist aggression and to gain freedom, encouraging Muslims all over the world to 'unite under the banner of Islam'. Xue envisioned the 'Chinese *Huizu* movement' as part of pan-Islamism, a local parallel to the Wahhabi and Sanussi movements, which 'aim to melt religious identity and *minzu* identity like steel into one whole, to form a type of large scale rejuvenation movement'.[70] In his interpretation, China's Muslims could gain ethnic status through politicisation of Islam, in which religious concerns seem almost secondary.

To further legitimise his advocacy of this pan-Islamic *Huizu* ethnicity, Xue added international references, translating freely from Muhammad Ali Jinnah's 1914 article in which the Indian Muslim leader supposedly wrote,

'In the 20th century Europeans see the religious bond uniting all *Huizu* [sic] as a characteristic feature of medieval Europe.'[71] In Xue's translation Jinnah rhetorically inquired into this Western ignorance, asking, 'Do they not understand the relationship between religion and the Muslims? Have they forgotten that Islam is not only a religion but at the same time is also a social race (*shehui zhi zhongzu*), a culture, a *minzu* . . . Islam is an ideal of one family.'[72]

Xue viewed the *Huizu* ethnicity in China as extremely heterogeneous, resulting from multiple Muslim migrations at different historical moments from different geographical areas and 'the variety of regional races and their different interests'. He included all the Muslims inhabiting China's entire territory in the category, dividing the *Huizu* into two basic groupings: the northwest (Xinjiang) *Huizu*, consisting of the turbaned *Huizu* (*chan Huizu*), Kazakh *Huizu*, Kirgiz *Huizu* and others; and the *Huizu* of the interior, including Shaanxi and Gansu, whom he called the *Dungan Huizu*.[73] The latter descend from the Tujue Turks with some additional admixtures of Mongols and other aliens. Yet the *Dungan Huizu* and the northwest *Huizu*, despite their different ancestries, because of 'their common belief have not formed separate kinds of *minzu* identity'. Regardless of racial differences and variation in their geographical environments, the shared religion, with its 'religious laws stipulating unity and prohibitions' caused them to 'form a type of [shared] *minzu* feeling, allowing religious identity to change totally into *minzu* identity'.[74]

As in his *Yuehua* article, in *Huizu Youth* Xue explained that the *Hui* had been subject to the cruel policies of the 'Manchu ruling classes', who had only one type of governance for the Muslims: extermination. In the Republican or Party-state era, 'the position of Islam and the *Huizu* has of course been greatly elevated', and Muslims have received assurances of protection and recognition. But the internal chaos in the country caused these promises to remain unfulfilled. To guarantee the survival of the *Huizu*, Xue believed, they needed closely related religious and ethnic reawakening movements, the former directed by imams and the latter by politically conscious intellectuals. Xue asserted unequivocally that the two should be organically intertwined, as there could be no *minzu* without religion. The example of the Manchus proved that for Xue: 'Why do the Manchus' *minzu* identity and *minzu* characteristics no longer exist? Speaking plainly, because they have no specific religion.'[75]

In Xue's analysis, the *Huizu* movement could not yet materialise because of two serious obstacles, the first being the backwardness of the northwest *Huizu*, who still 'live under the rule of the remnant feudal classes'.[76] This forced the interior (or Dungan) *Huizu* to take the lead in the movement and help to create a strong *minzu*, which could positively participate in the Chinese nation.[77] But to Xue's chagrin, the second obstacle, the division of the eastern Chinese *Huizu* into two vying camps, the *Huizu* faction and the Han believers faction, prevented the realisation of this goal.

Xue claimed that the Muslims in China meet all the criteria of a *minzu* set out in Sun Yat-sen's 'Three Principles of the People': common blood (*xuetong*); lifestyle, language, religion; and 'customs and habits' (*fengsu xiguan*). The common blood factor derived from the fact that 'the *Huizu* of the inner provinces are immigrant northwest *Huizu*' and because Muslims cannot marry non-Muslims.[78] Thus, there can be no traces of other *minzu* in the bloodlines of *Huizu*. Visible differences in appearance result from adaptation to local conditions, a biological phenomenon similar among humans to the 'Jiangnan orange changing into a tangerine in the Jiangbei'.[79]

The *Huizu* also met Sun Yat-sen's condition of a common way of life as they had been pushed into well-defined limits by centuries of oppression. Xue denied the significance of linguistic differences among Muslims in different parts of the country because Arabic constituted a true *lingua franca* for believers, regardless of their linguistic background. The last two criteria were naturally met, as Islam and its customs and habits created the foundation for *Huizu* ethnicity.

Xue also dismissed the argument of the Han believers faction that shared Han and *Hui* surnames in the interior, and their differences with Xinjiang *Huizu* surnames, proved common Han–Hui ancestry. Xue explained this not as a result of assimilation (*tonghua*), but rather an outcome of centuries of oppression: 'the policy of the Manchu Qing towards the *Huizu* was one of extermination. The *Huizu* of the inner provinces had no choice but to adopt Han surnames to avoid being massacred.'[80]

Xue believed the Han believers theory to be an extension of this same tactic of the *Hui* avoiding oppression by the more powerful *minzu* in the country: 'The Han believers theory is a theory of an oppressed *minzu* who have no other choice, a strategy designed to avoid being massacred.'[81] Instead, Chinese Muslims should imitate the example of Liu Zhi, who knew Islam to be equal to Confucianism and did not hide his Muslim identity. The modern *Huizu* should follow in his path to create an ethnicity as developed as the Han. Pretending to be one with the latter, who in fact despised the *Huizu* as backward and lowly, could only be a pathetic undertaking: 'If we plan to self-strengthen, first we must have self-confidence and self-sufficient abilities. In our hearts there can be absolutely no place for any capitulationist thoughts, and we all proceed from the basis of our *minzu* movement.'[82]

The movement, aiming at unity with other *minzu*, would need two stages. In the first, because of their cultural, political and economic inferiority to other peoples of China, the *Huizu* 'must adopt a strategy of keeping distance from others'.[83] This temporary cultural separatism would lead eventually to raising the *Huizu*'s qualities as a *minzu* towards the second stage, voluntary union with the previously more advanced *minzu*, clearly pointing at the Han.

Xue's radical stance on *Huizu* ethnicity brought immediate reaction from more traditionalist circles. One of those who took the time to reply was Liu Mengyang. Liu, twice as old as Xue, answered him in a published article,[84] stimulating Xue to a more systematic critique of the 'Han believers in Islam' idea and a more direct repudiation of its proponents. In the second issue of *Huizu qingnian*, published in October 1933, Xue took some personal shots at Liu in an article appropriately titled, 'On the question of the *Huizu* and Han believers in Islam'. Liu had stated that 'the *Huizu* in the *wuzu gonghe* concept are the people of Xinjiang' and that 'those in the inner provinces are Han who believe in Islam'. Xue replied that this was an entirely mistaken opinion, as *Huizu* 'refers to all the *minzu* practising Islam in China, and does not refer purely to the northwestern part of the *Huizu*'.[85] Liu, like his colleagues the Ding brothers, rejected the use of the character *Hui* to refer to Islam and Muslims, but Xue called that mere pedantry, for the character was well rooted in Chinese tradition and was a convenient way to describe the religion and its followers. It did not bother him that it derived from equating all Muslims in China with the *Huihe*. The name itself was of less importance than the recognition of the Muslims as an ethnicity: 'If Mr Liu considers *Hui* to be inappropriate and wants to rename the *Huijiao* and *Huizu* as *Yisilanjiao* and *Yisilanzu*, we are more than 100% in support of such a move and will strongly advocate it.'⁸⁶

In his article, Liu used Muslim genealogies from eastern China to refute Xue's assertion that Hui in the inner provinces were 'immigrants from the northwest'. Agreeing that this might be true, Xue nonetheless defiantly held that this did not mean that Hui and Han in China proper were of the same blood:

> Their [eastern China Muslims] genealogies clearly show that their ancestors migrated from the south, which of course is based on evidence, and therefore this argument is strong. The phenomenon of Han who believe in Islam is indeed true, but the Han who practice Islam have been subject to the Islamic prohibition laws. Generation after generation they married only other Muslims, and with time their bloodlines have become entirely separated from the bloodlines of the Han. After a thousand years, how can they still be talked about as Han?⁸⁷

This 'ethnogenesis by separation' added a new dimension to the discussion of the *Hui* ethnicity.

Xue's arguments became openly hostile when he described the 'Han believers in Islam' concept as an attempt to hijack the ancient Chinese Islamic ethnicity by a few elite intruders into its ranks:

> The Han who believe in Islam are a tiny phenomenon. Regardless of their location, nowhere do the *Huihui* want to say that their ancestors are Han ... Mr Liu says, 'Nowadays among those Muslims (*Huijiaoren*) in the inner provinces there are indeed some descendants of the *Huizu*, but to say that all the Muslims in the inner provinces are *Huizu* would be arbitrary.' So let me say this: Mr Liu is a Han who believes in Islam, but amongst our *Huizu* the Han are extremely few. Because of these minority Han, Mr Liu insists strongly on altering the bloodlines of our fifty million *Huizu*, hindering the *Huizu* revival movement. He would like to unconditionally surrender the great thousand-year-old *Huizu* to assimilation. Isn't this an arbitrary wrongdoing?⁸⁸

In paradoxical contrast to the common perception of the Nationalist government's sympathies at this time, Liu appeared to be in opposition to official policies, and Xue seemed to support them. Liu wrote that just because the government saw traces of ethnic sentiment in the religious bonds among Muslims, Muslims should nevertheless not 'consider ourselves to be *Huizu*'. For Xue this obviously resulted from Han Muslims' lack of historical experience of oppression and suffering, an important basis of *Huizu* ethnic consciousness: 'If we want to nourish the ethnic feeling of the *Huizu*, we should sincerely thank *Allāh* [that] the *Huizu*, oppressed for more than a thousand years, today can finally see the sky and sun. The Han who believe in Islam – what can they know about our suffering?'[89]

In Xue's interpretation, reconsidered in his debate with Liu, the *Huizu* constitute an ethnic group because of their shared culture derived from religion; the ethnic sentiment resulting from it; and the historical experience of hardship, oppression, discrimination and prejudice. The very developments that prompted Xue to propagandise the *Huizu* ethnicity proved the existence of such an ethnicity and, at the same time, resulted from it:

> If we say that the *Huizu* of the inner provinces do not consider themselves to be *Huizu* but say that they themselves are Han who believe in Islam, then why did all the Muslims of the inner provinces rise in an uproar against the publications of slanders against the *Huizu*? . . . Because the content of the slanders was a question of common blood (*xuetong*).[90]

Common blood made the *Huizu* protest against defamatory publications, and the government reacted positively to the pleas of the protesters not because it disliked offending Islam, but rather because it was afraid of ethnic separatism. The Han Muslims, like Liu, did not have to feel offended because they were 'descendants of the Yellow Emperor' and so outside of the *Huizu* pale.

For Xue, a *minzu* was a product of both common blood and, more importantly, of shared culture, psyche and religion, and the latter three factors made up the core of identity:

> The important factor in *minzu* construction is not a pure bloodline. It includes religion, habits and customs, and a way of life. Only in the case of a lineage is bloodline an indispensable factor. If you, Mr Liu, set your eyes on a lineage and talk about *minzu*, then wouldn't the scope of the *minzu* be identical with that of a lineage?[91]

Xue encapsulated his outlook on *Huizu* ethnicity and its movement in five points:

1. The Chinese *Huizu* is built on a religious basis, and not the foundation of a racial, regional, and historical *minzu*.
2. *Huijiao* and Islam, *Huizu* and Islamic nation (*Yisilanzu*) are equivalent in China.
3. The Chinese *Huizu* movement is a revival movement of politics, economy, culture and education. The movement of religious revival is its most important component.
4. The Chinese *Huizu* movement's goals include the elevation of the *Huizu*'s position, the promotion of *Huizu* intelligence, equality with other *minzu*, and eventual free association with other *minzu* in a unitary Chinese Republic.
5. Those *Huizu* who wrongly consider themselves Han believers in Islam have only religious sentiment but not religious identity and completely lack *minzu* sentiment and identity. We consider them to be not very different from Han believers in Buddhism, Christianity and Daoism.[92]

Xue understood the *Huizu* to be the Chinese branch of the great Islamic *minzu*, which encompasses all Muslim nations in the world. The *Huizu* should also be a full member of the Chinese nation, the *Zhonghua minzu*. In this they resemble the Indian Muslims, part of both the Islamic nation and of their Indian nation, and Turks, the vast majority of whom belong to both the Muslim *minzu* and the Turkish *minzu*. The word *Huizu* is just a historically rooted local equivalent of 'Islamic *minzu*', and its etymology from *Huihe* does not matter. Apparently, Xue defined *minzu* as a two-tiered phenomenon, allowing Muslims in China to act as full members of two cultures and polities, both China and the world of Islam. Just as their simultaneity in the late imperial era allowed them to be both Muslim and Confucian through the writings of the *Han kitāb* authors, now it allowed their masses to act as both Muslim and Chinese nationals.[93]

Neither Han Muslims nor Pan-Muslim: A Sinophone Muslim Ethnicity

The scholarly study of Hui history and culture in the Republican era grew rapidly, including an important contribution to the development of the *Huizu* theory by Jin Jitang (1908–1978), a Beijing Muslim.⁹⁴ Jin Jitang, like Xue Wenbo, was a younger member of the northern Chinese modernist Muslim circle centred around Chengda Teachers' College and, like Yin Boqing, was a collaborator of Wang Jingzhai. Not only did Jin publish one of the first systematic monographs on Hui history (*Zhongguo Huijiao shi yanjiu*, 1935), but he also provided the *Hui* public with a new optic on the *Huizu* controversy.

In his book and a subsequent article titled, 'The Islamic *minzu* theory' (*Huijiao minzu shuo*, 1936), published in *Yugong* magazine, Jin Jitang presented a third option, another vision of Muslim ethnicity in China. He wrote that the Sinophone Muslims were neither Han who believed in Islam nor the Chinese branch of a wider Muslim ethnicity encompassing both the inner provinces and the Turkic peoples of the far west. Yin Boqing himself wrote the preface to Jin Jitang's book, demonstrating that the debate over issues of Muslim ethnicity and religion could be conducted in a very civilised manner. Yin referred to the author, twenty years his junior, as a 'friend and young man of integrity'. Perhaps Yin had modified his views in the ten years between their two articles, for in the preface he wrote: 'Our people, who live in dispersal amongst three other religions, are immersed in and flow with their customs. The [threat of] assimilation is frightening, and I am afraid that a cautious conservatism may not be enough.'⁹⁵

Like Yin Boqing a decade earlier, Jin Jitang presented his arguments in an organised, coherent, modern Chinese prose, basing his case on critical and 'scientific' analysis of historical sources. This 'scientific' tone and methodology won his article the respect and attention it enjoys even today among Sino-Muslim intellectuals, who tend to dismiss Yin Boqing's arguments as 'not scientific enough', noting that Yin was not a trained 'scientist'.⁹⁶

Unlike Yin and Huang Zhenpan several decades earlier, but similar to Xue Wenbo, Jin thought that Islam has the power to create a separate ethnicity out of a multi-ethnic amalgamation of different peoples, as happened in China. He attributed this to the unique religious law that commands all aspects of believers' lives. For him, this proved Islam's greatness and superiority over other religions mentioned in Yin's text. To support his opinion he cited several relevant Qur'anic verses.

The novelty of Jin's argument lies in his stressing the ethnic divisions not only between *Hui* and Han, but also between *Hui* and the Uighurs of

Xinjiang, who at this time were only beginning to use that ethnonym again, after centuries of varying and contradictory usage.[97] In his book's opening chapter, titled, 'The difference between *Huihui* and *Huihu*', he named three distinctive Muslim groups in China: (1) the Gansu Huimin, who call themselves *Mumin* and not *Huihui* and are called *Manzi* ('southern barbarians') by local non-Muslims, because they emigrated from the south during the Liao and Jin dynasties; (2) the Xinjiang *Huimin*, who call themselves *Uighur* and who call the interior Muslims *Dungan* and the Chinese non-Muslims *Khitay*; and (3) *Huihui* of the interior, who call non-Muslims *Han'er ren*, a term coined under Mongol rule to refer to those Chinese who had lived under the Jin.[98] After analysing the historical records, Jin Jitang concluded that those who consider themselves the *Huihu*, or *Uighur*, and those who use the autonym *Huihui* must be two different *minzu*.

Like the Chinese Communists several years later, Jin addressed the ideological aspects of ethnic recognition. Unlike the Communists (but like Xue Wenbo), he grounded his arguments in Sun Yat-sen's 'Three Principles of the People'. He found Sun's five basic points much more relevant to the situation of the Sino-Muslims than Stalin's four criteria, for they met Sun's five principles of *minzu* recognition: differentiation by kinship and bloodline (*xuetong*), lifestyle, language, religion, customs and habits.[99] The need to press the Sinophone Muslims into a rigid set of standards forced Jin to bend his argumentation. For example, when discussing the linguistic uniqueness of the Chinese Muslims, he cited only examples of Arab or Persian loanwords and alleged differences in the accents of the Muslim inhabitants of Beijing and Tianjin. These instances hardly seem sufficient to consider the *Huihuihua* patois a separate language.

His arguments became particularly controversial when he discussed the separateness of *Hui* bloodline and kinship. Unlike Yin Boqing, who downplayed the role of foreign immigrants in the creation of the Sino-Muslim community, Jin stressed their importance and named numerous foreign ethnic groups implicated in the ethno-genesis of the *Hui*. He thus entered into the *Huizu* versus 'Han believers in Islam' debate:

> Since the introduction of the Han, Hui, Man, Meng and Zang theory, a debate has arisen as to the definition of the *Huizu*. Have the groups of

the *Huijiang* [southern Xinjiang] always belonged to the *Huizu*, and those inhabiting the inner provinces in China been Han who believe in Islam? Or is it that those in the *Huijiang* are *Huizu* and those in the inner provinces are not immigrants from the northwest but descendants of the *Huihe*? So the *Huizu* theory and the Han believers theory have been going on for the past 20 years and still have not been reconciled or resolved. Recently, the theory of Muslim ethnicity (*Huijiao minzu shuo*) has appeared, saying that those tens of millions of *Huimin* who live within the borders of China meet the five criteria of *minzu* formation of the nationalist doctrine (Sun Yat-sen's theory) . . . This process of *minzu* formation has been going on for centuries, and it is not a new phenomenon . . . Are the Chinese Muslims (*Huimin*) *Huizu*? The descendants of *Huihe* and immigrants from the northwest are Han who believe in Islam? [Or] a *Huijiao minzu*? . . . After considerable time spent researching this issue, I believe that the ancestors of today's *Huimin* were foreigners.[100]

In reasoning similar to Xue Wenbo's, Jin refuted Yin Boqing's suggestion that the influx of Han blood into the Hui's bloodlines resulted in their ethnic assimilation, and he seems not to believe that intermarriage with local Han women played any significant role. As Islam prohibits intermarriage with non-believers, or so Jin claimed, the Muslim bloodlines remained relatively free of external admixtures. And even if there were mixed marriages between Muslim men and Han women, the latter were obliged to convert to Islam, so their *xuetong* did not count as non-Muslim, and the offspring of those Muslim–Han marriages remained purely Muslim. Therefore, the Muslim bloodline had not undergone any significant attenuation. In Jin's words, 'The *Huizu* bloodline may be only augmented but never mixed, and the blood that circulates through it remains unchanged.' This peculiar interpretation of Muslims' genetic history in China suggests that there might be some religious quality to one's blood. Jin's interpretation also allows that by converting to Islam one's blood might transform into the appropriate Muslim blood, which then does not dilute the overall blood pool of the Chinese Muslims. Jin wrote, 'Bloodline (*xuetong*) might seem to be an abstraction, but when one looks at the facial features and figures of the Muslims, it is easy to notice the differences.'[101]

Jin's research thus constituted the first scholarly Chinese Muslim attempt to argue for a separate Sinophone Muslim ethnicity. As observed by Zvi Ben-Dor Benite, it effectively asserted that the *Hui* are an inseparable part of China and 'originally Chinese', because they have been melted into one nationality on Chinese soil under local conditions.[102] However controversial and perhaps questionable some of Jin's arguments might seem, his interpretation of Sino-Muslim ethnic status became popular among *Hui* elites in the later years of the Republic. Communist theoreticians used his article, and as the Communists rationalised their earlier treatment of the *Hui* as an ethnic minority Jin's writings entered the *minzu* canon of the Party and the *Huizu*.

Conclusion

After the Long March, during which Communist forces fought through many Muslim areas in northwest China, the CCP leadership settled in northern Shaanxi. With Mongols and Muslims virtually the only non-Han communities in the Shaan–Gan–Ning revolutionary base area, the *Hui* question became a burning problem for them. Constrained by the Stalinist criteria of nationhood (Rus. *natsiya*), the Party had to develop inventive ways of legitimising *minzu*, hoping to win the support of the frontier peoples.[103] Believing that Muslims were historically oppressed as a *minzu*, not a religious group, their specialists concluded that granting ethnic status to the Sino-Muslims would meet their strongest desires and cause them to support the Communists in their war against the Nationalists. With the legal banning of the term *Huizu* by Chiang Kai-shek in September 1940, the Communists decided that recognising the Sino-Muslims as the *Huizu* would encourage loyalty to their party.[104]

Despite controversies among the Communist theoreticians, some of whom shared the opinion that the *Hui* were only a religious group,[105] the Party eventually adopted the view that the *Huizu* was a national minority, though only in its initial stages of development of *minzu* identity and thus needing the Communist Party's political tutelage to achieve full-blown *minzu* consciousness. Li Weihan's reading of Jin Jitang's 1936 article allowed him to resolve the contradiction between Stalin's definition of a *minzu* and Mao's critique of Han chauvinist oppression of the *Huizu* under the Nationalists.[106]

The debate on Muslim religion and ethnicity dates to the last years of the Qing, and it reached its height during the Republican era, especially the crucial decade of 1926–1936. It still continues today, though in a much less intensive manner. In the People's Republic, the definition of the *Huizu* in strictly ethnic terms has been so thoroughly consolidated that calling it into question constitutes heresy. The state-sponsored 'minority schools' instil *Huizu* youth with the *Huizu* paradigm, while official representations of Sino-Muslim culture usually describe it as having '*minzu* characteristics and *minzu* flavour'. Like all *minzu* cultures other than the Han, the *Huizu* are presented to the non-Muslim public as something exotic, something into which one can only be born.

The official definition by the Communist Party of the Muslim communities in China as ten separate *minzu* has effectively pushed the study of Islam into the realm of ethnography. In the eyes of the Han majority, or at least in official discourse, Islam can only be a *minzu* phenomenon, not a living and universal religion but an exotic belief system belonging to a 'familiarly strange' *minzu*. This must be galling to those Sino-Muslim activists who invested so much effort into convincing both their co-religionists and other compatriots that Islam is an indispensable part of China, to be handled in a more sophisticated manner than a mere ethnic characteristic.

By labelling Islamic and Muslim history in China as a 'minority *minzu* history', the Party's doctrine has reduced Wang Daiyu, Liu Zhi and other authors of the *Han kitāb* to 'famous persons of *Huizu* history'. Clearly, the efforts of these great minds to create a full Islamic–Chinese synthesis, to be recognised and admired by all Chinese, have not been appreciated by the Communist government. Their categorisation as 'minority *minzu*' historical characters positions them as representatives of a 'backward *minzu*', to be led by the culturally superior Han, who entirely elide their intellectual refinement. Some Sino-Muslims understandably resent this underlying vision of the minorities' inherent backwardness in the Party's *minzu* policy.

Notes

1. The core role of the term *minzu* in modern Chinese political practice has caused Jonathan Lipman to call it a paradigm; see Lipman, *Familiar Strangers*,

pp. xx–xxv. By extension, all fifty-six officially recognised *minzu* in the PRC are thus paradigms unto themselves, including the *Huizu*. As is natural with paradigms, they are rarely questioned, especially in a political system like China's. For the current debates, see Chérif-Chebbi, Chapter 8, this volume.
2. Lipman, 'Hyphenated Chinese', p. 97. For a detailed discussion of the evolution of Sino-Muslim identity and different appellations given to Sino-Muslims, as well as policies towards Muslims throughout modern Chinese history, see Chang Chung-fu, 'Minzu guojia'.
3. See Gladney, *Muslim Chinese*, pp. 66–9. The so-called Stalinist criteria are a common language, a common territory, a common economic life and a common 'psychological make-up', i.e., a common culture. See Stalin, 'The nationality question and Leninism', pp. 348–72.
4. Lipman, 'White hats'.
5. Hedin, *The Flight of Big Horse*, p. v.
6. Effenberg, 'The Moslems of China', pp. 199–200. Effenberg gives the correct characters for *Huijiao*, but he translates *jiao* as 'emigrants' and the term *Huijiao* as 'Moslem emigrants abroad'.
7. For a detailed discussion of the development of this concept, see also Yamazaki, 'Kindai Chūgoku'.
8. Matsumoto Masumi, *Zhongguo minzu zhengce*, p. 266.
9. Leibold, *Reconfiguring Chinese Nationalism*, p. 154.
10. Atwill, *The Chinese Sultanate*, pp. 40, 207 n. 28. Terms coined by the Taipings include *Hanzu*, *Manzu* and *Mengzu*. See Crossley, 'Thinking about ethnicity', p. 10 n. 13.
11. Atwill, *The Chinese Sultanate*, p. 207 n. 28.
12. Du Wenxiu, 'Shuaifu Bugao', p. 123.
13. Matsumoto Masumi, *Zhongguo minzu zhengce*, pp. 270–4.
14. Huang Chengjun, 'Huanxing Huizhong', pp. 88–91
15. Huang, *Lun Huimin*. Hong Jun (1839–93) was a Chinese scholar-diplomat, Qing envoy to Russia, Germany and Austro-Hungary, and a Yuan era specialist. His critical edition of the Yuan history included translation of some works on Mongol history by Persian, English and French scholars, as well as information on the Muslims under Mongol rule and Muslim migration to China under the Yuan.
16. Millward, *Beyond the Pass*, pp. 197–203. I would like to thank Jonathan Lipman for this insight.
17. Ma Haiguo and Ma Yan, 'Shilun Yang Du', pp. 10–13.

18. He Zhiming, 'Qingmo minchu "wuzu gonghe"', pp. 129–34.
19. Ibid.
20. Cheng, 'Democracy is in its details', p. 331.
21. Zhang Juling, 'Qingmo minchu de Huizu baokan', pp. 25–37. Despite the non-religious character of *Zhengzong Aiguobao*, articles concerning pressing issues in the social life of Chinese Muslims were a regular feature. This drew the attention of Marshall Broomhall who, not knowing the personal details of those behind the paper, wrote in his seminal *Islam in China*: 'A recent article in a Peking paper called the Ai Kwo Pao eulogizes Islam to such an extent that it is suspected that the editor is himself a Moslem, or at least friendly to the claims of Islam', Broomhall, *Islam in China*, p. 295.
22. Gongheguomin, 'Huijiao Huizu bian'.
23. Ibid.
24. Ibid.
25. Ibid.
26. I would like to thank Jonathan Lipman for bringing this point to my attention.
27. I would like to thank Zhang Juling for alerting me to this fact.
28. Gongheguomin, 'Huijiao Huizu bian'.
29. Ibid.
30. Ibid.
31. Ibid.
32. Ibid.
33. Ibid.
34. Shou Jin, 'Huijiao Huizu zhi qubie', Part 1.
35. Ibid.
36. Ibid.
37. Shou Jin, 'Huijiao Huizu zhi qubie', Part 2.
38. Ibid.
39. See Ma's biography in Bai Shouyi, *Huizu renwu zhi*, pp. 1615–19.
40. See the Association's charter *Zhongguo Huijiao Jujinhui huizhang* quoted in full in Zhang Juling, 'Zhongguo Huijiao Jujinhui', pp. 16–18.
41. Ding Zhuyuan, 'Jinggao Huijiao Jujinhui', p. 14.
42. Cited in Zhang Juling, 'Zhongguo Huijiao Jujinhui', pp. 14–15.
43. See Yang Huiyun (ed.), *Huizu dacidian*, p. 448. Ironically, the only biographical information on Liu, a fierce opponent of the *Huizu* concept, may be found in a reference book titled, *The Great Dictionary of the Huizu*.

44. Liu Mengyang, 'Liu Mengyang zhi Wuzu Guomin Hejinhui'.
45. Ibid.
46. Ibid.
47. The date of Ding's death at the hands of Yuan Shikai's police is given as 18 July 1914 in his biography, authored by his grandson Ding Wenzhou, in Bai Shouyi (ed.), *Zhongguo Huihui minzu shi*, pp. 1121–4. However, Zhang Juling gives a more probable date of 19 August 1913 as the time of the execution and asserts that the paper was forced to close a month earlier. See Zhang Juling, *Lüyuan gouchen*, p. 268.
48. Yin Boqing, 'Huijiao yu Huizu bian'.
49. Ibid., p. 262.
50. Ibid.
51. Ibid., pp. 262–3.
52. Ibid., p. 264.
53. Ibid., p. 263.
54. Ibid.
55. Ibid., p. 264.
56. Ibid., p. 265.
57. Ibid.
58. The issue of Muslim proselytism remains a controversial one. A common assumption is that the Chinese Muslims were devoid of missionary ambitions and never carried out this type of activity on a wide scale in China. However, as can be seen in Yin's text, this view might not be totally correct, and the need to convert non-believers to Islam was even stressed by some progressive intellectuals. Chen Yuan cited the assumed lack of Sino-Muslim interest in proselytising in his influential 1928 article, 'Huihuijiao ru Zhongguo shilüe'. For more on Chen's article and its pivotal role in the subsequent internal Hui discussion of self-understanding, see Benite, 'From "Literati" to "Ulama"'.
59. Yin Boqing, 'Huijiao yu Huizu bian', p. 265.
60. Ibid.
61. This term, more precisely the 'citizens of the inner provinces with characteristic life habits' (*neidi shenghuo xiguan teshu zhi guomin*), was coined in 1946 by Sun Shengwu (1894–1975), a publisher of *Yuehua*, Chengda Teachers' College activist, ministry official, and member of parliament, who left for Taiwan after the communist victory in 1949. It was designed to guarantee special quotas for Muslims in the parliamentary elections without breaching the constitutional regulations of not distinguishing between citizens on the basis of nationality,

race, religion, gender, class and party affiliation. See Sun Shengwu, *Huijiao luncong*, pp. 141–4. See also Chang Chung-fu, 'Minzu guojia', pp. 423–6.
62. See Benite, 'From "Literati" to "Ulama"', p. 99.
63. Xue Wenbo, 'Guanyu wuru Huizu an'.
64. Ibid.
65. Xue's mention of the 'tens of millions of Huizu' was rooted in the popular late Qing and Republican-era Sino-Muslim assumption that Muslims constituted at least 10 per cent of the entire Chinese population, a community of some 40–50 million. Chinese Muslim elites have long believed that the numbers of Muslims were far higher than eventually determined by modern censuses conducted after 1949. This belief was perhaps partially derived from the omnipresence of Muslims in Chinese cities, but its origin lay more importantly in the Sino-Muslim intellectuals' desire to present their community as essential for the entire Chinese nation and as more influential than in reality. The inflated number of Chinese Muslims was also used in contacts with co-religionists outside China, helping the Sino-Muslim propaganda efforts. In his 1938 lecture in Cairo, Ma Songting, a famous imam and Chengda Teachers' College president, presented his listeners with a figure of 50 million Muslims. See Ma Songting, 'Zhongguo Huijiao'. When the Communists established their numbers to be closer to *c.* 10 million, most Sino-Muslims outside mainland China rejected that figure as Communist anti-Muslim propaganda. Muslim demographics remain a sensitive issue in the PRC. See Ting, 'Islamic culture in China', pp. 352–3.
66. Xue Wenbo, 'Fakanci'.
67. Xue's use of left-wing or even Leninist rhetoric does not necessarily imply that he sympathised with the Communist Party's agenda at this time (see his mention of 'Communist Party aggression', cited above). His arguments could be derived instead from Sun Yat-sen's principles of socialism and the 'people's livelihood'. Still, he later managed to ally himself with the Communist Party during the civil war. After the Communist victory he became a respected member of the establishment, working as an '*minzu* cadre' in Tibet in the 1950s.
68. Xue Wenbo, 'Zhongguo Huizu yundong', p. 7.
69. Ibid.
70. Ibid.
71. Ibid., p. 8.
72. Ibid.
73. Ibid.

74. Ibid.
75. Ibid., p. 11.
76. Ibid., p. 12.
77. On the internal differences among the *Hui*, both in eastern China and the northwest, and the evolution of a 'pan-*Hui*' identity, see Chao Chiu-ti, 'Shei shi Huizu?'
78. Xue Wenbo, 'Zhongguo Huizu yundong', p. 13.
79. Ibid.
80. Ibid.
81. Ibid. On this argument, see also Hua Tao and Zhai Guiye, 'Minguo shiqi'.
82. Ibid., p. 14.
83. Ibid., p. 11.
84. Unfortunately, I have not been able to locate Liu's article, as Xue Wenbo did not provide a reference.
85. Xue Wenbo (Dawude), 'Guanyu Huizu yu Hanren'.
86. Ibid., p. 10.
87. Ibid., p. 11.
88. Ibid.
89. Ibid.
90. Ibid.
91. Ibid., p. 13.
92. Ibid.
93. I borrow the term 'simultaneity' from Benite, *The Dao of Muhammad*, pp. 12–20.
94. Ben-Dor Benite writes of Jin as a 'young Chinese Muslim intellectual born to a Shandong family of gentry background'. See Benite, 'From "Literati" to "Ulama"', p. 99. In the *Chinese Encyclopedia of Islam*, Jin's biographical entry by Feng Jinyuan, 'Jin Jitang', p. 259, states that he was born in the Tongzhou district of Beijing.
95. See Yin Boqing's introduction to Jin Jitang, *Zhongguo Huijiao shi yanjiu*, p. 1. Yin, however, refrained from commenting on the divisive issue of ethnicity, writing instead of the necessity for scholarly studies of Muslim history in China.
96. There may be some doubt as to Jin's 'scholarly background'. Feng Jinyuan states that as far as modern non-religious education goes, Jin was trained only at the Beijing *Jifu Xuetang*, a middle school. However, thanks to arduous self-study he later taught on the 'question of Muslim history in China' at Chengda Teachers' College at Ma Songting's invitation. In 1949, after the Communist

takeover of Beijing, he enrolled at the North China Revolutionary People's University.

97. See Benite, 'From "Literati" to "Ulama"', pp. 99–100. Jin did not use the characters employed currently to transcribe the ethnonym Uighur into Chinese. In fact, it was only around the time that his book was published for the first time in 1935 that the local Chinese authorities in Xinjiang started identifying the local Turkic sedentary populations by this name in its modern Chinese orthography. The term Uighur was not associated with Islam prior to 1935, and applied, since the tenth century, to the primarily Buddhist, Turkic society centred in the Turpan oasis. It was used to distinguish this population from the largely Islamicised Turks living farther west. In the wake of the bloody Turkic uprising of the early 1930s, the Chinese authorities of Xinjiang under Sheng Shicai used the ethnonym Uighur as part of the Soviet-advised ethnic policy to placate the rebellious Turkic Muslims. The term Uighur itself was 'revived' by the Soviet ethographers working in the Soviet Central Asia and by exiles from Xinjiang in the region who used it as early as 1924. See Rudelson, *Oasis Identities*, pp. 5–6. There is some debate among scholars as to the exact date when the Xinjiang authorities officially declared the change of the previously used Chinese appellation for Muslim Turks, *chantou Hui* (turbaned Hui) to the new-old Uighur (*Weiwu'er*). Usually 1933, 1934 and 1935 are given, with Chinese scholars favouring the latter two possibilities. Zhao Haixia, 'Guanyu "chan Hui"', pp. 37–8, argues for the last months of 1934.
98. Jin Jitang, *Zhongguo Huijiao shi yanjiu*, p. 12.
99. Jin Jitang, 'Huijiao minzu shuo'.
100. Jin Jitang, *Zhongguo Huijiao shi yanjiu*, pp. 12–13.
101. Jin's work is discussed in Benite, 'From "Literati" to "Ulama"', pp. 101–2.
102. Ibid., p. 100.
103. On the development of CCP's Muslim policies in this period, see Matsumoto Masumi, *Zhongguo minzu zhengce*, pp. 284–93.
104. In September 1940, the Executive Yuan drafted a law prohibiting further usage of the word *Huizu*, explaining that the Muslims in China lack a defined territory of their own and are culturally identical with the non-Muslim Han. It further stressed that calling Muslims *Huizu* had led to conflicts and tensions. The law recommended that the Sino-Muslims be called *Huijiaotu*. See 'Xingzhengyuan ni tongling', 16 September 1940.
105. Gladney, *Muslim Chinese*, p. 89.
106. Leibold, *Reconfiguring Chinese Nationalism*, p. 154.

6

Selective Learning from the Middle East: The Case of Sino-Muslim Students at al-Azhar University

Yufeng Mao

In the early twentieth century, modern transportation increased the convenience of contacts with the heartlands of the Islamic world sought by Muslims in China, and these took varied forms. Importing or printing religious works, including textbooks, for example, could bring authentic Islamic teachings to the Chinese Muslim community. Principal contributors to this cause were the Xiexing Company of Shanghai, the Chinese Muslim Publishing House of Shanghai and the Chengda Teachers' College (*Chengda Shifan Xuexiao*) Publishing House in Beijing. Pilgrimage trips also became more viable, and some Muslim scholars, such as Imam Wang Kuan and Imam Wang Jingzhai, used these trips to study for short periods in the Middle East and to bring home books on Islamic studies. Finally, improved transportation naturally facilitated the dispatch of students to study in Islamic schools in the Middle East.

Such contacts allowed bilingual Muslim intellectuals to fulfil their self-proclaimed task of enlightening ordinary Muslims in China with accurate knowledge about Islam and the Islamic heartlands. But they had to select the information they chose to share and how they shared it, decisions that were based on many factors. In this chapter I use the story of three dozen Sino-Muslim students who studied at al-Azhar University in Cairo in the 1930s to illustrate Sino-Muslims' selective learning and transmission of Middle Eastern knowledge back to China.

Motivations for Sending Students to al-Azhar: The Muslim Modernist Vision

The first attempt to organise a group of Muslim students to study at al-Azhar resulted from the efforts of Muhammad Dazan, a visiting Afghan scholar at a mosque in Kunming, Yunnan, in the early 1930s. At the time, mosques in China occasionally hosted foreign Muslim scholars, such as Dazan, who taught the *Qur'ān* and other religious texts. In 1931, Dazan proposed that the Muslim Mingde Middle School in Kunming should send students to study at al-Azhar and wrote a letter of application to al-Azhar on the school's behalf. At his urging, the Mingde School then submitted a formal letter of its own. After two months, the school received a reply from al-Azhar agreeing to accept five students and to cover all expenses, including tuition, board, fees and stipends.[1]

The Yunnan branch of the Chinese Islamic Progressive Association (CIPA),[2] one of the most prominent institutions of the Islamic modernist programme, took on the responsibility for selecting the students. The selection examination tested candidates in two subjects, history and translation of Qur'ānic verses from Arabic into Chinese.[3] The first formally organised Chinese student group left Yunnan in November 1931.[4] It consisted of five people, including one Muslim English teacher who was appointed head of the team, three students from the Mingde Middle School, and one student from the Shanghai Islamic Teachers' College.[5]

In late 1932, Chengda Teachers' College in Beijing sent five students to study at al-Azhar. Imam Ma Songting, the Chengda headmaster, accompanied the students to Egypt, where he met several times with the president of al-Azhar (who was also Egypt's Minister of Religious Affairs) and with Egypt's King Fuad I. In a written request to the king, Imam Ma asked for 'guidance and assistance' from Egypt regarding Chengda's 'structure, teaching material, teachers, and finance'.[6] In reply, the Egyptian king agreed to donate a number of books, send two teachers to China, and to accommodate as many Chinese students as possible for study in Egypt. Other student groups soon followed. In 1934, the Mingde Middle School in Kunming sent another three students, and in the same year, Shanghai Islamic Teachers College sent five.

In 1935, however, the future of China's Egyptian study programme seemed to be in danger when the new president of al-Azhar turned down a request by Chengda Teachers' College to send a new group of students.[7] Therefore, in autumn 1936, Chengda's Imam Ma Songting paid another visit to Egypt to solicit assistance. His meeting with the new King Faruk and the president of al-Azhar was successful; King Faruk agreed to sponsor twenty more Chinese students to study at al-Azhar.[8]

Chengda was given the responsibility of selecting these twenty students, and the school scheduled two rounds of exams for candidates in June and July 1937. The first round would select ten Chengda students, and the second round would select ten students from other schools.[9] Candidates were tested on Nationalist (*Guomindang*) Party tenets, Islamic doctrine, Chinese, Arabic, history, geography, maths and sciences. They also participated in an oral interview and underwent a physical exam.[10] Because of the Marco Polo Bridge Incident (July 1937), which initiated an open state of war between China and Japan, the second round of exams for non-Chengda students did not take place. Instead, ten students were selected without an exam, four from the Shanghai Islamic Teachers' College, two from Xinjiang, one from Sichuan, one from Shanxi and three from Beijing. It is unclear what criteria were used for this selection or who made the decisions. In the end, largely due to the chaos of war, five of the students could not go, so the delegation departed with only fifteen students. In March 1938, this 'Delegation of Faruk Students' arrived in Cairo.[11] This would be the last organised group of Chinese Muslim students sent by Muslim civil society organisations to study at al-Azhar, bringing the total between 1931 and 1938 to thirty-three. Hai Weiliang transferred from India to al-Azhar in 1934, and a few students from the northwest studied at al-Azhar as individuals, but still the number did not exceed around three dozen.

Sending students to study at al-Azhar was a key component of an indigenous Chinese Islamic modernist programme. This movement in China, started during the last years of the Qing dynasty, aimed to rectify what activists saw as the backwardness of the Chinese Muslim community. They believed that ignorance of the true teachings of Islam, as well as the lack of integration of Chinese Muslim communities with Chinese society, lay at the root of the Chinese Muslims' difficulties. Consequently, their key goals were to improve knowledge of Islam among Chinese Muslims and to promote more effective and positive integration with Chinese society, an agenda combining religion with nationalism. To achieve the former goal, the programme sought contacts with the heartlands of the Islamic world. For the latter, the modernists promoted a vision of Muslims prospering within the framework of the Chinese nation (*Zhonghua minzu*), an entity first theorised by Liang Qichao early in the twentieth century (see Cieciura, Chapter 5, this volume).

Zvi Ben-Dor Benite sees the students' mission as part of the effort by twentieth-century Sino-Muslims to re-establish Chinese Islam's links to the Arab lands of Islam.[12] I argue that the missions also sought the empowerment of the Sino-Muslim community within China. In other words, the missions reflected the dual goals of the Islamic modernist movement: an Islamic revival and gaining Muslims their proper place in the new Chinese nation-state. Yu Ke, a frequent contributor to *Yuehua* magazine, articulated the modernist goals behind the missions in a long article titled, 'A few suggestions to the gentlemen studying in Egypt', written in spring 1932.

Yu Ke wrote that he was overjoyed to hear about the arrival of the five students in Egypt. He supported the assertion that studying abroad would revive Islam in China, because these students could help to clarify its religious doctrines in an age of ignorance:

> Islamic culture in China has declined a lot. This is known to everyone. Hundreds and thousands of things need to be reorganised and revived. If we, however, summarise the key work that needs to be done, it is only one thing: to clarify the doctrines [of Islam]. Without clear doctrines, any kind of effort will be baseless, incomplete, and futile in the end. I believe these gentlemen's goal in studying abroad is this [to clarify the doctrines of Islam]. Am I not right?[13]

Since the early twentieth century, reviving Islam in a religious sense has been one of the main goals of the modernist Muslim movement. Their activities have included promoting education for Muslim children, adopting written Chinese as a medium of religious texts, and importing religious texts from the Middle East to be translated into Chinese. Sending groups of students to al-Azhar, the Muslim world's premier university, constituted another big stride towards that goal.

In addition to hoping that the students would bring home a more refined understanding of Islamic religious teachings, Yu Ke argued that students should also study the history and educational achievements of the Islamic world. Moreover, they should try to keep up with new ideas and intellectual trends, as their compatriots in Japan and Euro-America had been doing since the late Qing. Yu Ke's comments show that some Muslims in China at that time looked towards the Middle East not only for authoritative judgements on religious matters, but also for intellectual and political inspiration in general. They knew that the Islamic heartlands, like East Asia, were a site of both imperialist aggression and indigenous modernism, and they wanted to reap its benefits within the transnational Islamic *umma*.

Curiously, at the beginning of his article, Yu Ke gave thanks to God that this mission would be a blessing 'for the Chinese Islamic religious community, fifty million Muslim compatriots, and even the Republic of China'.[14] Why was sending Chinese Muslim students to al-Azhar a blessing for the Republic of China? Given the context of the ongoing modernist movement, we can answer this question. Yu Ke, like other Sino-Muslim modernists, did not see the growth of Islamic teaching or the revival of the Muslim community as a potential obstacle to China's revival, as many contemporary Han intellectuals thought or even feared. As I have illustrated elsewhere, during this period, Sino-Muslim modernists saw Islam as a useful religion for China. Muslims would occupy a special role in the revival of China because of their exceptional characteristics, such as physical courage and strong group identity.[15] Since he claimed that 'fifty million' Muslims lived in China – a false statistic widely cited during this period, and even occasionally now – in his eyes they constituted one-fifth of the entire Chinese population. Yu Ke believed that if sending students to Egypt would help to revive the Muslim population in China, then it would also help the entire Chinese nation.

This ambition explains Yu Ke's usage of the Chinese term *xifang*, 'the West', to refer to the Middle East. Since the predominant mood among educated Chinese required learning from 'the West', Yu Ke argued that the Middle East, not just Euro-America, could provide inspiration for China's modernisation programme. His effort to highlight the importance of Muslims to China's national cause is consistent with the Sino-Muslim modernists' self-empowerment goals.

At the end of his article, Yu Ke used a medical metaphor, noting that these students were the first group of people to 'seek doctors and medicines' for the Chinese Islamic community, and therefore had the burden of bringing back 'written opinions' to 'guide' Muslims in China.[16] Many religious, intellectual and social trends animated the Middle East in the 1930s. Exactly which 'doctors' and 'medicines' might be brought back depended on the students, their experiences and calculations of benefit. Both products of, and actors in, the indigenous Chinese Islamic modernist programme, the students could not but be both inspired and limited by their visions. Moreover, their individual backgrounds, experiences in Egypt, and their relationship with the Nationalist state all powerfully influenced their selectivity in seeking education in Egypt and bringing its results back to China.

Individual Backgrounds

In their early twenties, having grown up in major metropolitan areas, these students received their education in new-style Muslim educational institutions that emphasised written Chinese and loyalty to the nation, as well as Islamic learning (see Matsumoto, Chapter 7, this volume). Moreover, they had access to and read the mushrooming Muslim periodicals that propagated modernist ideas. Despite this common background, however, their different life experiences shaped their overseas studies and their careers after returning to China. Some of them intended their study abroad to advance a broad Islamic revival in China and throughout the world. For others, studying abroad enabled them to win respect and equal social status for Muslims in Chinese society. The examples of Ma Jian and Na Zhong, both among the first group of students and both from Yunnan, illustrate these two impulses of the Islamic modernist programme.

For Ma Jian, studying abroad was unquestionably aimed at promoting an Islamic revival in China. He had grown up well versed in Islamic religious texts,[17] then between 1928 and 1929 he travelled to Gansu to study with Imam Hu Songshan, but found himself dissatisfied with the 'old' teachings he received.[18] In a letter written in 1929, he expressed the desire to study abroad because the outdated Gansu teachings 'could hardly deal with our complex society, not to mention counteracting other religions, including Christianity'.[19] For the young Ma Jian, then, studying abroad and improving

Islamic education in China would enable the Chinese Muslim community to adapt to the new times and to deal with challenges coming from other religions. This impulse dealt more with religious revival and reform than with improving the status of Muslims within Chinese society.

The novelty and exoticism of Cairo attracted the attention of other newly arrived students, but in Ma Jian's eyes, Cairo could only be a place for studying Islam. When he arrived in Egypt, the city immediately impressed him as a centre for Islamic studies. Three months after arriving in Cairo, Ma Jian wrote to Ma Fuxiang – a Muslim military commander, former provincial governor, Guomindang official, and patron of Islamic education – reporting on his impressions of Egyptian society in terms of ideological debates, politics, economics and education.[20] Similarly, in a letter from Egypt published in December 1932, Ma Jian detailed the universities, journals, Islamic associations and mosques in Cairo and concluded, 'Egypt is the most suitable place for studying Arabic language or religious subjects'.[21]

Because of his long-term dedication to Islamic studies, Ma Jian excelled immediately upon commencing his coursework. When the first group of students arrived in Cairo in 1932, the Arabic competence of the Chinese students clearly left much to be desired. Even though these students had studied Arabic prior to visiting Egypt, they still had only very limited Arabic listening and speaking skills. Taking an Arabic test when they first entered the university, the first group of students heard from the examiner that the results were not satisfactory.[22] These students therefore had to start at al-Azhar by studying Arabic intensively. After one year of training in Arabic, only Ma Jian received permission to take classes at the College of Theology; the other four students had to form a special class on their own and continue their language training.[23]

Ma Jian wanted his work to contribute to an Islamic revival in China. Communicating with his Arabic-reading audience in Egypt, Ma Jian did not try to hide his ambition to convert non-Muslim Chinese. In the 'forward' of his Arabic translation of *The Analects of Confucius*, Ma Jian wrote:

> I am Muslim and Chinese. As such I have the duty to make an effort to help those in the religion who do not understand Chinese to get a glimpse of philosophies and literature of China. Similarly, I should do my best to

spread the doctrines and laws of Islam in China, so that all people of my country come to know the truth of Islam and hopefully, if it is God's will, they will turn toward Islam.[24]

Clearly, for Ma Jian, Muslims shouldered the responsibility for converting other Chinese as an inescapable religious duty. In a *Brief Introduction to Islam in China*, he discussed Confucianism, Buddhism and Taoism, and concluded that Islam was superior to all three religions.[25] He lamented the limited influence of Islam on Chinese society, like a brilliant jewel that is hidden from sight due to lack of knowledge. Nonetheless, Ma Jian believed in Islam's potentially positive influence on China: 'If someone could reveal the truth of Islam to the earthly people [in China], then the light of Islam will shine into the hearts of the followers of polytheism and move them onto the wide road of the True Lord.'[26] Quite naturally in Ma Jian's view, Islamising China was his duty as a true Chinese patriot. His dedication to Islamic theological studies would thus contribute to his roles as both a pious Muslim and a patriotic Chinese citizen.

Having determined to translate the *Qur'ān* into Chinese, Ma Jian focused his education at al-Azhar on Qur'ānic studies. While in Egypt, he collected numerous Qur'ānic commentaries and started to translate the *Qur'ān* when he returned to China.[27] In addition to preparing himself for that work, Ma Jian also translated several Arabic religious works into Chinese during his eight years in Egypt, including *Huijiao zhexue* (*Philosophy of Islam*), published in 1934,[28] and Muhammad Abduh's *Islam and Christianity in Scholarly Culture*, published in 1936.[29]

Ma Jian's first translated work, *Huijiao zhexue* (*Philosophy of Islam*), based on Muhammad Abduh's *Risālat al-Tawḥīd*, reflected his own views as an activist of the Islamic modernist movement. On the one hand, Ma Jian's enthusiasm for Islam led him to choose to translate a book that focused on monotheism. On the other hand, as his biographer Li Zhenzhong points out, the choice of that book also reflected Ma Jian's own reformist thinking. The author, Muhammad Abduh (1849–1905), a famous Islamic jurist and reformist, had been the Grand Mufti of Egypt. Together with his teacher Jamāl al-Dīn al-Afghānī (1839–97), Abduh advocated political and religious reform in Arab and other Islamic countries. He insisted that Islam needed to move forward with the times and that religious faith did not conflict with social and scientific progress.³⁰ Ma Jian's choice of Abduh shows his pre-existing preference for modernist thinking, as well as his adaptation to the intellectual environment of Cairo.

While Ma Jian set his sights on theological studies, Na Zhong had very different ambitions and priorities. In a letter written to *Yuehua* magazine three months after arriving in Cairo to start his ten years of study there, Na Zhong described his motivation for studying abroad:

> My desire to study in Egypt started three or four years ago when I started to concentrate on Arabic. I saw the decline of Chinese Islamic education (*Zhongguo Huijiao jiaoyu*) and the corruption of teaching methods. [I thought] following bad old traditions without effort to reform was responsible for the continuous decline of our religion. As such, I wanted to go abroad and concentrate on theology, to prepare myself to contribute to Islam in China.³¹

Here Na Zhong described his goal in studying abroad as improvement of Islamic education in China. He did not, however, explain at that time what drew him to this goal. In an interview given much later in his life, Na Zhong revealed some personal experiences behind this specific ambition. During an outing when he was a young teenager, some non-Muslim classmates put pork on his plate when he was not paying attention. After he had finished his meal, they laughed and teased him with derogatory chanting, resulting in a big fight between Na Zhong and his tormentors. Na Zhong could not understand why they hated him simply for not eating pork, but he also had little knowledge of why he and other Muslims avoided it.³² After that experience, he decided to learn more about his religion and his heritage. Hearing from a history teacher that Arab Islamic culture had been very advanced and famous throughout the world, Na Zhong made up his mind to go abroad and learn more about the history and heritage of Islam.³³

Immediately after settling in Cairo, Na Zhong looked for introductory books on the basics of Islam, starting with a middle school textbook in Arabic. He read it from cover to cover, and it pleased him very much to discover basic knowledge of the Islamic religion, including why Muslims did not eat pork.³⁴ Na Zhong rejoiced in this new source of information but also felt saddened, realising that his community in China remained ignorant of what was common knowledge among middle school students in Egypt.[35] Na Zhong's story shows how one Chinese Muslim gained consciousness of his own community's ignorance regarding the Islamic religion. This anecdote sheds light on the educational focus of Muslim modernists in China, especially their goal of improving religious education. At the same time, Na Zhong's desire for respect from his non-Muslim Chinese compatriots translated into a thirst for knowledge of the Islamic heritage and the ambition to introduce it to non-Muslim Chinese society.[36]

In contrast to Ma Jian's dedication to Islamic theology, Na Zhong pursued Islamic history and civilisation. Though his original plan had been to study theology, he decided to focus on the history of Arab and Islamic civilisation shortly after he arrived in Cairo. In 1934, he published his translation of the middle school textbook noted above, titled *Islam*.[37] In 1936, after one year of preparation, Na Zhong passed a strenuous exam to become the first and only Chinese to obtain the 'scholar' (*'Alāmīya*) degree at the old campus of al-Azhar University.[38] After that, he studied at the College of History, specialising in Arab and Islamic history. He translated more works on Arab and Islamic culture into Chinese, including Muhammad Kurd 'Ali's *Islam and Arab Civilization*, parts of which appeared in *Yuehua* in 1936.[39] Na Zhong's acquaintance with a well-known Egyptian scholar, Ahmad Amin, not only helped him get permission to sit in classes at Cairo University,[40] it also led to Na Zhong's translation of Ahmad Amin's eight-volume *History of Arab Islamic Culture* later in his career.

The Egyptian Experience: Becoming 'Chinese Muslims'

Physical removal from their Chinese context and their position in Egyptian society both had profound impacts on the students. Both al-Azhar University and the city of Cairo were very cosmopolitan, full of Muslims from all over the world. In an Islamic world that increasingly associated Muslims with their national identities, not just membership in the Islamic *umma*, these Sino-Muslim students inevitably started to perceive Muslims in China as interacting with other Muslim communities based on national identities. In turn, they emphasised the importance of identifying with 'China' and 'Chinese Muslims' in their writings directed at their readers back home.

While these students had certainly possessed a clear Chinese identity prior to studying in Egypt, their awareness of their Chineseness was intensified by the experience of living abroad. They were 'Chinese' in the eyes of Egyptians, so their sense of pride – and sometimes humiliation – came largely from their own perception of that same Chineseness. The arrival of every group of Chinese students triggered much curiosity and attention from Cairo society. Students often found themselves followed by journalists, and curious Egyptians invited themselves to the students' dorms.[41] The students found themselves serving as spokespersons for China and its people, and the Egyptians treated them as a source of information on Chinese culture and history. The students received invitations to speak and write about China and Chinese Muslims, and to translate Chinese philosophical, historical and literary works. For example, a prominent scholar asked Ma Jian to translate the Confucian *Analects* into Arabic. That translation was first serialised in the Egyptian weekly *Victory Magazine*, and then published as a book.[42] At such times, their Chineseness became a source of pride.

At others, being Chinese constituted a source of embarrassment. In 1932, an Egyptian court asked Ma Jian to act as a translator for two Chinese defendants in an opium smuggling case. This experience led Ma Jian to comment that the two Chinese nationals' involvement in such a crime had 'humiliated China'.[43] Another student, Lin Changxin, complained about unfavourable Egyptian press coverage of China, as well as being subjected to prejudice from some Egyptians. In an article published in *Rendao* magazine, Lin wrote that such things were common. He expressed discomfort over the emphasis of the Egyptian media on the negative aspects of Chinese society such as opium smoking, bound feet and public executions.[44]

As mentioned above, another international development important for the students' self-perception was the increased classification of Muslims in Egypt by their national identities. As John Voll has pointed out, in the Islamic world 'one of the most dramatic reorientations that accompanied the twentieth-century transformations was a redefinition of the basic operating unit'.[45] While historically the Islamic *umma* had been a dominant identity for all Muslims, during this period the nation-state came to be accepted as the most important basis for group identity. After 1924, 'the Muslim world had become a series of states, and the sense of Islamic unity, though maintaining a substantial emotional appeal, was a shared sentiment rather than an organizational basis for specific programs'.[46] Within such a context, the students' identity as 'Chinese Muslims' strengthened as they interacted with Muslims claiming other national identities: Egyptians, Syrians, Indians and Muslims from the USSR. Since al-Azhar organised its international students by countries, the university asked these Chinese students to form a 'Chinese student mission' immediately after the arrival of the first group in 1932.[47] So right from the beginning, the students assumed an official identity at al-Azhar as 'Chinese' students, and soon started identify themselves to Muslims from other countries as 'Chinese Muslims'. In 1932, Na Zhong described the Chinese students' embarrassment when a Soviet representative to the World Islamic Conference in Palestine asked them why China had not sent representatives to this conference. 'We had no answer to that,' Na Zhong regretfully wrote back to China.[48]

Not only did the students see themselves as 'Chinese Muslims' in relationships with other Muslims, they also found themselves *de facto* representatives of 'Chinese Muslims'. In autumn 1934, Ma Jian was asked to give a speech in Arabic at the Islamic Confederation in Cairo on the subject of Islam in China,[49] a speech later published in Cairo under the title *Brief Introduction to Islam in China*.[50] Similarly, Pang Shiqian, head of the Faruk delegation, published an Arabic-language book in 1938 introducing the Chinese Muslim community.[51]

In his *Brief Introduction*, Ma Jian expressed pride in the Muslim community in China, while at the same time pointing out some of its problems. He said that despite some deviations, for the most part Chinese Muslims still followed the original doctrines of Sunni Islam. In his view, the Chinese Muslim community's geographic isolation ironically contributed to the authenticity of their beliefs and practices.[52] He listed the many difficulties facing Chinese Muslims in their effort to fulfil their religious duties, including a low level of education, poverty and distance from the heartlands of the Islamic world. Despite these obstacles, Ma Jian explained, Chinese Muslims worked hard to be good Muslims.

As representatives of 'Chinese Muslims', these students had to concern themselves with their community's image in the Islamic world. A few months after arrival, Ma Jian expressed regret that China had sent too few students to al-Azhar. He wrote that India had just recently sent twenty students, in addition to the thirty Indian students already there. Ma Jian lamented that India had lost her independence to British colonialism, whereas China was independent, yet China had sent only one-tenth of the number of Indians. 'I wonder what Muslim compatriots of our country think about this?' Ma Jian asked.[53] He blamed his 'Chinese Muslim' community for not attaching enough importance to Islamic education compared with Indian Muslims. He perceived the number of students at al-Azhar as an indicator of the relative strength of faith of Muslim communities.

For some of these students, education directly reflected national strength and became a matter of national pride. In *Nine Years in Egypt*, Pang Shiqian compared Chinese Muslims with Muslim communities in Egypt and in Syria. He wrote:

> The Chinese Muslim community is the most backward among all Muslim communities in the world. Take Egypt for example. Those with education are twenty percent of the population. In Syria it is forty percent. Chinese people who are educated are ten to twelve percent, but for Chinese Muslims only five to six percent of them are educated.[54]

When the students shared their Egyptian experiences with people back at home, they conveyed the sense that 'Chinese Muslims' had finally acquired an identity and a voice in the Islamic world. Hu Fangquan, another al-Azhar student, translated Ma Jian's book *Brief Introduction to Islam in China* (based on his Arabic speech) into Chinese and serialised it in *Rendao* over a period of several months. In the introduction, Hu wrote:

> This was the first time a Chinese person gave a speech in pure Arabic to an Egyptian audience ... This book is the first book published in Egypt that is written by a Chinese. For introducing the situation of Islam in China to world Muslim co-religionists, our colleague Ma Jian should be given much credit. Indeed, the joining of hands between world Muslims and Chinese Muslims has begun from here.[55]

For Hu, 'Chinese Muslims' had to connect with other Muslims based on national identities. Moreover, he and his colleagues in Egypt had the empowering experience of representing all 'Chinese Muslims'. Such self-avowed representation of all Muslims in China (including the Turkic Muslims of Xinjiang) was common among Chinese Muslim modernists and reinforced by the students' experience of Egyptian curiosity, and sometimes prejudice, regarding their homeland.

Under some political circumstances, it was expedient for many in the Middle East to treat these students from China as representatives of all Muslims in China. Na Zhong, who had expressed regret in 1932 over the lack of representation of Chinese Muslims at the World Islamic Conference, was able to participate at the 'Conference of the World Arab and Islamic Congress for the Defence of Palestine' in October 1938,[56] where he spoke as the representative of China:

> Gentlemen, I announce in the name of all Chinese Muslims, whose number exceeds fifty million, our identification with Muslims of the world, and our support for every resolution of this conference together with Muslims of the world, because the resolutions are for successful defence of the Palestinian cause ... I also announce in the name of my Muslim countrymen our denunciation of colonial policies aimed at eliminating Arab Islamic Palestine. And I reiterate in the name of Chinese Muslims our readiness to make effort and sacrifice for Palestine.[57]

In this speech, Na Zhong repeatedly insisted that he spoke in the name of all Muslims in China. He did not seem to doubt that fact, nor that all Muslims in China constituted one body. From the conference participants' perspective, the support of 'fifty million Chinese Muslims' would have been a great boost to morale. Apparently, the conference organisers welcomed the claim of representation, and they printed Na Zhong's speech in the proceedings of the conference, under the title 'Chinese Address'.[58] Both sides thus became complicit in seeing these young students as representatives of the entire Chinese Muslim community.

In their letters, speeches and memoirs addressed to Sino-Muslim readers at home, the students emphasised the 'Chinese' national identity of Muslims in China. Though intrigued and attracted by pan-Islamic identity and sentiments, they nonetheless conveyed to their Sino-Muslim readers the importance of being Chinese. A lengthy reflection by Pang Shiqian, after spending nine years in Egypt, shows the influence of pan-Islamic ideology on his thinking. Writing a diary on his long trip home, Pang reflected on the relationship between religious and national identities, and pointed out that 'nationalism had diminished religious enthusiasm' throughout the Islamic world.⁵⁹ He wrote:

> Islam used to know no nationalities. All were brothers as long as they belonged to the same religion. The *Qur'ān* says, 'All Muslims are brothers' . . . Prophet Muhammad said Arabs were not superior to others, and whites were not superior to blacks . . . Based on these teachings, Muslims used not to pay attention to nationalities. Recently, the world intellectual trend has been in favour of nationalism, and everyone sees his country as the main thing . . . As such, all regard the country as the priority, and religion the second. Based on the principle of not hurting the country, however, all try to fulfil duties toward religion. In the Islamic world, Muslims in India are the most enthusiastic toward the religion.⁶⁰

In this reflection, Pang struggled to reconcile his two potentially conflicting identities and ambitions. While he expressed nostalgia towards an older belief in universal Muslim brotherhood, he accepted the position that Muslims should do their best for the religion on the condition that they did not hurt the interests of their country.

Despite some qualms, the Sino-Muslim students for the most part emphasised that religious and national identities could be mutually enhancing. Upon his return to China from Egypt, Chengda Teachers' College student Jin Diangui said at the school's welcoming party:

> Our religion used to be powerful during the four Caliphs period and controlled a great many territories. It has been declining since then. Until today, Muslim countries have still not completely got rid of imperialism. All Muslim countries of the world, however, have awakened and are actively engaged in national revival movements (*minzu de fuxing yundong*).⁶¹

In this speech, the desire to regain the lost power of the Islamic empire and the attribution of the decline of the Islamic world to 'imperialism' reflected the influence of pan-Islamic thinking on Jin Diangui. According to Jin, however, nationalism did not conflict with the revival of the Islamic world. On the contrary, the national revival movements in different Muslim countries contributed to the broader programme of reviving the Islamic *umma*. According to Jin, the global Islamic revival movement had to be achieved through nationalist movements. As Chinese, their participation in the Chinese national revival programme was not a problem, but rather a necessary element of worldwide Islamic renewal.

Relations with the Chinese State

Good relations with the authorities of the Republic of China helped the students to exploit state resources for the advancement of their personal ambitions and the various causes of their Muslim communities. For the state, supporting these students at al-Azhar helped to gain the loyalty of Muslim elites and their collaboration in national(ist) causes. This collaborative relationship was not without conflict and tension. Students sometimes resented state control and policies to assimilate Muslims or deny Muslims representation in the political system. For their part, state authorities were wary of their lack of ideological control over Muslim students abroad. Al-Azhar students' selection of materials and ideas to introduce back home reflected precisely these concerns about their relationship with the state.

The Chinese Muslim students studying at al-Azhar certainly saw the advantages of maintaining a strong relationship with the Chinese state and intended to use state resources for the advancement of their communities. Some of the students, for example, had close contacts with the Chinese consulate in Egypt. Na Zhong earned extra income by working part-time as a secretary there.[62] Having a good connection with the state could thus help students towards their personal goals. Upon return, many of them became state employees or scholars at national universities, and some played pivotal roles in China's diplomatic relations with the Islamic world. For example, both Ma Jian and Na Zhong obtained positions in national universities; Zhang Bingduo was appointed to start an Arabic-language radio programme aimed at a Near Eastern audience; in 1939, Wang Shiming became the Republic of China's Vice-Consul in Saudi Arabia;[63] and Hai Weiliang served as a diplomat at the Chinese Embassy in Tehran.[64]

Chinese students at al-Azhar also involved themselves in a range of patriotic activities relating to the growing conflict with Japan, especially after the outbreak of full-scale war in July 1937. For example, for a period after the eruption of the war, several students – including Na Zhong, Lin Zhongming and Ma Xingzhou – translated news about China from the Egyptian newspaper *Al-'Aḥrām* into Chinese and distributed this mini-newspaper every day to Chinese living in Cairo who did not read Arabic.[65] Their most significant patriotic activity was a *hajj* trip in spring 1939 to counter the propaganda effect of the Japan-sponsored 'Northern China Muslim *Hajj* Delegation'. On 3 July 1941, the Egyptian branch of the 'Chinese Association for People-to-People Diplomacy' was established, and several Chinese students at al-Azhar became board members.[66] These activities afforded the students an opportunity to demonstrate the reconciliation of their religious identity with nationalist sentiments, and to show that their ties with the Islamic world could benefit the Chinese nation. They also served as propaganda tools for Sino-Muslim elites to show the loyalty of Muslims towards the Chinese nation (*minzu*) and the Chinese state.

Contacts with the state gained by the students in these study-abroad programmes also allowed them to exert influence on state policies relating to Muslim interests. In a memo to the Chinese government written by the 1939 student *hajj* delegation, the students suggested that the government establish a consulate in Saudi Arabia in order to take care of Chinese Muslim pilgrims during the *hajj*, promote trade and to prevent the Japanese puppet government in Beijing from doing the same.[67] Reports written by Hai Weiliang and Wang Shiming, who worked as diplomats at Chinese embassies in the Middle East, show efforts to influence China's relations with Middle Eastern countries.[68]

For its part, the Nationalist government was interested in providing resources to advance Muslim study abroad in order to co-opt students as future participants in domestic politics, and to exert control over their study and travel abroad. According to Derk Bodde, starting in 1939 the Chinese Ministry of Education began to grant students in Egypt annual fellowships of £20 sterling.[69] In the early 1940s, the Chinese Consulate in Cairo provided assistance to students seeking means to return to China, and even succeeded in persuading the American Army Air Corps to provide transportation for some of them.[70] The Chinese state also took advantage of the presence of Chinese Muslim students at al-Azhar to co-opt Muslim elites and to advance its own projects. This programme was not only an effective tool of people-to-people diplomacy, it also produced personnel, contacts and organisations that would become keys in the state's use of Islam and Muslims in Sino-Arab relations. More importantly, the Chinese state, wanting to mobilise domestic Muslim communities for the war against Japan and to support a pro-Chinese propaganda campaign in the Middle East, provided funding and support for the patriotic activities of the Chinese al-Azhar students.[71]

This collaborative relationship between the students and the Republic of China was not without conflicts. Especially after the mid-1930s, the Nationalist government tightened its control over civil society activities in an effort to enhance the power of the party-state. This tendency included increasing state control over the Muslim study-abroad programme, reflected clearly in efforts to exert ideological domination over the students. In 1934, a high-level Nationalist party official, He Yaozu, wrote a memorandum to Jiang Jieshi (Chiang Kai-shek) expressing concern over the overseas activities of Muslim civil society organisations. He mentioned that such activities could promote pan-Islamic sentiments and thus weaken the already weak national identity and nationalist sentiments of Muslims. This situation could be dangerous because of Japan's interest in exploiting pan-Islamic sentiments to win the hearts and minds of Muslims in China (see Matsumoto, Chapter 7, this volume).

To deal with the situation, He Yaozu suggested further promoting the idea that non-Turkic Muslims were Han Chinese with Islamic faith and intensifying exposure of Muslims to party doctrines (see Cieciura, Chapter 5, this volume).[72] From this point on, the government increased supervision and control over overseas activities by Muslim organisations, made clear in the examination through which students to al-Azhar were selected. The first group of students from Yunnan was tested on their knowledge of history and their Arabic-language skills. For the last group, the Faruk student delegation, 'party tenets' became the first item on the list of test subjects.

Responding to such official wariness, students and Sino-Muslim elites made efforts to demonstrate the loyalty of the overseas students to the state and argue that connections with the Islamic world were beneficial for Chinese national interests. An official Chinese Muslim delegation to the Middle East reported to Jiang Jieshi that the students in Egypt were patriotic Muslims: 'Here in Egypt are over thirty Chinese Muslim students. All of them are hardworking and self-motivated. They have strong nationalist consciousness and care a lot about their home country.' The delegation then argued that Sino-Egyptian relations could benefit from religious ties between Chinese Muslims and Egypt. Their report said: 'Their [the Chinese students'] expenses here are provided by Egyptian King Faruk. The [religious] sentiments are indeed touching ... The two old civilisations should have other ways of communication. However, it won't hurt to start with religious exchanges.'[73]

Despite the effort by Muslim elites to demonstrate the students' loyalty to the Chinese state, the Guomindang government continued to be wary about the lack of ideological control over students at al-Azhar. Such concerns may be seen in a report written by the Ministry of Education in December 1938 based on a survey of Chinese students conducted by Chinese diplomats in a number of countries, including England, the United States, Germany, France, Czechoslovakia, Turkey, Egypt and the Philippines. This report noted that there were thirty students in Egypt, twenty of whom were sent by the Chinese Muslim Association, while the other ten were refugee students from Xinjiang. The report lamented the lack of political indoctrination for these students, noting that, 'Very few students in Egypt knew anything about party tenets. Among the seventeen students surveyed, none knew about the "Five-Power Constitution". It is indeed shocking!'[74]

As a result of state engagement and surveillance, Muslim elites increasingly had to justify activities in the Islamic world in terms of serving national and state interests. In a report written in 1942, the Chinese Islamic Association asserted that the goal of sending students to Egypt was to train diplomats. A decade before, the Muslim students had defined the purpose of sending students abroad as bringing true Islamic teachings to China. By the early 1940s, the primary goal had become to serve the nation, and Islamic revival was no longer even mentioned. Aspiring to upward mobility within the political apparatus and aware of the government's distrust, the students emphasised nationalism and Islamic modernism, distancing themselves from pan-Islamism.

While at al-Azhar, the students certainly had contacts with various pan-Islamic and Islamic fundamentalist organisations. Ma Jian, for example, became a member of the standing committee of the Egyptian 'Confederation of Islam'.[75] Pang Shiqian had a relationship with the pan-Islamic Muslim

Brotherhood and was indebted to Hassan al-Banna, founder of that organisation, whose personal intervention made possible the publication of Pang's book, *China and Islam*.[76]

Nonetheless, such connections also had limits. At one point, members of the Muslim Brotherhood apparently expressed interest in setting up branches in China, but the Chinese students turned down this request, saying that they had already established their own organisations.[77] The students' decision was no doubt influenced by their perception that the Nationalist state would never tolerate such a pan-Islamic organisation in China. Ma Jian's choice to translate the work of a reformist theorist and the students' rejection of a close relationship with the Muslim Brotherhood resulted from a realistic assessment of what they could accomplish in Chinese society and what the Chinese government would tolerate.

Conclusion

The challenge facing many urban, educated Sino-Muslims in the early twentieth century resembled that facing the *Han kitāb* authors in the seventeenth and eighteenth centuries: to negotiate creatively the Sino-Muslims' place between Islam and China. Unlike the *Han kitāb* authors, however, Sino-Muslim intellectuals in the early twentieth century had greater access to the Islamic heartland, due (with appropriate irony) to transportation networks established by the imperialist powers. In Ben-Dor Benite's words, 'While Chinese Muslims of the early modern period bridged the gap between their world and the Islamic heartlands through genealogical tales, their twentieth-century contemporaries did so through travel.'[78] As a part of a broader Islamic modernist programme, Chinese Muslim students at al-Azhar University in Cairo went to Egypt to bring back home not only true Islamic teachings, but also means of empowerment for Muslims in China. Their decisions as cultural intermediaries were influenced by their personal backgrounds, their interactions with local Muslims, and their aspirations within the Republican state apparatus.

While in Egypt, these students remained part of the Muslim intellectual community in China. They contributed regularly to Chinese Muslim journals, received book donations from individuals and journal publishers,[79] and hosted Chinese Muslims visiting the Middle East. As expected, they also took the 'burden' of enlightening Muslims at home seriously. They translated and wrote on Islamic theology and published opinions and articles that offered suggestions on the directions to be taken by Muslims in China. In addition, the news reports they sent home functioned as a source of information on happenings in the Islamic world. In turn, the Chinese Muslim intellectual community took great interest and pride in these students. The editors of several journals, including *Yuehua*, *Rendao* and *Muyin yuekan*, solicited and published articles from them.[80] The students' activities were discussed in China, and their pictures appeared in the newspapers. Knowledge and texts brought back by these students were equated with 'food and medicine' for the Chinese Muslim community. An author named Yang Sishi called on readers to look for answers to their religious questions in the Egyptian journal *Nur al-Islām* sent back by the students, because through *Nur al-Islām*, 'all opinions about Islamic education and religious affairs have been introduced to us'.[81] The presence of these students at al-Azhar, therefore, held both practical and symbolic importance for the Chinese modernist programme. Undoubtedly, their decisions with regard to what to introduce to their fellow Sino-Muslims had profound influences on the changing identities of the Sino-Muslim population.

Notes

1. Gao Fayuan, *Musheng houyi*, p. 63.
2. See Cieciura, Chapter 5, this volume.
3. Na Zhong, audio interview.
4. Na Zhong, 'Jinian Ma Jian'.
5. Gao Fayuan, *Musheng houyi*, p. 63.
6. Zhao Zhenwu, *Xixing riji*, pp. 95–6.
7. Zhao Zhenwu, 'Sanshinian lai zhongguo Huijiao', p. 4.
8. Pang Shiqian, *Aiji jiunian*, p. 21.
9. Pang Shiqian, 'Faluke liuai', p. 27.
10. 'Beiping chengda shifan xuexiao', p. 12.
11. Pang Shiqian, 'Faluke liuai', p. 26.
12. See Benite, 'Nine Years in Egypt'.
13. Yu Ke, 'Wo suo gongxian', p. 11.
14. Ibid.
15. Gu Jiegang, the great folklorist and historian, included his strong version

of this opinion in his writings of the 1930s and 1940s. See Schneider, *Ku Chieh-kang*.
16. Yu Ke, 'Wo suo gongxian', p. 11.
17. Li Zhenzhong, *Xuezhe de zhuiqiu*, p. 285.
18. Ma Jian, 'Liugan diansheng', p. 30.
19. Ibid.
20. Ma Jian, 'Ma Zishi jun zhi laihan'.
21. Ma Jian, 'Aiji tongxin', p. 11.
22. Gao Fayuan, *Musheng houyi*, p. 80.
23. 'Zhongguo xuesheng ruxue', p. 14.
24. Muhammad Makin [Ma Jian] (trans.), *Kitāb al-Hiwār*, p. 6.
25. Li Zhenzhong, *Xuezhe de zhuiqiu*, p. 49.
26. Ma Jian and Hu Fangquan, 'Zhonghuo Huijiao gaiguan', p. 9.
27. Na Zhong, 'Jinian Ma Jian'.
28. Li Zhenzhong, *Xuezhe de zhuiqiu*, p. 37.
29. '*Huijiao Jidujiao yu xueshu wenhua*', p. 9.
30. Li Zhenzhong, *Xuezhe de zhuiqiu*, p. 37.
31. Na Zhong, 'Na Zijia jun', p. 36.
32. Na Zhong, audio interview.
33. Ibid.
34. Ibid.
35. Ibid.
36. This modernist ambition reiterates that of the *Han kitāb* writers: to represent Islam as a civilised *dao* within Chinese society, rather than a barbaric, foreign, absurd teaching. See Lipman, Chapter 1, and Frankel, Chapter 2, this volume.
37. Gao Fayuan, *Musheng houyi*, p. 125.
38. Ibid., p. 100.
39. Na Zhong, 'Shizijun zhanzheng zhong'.
40. Gao Fayuan, *Musheng houyi*, p. 90.
41. Ibid., p. 92.
42. 'Ma Zishi zuijin', p. 37
43. Ma Jian, 'Aiji tongxin', p. 13.
44. Lin Changxing, 'Shanghai Kailuo jian', p. 21.
45. Voll, *Islam: Continuity and Change*, p. 149.
46. Ibid., p. 152.
47. Na Zhong, 'Na Zijia jun', p. 38.

48. Ibid., p. 38.
49. 'Ma Zishi zuijin', p. 37.
50. Li Zhenzhong, *Xuezhe de zhuiqiu*, p. 62.
51. Pang Shiqian, *Aiji jiunian*, p. 68.
52. Ma Jian and Hu Fangquan, 'Zhongguo Huijiao gaiguan (4)', p. 3.
53. Ma Jian, 'Aiji tongxin', p. 13.
54. Pang Shiqian, *Aiji jiunian*, p. 17.
55. Ma Jian and Hu Fangquan, 'Zhongguo Huijiao gaiguan (1)', p. 8.
56. Gao Fayuan, *Musheng houyi*, pp. 105–7.
57. 'Kalimat al-Sīn', reprinted in Gao Fayuan, *Musheng houyi*.
58. Ibid.
59. Pang Shiqian, *Aiji jiunian*, p. 68.
60. Ibid., p. 68.
61. Jin Diangui, 'Huanying Jin Ma erjun'. Jin Diangui uses the popular term *minzu* to indicate Chinese nationality, not the 'minority nationality' definition that became standard in China after the 1950s.
62. Gao Fayuan, *Musheng houyi*, p. 101.
63. Ma Kainan (Yusuf), 'Foreign relations', p. 80.
64. Hai Weiliang, 'Yilang zhi zongjiao'.
65. Gao Fayuan, *Musheng houyi*, p. 103.
66. Tian Pu and Feng Wu, 'Zhongguo guomin waijiao', p. 24.
67. Ma Jian and Pang Shiqian, 'Memorandum to the Foreign Ministry'.
68. Hai Weiliang, 'Yilang zhi zongjiao'. See also Wang Shiming, 'Jiaqiang zhongai'.
69. Bodde, 'China's Muslim minority', p. 284.
70. Pang Shiqian, 'Faluke liuxuesheng', p. 27.
71. For example, the government provided all the funds for the student *hajj* delegation.
72. Wang Zengshan, Cable to Jiang Jieshi [Chiang Kai-shek]. See also Cieciura, Chapter 5, this volume.
73. Wang Zengshan, Cable to Jiang Jieshi [Chiang Kai-shek], pp. 702–3.
74. Wang Huanchen, *Liuxue jiaoyu*, pp. 2079–80.
75. Ma Jian and Hu Fangquan, 'Zhongguo Huijiao gaiguan (1)', p. 8.
76. Pang Shiqian, *Aiji jiunian*, p. 68.
77. Ibid., p. 69. An organisation calling itself 'the Muslims' (*Yihewani*, Ar. *Ikhwan*) had been founded in Gansu in the last Qing decades, but it had no formal ties with the Egyptian group of the same name.

78. Benite, '"New Year's in Egypt"'.
79. 'Zhongguo xueshengbu tushuguan'.
80. For examples, see Hu Fangquan, 'Zhonguo liuai', pp. 32–3; and 'Jieshao muyin yuekan', p. 19.
81. Yang Sishi, 'Duiyu Aiji huiguang yuekan', pp. 11–13.

7

Secularisation and Modernisation of Islam in China: Educational Reform, Japanese Occupation and the Disappearance of Persian Learning

Masumi Matsumoto

Before the twentieth century, Persian learning was very important in the madrasa (*jingtang*) curriculum of China. According to tradition, Hu Dengzhou arranged the Thirteen Classics (*shisan-ben jing*) in the late Ming, seven books in Arabic and six in Persian.[1] After mastering Arabic, compulsory for citing and understanding the *Qur'ān*, students learned Persian to pursue the path of human completion, to reach directly the true essence of existence, God. The Persian curriculum stage usually proved to be the most difficult, for it took more than ten years for students to master all of those thirteen texts in foreign languages. The madrasa students and *ahong*s[2] spoke Chinese in its many varieties, but most were illiterate in Chinese characters.[3]

In recent years, scholars have demonstrated that 'traditional' Islam in China, usually called Old Teaching (*laojiao*) or the Traditional Way (*gedimu*, from Ar. *qadīm*), was profoundly affected by the concept of 'unity of being' (*wahdat al-wujūd*), inherited from the philosophical and ontological discussions of Ibn Arabi (1165–1240), Jāmī and other Sufi thinkers. The 'unity of being' was a universalist Islamic explanation of all varieties of existence as flowing from one single divine essence. Before the twentieth century, *wahdat al-wujūd* thinking prevailed throughout the Islamic world, including Africa, India and South East Asia.[4] Islam in China was no exception.

In modern times, however, the madrasa curriculum in China has changed gradually with the expansion of Islamic modernist and reformist movements, and Persian learning slowly disappeared from the curriculum, with the exception of particular villages in North China. This chapter explores why Persian learning was discarded in the process of secularisation of Islam in China – in the context of educational reform and Japanese imperial domination – and why traditional Persian learning has been preserved only in places such as Tianmucun (or Muzhuangzi) in Tianjin and Ding Zhuangzi and Cao Zhuangzi in Hebei.

Madrasa Education in Contemporary China

As an introduction, let us consider Islamic education in contemporary China. Nowadays, very few madrasas anywhere in China maintain the traditional learning, including Persian learning. In almost all the mosques that call themselves 'traditional' (*gedimu*), everywhere in China, they teach only Arabic as a religious language. Beginning in 1957, the Anti-Rightist Campaign and Anti-Religion Campaign forced the end of both Arabic and Persian learning. After those campaigns, Islamic schooling revived for a few years, but was again terminated or muddled during the Great Proletarian Cultural Revolution (1966–76), when religious activities were condemned and clerics and religious students persecuted. After that ten-year turmoil, the madrasas revived throughout China's Muslim communities in the 1980s and 1990s. The new madrasas, mostly funded by community members, were named Sino-Arabic schools (*Zhong-A xuexiao*) or Islamic schools (*Yisilan xuexiao*).

Since 1999, I have visited more than thirty Sino-Arabic schools in nine cities, provinces and autonomous regions. Most of them taught only Arabic as a religious language. Their curricula stressed Chinese literacy as the most important tool of common sense and communication, taught both Islamic law and domestic civil law, and attempted to stimulate their students' 'national awareness' (patriotism) in order to 'develop Muslims' status'. By the end of the 2000s, most madrasa students (called *mullah* or *khalifa* in China) finished a nine-year compulsory secular education following the initiation of the Compulsory Education Act in 2005. Those who failed the high school entrance examinations, those too poor to afford the tuition of secular high schools, and those from pious family backgrounds came to these Sino-Arabic schools for spiritual knowledge and job opportunities. Some of them have become Arabic interpreters and traders, earning relatively good salaries, and some have settled down in bigger cities and acquired urban residential registration (*hukou*). Commercial and international coastal cities such as Yiwu and Guangzhou, where cheap commodities for developing countries are traded, have demand for Arabic-speaking personnel.[5] In general, these Sino-Arabic schools charge little or no tuition fees.[6] Therefore, Muslim children from poor but pious families, particularly in the northwest, Yunnan and Henan, make use of Islamic schooling opportunities to acquire training for a better future, both in the present world and in heaven.

A Brief History of Persian Learning in China

Persian was likely the first literary language for the Sino-Muslims because of their ancestral roots in Central Asia and because of its general use as a *lingua franca* of Muslim trade routes from the Mediterranean to East Asia. Sayyid Ajall Shams al-Din (1211–79, called Sai Dianchi in Chinese), the conqueror and first governor of Yunnan under the Mongols, came from Bukhara, a city with a strong Islamic legacy and focus on Persian texts. Many Muslim soldiers, engineers, scientists and merchants also came from Central Asia with the Mongol armies and settled down in scattered areas in China. Most of them were male, so they married local women in China and began a long process of acculturation. Many Persian words have remained in use in Sino-Muslim communities as reminders of that legacy. Clerics are *ahong* (Per. *akhūnd*), friends are *dusuti* (Per. *dūstī*), worship is *namazu* (Per. *namāz*) and so on.[7]

Sufi influence, which encompassed considerable Persian learning, can be traced back to the Ming era or even before. Some scholars claim that Sufi teachings had already arrived by the late Yuan, based on an inscription found in Qaraqorum in Outer Mongolia.[8] A Chinese inscription, the *Laifuming*, erected in 1528 at the Ji'nan South Mosque (Shandong), clearly indicates that *waḥdat al-wujūd*, the 'unity of being,' had affected Muslims in Shandong by the mid-Ming along with the adaptation of Confucian and Daoist concepts.[9]

In addition to Hu Dengzhou's thirteen texts, madrasa students learned the *Qur'ān* and Chang Zhimei's *Hawā* and *Minhāj al-ṭalab*.[10] Though other combinations of texts might have been used, we can recognise that on a foundation of Arabic literacy and knowledge, Islamic philosophy, theology and ontology were taught through Persian Sufi writings, particularly Jāmī's.

We may conclude that the ultimate goal of the madrasa students was the mastery of Islamic knowledge through Persian, including complex stages of self-training to reach the ultimate goal, God, the essence of existence.

Though Chinese scholars divide madrasa education into several local schools – Shaanxi, Shandong, Nanjing and Yunnan – in accordance with variations of Arabic and Persian texts and their different stresses on Chinese literacy, the basic curriculum was generally the same throughout the Chinese culture area.

The *Han kitāb* corpus, written in Chinese, annotated, interpreted and translated those books.[11] The *Han kitāb* was written for two audiences: male Muslims, illiterate in Arabic or Persian but literate in classical Chinese, who desired deeper understanding of Islam; and non-Muslim Han and Manchu elites who had only literacy in classical Chinese. The *Han kitāb* apologia explained Islam for the Sino-Muslims, often targets of discrimination and suspicion because of their 'peculiar' dieting, fasting, prayers, frequent bathing, funeral rituals and endogamy. Through the *Han kitāb*, Sino-Muslims with Chinese literacy could explain to non-Muslim elites that Islam and Confucianism were 'almost the same' in ontology; in human values such as love, filial piety, etiquette, courtesy and hospitality; and in loyalty to their earthly lord, who ruled as the shadow of God, the ultimate Master (*zhu*) that created all existence (see Lipman, Chapter 1, this volume). Since the emperor, the sovereign ruler, was also created by God and had the essence of God, all Muslims in his imperial territory had to obey him. This theology encouraged dual loyalty towards the emperor and God, and Sino-Muslims could lead stable and safe lives under the rule of the emperor.[12]

Many scholars in the contemporary era praise the *Han kitāb* as evidence of dialogue between two great civilisations, Islam and China.[13] We may also suspect that after the Ming era, Sino-Muslim intellectuals with Chinese literacy preparing for the civil or military examinations became more numerous, but many were not able to reach the highest degree (*jinshi*) and thus achieve official rank. However, having acquired literacy in classical Chinese, they became mediators between Muslim and Chinese-Manchu society to avoid conflict. Sino-Muslim intellectuals thus became buffers to protect the spiritual world of China's Muslims, which stressed Arabic and Persian learning and granted respect to Arabic and Persian literates rather than to Chinese literates.

Sufi orders (Ar. *ṭuruq*) were introduced into northwest China in the seventeenth and eighteenth centuries, and acquired many followers. The personal veneration of the Sufi master, called *shaykh* or *murshid* in Arabic (Per. *pīr*, Ch. *laorenjia*) attracted many Muslims in the region, where barren soil and inadequate rainfall created harsh conditions. *Shaykh*s became spiritual mentors for many poor but pious Muslims, who wanted directly to perceive the real existence of God through the *shaykh*'s teaching and intercession. Some *shaykh*s performed miracles (Ar. *karāmāt*), and their lineal descendants could inherit their mystical power (Ar. *baraka*). The *shaykh* might be considered a Sufi saint (Ar. *walī*), and his tomb (Ch. *gongbei* from Ar. *qubba* via Per. *gunbad*) might become a site of worship. Sufi orders in northwest China made use of Persian texts such as *Mirsād al-ibād* for educating *ahong*s.

What did 'Literacy' mean in the Pre-modern Era?

Returning to non-Sufi Muslim congregations, students in their madrasas required ten years or more to master the two religious languages and then study Islam's complex theory, not in their native Chinese but in written Arabic and Persian. Some scholars claim that 99 per cent of madrasa students were illiterate or semi-illiterate in Chinese before the twentieth century.

Prior to the 1950s, Sino-Muslims could follow two different routes to 'literacy'. Indeed, two different kinds of pedagogy had co-existed for more than 500 years. One could learn mainly Chinese texts to acquire Chinese literacy or learn both Arabic and Persian at a madrasa, usually located in a mosque. Most Muslim families preferred the latter, because Chinese literacy was held to lead to assimilation into Chinese culture, which sometimes discriminated against Muslims.

Most *ahong*s, the community leaders, asserted that Islamic study was the best, for Chinese learning could lead directly to unbelief (Ar. *kufr*).[14] Ma Fulong, a modern *ahong*, pointed out three reasons for preferring Islamic knowledge. First, the Qing regime, sponsor of Chinese knowledge, had brutally suppressed the Muslim uprisings in the northwest and Yunnan. Second, those literate in Chinese were apt to be conspirators with the regime and betrayers of the Muslims. Third, *ahong*s wanted to defend the purity of Islamic doctrine, protecting Islam from superstitions and heresies. For example, some *ahong*s prohibited Muslims from watching Chinese drama.[15]

Similarly, according to the memoir of an *ahong* in Shaanxi, mosque education was good enough to aim at human perfection and to prevent assimilation with the Chinese.[16]

Some Sino-Muslim families prepared their sons for the military rather than the civil examination, because a military career was perceived as less assimilated to Chinese ways.[17] Muslim military officers had more opportunities to be promoted in Chinese society and were expected to mediate between Muslim and non-Muslim societies. Ma Fuxiang (1876–1932), for example, a powerful and influential Muslim warlord in the northwest during the Republican era, held a Qing military examination degree. After defeating Muslim uprisings in the northwest in 1895, he contributed to the security of Muslim society not only in his native northwest, but also in North China. Even though he and his family members might be judged as traitors because they suppressed or massacred Muslims, Ma Fuxiang was promoted to be head of the Mongolian and Tibetan Affairs Commission (*Meng-Zang weiyuanhui*) of the Nationalist government and played the role of mediator between Muslims and non-Muslims. The employment of 'obedient' Muslims like Ma Fuxiang to control 'disobedient' Muslims was a conventional divide-and-rule policy of various regimes that controlled China.

However, some Sino-Muslim families – those who could afford the cost of long-term schooling – educated their sons in Chinese to become literati or bureaucrats, because such literati could also be mediators between the Muslims and non-Muslim society. Among Muslims with Chinese literacy, some became doctors, and in the twentieth century some became journalists. Training some Muslim leaders with Chinese literacy also worked as a tactic of community survival when negotiation with local power-holders or the central regime became necessary. Such leaders were expected to keep Muslim society peaceful, to ensure a calm and autonomous religious life. Muslim society hoped not to be in conflict with secular power or non-Muslim neighbours, ignorant of Islam and potentially prejudiced against Muslims.

Modern Sino-Muslim Literati

Some Sino-Muslims literate in classical Chinese travelled to Japan after the Qing abolished the civil service examination in 1905, joining other Qing students, many of whom later became members of the anti-Qing Revolutionary

Alliance (*Tongmenghui*). In Tokyo, Muslim students established the Muslim Educational Association of Students in Tokyo (*Liudong Qingzhen Jiaoyuhui*) and published one issue of a bulletin, *Xinghuipian* (see Cieciura, Chapter 5, this volume). Many of the members of this association entered university prep schools, crash courses for Chinese students or special military schools designed for Chinese students attached to the Japanese Army.

In *Xinghuipian*, published in 1908 for circulation in China, we can observe three repeated assertions: (1) we must reform Islamic education and Islam itself as a contribution to the birth of the Japan-like nation-state of China; (2) through our association, we must unify and connect China's millions of Muslims, who formerly had no intimate relationship to one another; and (3) we must condemn the anti-modernist 'stubborn *ahong*s' who cling to the tradition of the Thirteen Classics in Arabic and Persian.

Regarding the first, Zhao Zhongqi asserted the importance of Chinese literacy in order to prevent Muslims from remaining isolated or segregated from Chinese society. On the subject of unification, Bao Tingliang argued that the overseas Sino-Muslim students needed to gather population data on China's Muslims, undertake social investigation of Muslim communities and exert leadership over Muslims, who continued to be discriminated against and regarded as dangerous because of numerous 'rebellions' against authority in the northwest and Yunnan during the nineteenth century. Addressing education, Cai Dayu criticised the *ahong*s shallow knowledge of the *Qur'ān* and Sino-Muslims' ignorance of Arabic. When the members of the association made the acquaintance of Captain Fadli, an Egyptian officer who also sojourned in Japan, Cai felt ashamed of being ignorant of Arabic.[18] These Muslim intellectuals with Chinese literacy strove for community survival in the emerging framework of a Chinese nation-state as well as consciousness of the transnational *umma*, in which Muslims communicated in Arabic (see Mao, Chapter 6, this volume).

In general, any kind of discrimination has to be attributed to those who discriminate. But as minorities in Chinese society, these intellectuals, 'representatives' or defenders of the Sino-Muslims, could not blame either Han or Manchus, so they blamed their own community leaders, the clerics. The *ahong*s stood accused of 'backwardness' (i.e., illiteracy in Chinese), outmoded attachment to complicated Sufi theories of 'pure and true existence', and indifference to the improvement of the daily lives of ordinary Muslims, many of whom lived in poverty and suffered discrimination. In order to make Muslims' presence in China more stable and safe, modernist Muslim intellectuals demanded the introduction of new schools, the reform of pedagogy, and the fostering of 'modernised' religious leaders bilingual in Arabic and Chinese. However, no members of the Tokyo-based association mentioned Persian, which presumably they had never learned because they had acquired Chinese (rather than 'Islamic') literacy. The education they had received in the mosque taught them the value of Arabic, but not Persian.

Experience of the Pre-modern Madrasa

What had fostered those 'stubborn *ahongs*' in China's madrasas? We have a description from Wang Jingzhai (1879–1949), one of the most influential modern *ahongs*, who came from a poor family in Tianjin. Of course, since he was a reformist, we should not entirely trust his portrayal of his adversaries. Wang was one of the rare people who obtained Chinese literacy as well as Arabic–Persian linguistic mastery. He dared to translate the *Qur'ān* into Chinese to make God's message clearer to Chinese users, though almost all conservatives condemned him, stating that Qur'ānic translation was prohibited by Islamic law. He also translated Sa'dī's *Golestān* from Persian into Chinese and published a journal, *Yiguang* (*Light of Islam*), from 1927 until 1939, becoming one of the most important leaders of the Sino-Muslim modernists. He migrated to Chongqing with the strategic retreat of the Nationalist government during the Anti-Japanese War.

According to Wang's memoir, most madrasa students of his generation in northern China came from economically poor conditions. Many discontinued their studies because of the difficulties in understanding two foreign languages and Islam's complicated theology, but also because of poverty and difficulties in human relations among students and *ahongs*. Students moved from mosque to mosque in search of better learning conditions and more qualified teachers. In many cases, *ahongs* possessed only low levels of knowledge of Arabic and Persian, particularly in oral pronunciation. Wang Jingzhai, who had studied in the Middle East, complained about how far such *ahongs*' linguistic ability was from native level.[19]

Another 'insider' accusation against the *ahongs* came from Changde, in

Hunan, where Shan Guoqing decided to reveal the reality of his madrasa education. According to him, the old school *ahong*s never accepted educational ideas brought by Chinese-literate bureaucrats. They also denounced Islamic reformers and contested their Qur'ānic interpretations, saying that those reformers entirely lacked Islamic knowledge. Some of these 'corrupted' *ahong*s, he said, accepted money from the rich, at the same time denouncing Islamic reformers as 'heretical Han'. Shan concluded that the 'elders' (*xianglao*), the most influential men of the community, manipulated those *ahong*s to preserve their vested interests.[20] In any case, frequent conflicts occurred between conservatives and reformers, and this antagonism divided Sino-Muslim society, quite contrary to the reformers' ideals.

However, madrasa learning increased a man's prestige in these communities, for most Sino-Muslims were not literate in any language. Islamic culture appreciates knowledge of Islam, and those who had a religious background were praised, respected and trusted. The pre-modern Islamic curriculum continued for more than 400 years, passing down precious texts brought from the Middle East and Central Asia, in spite of numerous crackdowns, uprisings and conflicts. The traditional *ahong*s tenaciously preserved their texts, rituals and sense of Islamic ethics as cultural treasures, reminding Sino-Muslims of their roots, pride and distinction from the vast non-Muslim population surrounding them.

The Start of Reformist Schooling

As late as the beginning of the People's Republic (PRC), the pre-modern Thirteen Classics curriculum continued among the traditional non-Sufi Muslim communities in China. This was in sharp contrast to, or even conflicted with, the ideas of Islamic reformists or modernists, who promoted a modern curriculum that included literacy in Arabic and Chinese, law, science, geography, Chinese national history and national consciousness, and so on. Reformers founded schools such as the Shanghai Islamic Normal School (*Shanghai Yisilan Shifan xuexiao*), the Mingde High School (*Mingde zhongxue*) in Yunnan and the Chengda Teachers' College (*Chengda Shifan Xuexiao*). The Chengda Teachers' College in particular was associated with the Guomindang's strategic retreat and migration in the face of Japanese aggression after 1938 and was promoted to be a 'national' school in Guilin in 1940.

Religious leaders fostered there followed either Guomindang or Communist Party (CCP) leadership after 1945, and Chengda Teachers' College graduates divided into two political camps after 1949. Those who followed the Guomindang became leaders of the Chinese Islamic Association (*Zhongguo Huijiao Xiehui*) in Taiwan, while those who accepted the Communist regime worked within its institutions.

According to contemporary assessment, the four great *ahong*s of the Republican era were Wang Jingzhai, Ma Songting, Ha Decheng and Da Pusheng. Ma was one of the founders of the Chengda Teachers' College, while Ha and Da were famous *ahong*s with experience in Shanghai, the international port city where Muslims gathered from all over the world. All were 'patriotic' Islamic reformers, modernists and anti-Japanese propagandists. They worked together with Muslims literate in Chinese and sometimes with non-Muslim literati to improve the fragile status of the Sino-Muslims in the new era.

After visiting the Middle East in the 1920s, they introduced a popular (but probably false) *ḥadīth*: 'Loving the state is part of [Islamic] faith'. This *ḥadīth* had become very popular among Islamic modernists in the Middle East from the end of the nineteenth century as part of their anti-imperialist and nation-building agenda to be implemented through modern education. Islamic modernists in China made efforts to integrate the Sino-Muslims as members of the Chinese nation, inculcating patriotism by stressing that *ḥadīth* as the Prophet's words.[21]

As China's Muslim literati were traditionally divided into two categories on the basis of literacy in Chinese or Arabic, so too were modern Islamic reformers. Most of the Arabic literates had experience in the Middle East when they made the pilgrimage to Mecca at the beginning of the twentieth century, at a time when Middle Eastern modernists generated discourses of anti-imperialism and Islamic reform. Some Chinese literates, on the other hand, had studied in Japan prior to the 1911 revolution. Unlike the traditionalists, these two groups of modernist literati both advocated modernisation of Islam in China, promoting: (1) national education for national unification; (2) Chinese and Arabic bilingual literacy among Muslim children; (3) the improvement of Sino-Muslim economic conditions; (4) the publication of Islamic journals and the translation of the *Qurʾān* into Chinese; and (5) the unity of China's Muslims. This last was particularly stressed because of the proliferation of competing factions and schools. They also advocated dispatching Muslim representatives to the national parliament in 1936.[22]

Reasons for the Presence of Islamic Reformers

'The Chinese modern' came largely from the outside. Unequal treaties brought Christian missionaries, the collapse of old-style gentry education and the civil service examinations, the introduction of modern education, occupation troops, foreign concessions in many cities, a modern transportation system and more. Because of the open-door policy of the late Qing, many Islamic books were brought from Egypt, Turkey and especially from India, which had Islamic Institutes subsidised by Great Britain.[23] Furthermore, the nineteenth-century development of steamship transportation made travel to the Middle East and the pilgrimage to Mecca more convenient and gave Sino-Muslims access to communication from all over the Muslim world (see Petersen, Chapter 4, this volume).

In sharp contrast, the overland route was abandoned because of the treaties to regulate the Qing–Russian frontier. After 1917, the Russian Revolution and the formation of the USSR increased border security, while Islamic schools in Central Asia changed dramatically under the modernist, atheist Soviet regime. That is, the sea route overwhelmed the old land route in terms of modernity, safety and speed. At the same time, it renewed the 'authentic' linguistic status of Arabic, at the expense of Persian, which was associated with Central Asia.

The four great *ahong*s were all multilingual. Wang Jingzhai, for example, had been educated in the traditional curriculum, including Persian, and he acquired Chinese literacy by reading newspapers and journals.[24] But conventional Sino-Muslim histories name no prominent *ahong*s without Chinese literacy, for they stress reform, modernity, patriotism and anti-Japanese sentiments. The official historical discourse conforms to this assessment, so contemporary scholars on the Sino-Muslims – Chinese, Japanese (including this writer) and Western – have paid little attention to traditional *ahong*s without Chinese literacy. That is, contemporary scholars cannot read vernacular writings in Sino-Arabic *pinyin* (*xiaoerjing* or *xiaoerjin*),[25] and most cannot read Persian, so they do not focus on the traditionalists' discourse of *wahdat* *al-wujūd*, the unity of being. Religious leaders who had Chinese literacy and resisted imperialism have left their names in printed histories, but we must also examine the cultural heritage left by those 'illiterate' clerics. Might they have been subalterns in the semi-colonial and post-colonial context of twentieth-century China?

Sino-Muslim literati who succeeded in becoming civil or military bureaucrats could not understand the deep meaning of Islamic teachings embodied in Arabic and Persian texts. Their Arabic was poor, reaching only the level of reciting the *Qur'ān* and sounding out simple texts. Learning Persian required even more time and would have interfered with their acquisition of Chinese literacy, so they maligned it as obsolete and irrelevant to complex modern times. But when I looked at the classical texts preserved carefully at ordinary mosques or in private homes, I found many letters written in *xiaoerjing* inserted among their pages. We may thus conclude that madrasa students and imams constituted another kind of literati, and that they received the respect of their communities.

In the late Qing and Republican periods, it was common for a Muslim family to allocate sons to various fields. If one was judged to be brilliant, he was encouraged to study for the military or civil examinations. Another might be persuaded to be a madrasa student to earn the family prestige within the Muslim community. An *ahong* in the family also promoted intercommunity communication through personal mobility, information on trade, calculation of commercial and personal risk, and exchange of brides. Muslims were especially vulnerable to risk because of the repeated rebellions and defeats in the northwest and Yunnan. Even though Muslims in other regions were not directly affected, they had to manage the risk and perform as obedient subjects to the Qing and then Republican authorities.

In order to improve madrasa education, Sino-Muslim modernists presented a strong critique of the traditional Islamic curriculum, especially Persian learning. They believed that Sufi teachings, based on Persian knowledge, had little modern relevance and took too long to master.[26] Instead, they advocated 'efficiency', 'results', enlightenment and the advancement of the individual. At the same time, Muslim communities came under pressure from imperialism, political turmoil, the trend of national integration and campaigns for the alleviation of poverty.

On the exclusion of Persian learning from the curriculum, a Muslim teacher in Hunan wrote in 1925:

> It is important to ponder the contents of Muslim children's textbooks. There is a linguistic competition between vernacular Chinese (*baihua*) and Persian. If we depend upon the *Qur'ān*'s teaching, its translation into vernacular Chinese should be argued, because it seems to be easier for children to learn it. Needless to say, the children's mother tongue is colloquial Chinese. If we use Persian, the teaching method might be an indirect one in order to know the meaning of the Persian texts. Then learners need more skills for detailed translation of Persian. However, even if children try to learn Persian, they soon forget it, and children also feel it to be torture . . . Isn't it strange to teach the contents of Islamic texts to Chinese children by using Persian? . . . They are mumbling Persian phrases without knowing the precise meanings . . . Now the Isolation Pact to prohibit overseas communication has been abolished, and most imported Islamic textbooks are in Arabic . . . Persian books include many false *ḥadīth*. It is time for us not to depend on Persian but to learn Chinese characters in order to improve our life level . . . Of course, we do not intend to abolish all Persian learning.[27]

Gradually, the Persian curriculum disappeared in the 1920s and 1930s in the reformers' schools. The Chengda Teachers' College in Ji'nan, Shandong, had three Persian classes per week in 1927, but gradually reduced them after their migration to Beiping in 1929, eliminating them by 1936.[28] In the northwest, the Muslim Provincial Normal School provided two Arabic classes and four Chinese classes, but no Persian class in 1934. Thereafter, even more stress was put on Chinese learning with five classes, while Arabic was reduced to only one.[29]

In addition, the concept of 'responsibility' was introduced into Sino-Muslim education. At that time, it meant roughly the ability to respond to challenges, especially from Christian missionaries, some of whom came to China with tactics specifically designed to convert Muslims. Sometimes they used the Arabic Bible to refute the 'mistakes of Islam'.[30] Some missionaries learned Arabic well enough to deliver sermons in that language and distributed tracts among madrasa students. We have, however, no evidence that they distributed Persian texts. According to the missionaries' understanding, Islam consisted only of Arabic knowledge, and they ignored Persian. This stemmed partly from the missionary methodology of Samuel Zwemer, the founder of the Arabia Mission, and partly from their serene confidence in the supremacy of Christianity over Islam.[31] Ironically, Japan also dispatched converted Muslim 'missionaries' to China and advocated the development of Islam through Islamic journals in the 1920s.[32] Sino-Muslim elites believed their co-religionists, particularly illiterates, to be quite vulnerable to those challenges.

As early as the mid-nineteenth century, Ma Dexin and Ma Lianyuan of Yunnan wrote books to refute the Christian doctrine of the Trinity, asserting what they saw as a contradiction between that idea and Islam's more straightforward claim of God's singularity (Ar. *tawhīd*). Ma Dexin and Ma Lianyuan had luck, intelligence, education and resources enough to publish such books in both Arabic and Chinese, but others were not able to do so because they lacked linguistic ability and financial support from Muslim donors. The Yunnanese *ahongs*' response indicates that traditionalists felt the responsibility to react, whether challenges came from reformers or Christian missionaries. This phenomenon clearly stems from the modern condition, in which individuals establish a modern self, not entirely immersed in the community and potentially separated from religious techniques designed to reach God.

In the northwest, severely damaged after the Muslim uprisings (1860–78 and 1895), the *Ikhwan* (Ch. *Yihewani*), introduced by returned pilgrim Ma Wanfu (1853–1934), became dominant through the support of Muslim warlords who emerged from the Qing military. Ma Wanfu's campaign to return to the original *Qur'ān* was clearly influenced by Islamic reform movements in the Middle East. The *Ikhwan* and the warlords did important work to end the continuous conflicts among Muslims in the region, especially those among conventional mosques and various Sufi *menhuan*.[33]

In the generation after Ma Wanfu, the *Ikhwan* advocated both Arabic and Chinese studies, and they continued to condemn the Sufis' mystical theories and curriculum, which included Persian learning. Like the Islamic reformers or revivalists in the Middle East, they denied the validity of Sufism, which had not existed at the time of Prophet Muḥammad's revelation. In the modern trend of 'purification' of Islamic doctrine, Persian learning gradually diminished in the northwest, except among Sufis.

Three Villages: Maintaining Persian Training in North China

In my introduction, I mentioned three Muslim villages in Hebei and Tianjin that still maintain Persian learning in their madrasa curriculum. In oral interviews, their leaders told me the following story about their educational history. After 1978, with the initiation of the PRC's reform and opening policy, old *ahong*s were restored to honour and once again took the lead in Muslim communities. In the aftermath of the Cultural Revolution, Muslims argued about what kind of education would be most valuable in the new age of 'freedom of religion'. Old *ahong*s wanted to revive traditional learning and brought out the Thirteen Classics, which had been preserved in secret for more than ten years.[34] Community members agreed, and the revival included Persian learning in the old style. They also began to teach the doctrine of unity of being again. Chinese scholars claim that this curriculum remains characteristic of 'the Shandong school' of Islam in China.

On the other hand, in other parts of Shandong, that tradition died out after 1949. According to another old *ahong* (b. 1919), interviewed in Ji'nan, Shandong, in 2008, Persian study was called *daoxue*, 'study of the way', the path to human perfection, or *xinglixue*, 'study of nature and principle', both terms associated with Neo-Confucianism. He completed his madrasa study around 1947, so the period of his Persian learning coincided with Japan's occupation (1937–1945). Thereafter, he became an *ahong* at the Huihuiying mosque in front of Zhongnanhai, later the headquarters of the Communist Party leadership in Beijing. That mosque was destroyed after the establishment of the PRC. He remembered:

> Japan's regime was good because they didn't interfere in our affairs. We Muslims were under the special protection of Japan. The Guomindang were much worse. They destroyed our mosques and tried to control us. They sometimes tried to massacre Muslims, suspecting that poor Hui people were bandits.

Even after 1949, he recalled, Persian learning continued in the madrasa until the outbreak of the Cultural Revolution in 1966, when he served as *ahong* in a mosque in Jiyang, Henan, for two years, then gave up teaching during the ensuing eight years of turmoil and worked as a farmer in his home village. After 1978, he returned as *ahong* to the Shijiacun mosque, near Dezhou, Shandong. Because of the hiatus in mosque education during the ten years of the Cultural Revolution, many madrasas gave up Persian. Former madrasa students who had only Arabic knowledge – they had not yet reached the level of Persian – were sent to the countryside. After 1978, they became 'instant *ahongs*' when the mosques reopened. I was puzzled by this life history, so different from the official histories of both the Nationalists and the Communists. Particularly, the memory of Japan's occupation differs considerably from the two party lines, so I shall try to resolve the question.

As mentioned above, according to Wang Jingzhai's 1937 description, there was strong antagonism between 'conservatives' and reformers in Hebei and Tianjin before the Japanese invaded north China in 1937. The conservatives included almost all the *ahong*s, who stuck to the curriculum based on the Thirteen Classics. Wang Jingzhai was one of the exceptions. He managed to acquire Chinese literacy and also travelled to Mecca and even entered al-Azhar University in Cairo, a headquarters of Islamic reformers and anti-Sufi ideology (see Mao, Chapter 6, this volume). He continued to advocate Islamic reform in China, but was ignored or dismissed by the major *ahong*s, their followers and mosque administration committees. He persisted, translating the *Qur'ān* into Chinese in Beijing from 1926 to 1928.

Then, in 1929, the modernist, reformist Chengda Teachers' College moved to recently re-named Beiping from Ji'nan, Shandong. Conservatives rejected Wang's translation of the *Qur'ān*, so his mosque became one of the reformers' headquarters. Modernist students, Muslims literate in Chinese, and reformist *ahong*s such as Ma Songting innovated in curriculum design, creating a modern Sino-Muslim education to foster three kinds of leaders: reformist *ahong*s, modern schoolteachers, and leaders for the newly created Muslim associations, committees and periodicals. Their centre was the Chengda Teachers' College.[35]

Japan's Phony Associations and Policy towards Islam

Before and during the war in China, Japan's military governments conducted numerous intrigues towards Muslims in China. Following Japan's victory over Russia in 1905, not only the pan-Asianists (J. *Ajiashugisha*), but also the Japanese Army, particularly General Utsunomiya Tarō, paid special attention to Islam in order to rule Asia by replacing the Western empires.[36] Many patriotic agents were dispatched as 'volunteers' to China to collect information, and some of them, such as Kawamura Kyōdō, Tanaka Ippei and Sakuma Teijirō, converted to Islam in the 1920s. Officially and unofficially, Japanese scholars and intelligence agents investigated Islam, which historically had not existed in Japan. Knowing about Islam in order to rule over Muslims became an important issue in Japan's expansion of power in Asia, starting with Manchuria and north China, but later including South East Asia. Japanese leaders concentrated particularly on understanding the 'unknown' Islam in China for its geopolitical importance, and they made it a national project.[37]

After the Mukden Incident in 1931, Japan occupied northeast China and fabricated the puppet state of Manchukuo, in theory an ideal, moral and harmonious 'heaven' that included heterogeneous ethnicities: Manchus, Han, Mongols, Koreans and Japanese. Needless to say, the real ruler of the puppet state was the Japanese Army, which tried to make use of Muslims, propagandising Japan as a good friend and protector of Islam. This policy constituted part of the Japanese Army's 'northern strategy' to confront Communism and resist the Soviet Union in Manchukuo. Islam played the part of a buffer as well as a tool of divide-and-rule in East Asia.[38] In this context, both civilian and military agencies utilised a small number of Tatar Muslim refugees in Manchukuo and Japan.

The Shigekawa Agency (J. *Shigekawa kikan*)[39] was in charge of the appeals to Muslims from September 1937, just after the invasion of north China. The Japanese authorities ordered Muslims in occupied Beijing to form an Islamic Association of Beijing (*Beijing Huijiao Hui*) in place of the old Beiping Muslims Association (*Beiping Huimin Gonghui*). Wang Ruilan, the prominent but non-reformist *ahong* of Beijing's largest mosque, became the religious leader of this puppet association. In February 1938, the Shigekawa Agency initiated, and Major Shigekawa himself headed, the All-China Islamic Union (*Zhongguo Huijiao Zong Lianhehui* to unite all the Muslims in the occupied zone. Most of the Islamic reformers, such as Wang Jingzhai, Ma Songting and Shi Zizhou, escaped from Beiping following the Guomindang's (GMD) westward retreat to participate in anti-Japanese resistance. Those Muslims who remained in the occupied zone included merchants, Chinese-style literati, journalists, conservative *ahong*s, madrasa students, women and so on. The Japanese authorities organised them under the All-China Islamic Union, making a special policy to conduct modern education in Chinese, preferential measures and political–military training. Muslim youth at the Japanese training centres bowed daily towards the Imperial Palace in Tokyo to pay respects to the emperor of Japan.

Some Muslims found that this act violated the principle of *tawhīd* (oneness of God), and it resulted in Muslim hatred towards Japan.[40] Tang Yichen, a Muslim literate in Chinese, became the secretary of the All-China Islamic Union. He wanted to improve Muslims' living standards and educational levels by drawing financial assistance from the Japanese Army.[41] Under Japan's surveillance, the Union planned to establish a development bank, to be called the Industrial Bank of the Northwest (*Xibei Xingye Yinhang*, J. *Seihoku Kōgyō Ginkō*), using capital from Japanese investors, and also to open a trading company, *Huilong Gongsi* (J. *Kairyū Konsu*), to co-opt the commerce of Muslims in north and northwest China and Inner Mongolia.[42]

The Japanese rulers took modernisation of education for Muslims as one of their most important tasks. Making use of Muslims literate in Chinese, who became collaborators, the Union and the puppet governments of occupied China advocated the promotion of 'modern' education, including Arabic and Japanese language classes.

Those schools were under strict surveillance by the Japanese Army, but community leaders had no choice but to persuade Muslims to send their children to elementary schools run by the puppet government, saying that 'elementary schools are more efficient [than madrasas]'.[43] As modernists, they also declared the necessity for women's elementary education.[44] For example, an article in *Huijiao zhoubao*, a weekly paper issued by the All-China Islamic Union, described the problem as follows:

> The pedagogy of fostering *khalifa* (madrasa students) has not been improved. This pedagogy continued for a thousand years and fostered a lot of *'ālim* historically. However, the world has to change in the course of time . . . The only requirement is to change the pedagogy of fostering *khalifa* . . . What is

the old life like? It is a passive, parasitic and unstable life. If life is unstable, no type of business will be successful.[45]

However, almost all the Muslims in the occupied area were illiterate in Chinese. Shi Zizhou, a famous Muslim intellectual and Islamic reformist from Tianjin, accompanied the Guomindang as they retreated to Chongqing after 1938. There he wrote that Muslims in Tianjin had been reluctant to send their children to modern elementary schools, even though Muslims literate in Chinese, such as Shi and Wang Jingzhai, had made consistent efforts to enlighten Muslims by publishing journals in Chinese.[46] We can observe how the Union and Muslims literate in Chinese, those who became collaborators with Japan, were irritated by other Muslims' indifference to modern education, which encouraged pursuit of material happiness, wealth and social success.

Even though most people in the occupied area hated Japan's behaviour and dominance, some people eventually gave up resistance, sometimes in order to improve their poverty and lack of education. In contrast, others established anti-Japanese guerrilla forces. Because of the relatively small number of Japanese personnel assigned to control the vast occupied area, the occupation governments used pro-Japanese Chinese elites and military to sustain the occupation. Japan's aims in the occupation were clear. Even though the Sino-Japanese War broke out accidentally in July 1937, Japan followed the 'Manchukuo way' of ruling in the occupied area of north China. There, Japan wanted to concentrate food as well as natural and human resources to continue the war against the Guomindang and Communists, whose forces had to be eliminated to ensure the occupied zone's security.

Japan took a conciliatory position towards the Muslims in the occupied areas and declared that Japan would never intervene in Islamic doctrine or teaching. According to this policy, the traditional rituals, beliefs and curriculum were preserved, especially in the Tianjin area.[47] Japanese agents and policymakers worked towards the unification of Muslims under their control, but did not concern themselves with the content of the belief or values, especially those that appeared in Persian writings. The Japanese were interested only in resource extraction and security, and they had to neutralise any anti-Japanese guerrillas, so they appointed Muslims literate in Chinese to supervise security within the Muslim communities. In the face of the absolutely dominant armed forces of Japan, these Muslims had no choice but to become mediators among clerics, ordinary Muslim people and the Japanese occupation.

However, Muslims literate only in Arabic and/or Persian asserted that they were indifferent to policy and interested only in defending Islamic belief (*buzhengguo, zhengjiao*). In the philosophy of *wahdat al-wujūd* (the unity of being) or *daoxue*, Muslims aimed towards human perfection, a peaceful society and a focus on God. Based on their long experience with the Qing and Republican regimes, they realised that they would not be able to overturn any regime that possessed strong military force. This did not change under Japan's rule, and these Muslims maintained their stance of non-resistance.

Some community leaders did actively collaborate with Japan. According to an interview with Wang Yingqi (b. 1933), most mosques in the Tianjin area were preserved and Muslims not massacred because of an *ahong* named Li:

> The chairman of Japan's agency in Tianjin had an intimate relationship with Li ahong in Tianjin. Li's brother Li Wenhan was in charge of the Ji'nan South Mosque. When Japan invaded Ji'nan, one Muslim was about to be executed. When Li in Tianjin appealed to the Japanese Army, the Muslim was released. Li ahong had such power and influence. When Japan invaded Jining in December 1937, Li Wenhan was ordered to clean up the East Mosque of Jining, and they welcomed the Japanese Army by serving them tea. He spoke to the Japanese officers: 'We Muslims are obedient to Japan. We are good people.' Because of Li ahong, the Japanese Army did not kill Muslims, but there were some exceptions. The Japanese Army massacred twenty-nine 'disobedient' and innocent Muslims (including the ahong, madrasa students and children) at the Jining West Mosque, because the ahong there did not welcome the Japanese Army but rather closed the door of the mosque. The ahong hated Japan because his wife's parents had been killed by Japanese in Harbin.[48]

The interviewee, Wang Yingqi, was the son of Wang Enrong, the *ahong* murdered by the Japanese Army at Jining. In his analysis, the incident of the Jining West Mosque served as a warning to Muslims in the occupied zone. The 'influential' *ahong* Li was Imam Li Xizhen of the Tianjin Ximenbei

South Mosque, one of the high-level leaders of the All-China Islamic Union in 1939.[49] In spite of pro-Japanese Muslim elites' efforts to promote modernism, the traditional Thirteen Classics curriculum was preserved, and madrasa students were fostered as usual in the safe haven of Tianjin. On the other hand, Islamic reformers, the adversaries of those 'conservatives', advocated patriotism and published Islamic journals in Chinese from their exile in Yunnan, Chongqing and Guilin. Ironically, the conservative *ahong*s in the occupied zone were happy to be rid of their contentious antagonists, thanks to the Japanese invasion and occupation.

Let us consider the Muslim village of Tianmucun, near Tianjin, in 1940. Of the village's population, around 4,000, 73 per cent engaged in farming, while 24 per cent lived by trade outside the village. Only three small private schools taught Chinese, and there were three madrasas. Almost all the residents of the village were pious Muslims eager to learn about Islam but reluctant to learn Chinese. The mosques filled for the five daily prayers.[50] We may conclude that Muslims in the village piously followed the conservative *ahong*s, who appreciated the traditional curriculum of the Thirteen Classics.

In 1949, after the defeat of Japan and the Communist victory in the civil war, some reformers migrated to Taiwan, following the GMD, so the reformist camp divided into two. Those who stayed in the PRC were ordered to establish and support the Chinese Islamic Association under the surveillance of the Communist Party. We need not wonder what happened to both reformers and conservatives after 1966, with the beginning of the Great Proletarian Cultural Revolution.

Conclusion

All over the Muslim world, including China, modernity almost always eliminated the philosophy and curriculum of *wahdat al-wujūd*, the Sufi-inspired 'unity of being'. The Persian language came to be considered a barrier to modern reform. In China, it disappeared first in the northwest, where local Muslim warlords supported the reformist, fundamentalist Ikhwan. But even after 1949, conventional mosques in some parts of north China preserved Persian learning until the beginning of the Cultural Revolution. But that catastrophic ten-year break eliminated traditional pedagogy, and *ahong*s with Persian knowledge disappeared. The only exceptions that I have been able to find are those three north China villages. An Iranian TV crew went to the mosque in Tianmucun to verify their possession of copies of the great Sufi textbook *Ashi"at al-Lama'at*. Iran, not surprisingly, is one of only a few Islamic countries where the philosophy of *wahdat al-wujūd* is preserved in its original Persian texts.

We certainly cannot explain the entirety of twentieth-century Sino-Muslim history by examining the fate of *wahdat al-wujūd* thinking. But we should consider that this philosophy did enable the acceptance of multicultural values through its stress on the oneness of all being, and thus of all humankind. Indeed, when 'unity of being' disappeared from the curriculum, multicultural values also seemed to die out among north China Sino-Muslims, leaving only the identity politics of the *Huizu*. The two contradictory trends – Islamic revivalism, on the one hand, and secularisation and nationalisation, on the other – have remained in tension throughout modern history. Beginning with the *Han kitāb* in the Qing period and continuing through the religious disputes of the Republican period, they remain focused today on the same problem: how to produce Islamic understanding in Chinese.

After the collapse of traditional examination system education – that is, after 1905 – modern education gradually expanded its influence and attraction. At the same time, Muslims were faced with many diverse pressures, including imperialism, challenges from Christian missionaries, printing technology and postal services, the vernacular Chinese movement (which brought the concepts and charms of modernity), ease of physical and social mobility due to development of transportation and communication, translation of foreign publications, the birth of the anti-religious USSR, and the Anti-Japanese War. This complex and rapidly changing environment may be compared with the IT revolution and globalisation of our age, deeply dividing those who have joined the trend from those who have refused, resisted or failed. Persian learning was judged inefficient, irrational and dogmatic, and the traditional curriculum was discarded. Reformists advocated such modern slogans and secular goals as overcoming poverty, progress through modern education, patriotism and nationalism, success in individual life, and anti-imperialism. Thus, metaphysical philosophy aimed at human perfection through direct approach to God was almost entirely abandoned.

With the irony of history, however, I have argued that Muslims' non-confrontational attitudes towards Japan and Japan's ignorance of Islam preserved the traditional Thirteen Classics style of education, including Persian learning, in some parts of north China. This phenomenon cannot be explained as part of the dichotomy of 'bad' imperialism and 'good' patriotism. Under the PRC, some north China Muslims defended the Thirteen Classics, often at high cost to themselves, against the turmoil of the Cultural Revolution. We might analyse this as resistance against the secular regime, politically and linguistically dominated by non-Muslim atheists.

In conclusion, we must acknowledge that this tradition will soon disappear, and the Thirteen Classics will be preserved only for research in museums and libraries and to propagandise Sino-Iranian cultural relations for the sake of petroleum and trade. Because the study of the Thirteen Classics requires many years and two foreign languages, it will be judged to be inefficient as well as opposed to modern secularisation. Moreover, Islamic reformist ideas – advocated by the *Ikhwan* and the more recent fundamentalist *Salafiyya* (see Chérif-Chebbi, Chapter 8, this volume) – now claim to be 'true' Islam because they have been brought directly from the Muslim heartlands and assert their unique, legitimate basis in the *Qur'ān* and *ḥadīth* rather than Persian Sufi texts. This examination of twentieth-century Sino-Muslim education leads me to define the new 'authentic' trends as newly invented traditions gradually replacing older texts and religious ideas.[51] As a Beijing Muslim intellectual told me, commenting on the differences between the old Nationalist policies and the Communists' *Huizu* policy: 'The Guomindang treated us as citizens, equal before the law. The Communist Party treats us as a minority *minzu*, and the *zu* initially meant "those on the outside".'

All three theories formulated by modern Sino-Muslim intellectuals must be seen as consciously political projects, designed to uplift the Muslims' position vis-à-vis the state and non-Muslim compatriots. No ultimate judgement is possible as to whether they are correct or incorrect. The current status of Sino-Muslims in mainland China as the *Huizu* national minority has more to do with the military victory of the Communists in 1949 than with the existence of any final proof that the Sino-Muslims are indeed *Huizu* rather than Han believers in Islam, members of a pan-Islamic nation or 'citizens with characteristic customs and habits'.

Notes

1. Zhao Can, *Jingxue xichuan pu*.
2. From Per. *akhūnd*, these are the religious leaders or clerics in Chinese Muslim communities.
3. *Han kitāb* scholars such as Wang Daiyu, Ma Zhu, Liu Zhi, Ma Dexin (Fuchu) and Ma Lianyuan wrote texts in Chinese as commentaries on Islamic philosophy, ontology, jurisprudence and ritual, but ordinary madrasa students and their teachers could not read them.
4. Green, 'Emerging approaches', pp. 123–48.
5. Simpfendorfer, *The New Silk Road*; Matsumoto Masumi, *Isurāmu e no kaiki*; Matsumoto Masumi and Shimbo Atsuko, 'Islamic education'.
6. Matsumoto Masumi, *Isurāmu e no kaiki*; Matsumoto Masumi, interview with *ahong*s in Zhaotong, Yunnan.
7. Yang Zhanwu, *Huizu yuyan wenhua*.
8. Uno Nobuhiro, Matsuoka Hitoshi and Matsuda Koichi, 'Genchō kōki'; Yajima Yoichi, 'Genchō ki', pp. 81–90.
9. Matsumoto Akirō, *Chūgoku Isurāmu shisō*, pp. 1–22.
10. Yang Huaizhong and Yu Zhengui, *Yisilan yu Zhongguo wenhua*, pp. 347–68.
11. On the *Han kitāb*, see the relevant works of Matsumoto Akirō in the Bibliography.
12. Masumi Matsumoto, 'Esunishiti'.
13. Murata, *Chinese Gleams*; Benite, *Dao of Muhammad*; Liu Yihong, *Huiru duihua*.
14. Da Xinwu, 'Zhongguo Yisilanjiao'.
15. Ma Fulong, *Ma Fulong ahong zishu*, p. 25.
16. Huang Dengwu, *Zhongguo jingtang jiaoyu*.
17. Ando Jun'ichirō, 'Chūka minkoku ki'.
18. For information on Ahmad Fadli and his relationship with Japan, see Roussillon, *Identité et modernité*. Fadli had a strong personal relationship with General Utsunomiya Tarō, for which, see Esenbel, 'Utsunomiya Tarō' and Cai Dayu, 'Liudong Qingzhen'.
19. Wang Jingzhai, 'Wushi nian'.
20. Shan Guoqing, 'Wo jiao dangju'.
21. Matsumoto Masumi, 'Chūgoku no Isurāmu' and 'Rationalizing patriotism'.
22. Guomin zhengfu, 'Guomin dahui'.
23. Wang Jingzhai, 'Fayang Yisilan'.
24. Wang Jingzhai, 'Wushi nian'.
25. *Xiaoerjing*, one of the earliest phonetic representations of Chinese, transliterates

local Chinese pronunciation using the Arabic alphabet. Learning Chinese characters took a long time, while learning the Arabic alphabet was relatively easy, so some Sino-Muslims wrote their spoken vernacular in the Arabic script in which they were literate. *Ahong*s, students and others exchanged many letters in *xiaoerjing*, and textbooks for illiterate women were published in *xiaoerjing*. I have observed that in many *nüxue* – women's madrasas – in Linxia and Lanzhou, older and illiterate women learn *xiaoerjing* both to express themselves and to read religious texts. However, because *xiaoerjing* is phonetic, it differs in accordance with local dialect and thus can be very difficult to decipher.

26. Ding Shiren, '20 shiji Hezhou'; Chao Chiu-ti, *Linxia zongpai*.
27. Changde Huijiao Jiaoyu Puzhuhui, *Huiwen duben*.
28. Ma Songting, 'Zhongguo Huijiao'.
29. Ma Fulong, *Ma Fulong ahong zishu*, p. 26.
30. Zwemer, 'Islam a missionary problem', p. 184.
31. Masumi Matsumoto, 'Protestant Christian missions'.
32. Masumi Matsumoto, 'Sakuma Teijirō no tai Chūgoku'.
33. Lipman, *Familiar Strangers*, pp. 201–11.
34. Matsumoto Masumi, interview with H *ahong* and D *ahong*, 21–2 February 2013, at Tianmucun, Tianjin.
35. Ma Songting, 'Zhongguo Huijiao'.
36. Esenbel, 'Utsunomiya Tarō'.
37. Matsumoto Masumi, 'Sakuma Teijirō no tai Chūgoku'.
38. Sakamoto Tsutomu, *Nitchū sensō*; Gaimushō, 'Kakkoku ni okeru'.
39. This unit, headed by Major Shigekawa Hidekazu, inherited the functions of the Doihara Agency, part of the Japanese Army. The Shigekawa Agency came to be in charge of secret activities in Beiping and Tianjin after 1935. Its activities included dealing in opium and fabricating staged insurgencies, so it began to treat with Islam. According to Ando Jun'ichirō, 'Nitchū sensō', professional Muslim agents such as Kawamura Kyōdō and Sakuma Teijirō had no connections with this agency.
40. See the works of Shimbo Atsuko listed in the Bibliography.
41. Yamazaki Noriko, 'Nitchū sensō ki'.
42. Gaimushō, 'Kakkoku ni okeru'.
43. 'Jiaoyu jiyao'.
44. Zai Wei, 'Nüzi jiaoyu'.
45. Di Jingxiu, 'Gaishan halifa jiaoyu'.
46. Shi Zizhou, 'Huijiao jiaozhang'.

47. Tianjin qu benbu, 'Fenhui zhangcheng'; Ando Jun'ichirō, 'Nitchū sensō'.
48. Masumi Matsumoto, interview on 7 September 2010 at Ji'nan. Concerning the Japanese Army's massacre of Muslims at the Jining East Mosque, see Wang Yingqi, 'Fasheng zai qingzhensi li'.
49. Zhongguo Huijiao Zong Lianhehui, 'Zhongguo Huijiao'.
50. Mu Chengzhu and Mu Chengren, 'Mujiazhuang'.
51. Lipman, 'White hats'.

8

Between 'Abd al-Wahhab and Liu Zhi: Chinese Muslim Intellectuals at the Turn of the Twenty-first Century

Leila Chérif-Chebbi

Introduction

Two polar tendencies appear to attract contemporary Chinese Muslim intellectuals as they express their ways of thinking and representations of their Islamic faith in China, tendencies we may loosely identify with 'Liu Zhi' and ''Abd al-Wahhab'. We must deal with these as opposite poles of a spectrum. The Liu Zhi tendency includes those who try to talk about a Chinese Muslim culture, even a Chinese Islam, as a syncretic religion, a 'Neo-Confucian Islam',[1] a religion inscribed in a historical and cultural context with interpretations adapted to the times. 'Abd al-Wahhab, on the other hand, represents those who want to know and talk about Islam as a unified transcultural religion, born and defined outside China in the Arabic language, a religion that reflects ahistorical truth, meanings given by God once and for all at the time of the Prophet.

Intellectuals are here understood as those who produce ideas, diffuse them, receive recognition from a public, and act as intermediaries between the public and their ideas.[2] Today's Chinese Muslim intellectual traditions derive from a long historical process, beginning no later than the mid-seventeenth century.[3] The process, which began with Wang Daiyu and was refined by Ma Zhu, Liu Zhi and many others, has continued through the twentieth century, so Liu Zhi and his colleagues continue to inspire Chinese Muslims, especially lay intellectuals. In contrast, the admirers of 'Abd al-Wahhab (1703–92), founder of the reformist scripturalist religious school known as Wahhabiyya, mostly religious professionals or private school teachers, take their inspiration from Chinese Muslim reformists in the first part of the twentieth century, both fundamentalists and modernists, and from outside China, first in political Islam and later in Saudi-inspired Salafism.

The first part of this chapter constitutes an anthropological survey of contemporary Chinese Muslim intellectuals: who are they and how do they act? The second will explain how they arrange themselves along the spectrum between those poles of attraction, from a China-centred tradition to an exogenous Islamic tradition, and how they manage to cooperate and find a middle ground between what appear to be opposite aspirations.

For three decades, and most markedly since 2004, there have been dramatic changes inside China concerning the definition of the intellectual, one who is allowed or able to produce intellectual discourse. Since the 1980s, the Communist party-state has softened its grip on public discourse by allowing, or at least tolerating, many Islamic magazines, reviews and books to be published by private institutions or individuals. The Internet has radically enlarged the number of people who can produce discourse as well as the public who can receive it. By 'Chinese Muslim intellectuals' we intend here members of the mainly Chinese-speaking *Huizu* as well as other smaller Sinophone Muslim populations such as the Dongxiang, Salar and Bonan who live in close contact with the Hui. Conversely, the Turkic- and Farsi-speaking peoples of Xinjiang share a Central Asian culture of Islam that has few ties with Chinese Islamic culture except those created by the state, so those Xinjiang peoples fall outside the scope of this chapter.

Contemporary Chinese Islam has received scant and fragmented attention in Western and Chinese scholarship, so this chapter constitutes a preliminary and incomplete survey of Muslim intellectuals in today's China. It rests on one of the richest primary sources, the Chinese Internet, which links many of those intellectuals to one another and constitutes a national agora for debate. We must thank the desire to teach and publicise knowledge that leads Muslim websurfers to publish online many previously printed materials that would have been unavailable without them. This chapter rests on many years of collecting printed material, taking interest in who is writing and translating, and why. As a result, I have developed long-standing friendships among the actors in China's Islamic revival, enabling me to decipher pen names, to identify Internet authors and to decide who is important. Finally, I have been able to interview many people directly, both inside and, even more important, outside the academic sphere.

Who are the Intellectuals Today?

Three different categories of Muslim intellectuals emerged in China at the dawn of the twenty-first century: (1) academics, officially authorised scholars; (2) religious professionals, who, though quite numerous, publish less because their roles as imams or *ahong* oblige them to perform many religious and social functions; and (3) private lay thinkers, the latest to appear but also the most popular.

During the Great Leap Forward and the Cultural Revolution (1958–76), an entire generation was unable to express itself or even think about itself as Muslim, so contemporary intellectuals could be described as being two generations: grandfathers and grandsons, with few fathers in between. The older generation, now disappearing, was trained from the 1930s to the early 1950s. Many died during those 'twenty years of trouble', including scholars such as Pang Shiqian (1902–58),[4] Chen Keli (1923–70)[5] and Ma Jian (1905–78),[6] but some survived and since the early 1980s have resumed their writing.

Academics: a constrained discourse

Some older scholars had no choice but to follow the state-imposed rhetoric for decades, but they produced important reference works. Ma Tong (b. 1929), for example, wrote an authoritative work on Chinese Islamic groups,[7] using their internal documents and oral histories, but much of his descriptive work, like that of his colleagues, stopped after 1958. Feng Zenglie (1926–96) studied the nineteenth-century Hui uprisings[8] as well as the 'traditional non-Sufi' (*gedimu*, from Ar. *qadīm*) religious groups[9] and Chinese Muslim literati, but he, too, could not evade references to the officially required discourse of *minzu* as a component of Chinese Muslim identity. Bai Shouyi (1909–2000) was an outstanding historian of China and worked, mainly before 1949, on *Huizu* history, similarly constrained by state-imposed paradigms.[10]

Some scholars belong to the generation in between, which means that most of their learning and all of their careers took place under the Communists. Yang Huaizhong (b. 1934) began to study the *Huizu* during the Cultural Revolution and became chief editor of *Huizu yanjiu* (*Journal of Hui Muslim [Minority] Studies*). Yu Zhengui (b. 1946), a colleague with whom he produced two books,[11] became vice-president and general secretary of the Islamic Association of China, leaving Ningxia and academe for a more political and influential post in Beijing. Another important intellectual, Lin Song (1930–2015) – the son of an Azharite[12] from Shadian in Yunnan – is famous for his rhymed translation of the *Qurʾān* and other Chinese works on the *Qurʾān* and Islamic culture. Much respected among Chinese Muslims, he has written numerous articles in Muslim newspapers and prefaces to co-religionists' published books.[13]

The youngest generation of Chinese Muslim scholars, some of whom studied outside China, positions itself farther from state power and has been more active in socio-religious activities and as academics. As practising Muslims, they try to produce positive knowledge about Islam in China – especially stressing their own religious group, if they belong to one – and they often describe the compatibility of Islam with the Chinese world order.

Examples from northwest China would include Ma Mingliang (b. 1961), from the Salar *minzu*, born in Xunhua in Qinghai province, who studied at the Minzu University of China before going to Kuwait University in 1987. After returning to China, he first taught in his home province, then in Ningxia, finally becoming head of the Department of Islamic Research at Northwest Minzu University in Lanzhou (Gansu) in 2005. In 2012, he received a prize from the Central Minzu Commission (*Zhongyang Minzu Weiyuanhui*) for his work.[14] Ma Mingliang is also very popular inside Muslim circles because he often participates in conferences and meetings held outside the official academy at private schools and mosques.

Ding Shiren (b. 1966), born in Lintan (Gansu), is now professor in the Department of Philosophy of Lanzhou University (Gansu). Quite unusual among Chinese scholars, he did not receive his BA or doctorate at a Chinese university, but rather studied at the Lanzhou Islamic Institute beginning in 1984 and was sent to the International Islamic University in Islamabad, Pakistan, in 1986, where he received his doctorate in 2003, returning to

Lanzhou to teach at the university. Since 2008, he has edited a professional journal, *Islamic Culture*,[15] which publishes the contributions of many non-academic scholars.

A remarkable representative of this new generation of intellectuals is Ma Qiang (b. 1972), from Xiji in the Ningxia Hui Autonomous Region, who earned his doctorate in anthropology at Guangzhou's Zhongshan University. Currently a professor at the Center for Studies of Northwest Minzu at the Xi'an Normal University and a practising Muslim, he is said to have petitioned for (and won) a *halal* dining hall at Zhongshan University in Guangzhou.[16] His interests are diverse, focusing on contemporary Muslim communities and new forms of religious practice. Unusual in an academic culture that valorises local scholars studying their own places, Ma Qiang has published on Muslim communities in Guangzhou,[17] Xi'an,[18] Lanzhou and Ningxia, as well as Chinese converts to Islam in China and Malaysia.[19]

These academics produce official and normative intellectual discourse and serve as references not only in academic circles, but also amongst the mass of Chinese Muslims, especially those involved in practise and dissemination of knowledge. Ma Mingliang demonstrates that Chinese Muslim intellectuals are not defined only as members of one *minzu*, but rather belong to a larger Chinese Islamic culture, common throughout the Chinese culture area. That huge zone could be divided into three regional subcultures: the northwest; the northeast, central and coastal China; and the southwest and south. All the Muslims of this vast area share similar ways of organising themselves into religious groups and read works by the same intellectuals, whereas the Turkic-speaking peoples of Xinjiang have their own academic culture and influential figures.

Religious scholars

*Ahong*s and other religious professionals associated with mosques have experienced the same generational gaps as academic scholars. They stopped working for nearly twenty years during the Great Leap Forward and Cultural Revolution, and many suffered direct persecution. Some died, and the survivors have been granted official positions and treated with utmost respect, even if they have to be helped by younger colleagues. Ma Songting (1895–1992), for example, was categorised as one of the 'Four Great Imams' of the

Republican era (1912–49), then survived until the 1990s and played a symbolic role, serving the government and receiving public honours in return.[20] We may divide the religious professionals into two groups: 'political' *ahong*s, who aid the state by supervising practice and doctrine; and a new generation of younger *ahong*s.

*Ahong*s working for the government, acting and writing in order to please it, denouncing activists who 'trouble social harmony', and enjoying privileges in return, are nicknamed 'political *ahong*s' (*zhengzhi ahong*). Like academics, they create and control a normative discourse. They publish books of sermons delivered at Friday communal prayers,[21] and, since 1996, have even organised nationwide sermon-writing competitions, and later at the provincial level.[22] The soft but extensive control exerted by the Islamic Association of China (*Zhongguo Yisilanjiao Xiehui*, hereafter abbreviated as *Yixie*) has generated eagerness to participate in those competitions and publish sermons pleasing to the authorities, for winning a prize can boost a young *ahong*'s career. The *Yixie* was founded in 1953 by the Communist Party and included Muslim religious professionals, directors of religious groups, scholars and political leaders. Since the 1980s, it has created branches at every administrative level, from province to small town, enforcing state control over all Islamic institutional and social life. It is the major institutional mediator between the governmental administration and Muslim people in the realm of religion.

From the 1980s to the mid-1990s, the *Yixie* resumed its activities but still did not dare to impose its own normative discourse. But since the mid-1990s, it has begun to control textbooks and teaching materials for all levels of religious education and to dictate the interpretation of the sacred books. The *Yixie* apparently seeks to control the process called *jiejing*,[23] 'explaining the Scriptures' – Qur'ān and *ḥadīth* (*Shengxun*) – the official term preferred by the state over *jiangjing* 'discussing/disputing the Scriptures'. The latter term, widely used among Chinese Muslims, refers to a theological debate or discussion. As one *Yixie* official said, 'explaining' the Qur'ān must 'match society's progress'.[24]

The most remarkable of the 'political *ahong*s' is Chen Guangyuan (b. 1932), appointed imam of the only mosque to remain open during the Cultural Revolution after 1966 (to welcome foreign Muslims) and later head of the *Yixie*. He was proud to stress in a sermon that he did not suffer during the Cultural Revolution because he always behaved properly.[25] He authored *An Ahong's Manual for the New Age*,[26] a *vade mecum* of good practice congenial to the state. This manual demonstrates the growing interest of state power in managing Islamic behaviour and knowledge.

Ahong Ma Xian (b. 1929) from Ningxia, pupil and son-in-law of the famous *Ikhwan*[27] imam Hu Songshan (1880–1956),[28] went to Beijing in 1952 to specialise in religious and Arabic studies. He was able to work in religious affairs even during the Cultural Revolution, mostly on Arabic translations, but could not escape twice being sent to the countryside for 're-education through labour'. As one of the vice-presidents of the *Yixie* after 1981 and general secretary from 1987 to 1993, he was a main leader of the *Yixie*'s effort to revive religious institutions and to harmonise relations among religious groups.[29] Ma Xian remains vice-president of many official associations. He authored *Questions and Answers: General Knowledge of Islam*, among other books, and has written many articles.[30] He also translated a collection of *ḥadīth*, published in 2002,[31] as a major task of contemporary fundamentalists lies in making religious texts available to Muslims without intermediaries. This applies especially to the *ḥadīth*, considered the most reliable religious reference after the *Qur'ān*, transcending exegesis of the four main legal traditions or, in China, traditional imams' explanations. Today all six main collections of *ḥadīth* are available in Chinese translation.[32]

A new generation of imams has appeared, educated in modern schools in China, in private religious schools or in Islamic studies institutes, many of whom studied abroad. Often called *Salafis* because of their training in Saudi Arabia and their uncompromising attitude, even if they deny it, these *ahong*s constitute the core of the 'Abd al-Wahhab tendency. During the 1990s these new graduates were reluctant to take charge of a mosque community, and those communities would have preferred an old-style *ahong*, someone who understood their customs and daily problems, and with enough life experience to be a moral guide. Since then, however, having matured, they appear to be accepting leading roles in mosques. Yunnan province, for instance, has a number of imams who studied in Saudi Arabia. Recently many articles and discussions have appeared online about *ahongs*' obligations and duties, criticising conservatism, and encouraging them to take part in the new era.[33] Two books were published on *ahongs*' lives and duties, titled *The Ahong's*

Burden[34] and *One Imam's Ten Years of Soul-searching*;[35] we should note that both authors have been awarded prizes in sermon competitions.

Some *ahong*s have also become web activists, 'online *ahong*s' (*ahong zaixian*), giving advice ranging from very private concerns to theological interpretations, as is common elsewhere in the Muslim world. The site that first developed this kind of advice has classified its answers by topics: doctrine (76 answers); holy books (11); sharing faith with others and conversion (66); Islamic family (212); Islamic education (9); Islamic society (271); and legal matters such as funerals, prayers in times of trouble, travels and holy days (167).[36] As evidence, the social topics are particularly worth Chinese Muslims' attention. Internet advice has given online *ahong*s unprecedented regional and nationwide influence that was impossible before the Internet. For example, 'China Muslims'[37] started its webzine with a portrait of a new imam, *ahong* Alif, who stresses that websurfing has not changed his identity as an *ahong*, but just adapted it to the new communication era: 'We must use new means to build new *jama'a* (community), and the Net is a good choice.'[38] Along with written advice, the web offers Chinese Muslims filmed conferences, lectures and sermons by *ahong*s and other intellectuals. However, since the late 2000s, online materials, especially filmed sermons, have been disappearing due to enhanced state control on Internet content.

These new *ahong*s experience more diversity and discontinuities in their careers and activities than their older colleagues, who intended life-long careers as religious professionals once they 'donned their cloak' (*chuanyi*), a Chinese Muslim expression for the graduation of *ahong*s, who wear a green coat at their ordination ceremony.[39] The new religious professionals, having studied outside China, in private Muslim schools or in governmental institutes, can become teachers in private schools, writers or translators before taking the office of *ahong*. They can also start their career as *ahong*, go abroad later to improve language and religious knowledge, and then return to China as teachers or even earn an advanced degree.[40] They find it hard to accept staying in one place for years with a modest salary and attached to one congregation, when a learned young man might gain a nationwide audience, travel across China for conferences at schools, mosques or even universities, write books and articles, and appear in filmed sermons or lessons. One Lanzhou *ahong* was even running a business in Guangzhou, 2,200 km from home, commuting by plane to combine his two occupations. The multi-occupational and discontinuous careers of these new *ahong*s make them more similar to the third category of intellectuals than their predecessors.

Laoshis *or 'scholars without positions'*

The third category can be called 'scholars without positions', or the *laoshi* category. *Laoshi* (teacher) is the honorific title given to those who have acquired intellectual status without having received an official title. They do not obtain state college or university degrees or, if they do, they are not involved in official academic research. The older generation of *laoshi*s includes retired public officials as well as high school and middle school teachers. Younger *laoshi*s may have a mosque or a private Muslim school education, but some are eager to go to university and join China's top intellectual circles. Some want to write doctoral dissertations. They are all committed to religion and related cultural activities. Many believe that they have revived and modernised the knowledge and the propagation of Islamic faith amongst Muslims.

Most of the 'scholars without position' work as private school teachers or headmasters. The older generation, founders of China's 'Sino-Arabic' schools (*Zhong-A xuexiao*), or 'popular' schools (*minban xuexiao*),[41] include people like the Henan *ahong* Huang Wanjun (1919–2013), who taught undercover in the 1970s in Inner Mongolia and established the first Muslim school in Henan in 1978.[42] He opened modern Arabic learning to female students, whereas female *ahong*s studied primarily the Persian language in central China. Huang Wanjun's example, encouraging his pupils to spread female education,[43] was first followed in Linxia (Gansu), then in Ningxia and Yunnan, and later all over China.[44]

Ma Enxin (b. 1927), from Yunnan, first studied in a village mosque school, then went to a modern Muslim school in the Weishan area of western Yunnan – Ma Zhu's home region (see Lipman, Chapter 1, this volume) – from 1947 to 1950. He specialised in Arabic translation, and in 1956 taught at the Kunming Normal School. In 1958, he was sent for re-education by labour for four years, worked in transport, was jailed after the 'Shadian incident' in 1975,[45] and freed in 1978. He taught at mosques, at the government's Kunming Islamic Institute for two years after its creation in 1987, and at the Islamic Cultural Center of Najiaying village up to 1997, when he retired because of health problems. He published some twenty-five books, mainly translations of Islamic doctrine, and booklets concerning rituals as well as political Islamic writings, mostly in collaboration with Hong Kong Muslims.[46]

A third member of the older generation, Bahā' al-Dīn Ma Zhixin (1934–2012), known as *Baha Ahong*, grew up in a Sufi family near Linxia in Gansu. Educated in mosque schools, he was jailed in 1958 and released one year later. In 1972, he began to teach an evening class, undercover, to four students, two males and two females. His teaching expanded and, in 1980, he officially founded the Linxia Sino-Arabic School with 120 students, one building for male students, another for female students. His school became the most important and successful of its kind, graduating more than 5,000 students, at least 600 of whom studied outside China. Graduates became translators, businessmen linked with the Muslim world and teachers in similar 'popular' schools. Some became imams in charge of mosques, others studied and taught at governmental Islamic institutes, and a few entered the official universities. In 2007, due to its success and under governmental pressure, the school accepted state financial help and became the Linxia Foreign Language School.[47]

Ma Zhixin's goal, like that of the Republican era modern Muslim schools (see Cieciura, Chapter 5, and Matsumoto, Chapter 7, this volume), lay in educating faithful Muslims, literate in both Chinese and Arabic, able to work in various milieus. He defined his mission as 'to teach, but more important, to educate people, and for both students and teachers, to put moral education in first place', thus conforming to both Chinese and Islamic traditional culture and values.[48] In his view, ethics, even more than knowledge, must leave its imprint on young Muslims.

Honorary director of his school since 1997, Ma Zhixin spent much time travelling inside and outside China,[49] meeting people, giving lectures and lobbying for his school. He also opened a female branch, whose headteacher after 1989 was his first female pupil, Ma Xiulan, who still firmly dominates the female school, earlier called the Sino-Arabic Girls' School and today Linxia Foreign Language Institute branch school. This older generation, as these examples show, dedicated itself to work as religious professionals, or *ahong*, though only one of them remained employed as an *ahong*. The two others took a less traditional path, deepening their influence on the new generation.

Let us also examine the new generation, the men who run the 'Islamic Study City' (*Yisilan xueshu cheng*) or the 'Islamic bookstore' (*Qingzhen shuju*)[50] website in Beijing, founded in 2003.[51] They say they originated from provincial towns and studied in mosques or private Sino-Arabic schools. After their studies, they went to Beijing in search of knowledge and culture, that is, Chinese culture. Unable to pay high fees or to pass the university entrance exams, they became auditors at Beida, China's premier university. Eager to share their knowledge with their co-religionists, they built their website to sell books, CDs and DVDs online, printing their own works and reprinting old Sino-Muslim and Islamic books. They participate in conferences and academic meetings to collect books. They also locate and provide articles from libraries on demand. Alongside cultural openness and a thirst for knowledge, they remain deeply committed to religious orthopraxy.[52]

One representative of this new generation travelled a great distance. Kang Youxi (b. 1969) came from a very poor Sufi family in Ningxia. Sent to Wuzhong to be educated in a mosque's boarding school, he later chose to study with diverse imams: Sufi, traditional non-Sufi and Wahhabi-inspired. He went to Linxia and studied there before joining the Linxia Sino-Arabic School in 1989. With the founder's financial help, he went to Beijing to pursue knowledge from 1991 to 2000, following courses as an auditor. He translated a collection of *ḥadīth*, the *Ṣaḥīḥ al-Bukhārī* (*The Authentic al-Bukhari*),[53] and booklets of Sufi inspiration. Surprisingly, he then left China and settled in the United States in 2000, where for some time he headed a website for Chinese Muslims living in America and was the editor of a few religious books, undertaking his own translations. His autobiography[54] provides insightful and lively reports of Chinese Muslim activism, including his report on the May 1989 demonstrations in Linxia against a book insulting Islam:

> When I was studying the Scriptures in Linxia, one day, suddenly, the ahongs of the mosques gathered all the religious students [*manla*, from Ar. *mulla*] and the mosques' congregations (*fangmin*) to take to the streets to demonstrate and express their condemnation. They explained it was aimed

at asking the government to enforce the Constitutional right to respect religion, and to punish *Xing Fengsu*'s [Sexual Customs] authors and publishing house, because the content of the book profoundly and grossly insulted Islam.⁵⁵ At that time, I did not understand anything about demonstrations . . .⁵⁶

As noted above, this new generation were educated at mosques or Muslim schools, but it did not suffice for them to feel fully educated. To consider him- or herself a learned person, a Muslim in a more open and developing China cannot rest entirely on religious knowledge. This attitude is similar to that of young imams who have diversified their careers.

Other non-academic scholars have become magazine journalists and publishers. In 1992, Han Haichao, officially registered in the Salar *minzu*, founded *Kaituo*, one of the longest-lasting Chinese Muslim private magazines, in Lanzhou, Gansu.⁵⁷ Though its staff has changed, Han Haichao has remained in charge, getting in touch with China's main Muslim intellectuals and asking them to send articles. His publication is one of very few Muslim magazines, except those produced by local branches of the government-sponsored *Yixie*, to receive official approval. He clearly states that if any article criticises government policy or fuels Muslim religious animosities, he will not publish it.⁵⁸ In China today, anyone who aims to keep writing or publishing must adopt those principles.

In the intricate milieu of Muslim intellectuals, we may also find writers and essayists such as Yisima'er ('Ismāʿīl) Zhang Chengqian, a relative of the great imam Wang Jingzhai (1879–1948). Without a proper religious education, Zhang Chengqian published a number of books: *The Call of Islam* (1992);⁵⁹ a commentary on the *Qurʾān* (2005);⁶⁰ and *Peaceful Belief and Humankind's Final Goal* (2012).⁶¹ His books created a buzz in China because they express open-minded, progressive and controversial views, focusing solely on the *Qurʾān*'s text and asking readers to take a critical distance even from the *ḥadīth*. Zhang Chengqian has been accused of being an Ahmadi;⁶² a charge of heterodoxy by fundamentalists who consider Ahmadis to be non-Muslims.

Other *laoshi*s work as webmasters. After being a journalist in official media, Ma Yuming, from Lanzhou, known as Xiao Ma A-ge, with other young activists founded a Muslim newspaper and then the website www.2muslim.com, opened in October 2003),⁶³ one of the most successful and richest in content of Chinese Muslim sites. Wuhuaguo (a pseudonym),⁶⁴ from Xi'an, studied in Lahore, Pakistan, and authored many books on Islam. He actively promoted conversion, and for this purpose created a Muslim website⁶⁵ in December 2002 to publicise his views and to encouragement conversion. Having created considerable enmity with his unorthodox views,⁶⁶ especially in his hometown of Xi'an, he left both his website and Xi'an in 2008, becoming a small town mosque's *ahong* in 2010.

These self-made scholars have been important in shaping contemporary Chinese Muslim opinion. Their influence is wider than that of academic scholars because they have greater access to their Muslim audience; they are less intimidating than famed scholars or solemn imams. They are less committed to the authorities' official discourse than academics or even successful *ahong*s. The general public can also consult these *laoshi*s on questions of religion and morals, especially on the web. They have more venues in which to express themselves – private publications, magazines, conferences and the Internet – whereas academics or official *ahong*s must be more circumspect, even if they can publish or speak in private institutions.

One category extends over all three categories described above, the people called scholars (*xuezhe*), a group that could include academics, religious professionals and non-academic intellectuals. For Muslims, the term carries respect for both religious knowledge and the ability to express it within the Chinese language and culture. A religious scholar not at ease with Chinese will be called *erlin*, transliterating the Arabic word *'ālim*. Contemporary Chinese use *xuezhe* to describe the seventeenth–twentieth-century scholars discussed in the previous chapters, including those who went to al-Azhar during the 1930s and 1940s. It now includes not only the oldest generation's most respected intellectuals, such as Ma Enxin and Ma Zhixin, but also the new generation of intellectuals, such as Zhang Weizhen (b. 1963), Qi Xueyi and others.⁶⁷

The new generation, after its appearance during the 1990s, has gained recognition for its intellectual value among Muslims since the millennium. Reversing the shift observed by Zvi Ben-Dor Benite, from literati to *'ulema* during the first part of the twentieth century,⁶⁸ in the 2000s many intellectuals shifted back from *'ulema* to literati. Benite observed a shift at the beginning of the twentieth century from literati expressing themselves exclusively inside Chinese culture and aiming to underline the compatibility of Islam with China's culture and world order, to *'ulema* who wanted to learn outside and to (re)link Chinese Islam to the Muslim heartlands. Fifty years later, referring to those *'ulema*, many Chinese Muslims studied either in the outside Muslim world or studied from it. But in the twenty-first century, they have shown a desire to return to the Chinese cultural milieu, or to adapt Islamic knowledge to China; that is, after acquiring *'ulema* status they desire literati recognition.

We cannot conclude our analysis of these categories of intellectuals without noting that one category is almost completely missing, namely women. Very few women have entered Chinese Muslim intellectual circles, with the exception of a few professors and researchers, but they rarely intervene in social and religious activities. Perhaps as they do not wear a veil, which during the last twenty years has become the major symbol of women's religious commitment, these female academics are not considered relevant to Islamic intellectual work. The female imams (*nü ahong*) teach but do not write essays. We also found a handful of schoolteachers, like Ma Xiulan,[69] who perfected her Arabic in Beijing and later Malaysia. She authored three translations, two of them on Muslim women's issues, and in 1994 founded a monthly magazine, *Muslim Women* (*Musilin funü*), which published forty-six issues and is said to have had a great influence on women[70] and converts.

One main dividing line within all these categories is the opposition between secular or academic knowledge, on the one hand, and religious activism, on the other, sometimes combined with a popular rejection of Hanification, assimilation to Chinese culture (*hanhua*). Now we may explore their positions and how they managed to achieve a level of compromise.

Liu Zhi and 'Abd al-Wahhab: Secularised Academics versus Devout Muslims?

Let us now investigate how Chinese Muslim intellectuals have arranged themselves between the two poles constituted by Liu Zhi and 'Abd al-Wahhab. This means taking a position between a national Chinese Islam entirely compatible with Chinese nationalism, and a transnational (transcultural) idea of religious praxis and doctrine, a universalising religious orthodoxy and orthopraxy that might condemn or negate local cultures and praxis.

The inheritors of Liu Zhi

Chinese Muslim intellectuals, especially the secular and non-practising scholars, insist on the existence of a national Islam rooted in Chinese culture. The other chapters in this volume describe the issues and transformations of this stance, as do earlier publications, such as Kristian Petersen's article 'Reconstructing Islam',[71] James Frankel's *Rectifying God's Name*[72] and Sachiko Murata's *Chinese Gleams of Sufi Light*.[73] This Chinese Islam was defined during the seventeenth and eighteenth centuries by scholars who called themselves 'Islamic Neo-Confucians' or 'Muslim literati' (*Huiru*).[74] With a few exceptions, these authors were secular literati who did not take up religious positions. Writing in Chinese, they aimed to explain Islam to co-religionists educated in Chinese and to non-Muslims, in order to make it compatible with orthodox Chinese philosophical views. Liu Zhi, whose book was included in the catalogue of the *Siku quanshu*,[75] appears as the most perfect master of so-called syncretism. This chapter does not aim to discuss these past scholars' actual accomplishments, but rather to stress the importance of this classical Muslim literature for contemporary scholars and to underline its place in the debate on national 'Chinese Islam'.

For the supporters of Liu Zhi, mostly Muslim academic scholars, Islam has become part of Chinese culture. As Yang Huaizhong and Yu Zhengui wrote, 'The Islamic culture of China is a branch of the world's Islamic culture and at the same time it is also a constitutive part of China's civilization.'[76] Could those words have been written by a non-Muslim Chinese scholar? To express these views Muslim intellectuals walked along a twisted path between considering Islam as a universal religion and as a patrilineal religion transmitted by blood. Therefore, many Sino-Muslims, called *Huizu* in the 'ethnicity classification' categories of the People's Republic of China, have found it crucial to claim foreign origin and some physical (genetically transmitted) features that would distinguish them from non-Muslim Chinese, usually called Han.[77] The question of Han who converted to Islam outside marriage ties, in considerable numbers in some places, is still a sensitive topic for Chinese Muslims, except for some freelance essayists.

As discussed by Cieciura (Chapter 5, this volume), the debate about Islam and Muslims started during the Republican period. Is Islam (*Huijiao*) a culture of one specific people (the *Huizu*)? Or is it a religion of different peoples that settled in China, like Buddhism or Christianity?[78] After 1949, the Communists closed the debate for nearly fifty years by creating the rigid categories of 'minority *minzu*' (*shaoshu minzu*), among them the *Huizu*. In this they met the expectations of some Sino-Muslims, who did not want to be considered as Han (Chinese) who believed in Islam.[79] The Communists created – or 'differentiated' (*shibie*) – other minority groups of Islamic faith, such as the Dongxiang, the Salar and the Bao'an *minzu*, incorporating some Muslim Mongols, some Muslim Tibetans, the Utsat (Malays) of Hainan and Muslim Thais into the *Huizu*, but excluding others. During the Cultural Revolution, Islam was considered to be an element of minority folklore that would naturally disappear with social evolution.

From the late 1950s to the 1980s, Chinese scholars had little or no access to foreign academic literature and consequently had references only inside their own *minzu* paradigm. The *Huizu* historian Bai Shouyi and the Han sociologist Fei Xiaotong (1910–2005),[80] both trained before 1949, constituted the highest authorities. Since the 1980s, some scholars have been able to slowly extricate themselves from the 'minority trap' that had forced them to refer consistently to 'minority culture, folklore and customs' when considering Islam. Many academic works bearing *Huizu* in their titles actually deal with Muslims and Islam in China.

The *minzu* paradigm traps Islam in fixed *minzu* boundaries and makes it difficult or even impossible to develop connections outside the *minzu*. It separates Hui Muslims from other domestic Muslim minorities, like the Uighurs, and it causes the conversion of non-Muslim Chinese to look odd. For instance, Wuhuaguo (a pseudonym), the founder of a website mainly devoted to conversion, explains[81] that if Islamic proselytism cannot develop, it is because the Han consider Islam as the *Huizu* minority's religion, so who would dare to convert to Islam? Some Sino-Muslims themselves do not want to proselytise for the same reason. Islam has been ethnicised (*minzuhua*), although historically over the centuries of Islam's presence in China, people from various cultures – Chinese, Mongol, Manchu, Tibetan, Thai and more – chose to believe in Islam. Wuhuaguo differentiates three processes of diffusion of Islam: (1) the settling of foreign Muslim merchants, soldiers, craftsmen and others from the Tang to the Yuan dynasty, who married local women; (2) conversion of non-Han, mainly Mongols and Manchus; and (3) the conversion of Han. In private he went further to argue that there are so many Muslims in China today because Han converted in great numbers.[82] He thus questions the presumption of 'blood transmission' in the history of the *Huizu*.

From minzu *to Muslim*

Today, the discourse shifts from *Huizu* to Muslims, depending on the Islamic practice of the Muslim academic professionals and officials, and also on their desire to please the atheistic Communist authorities or their fellow Muslims. A typical example of this shifting discourse is the English translation of the title of the academic journal *Huizu yanjiu*. When founded in 1991, it was translated as *Researches on the Hui Nationality*, but in 2004, without any change in the Chinese title, it became the *Journal of Hui Muslim Minority Studies*. In the process of (re)interpreting China's Islamic history, scholars have done many studies about Liu Zhi and the seventeenth–nineteenth-century 'Muslim literati'. The Qing period texts have been reprinted in simplified characters or in vernacular Chinese (*baihua*) for clarity, and old manuscripts have been edited and re-published by both academic and non-academic Muslim scholars. An abundant literature utilises commonplace phrases such as 'using Confucianism to explain Islam' (*yi Ru shi Yi*)[83] and 'using Confucianism to comment on the Scriptures' (*yi Ru quan Jing*).[84] To its opponents, this Neo-Confucian expression of Islam – the past four centuries of Chinese-language literature on Islam – appears to be 'opposing the Scriptures and diverging from [correct] customs' (*fan Jing yi su*).[85] The contemporary Muslim community's most respected academic scholar, Lin Song, has refuted this assessment,[86] denying that this Chinese-language literature embodies unorthodox views. In conclusion, the recent shift from understanding Islam as an ethnic religion to recognising it as a universal religion parallel to or inside Chinese culture has eased the way towards a middle ground between the poles of my title: a Chinese culture of Islam and a universal religion unlikely to accommodate any syncretism or local accretions.

The 'Han Studies faction'

Apart from the numerous scholarly studies devoted to a specific Chinese national expression of Islam, one of the most surprising developments of Liu Zhi's heritage was the Xidaotang (The Hall of the Western *Dao*). Xidaotang is a religious group founded in Lintan, Gansu, at the dawn of the twentieth century; its ideology and expressions blend the writings of Liu Zhi with Sufi practices and organisation. Previously called the 'Han Studies faction' (*Hanxuepai*) in Gansu, its adherents used to live together in communes, sending envoys outside for lucrative commercial activities, especially with Tibetans, and put a special emphasis on the education of both men and women.

The Muslim warlord Ma Anliang attacked the Xidaotang in 1914, looted its wealthy central commune, and killed its founder Ma Qixi (1857–1914), calling him and his followers heretics. Another master took the lead, and the order revived and flourished due to its commercial ties with Tibet, for which Xidaotang followers learned Tibetan in school. The nascent People's Republic of China cracked down on the Xidaotang in 1954, a time when there was, as yet, little repression against Muslims. Though the Xidaotang was reported extinct at the beginning of the 1980s,[87] it nonetheless again regenerated and developed at an amazing speed. It has recovered its wealth, re-educated its children and revived a very active community life in Lintan. To describe their communal life and their organisation, an American scholar jokingly called it a 'kibbutz', a comparison that had great success in China.[88]

Contemporary researchers and many Muslim intellectuals developed a fascination with Xidaotang studies. Chinese scholars went to Lintan, the Xidaotang's centre, for symposiums and research visits.[89] The Xidaotang's heritage of historical documents has been published by the organisation's current *shaykh*, Min Shengguang (b. 1936), including the first master's writings and a broad collection of secondary works.[90] More useful for the government, he is one of the vice-presidents of the *Yixie* and has developed a very patriotic discourse. The Xidaotang represents the acme of 'Liu Zhi' Chinese Islam in the northwest, being expressed in Chinese, based on Liu Zhi's own writings, and maintaining the form and style of northwestern Sufi brotherhoods.[91] In that sense, it certainly deserves attention. However, considering the small number of its adherents and its few converts, it has little influence on Islam in China outside southern Gansu.

Intellectuals and Chinese Islamic tradition

It is not only non-practising *Huizu* academics that underline a Chinese culture of Islam, but also practising Muslim academics and intellectuals, some having studied abroad in Pakistan or Saudi Arabia. They feel more attached to their Chinese religious solidarities, whether Sufi or traditional Islam (*gedimu*), and undertake fieldwork on Islam in China, promoting the study and appraisal of local Islamic knowledge and scholars. As one of those scholars commented, 'You have to go to the rural areas, talk many times with ahongs, and they will let you know their traditions, their rich and wide knowledge preserved through centuries.' In private those intellectuals criticise the 'Abd al-Wahhab tendency for not undertaking more than superficial fieldwork. For them, the 'Abd al-Wahhab tendency not only does not pay enough attention to Islam as actually practised in China, but has also acquired only a superficial and partial knowledge of classical Islam, including the *sharī'a* (Islamic law).[92]

The inheritors of 'Abd al-Wahhab

The followers of 'Abd al-Wahhab form the other pole of contemporary Chinese Muslim thought. A new assembly of intellectuals and religious activists has emerged, mostly trained in Sino-Arabic schools and later abroad (mostly in Pakistan, Egypt and Saudi Arabia), who were initiated into political Islam in the late 1980s, and later into Saudi Arabian Wahhabism and Salafism. During the 1990s, they tried to deny the validity of culturally Chinese Islam by raising the flag of universal Islamic unity and uniqueness, expressed in only one language, Arabic. Because of their religious inspiration, other Chinese Muslims called them *Salafiyya*, referring to a religious trend that had appeared earlier in China, at the end of the 1930s.

Generally speaking, the transnational, transcultural *Salafiyya* has a common creed based on strict adherence to the concept of God's oneness (Ar. *tawhīd*). It rejects the role of human reason, logic and desire, and advocates following only the guidance of the *Qur'ān* and the Sunna, without any imitation of earlier scholars or cultural adaptation.[93] Salafis consider other sources of explanation or traditions – for example, the four legal schools of jurisprudence – to be useless at best, if not condemnable innovations. Education must lead Muslims to master the original texts of the *Qur'ān* and the *ḥadīth*, and therein lies the significance of the numerous Sino-Arabic schools – called 'proselytising' (Ar. *da'wa*) schools by some Muslims – established by fundamentalist Muslims in China, generally located outside individual mosques in order to overcome factional affiliations.

Historical Wahhabi-inspired movements in China

'Abd al-Wahhab followers are called 'Salafis' in China. In that context, the Chinese word *Sailaifeiye* refers to two different movements of Wahhabi–Salafi trends, born at different historical times. The first is the 'historical Salafiyya', referred to in China as a religious solidarity or faction (*jiaopai*). It appeared in Linxia, Gansu, in the late 1930s as a breakaway from a previous Wahhabi-inspired trend, the *Ikhwan* ('Brothers'). Deeply influenced by Wahhabism during his pilgrimage and studies in Mecca, Ma Wanfu (1853–1934), founded the *Ikhwan* at the end of the nineteenth century. He and his supporters opposed traditional Islam and Sufi orders, which they considered deviant. Though influenced by Wahhabism, the *Ikhwan* did not claim to have left the mainstream Hanafi school of jurisprudence, and therefore won an early twentieth-century Muslim warlord's political support. Eventually, the evolving *Ikhwan* rejected any link with Wahhabism in order to influence Chinese Muslims, whose prejudices against Wahhabism rose to a high level because Wahhabis destroyed historical heritage sites and places of popular worship in Mecca and Medina – including the houses and tombs of the Prophet's family – in 1806 and 1925. The *Ikhwan* has managed to keep popular and political support for a century and still maintains a position of influence inside the Chinese government's administration of religions.[94]

The 'historical *Salafiyya*' appeared in 1936 in Linxia, led by two *Ikhwan* imams who responded to Wahhabi propaganda in Saudi Arabia during their pilgrimage and began their own proselytisation work. For years the *Salafiyya* remained quite local, due to both Muslim warlords' and the *Ikhwan*'s determined opposition. Other Chinese Muslims often call the historical *Salafiyya* by the Chinese name *Santai* (Three Elevations), for they raise their hands thrice during prayers while others do so only once. Following the Communists' rise to power in 1949, the crackdown on the *Salafiyya* stopped, but its development remained slow after the late 1950s, when the regime banned nearly all religious activities for twenty years.

The historical *Salafiyya* has produced no great intellectuals working in Chinese, because of regional limitations and its insistence on reading core sources only in Arabic. A southern Chinese convert, in the late 1990s, stated that the historical *Salafiyya* headquarters mosque in Linxia, the Xinwangsi mosque, was led by an imam who could hardly be understood because he spoke only the local dialect. Moreover, he had not been well trained in Chinese writing.[95] In Linxia itself, the historical Salafi headquarters has a rival, the Qianheyan mosque. This mosque, closely linked with Saudi Arabia, was magnificently rebuilt in the 2000s and runs a modern religious school for both males and females. The 'historical Salafis' do call themselves Salafis; though facing much opposition from fellow Muslims, they are recognised as a legitimate religious group by the Chinese government.

'Neo-Salafis' in the late 1980s

In contrast, the more recent Wahhabi–Salafi movement is not a formally constituted religious group, but a trend composed of members of the older generation of *laoshi*s, who evolved with China's opening to the Muslim world in the late 1980s, as well as a new generation of former students of religious schools and international Islamic universities. This new generation of 'Abd al-Wahhab inheritors also includes young *Ikhwan* adherents trained outside China or influenced by globalised Salafism. All refuse to be called 'Salafi', saying that they identify with Islam and nothing more. Often disadvantaged by poor education in Chinese, they did not dispute directly with intellectuals advocating 'national Islam'. In private, academic scholars mocked these Salafi intellectuals, saying that their translations and essays are very badly written. During the 1990s, this new trend propagated primarily foreign Muslim views by translating into Chinese large numbers of religious works, explanations of Islam, law textbooks, teaching materials, proselytisation booklets and essays, mostly from Arabic and to a lesser extent from English.

The earlier generation of Muslim activists, due to ties created with the Middle East in the 1990s, includes defenders of 'Abd al-Wahhab. Bahā' al-Dīn Ma Zhixin, founder of China's most famous private Muslim school, careful to avoid identification with any Islamic group, has been called 'Salafi' by some opponents, who accused him in addition of having his school financed by Saudi Arabia.[96] In a posthumous tribute, a Saudi religious professor praised him as a reformer and a proselytiser influenced in his religious reformist views by Muhammad ibn 'Abd al-Wahhab. This professor added that Baha al-Din Ma Zhixin hoped that Chinese Muslim people could publicly acknowledge the 'Wahhabi doctrine' and not criticise it.[97]

The other great teacher and translator from Yunnan, Ma Enxin,[98] also expressed his utmost admiration, explaining that 'Abd al-Wahhab was slandered by European colonialists and by some servile Muslims, that he wanted to purify religion, to restore the creed of God's uniqueness, and to restore a practice of Islam similar to the practice of the first three generations after the Prophet Muhammad (that is, the *Salaf*). In his long defence of 'Abd al-Wahhab's teachings, Ma Enxin exposed the classical defence of the Saudi clerics,[99] who claim that Wahhabism is a reformist branch of the mainstream Hanbali school of jurisprudence, one of the four schools recognised by all Sunni Muslims. Therefore, those clerics evade, as did Ma Enxin, the main accusation thrown against Wahhabi–Salafis, that of denying the traditional schools and creating another sectarian group, introducing discord (Ar. *fitna*) amongst Muslims. It must be underlined that some Saudi clerics do now recognise followers of a 'Wahhabi doctrine', taking pride in what was, and still is, a negatively regarded name in the traditional Muslim world.

Members of the new 'Abd al-Wahhab trend deny the name 'Salafi', thus opposing the 'historical Salafis' described above. This new generation, with its new practice and new sources of inspiration, tends to create currents or schools inside their original religious group, Salafi or *Ikhwan*. They argue they are renewing methods of teaching, addressing all religious groups, and attending to women's education. In the northwest, women traditionally did not go to the mosque for prayer and did not receive religious education outside their homes. The Neo-Salafis claim new and modern inspiration from the Muslim world. Having translated political Islamic thinkers during the 1990s – mainly the Egyptian Muslim Brotherhood and the Pakistani advocate of an Islamic state, Abu al-'Ala' al-Mawdudi (1903–1979) – they support a promoter of a moderate Islam, a 'Middle Way',[100] the 'Global Mufti' Yusuf al-Qaradawi (b. 1926).[101] A former Egyptian Muslim Brotherhood sympathiser based in Qatar, a prolific writer and an endless source of inspiration for Neo-Salafis all over the world, Qaradawi has made efforts to develop a *fiqh* (Islamic jurisprudence) addressed to Muslim minorities, especially in Europe. His works have been translated into Chinese, he was invited in China in 2009, and he often receives Chinese Muslim visitors. These Chinese Muslim reformists are particularly denounced when they appear inside the well-organised traditional *Ikhwan* group, where they are maligned as 'Wahhabis' or 'Salafis'. Debate is heated even in the *Ikhwan*'s core centre of Xining, Qinghai, where the reformists denounce the traditional *Ikhwan* as attached to its old textbooks and as refusing to evolve from tradition.¹⁰²

Why do Salafis cause so much enmity? First, among their fellow Muslims, Chinese Salafis caused discord because the 'historical Salafis' adopted divergent rituals (the *Santai*) and because so-called Salafis are perceived as quite rowdy and intolerant. Second, being strongly attached to Arabic as the unique source of correct doctrine, they refuse the influence of local cultures on faith and creed, insisting that Islam is not a minority religion.¹⁰³ So they do not discuss Liu Zhi and refer only to Arabic sources. They also denounce the Ahmadis, Baha'is and Shi'ites, all considered heretics or enemies in the Sunni Muslim world, especially by the Saudi Wahhabis, whereas they were never an issue in China, where they never appeared, except a very small number of Ahmadis. Third, Salafis try to avoid contact with non-Muslims and even more carefully avoid those they consider to be bad Muslims, whom they call hypocrites (*munafeige* from Ar. sing. *munāfiq*).¹⁰⁴ This retreat from contact with others led Chinese Muslims to apply the name 'Salafi' to every Muslim activist who does not want to follow mainstream attitudes and who does not want to obey the authorities' control and gain their approval.

Actually, frontiers between schools and religious trends are shifting among the younger generation. As Ma Qiang observed, globalisation has introduced many changes:

> Chinese Islam received the influence of foreign Islamic ways of thinking and activities, so a phenomenon of new factions (*xin paibie*), of denying factions (*wu paibie*), of mixed factions (*hunhe paibie*) appeared. Inside and between the religious groups, a new reformism is transforming conventional distinctions. Moreover, amongst the traditional groups appeared an anti-sectarian trend of 'Old faction no longer old, new faction no longer

new' (*Laopai bu lao, Xinpai bu xin*). New intellectual trends and activities in the Arab world and in South and Central Asia have powerfully influenced Chinese Islam, including the Tabligh movement, reformism in religious law, the Taliban movement, and Sufi thinking – and in response, Chinese Muslims often follow blindly or do not know what to do.[105]

At the beginning of the 2000s many Chinese Muslims, especially in their online identity, claimed to be 'no school, no faction', putting themselves above traditional Chinese Muslim religious groups, relying only on the *Qur'ān* and the Sunna. This labelling seems to have been largely abandoned later, for their vague and polysemic definition could put together Neo-Salafis and others considered as unorthodox, as discussed earlier, claiming to rely only on the *Qur'ān* to interpret Islam.

Intellectuals in Search of Reconciliation

Many factors have forced Chinese Muslims away from the two poles of this intellectual spectrum towards a middle way. The boundaries among social categories of Muslim intellectuals, their religious affiliations and their ways of thinking have eroded. The defiance of militant Salafism, too, has contributed to a desire for compromise. The constant pressure and presence of state authority – for example, the transformation of the Linxia Sino-Arabic School into a public school – also militated in favour of less overt resistance to that authority in the 2000s. Islam in China cannot be cut off from its foreign inspiration, but it also cannot be uprooted from Chinese soil or removed from the supervision of the state.

Evolution of the nationalist idea of Islam

The 1990s were a decade of acquaintance with 'Abd al-Wahhāb's heritage, a decade of learning the Wahhabi–Salafi doctrine, forging and maintaining ties through studies and visits abroad and pilgrimage, translating articles and books. The twenty-first century, however, has become a time to assimilate and consider those new experiences and ideas from abroad in the real context of contemporary China. Given the realities there, Muslims cannot avoid exchanges with Chinese society and the state authorities. Moreover, 9/11 made both political Islam and Saudi Wahhabism appear appalling in the eyes of Chinese society at large. Conversely, China's development, much admired in the Arab world, and China's confrontation with the Middle East's crude realities, may have encouraged Chinese Muslims to reconsider their position on national Islam. At least, they could no longer appear so strongly attached to the Salafi–Wahhabi version of Islam.

Indigenisation of culture and oneness of religion

Chinese Muslim intellectuals had to escape from the contradictions in discourse and attitude between a national, syncretic Islam (the 'Liu Zhi' tendency) and a religion fixed since the Prophet and the first three generations of followers (the ''Abd al-Wahhab' tendency). To that end, they must first explain this dichotomy, as was attempted in Lanzhou University's review, *Islamic Culture*:[106]

> Islam, since it flourished in the 7th century on the Arabian Peninsula and spread outward all over the world, has become an international or world religion. Followers of Islam, based on its fundamental teachings and values, created diverse Islamic cultures and civilizations, so under the guises of diversity lay the unified and unchanging Islamic teachings. It shows that religion constitutes the core of Islamic culture, while the culture is a spiritual and material expression of Islam. Since Islam, as believed by its followers, is a revealed religion and protected by Allah [God], no one can interfere to change it. So any localization or indigenization is unacceptable from an Islamic point of view, though localization or indigenization of Islamic culture is preferable but necessary [sic]. This article is to differentiate between Islam and Islamic culture, highlight basic characteristics of each concept, and discuss the impasse of indigenization of Islam as a revealed religion.[107]

Actually, the author makes a clear distinction between a culture of Islam, which could be indigenised (*bentuhua*), and Islamic doctrine, which is singular and unalterable. Establishing a dichotomy between concepts of culture and religion enables a functional reconciliation between the two tendencies of Chinese Islam. The term indigenisation, quite recent in Chinese Muslim vocabulary, may now be found in the writings of many Muslim intellectuals to describe their ancestors' acculturation.

Dialogue of cultures

A Chinese Islamic culture, with its *Han kitāb* writings, can be placed in equality with the Han Chinese spirit and philosophy. In this vision, Islam should no longer be viewed as an underdeveloped minority folklore, but rather as a religion on a par with Chinese culture and with other religions. Articles, books, symposiums and conferences have been devoted to this issue. Cultural dialogue constitutes a reaction, on the one hand, to government policy that treats the five recognised religions in China (Buddhism, Daoism, Catholicism, Protestantism and Islam) as a whole and wants them to act in harmony. On the other hand, it also reflects the anxieties of Muslims about the rapid growth of Christianity among Chinese people and their very low level of attraction to Islam, though conversion is regarded with pride and converts are much respected when they write essays and articles.[108] These internal preoccupations merge with international tendencies. Dialogue of religions as well as dialogue of civilisations is a worldwide phenomenon, which has also reached Chinese Muslims.[109] Some Chinese Muslim intellectuals specialised in those studies, glorifying a cultural dialogue in which Islam and Chinese Muslims have a pivotal place.[110]

Generally, since the 2000s, Muslim intellectuals do invoke Western references in their writings, and dialogue has transcended the academic milieu. Muslims open dialogue with believers of other faiths and publish it online, for example, Wuhuaguo debating with a Christian[111] or a Xining *ahong* with a Buddhist.[112] During the 1990s, activists imitated foreign Muslims and talked with prejudice about the West, its negative habits and its corruption,[113] but during the 2000s, academic Western references have provided a higher scholarly value for their writings.[114]

In order to create an intellectual ground for discussions about Islamic culture and faith, devout Muslim academics work with religious and private scholars, mostly heirs of 'Abd al-Wahhab. They organise scores of joint conferences that include university professors, religious professionals from diverse factions and affiliations, and lay intellectuals, such as Muslim journalists and private school teachers. Those professors are even nicknamed 'imam professors' by some of their disgruntled (Han) colleagues. Before the late 1990s those meetings appeared to be disputes and debates between practising

Muslims and non-religious scholars. Today, they have merged into meetings where, surprisingly, imams sometimes deliver religious lessons on the *Qur'ān* and *ḥadīth* without any discernible secular content. The boundary between academic knowledge and proselytising discourse has apparently become quite flexible.

This new collaboration is particularly noticeable at Lanzhou University, which, in 2007, convened a huge conference on Chinese Muslim 'scripture hall education' (*jingtang jiaoyu*), attended by many of Linxia's imams.[115] This conference was followed by a second in Hong Kong in 2009.[116] The university's journal, *Islamic Culture*, publishes articles by academics – mostly practising Muslims – as well as by imams and *laoshi*s (non-academic intellectuals).

Occasions for diverse Muslim intellectuals to meet at conferences also take place in private Muslim schools, in Yunnan (e.g., Najiaying and Zhaotong) and Gansu. Najiaying invites provincial Muslim university students to weeklong summer conferences. Participants are not forced to orthopraxy, but the show put on by some of Chinese Islam's stars and the warm atmosphere of the Muslim village may leave a very positive impression in their minds. In 2010, Zhang Weizhen participated as a main speaker; his Najiaying speech was filmed and made available on the Internet.[117]

Zhang Weizhen, an exemplary evolution

To illustrate this analysis of the evolution of contemporary Chinese Muslim intellectuals from the late 1980s to the late 2000s, let us trace the career of the famous scholar Zhang Weizhen, whose pen name is Hange.[118] Originally trained at the Linxia Sino-Arabic school, he acquired the status of scholar (*xuezhe*) when he became one of the first Chinese to study (1986–1992) at the Islamabad International Islamic University in Pakistan.[119] After his return, he taught at his alma mater before moving to and later becoming director of the Guanghe Sino-Arabic School, near Linxia, considered a more fundamentalist school. In 1996, rumours flew that Zhang Weizhen was a Salafi influenced by Saudi Arabia. In 2004, he abruptly resigned from Guanghe to become head of the affluent Yunnan Najiaying Islamic Culture Institute, where Ma Enxin also taught. In 2009, he returned to Gansu to lead the Linxia Sino-Arabic School, taken over by the state in 2007 and renamed the Linxia Foreign Language Institute.

Zhang explains that the first task of the Linxia Sino-Arabic School was to rebuild the faith, so severely damaged by the Cultural Revolution. But the school had evolved, because not every student can become an *ahong* or a scholar, so the school now trains 'experts' who become interpreters or businessmen. As Ma Zhixin said before him, the greatest aim of the school lies in training sincere Muslims, *hege de Musilin*. In this phrase, *hege* – 'to meet the required standard' – refers also to a transliterated Muslim term, *hange Musilin*, from the Arabic *haqq*, 'truth', indicating a sincere Muslim.[120]

Zhang Weizhen's early publication titled, *Restore the True Spirit of Islam* (1993),[121] is a collection of brief texts of two or more pages. He quotes largely Hasan al-Banna (1909–49) and Sayyid Qutb (1906–66), respectively, founder and eminent member of the Egyptian Muslim Brotherhood. The former was assassinated, the latter executed by Nasser. Zhang wrote chapters on them, as well on Jamāl al-Dīn al-Afghānī (1838–97), whom he called the first reformer and modernist activist. All these authors were noted Muslim political activists and important sources of political Islam, a sign of its intellectual influence during the 1980s, before the rise of Saudi Salafi–Wahhabism in China a decade later.

Zhang criticised the state's ideological contention that Islam be considered a constitutive element of *minzu*.[122] Furthermore, one of his longest essays was devoted to an enquiry on women's place in society in a rural Chinese village. He pointed out that if women did not work outside the home, the reverse of what the Communist Party had encouraged women to do, they could live quietly, devoting themselves to family and the education of children, strengthening both family and society.[123] This is a standard discourse in modern Islamic thinking: not to force women to stay at home, but rather to persuade them to do so for the sake of themselves, their families and society.

Zhang Weizhen continues to publish, under his pen name, translations of Yusuf Al Qaradawi, considered a quietist and consensual thinker. Under his real name, he translated (in collaboration with Ma Yulong) an abridgement by a Saudi author of the mystical imam al-Ghazālī (1058–1111).[124] His attitude evolved from religious activism outside the public sphere to the quieter attitude of an institutional scholar, translating and widening his reflection to include comparative religions under the influence of the 'dialogue of civilisations'.[125] He still argues with some Muslim modernists such as Zhang Chengqian and Wuhuaguo, who give personal interpretations of Islam and the *Qur'ān*, freeing themselves from the authority of the *ḥadīth*, which remain so important for Salafis.[126] On the other hand, he regularly writes articles in the academic review *Islamic Culture*. He gives lectures in many places and writes introductions for books and interviews as headmaster of the Linxia Foreign Language Institute.

Interviewed in spring 2013, he explained his intellectual path by his long-standing desire to be a scholar. He was much interested by the situation in Tunisia, trying to understand, through scarce information, the actual debate between secularists and Islamists writing a new constitution, and women's mobilisation to maintain an equal status with men. In summary, Zhang Weizhen has undergone an exemplary evolution and benefits from a very high media profile amongst Chinese Muslims and Muslim intellectuals.

Conclusion

Changing attitudes towards intellectual dialogue and social networking demonstrate the evolution of every side of contemporary Chinese Muslim intellectual life. Secular academics despised Wahhabi-influenced intellectuals as uneducated and accused them of endangering the *Huizu* vis-à-vis Chinese society and the state by their uncompromising attitude. Wahhabi intellectuals gradually evolved towards more socially acceptable behaviour in order to attract followers and slowly gain status. The activities and intellectual debates described earlier could lead us to think that Chinese Muslims enjoy total freedom of expression. Actually, they must not cross a red line: they must not criticise the Chinese state, its laws, and the Communist Party's policies and directions. Muslim intellectuals remain well aware of that line and its importance for their intellectual lives. Moreover, the Chinese state has placed a ban on non-authorised publications, including some Muslim publications, leading to a slow disappearance of private and unofficial publications, and closing some bookstores for selling them. It also exerts a tighter control on Muslim websites, banning some of them and removing many texts and all the preachers' self-made videos. It makes studying contemporary Chinese Muslim intellectuals a race to preserve primary sources before they disappear.

This preliminary enquiry into contemporary Chinese Muslim intellectuals certainly calls for further studies. The intellectuals have adapted to the '*minzu* paradigm', to political Islam when China began to open, to dialogue with other religions, and to demands to be recognised outside the narrow circle of Sino-Muslim studies. Their thinking deserves inclusion in studies of new intellectuals in the Muslim world and ought to be noticed and analysed by both Sinologists and Islamicists. Reform and adaptation of Islam in China has been a centuries-long process. Its dynamics today echo back to seventeenth- and eighteenth-century reflections. Those reassert the main issue of Islam in China: how to adapt and reform in order to survive inside China while remaining active participants in the world of Islam.

Notes

1. Murata, 'The unity of being'.
2. Zeghal, 'Intellectuels de l'islam', p. 23.
3. See Lipman, Frankel, Tontini and Petersen, Chapters 1–4, this volume.
4. Benite, '"Nine years in Egypt"'.
5. Ma Jitang, *Chen Keli zhuan*; Chérif-Chebbi, 'Chen Keli'.
6. Li Zhenzhong, *Xuezhe de zhuiqiu*.
7. Ma Tong, *Zhongguo Yisilan jiaopai yu menhuan zhidu shilüe*. and *Zhongguo Yisilan jiaopai yu menhuan suyuan*.
8. Feng Zenglie, *Qingdai tongzhi nianjian*.
9. Feng Zenglie, 'Yisilan zhexue'.
10. Bai Shouyi, *Zhongguo Yisilan shi cungao*; *Huizu zongjiao wenji*; and *Zhongguo Huihui minzu shi*.
11. Yang Huaizhong and Yu Zhengui, *Yisilan yu Zhongguo wenhua*; and *Zhongguo Yisilan wenxian*.
12. Lin Xinghua (1908–2001) went to al-Azhar in 1934 and stayed for nine years in Egypt. After his return, he taught Arabic in his home province of Yunnan, then went to Beijing to work in the Institute of Foreign Languages. He retired in the 1980s to his home village; see Na Lanzhen, 'Huainian "shiji" laoren'.
13. See at: http://baike.baidu.com/view/316670.htm. This quite complete biographical article can be found at many sites.
14. Ma Mingliang, *Yisilan wenhua xinlun*. His biography can be found at: http://www.yslzc.com/rw/Class124/rw1/201201/37735.html.

15. Ding Shiren, Ding Jun and Hu Long, *Yisilan wenhua*. His colleagues studied abroad in Saudi Arabia and Pakistan.
16. See at: http://www.2muslim.com/forum.php?mod=viewthread&tid=3523.
17. Ma Qiang, *Liudong de jingshen shequ*; and *Minguo shiqi*.
18. Ma Qiang, *Huifang neiwai*.
19. Ma Qiang, *Kuayue bianjie*.
20. Sai Shengbao, 'Aiguo zhuyizhe'.
21. *Wo'erzi yanjiang ji*; Zhongguo Yisilanjiao Jiaowu Zhidao Weiyuanhui, *Xin wo'erzi yanjiang ji*. Other books, including two volumes of anthologies of *wa'z* competitions, have been published since.
22. See at: http://xn.2000y.net/824553/index.asp?xAction=xReadNews&NewsID=1034.
23. *Zhongguo Musilin*, pp. 4–7, for the tenth anniversary of the work on 'explaining the *Qur'ān*'.
24. See at: http://www.jxmzj.gov.cn/llyd_1/shmwz/201110/t20111007_176438.htm.
25. Chen Guangyuan, 'Zenyang danghao yiming ahong'.
26. Chen Guangyuan, *Xin shiqi*.
27. The *Ikhwan* reformist movement was founded at the end of the nineteenth century. Inspired by Wahhabism, it nonetheless retained China's dominant Hanafi school of law and is today one of China main Islamic currents.
28. Lipman, 'The third wave'.
29. Min Junqing and Ding Kejia, 'Wuben hengyi lishen'.
30. His collected writings have been reprinted in two volumes, Ma Xian, *Bihai tanzhu*.
31. Muhammad Fuad 'Abd al-Baqi, *Shengxun zhuji* (trans. Ma Xian). The same text, an anthology of the two main *ḥadīth* collectors, al-Bukhari and Muslim, composed by a modern Egyptian scholar (1882–1968) and classified by topics, was previously translated by a 'popular' (*minjian*, i.e., non-institutional) Islamic teacher and had a wide diffusion in China, which underlines the importance of those translations: Muhammad Fuad 'Abd al-Baqi, *Shengxun zhuji* (trans. Muhammad 'Uthman). The question remains, did Ma Xian intend to give an 'official' interpretation of this *ḥadīth* collection?
32. Qi Xueyi, 'Zhongguo de shengxun yijie'.
33. For instance, see 'How to be a *hege* ['trustworthy', from Ar. *ḥaqq*, truth] *ahong*', at: http://www.2muslim.com/forum.php?mod=viewthread&tid=104937;

for a more academic article, see Ma Qiang and Hu Qunqiong, 'Quanqiuhua beijingxia'.

34. Ma Guibao, *Ahong zhi zhong*. Though most chapters are lessons on Islam and ethics, this collection of published articles also includes an autobiographical essay.
35. Liu Xueqiang, *Yiwei ahong de shinian xinlu*, a collection of moral stories both collected from his own life experience and gleaned from others.
36. See at: http://www.islamcn.net/ask.
37. See at: www.2muslim.com.
38. 2Muslim, 'Ailifu'.
39. Actually, the Anti-Rightist Campaign (1957–1959), the Great Leap Forward and the Cultural Revolution interrupted or ended older *ahong*s' professional lives as well.
40. See the example of Qi Xueyi, who had mosque training, then went in 1987 to Pakistan and Saudi Arabia, returned to serve as imam in 1995, translated the *Saḥīḥ al-Bukhārī*, later took a Master's degree in Saudi Arabia, then a PhD in Shanghai in 2007, becoming the first *ahong* to obtain this diploma, see at: http://news.xinhuanet.com/zgjx/2007-06/19/content_6261912.htm.
41. Ding Jun, 'Civilian-operated'.
42. Mu Zhi, 'Zhongguo Yisilan'. Mu Zhi is the pen name of Chen Yufeng, from Henan, who studied with Huang Wanjun and in the northwest, went to Egypt, and headed the *Taqwa* College in Shadian (Yunnan). He is now head of the Zhaotong Sino-Arabic specialised training school in northeastern Yunnan.
43. In the early 1990s, I met young female teachers from Inner Mongolia in remote Weizhou (Ningxia), teaching without salary '*fi sabil Allāh*' (to serve *Allāh*), and ready to go elsewhere to propagate Islamic education.
44. Jaschok and Shui, *The History of Women's Mosques*, pp. 101–3.
45. After many incidents during the Cultural Revolution, some caused by their refusal to raise pigs – an extreme humiliation – the Muslims of Shadian, Yunnan, protested their harsh treatment by taking up arms against the state. The People's Liberation Army attacked and razed the village in July 1975, claiming perhaps 1,000 lives. Gladney, *Muslim Chinese*, pp. 137–40. Shadian has since been rebuilt, with considerable state investment, including a huge central mosque.
46. Hu Dawud and Salih Li, 'Danbo mingzhi'. A 43-minute film on Ma Enxin, produced by the major Hong Kong Muslim site, 'Light of Islam' *Yisilan zhi guang*, (www.noorislam.com), divided into episodes, may be found at: http://

www.tudou.com/programs/view/JeH0TngZVoc. See also an anthology of his articles, Ma Enxin, *Ma Enxin wenji*.
47. Officially approved main achievements are listed by Ding Jun, 'Civilian-operated, pp. 22–6.
48. Ma Zhixin, 'Jiaoyu yu zongjiao cishan'.
49. His death in 2012 was not only widely noted on the Chinese Muslim web, but was also marked by prayers in foreign countries where his students used to go, including educational institutions in Saudi Arabia, Islamabad International Islamic University (IIUI) in Pakistan, and Yala Islamic University in Thailand.
50. See at: www.islambook.net.
51. Ho, 'Islamic axis as transborder connectivity'.
52. Interview with one of the founders, born and raised in Shanxi, July 2006.
53. *Buhali shengxun* was published earlier in two volumes, in 1999 and 2001. The work has been criticised for grammatical and character mistakes. Another translation by the Linxia former *ahong* Qi Xueyi (see n. 32), who studied in Saudi Arabia, revised by Ding Jun, a former student at IIUI and Medina University and now professor at the Northwest University for Nationalities, was published in four volumes in 2008 and republished in 2012.
54. Kang Youxi, *Wuwei de mengxiang*.
55. Gladney, *Muslim Chinese*, pp. 1–9.
56. Kang Youxi, *Wuwei de mengxiang*, p. 111.
57. Zhao Guojun and Ma Guifen, 'Ershi shiji bashi niandai', pp. 86–90. On *Kaituo*, see Yang Wenjiong, 'Wenhua zijue yu jingshen hewang'.
58. 'Di wujie Musilin baokan'.
59. Zhang Chengqian, *Yisilan de zhaohuan*.
60. Li Jingyuan, *Gulanjing yizhu*. See a mild criticism by Zhang Weizhen, recalling his first commitment to Islam, in *Gaoyuan*, available at: http://www.yslzc.com/zazhi/gy/dishibaqi/200806/26184.html.
61. Zhang Chengqian, *Heping xinyang*.
62. See an analysis of his *Qur'ān* commentary demonstrating his Ahmadi inflence, Li Shanmu, *Lun hunhe de zongjiao*.
63. 'Xiao Ma A-ge'.
64. *Wuhuaguo*, meaning 'fig', is his pseudonym, referencing the *Qur'ān*'s *Surat al-Tīn* ('The Fig', *sura* 95). His real name is Hong Lu.
65. See at: www.xaislam.com.
66. For instance, in an answer online to a Hui woman in love with a Han, he opined that it was possible to marry him if she was not a Muslim believer, but

if she believes in Islam, it is forbidden. Other Muslims in Xi'an told me in 2006 that he allowed people to perform prayers in Chinese, and they expressed a stern condemnation of his actions.

67. See an interesting debate that took place in 2008, 'Zhongguo Musilin you yige xuezhe qunti ma?'
68. Benite, 'From "literati" to "ulama"'.
69. Rosati, *Musilin funü zongjiao yishi*, pp. 70–9, 86–7.
70. Ibid., pp. 58–9; and see at: http://www.muslem.net.cn/bbs/article-7411-1.html.
71. Petersen, 'Reconstructing Islam'.
72. Frankel, *Rectifying God's Name*.
73. Murata, *Chinese Gleams*.
74. Murata, 'The unity of being'.
75. Liu's ritual treatise *Tianfang dianli* was analysed in the *Siku Quanshu* catalogue, bringing it great prestige among Sino-Muslims despite the editor's negative judgement. See Frankel, Chapter 2, this volume.
76. Yang Huaizhong and Yu Zhengui, *Yisilan yu Zhongguo wenhua*, p. 3.
77. Lipman, 'White hats, oil cakes and common blood'.
78. Benite, 'From "literati" to "ulama"'.
79. See Cieciura, Chapter 5, this volume.
80. Fei Xiaotong was trained in China by foreign anthropologists and studied with Bronislaw Malinowski at the London School of Economics from 1935 to 1938.
81. Wuhuaguo, 'Yisilan zai Zhongguo chuanbo'; see also his book, *Musilin xiwang zhi lu*.
82. Interview in Xi'an, July 2006.
83. For instance, Lin Song, *Huihui lishi yu Yisilan wenhua*, pp. 182, 191.
84. See, among others, Sha Zongping, *Zhongguo de Tianfang xue*, and the collection 'Ruhua haishi huaru'. The latter is a compilation of articles edited by the staff of the Zhongwen Yisilan xueshu cheng (Chinese Islamic Study City, at www.islambook.net); see particularly the bibliography, pp. 194–220.
85. Liang Xiangming, '"Yi Ru quan Jing"'.
86. Lin Song, 'Cong *Tianfang dianli* kan'.
87. Li Xifeng, 'Xidaotang'.
88. Ma Tong, 'Jibuci yu Xidaotang', pp. 177–83.
89. For a summary of publications on the Xidaotang, see Gao Zhanfu, 'Zhongguo yisilanjiao Xidaotang'.

90. Min Shengguang, *Ma Qixi shilian shangshi*; and *Zhongguo Yisilanjiao Xidaotang*.
91. On commonalties and differences between the Xidaotang and the Sufi orders, see at: http://blog.sina.com.cn/s/blog_5ef66f4b0100oksd.html.
92. Interviews regarding the current notion of *xuezhe* with imams, professors and lay intellectuals in Lanzhou, Xi'an, Beijing and Yinchuan, May and June 2013.
93. Wiktorowicz, 'Anatomy of the Salafi movement'; see also Meijer, 'Introduction'.
94. Chérif-Chebbi, 'Brothers and comrades'.
95. Hengli, '*Xibei xingji*'. The text, written by a southern convert who discovered northwestern regional Islamic culture, is accessible on numerous sites.
96. 'Linxia de ahong (6)'.
97. See at: http://dev.gansudaily.com.cn/system/2012/03/01/012391850.shtml.
98. Hu Dawud and Salih Li, 'Danbo mingzhi'.
99. Mouline, *Les clercs de l'islam*, pp. 18–21.
100. Yusuf al-Qaradawi, *Khutab al-shaykh*.
101. Skaovgaard-Peterson and Graf, *Global Mufti*.
102. 'Yiwei meiti jizhe'.
103. Zhang Weizhen, *Huanyuan Yisilan zhen jingshen*, pp. 8–12.
104. Gladney, 'The Salafiyya movement'.
105. Ma Qiang, 'Quanqiuhua beijingxia'.
106. Ding Shiren, 'Yisilan wenhua'.
107. Ibid., p. 2.
108. See, for instance, Zhang Zaili, *Zhida linghun*.
109. For instance, Yao Jide, 'Wenming duihua', written by a Muslim professor at Yunnan University.
110. Ma Mingliang, 'Yisilanjiao de Zhongguohua'; see also 'Yi Ru quan Jing' and 'Dangjin Zhongguo tong Yisilan guojia'.
111. Wuhuaguo, 'Yu yige Jidutu'.
112. 'Yu Jinbiao ahong'.
113. Zhang Weizhen, *Huanyuan Yisilan*, pp. 72–81.
114. Zhang Weizhen, 'Shilun Yiben Taimiye', pp. 30–9. On the issue of the medieval author, Ibn Taymiyya, considered to be a precursor of fundamentalist Islam, the author quotes John Locke and Francis Bacon.
115. See at: http://www.2muslim.com/forum.php?mod=viewthread&tid=38484&extra=page%3D1.
116. See at: http://www.mslwhyp.com/news_view.asp?id=81.
117. See at: http://www.islamcn.net/sv/list/list3_2.html.

118. *Hange* is the Chinese transliteration of Arabic *haqq* (Truth); it was the pen name of the martyred Ikhwan imam Chen Keli (executed in 1970).
119. 'The university was created to produce scholars and practitioners who are imbued with Islamic ideology, whose character and personality conforms to the teachings of Islam, and who are capable of catering to the economic, social, political, technological and intellectual needs of the Muslim Ummah.' See at: http://www.iiu.edu.pk.
120. 'Fangtan Hezhou cheng'.
121. The introduction is by the founder of the Linxia Sino-Arabic School, Ma Zhixin.
122. Zhang Weizhen, *Huanyuan Yisilan*, pp. 8–12, in a chapter on relations between nationality (*minzu*) and religion.
123. Ibid., pp. 29–41.
124. Shami, *Al-Ghazali's Revival*.
125. See the introduction to a translation of Yusuf al-Qaradawi published in 2010, available at: http://www.islambook.net/shop/sort_book.asp?productno=6826.
126. See at: http://hi.baidu.com/mushafuer/item/40f6dab2cced9570254b0949; and Zhang Weizhen, 'Zenyang duitai shengxun?'

Bibliography

2Muslim, 'Ailifu: Zouzai tietu de daolushang' ('Alif: walking on a clearly designed path'), *Zhong Mu wangyou* (*Chinese Muslim Netsurfer*), No. 1 (December 2005), available at: http://www.2muslim.com/forum.php?mod=viewthread&tid=151 32.

Abou El Fadl (Khaled Abu al-Fadl), 'Islamic law and Muslim minorities: the juristic discourse on Muslim minorities from the second/eighth to the eleventh/seventeenth centuries', *Islamic Law and Society*, 1(2) (1994): 141–87.

Abt, Oded, 'Muslim ancestry and Chinese identity in Southeast China', PhD dissertation, Tel-Aviv University, 2012.

Ames, Roger and Henry Rosemont, Jr, *The Analects of Confucius: A Philosophical Translation*, New York: Ballantine, 1999.

Ando Jun'ichirō, 'Chūka minkoku ki ni okeru Chūgoku Isurāmu shin bunka undō no shisō to kōzō' ('Thought and structure of the new culture movement in Chinese Islam during the Republican period'), in *Chūgoku no Isurāmu shisō to bunka* (*China's Islamic thought and culture*), *Ajia yūgaku*, No. 129, Tokyo: Bensei Shuppan, 2009.

Ando Jun'ichirō, 'Nitchū sensōki no Chūgoku tairiku ni okeru Kaikyō kōsaku to Kaimin shakai: Kahoku o chūshin ni' ('"Islam work" and Muslim society on the Chinese mainland during the Sino-Japanese War: Focus on North China'), presented at the conference, 'Japan's Wartime "Lama Work" and "Islam Work",' Tokyo University of Science, 1 December 2012.

Ansari, Muhammad Abdul Haq, *Sufism and Shariah: A Study of Shaykh*

Ahmad Sirhindi's Effort to Reform Sufism, Leicester: Islamic Foundation, 1986.

Atwill, David, *The Chinese Sultanate: Islam, Ethnicity, and the Panthay Rebellion in Southwest China, 1856–1873*, Stanford, CA: Stanford University Press, 2005.

Aubin, Françoise, '"En Islam chinois: quels Naqshbandis?' in Marc Gaborieau, A. Popovic and T. Zarcone (eds), *Naqshbandis: Cheminements et situation actuelle d'un ordre mystique musulman*, Istanbul and Paris: Éditions Isis, 1990, pp. 491–572.

Aubin, Françoise, 'Reflections on the Fletcher legacy', the Joseph Fletcher Memorial Lecture, Harvard University, 21 June 2006, available at: http://blog.sina.com.cn/s/blog_a5faae600102v0xh.html, last accessed 14 September 2015.

Bai Shouyi, *Huizu renwu zhi – Qingdai (Records of* Huizu *Biographies: Qing Period)*, Yinchuan: Ningxia Renmin Chubanshe, 1992.

Bai Shouyi, *Huizu zongjiao lunji (Collected Essays on* Huizu *Religion)*, Beijing: Beijing Shifan Daxue Chubanshe, 1992.

Bai Shouyi, *Zhongguo Yisilan shi cungao (Manuscripts on the History of Islam in China)*, Yinchuan: Ningxia Renmin Chubanshe, 1995.

Bai Shouyi (ed.), *Zhongguo Huihui minzu shi (History of the* Huizu *of China)*, Beijing: Zhonghua Shuju, 2003, 2 vols.

Bai, Limin, *Shaping the Ideal Child: Children and Their Primers in Late Imperial China*, Hong Kong: Chinese University of Hong Kong Press, 2005.

Bao Tingliang, 'Zongjiao gailiang lun' ('On religious reform'), *Xinghuipian* (1908), pp. 31–40.

'Beiping chengda shifan xuexiao zhuban Faluke Zhongguo liuai xueshengtuan zhaokao jianzhang' ('Rules for selecting the King Faruk student delegation to study in Egypt, set by *Chengda Shifan Xuexiao* in Beiping'), *Yuehua*, 9(12) (April 1937): 12.

Benite, Zvi Ben-Dor, 'From "literati" to "ulama": the origins of Chinese Muslim nationalist historiography', *Nationalism and Ethnic Politics*, 9 (2004): 83–109.

Benite, Zvi Ben-Dor, *The Dao of Muhammad: A Cultural History of Muslims in Late Imperial China*, Cambridge MA: Harvard University Asia Center, 2005.

Benite, Zvi Ben-Dor, 'Follow the white camel: Islam in China to 1800', in David O. Morgan and Anthony Reid (eds), *New Cambridge History of Islam*, vol. 3, Cambridge: Cambridge University Press, 2010, pp. 409–26.

Benite, Zvi Ben-Dor, '"Nine Years in Egypt": Al-Azhar University and the Arabization of Chinese Islam', *HAGAR, Studies in Culture, Polity and Identities*, 8(1) (2008): 105–28.

Benite, Zvi Ben-Dor, 'The Marrano emperor: the mysterious bond between Zhu Yuanzhang and the Chinese Muslims', in Sarah Schneewind (ed.), *Long Live the Emperor! Uses of the Ming Founder across Six Centuries of East Asian History*, Ming Studies Research Series No. 4 (2008), pp. 275–308.

Bodde, Derk, 'China's Muslim minority', *Far Eastern Survey*, 15(18) (11 September 1946): 281–4.

Bowering, Gerhard, 'Covenant', in Jane Dammen McAuliffe (ed.), *Encyclopaedia of the Qur'an*, Leiden: Brill, 2001, pp. 464–7.

Brokaw, Cynthia J., *The Ledgers of Merit and Demerit: Social Change and Moral Order in Late Imperial China*, Princeton, NJ: Princeton University Press, 1991.

Broomhall, Marshall, *Islam in China: A Neglected Problem*, London: Morgan & Scott, 1910.

Cai Dayu, 'Liudong qingzhen jiaoyuhui xu' ('Introduction to the Muslim Educational Association of Students in Tokyo'), *Xinghuipian* (1908), pp. 75–9.

Calder, Norman (ed.), 'Law', in *Interpretation and Jurisprudence in Medieval Islam*, Aldershot and Burlington: Ashgate Variorum, 2006.

Calder, Norman (ed.), 'The limits of Islamic orthodoxy', in *Interpretation and Jurisprudence in Medieval Islam*, Aldershot and Burlington: Ashgate Variorum, 2006, pp. 66–86.

Chang Chung-fu, 'Minzu guojia zuqun yishi yu lishi jieshi de hudong yiyi: Yi Haixia liang'an "Huizu" rending wei li' ('Nation-state, ethnic identity, and the interaction of meanings in historical interpretation: the example of definition of the *Huizu* on the two sides of the Taiwan Strait'), in Yu Miin-ling (ed.), *Liang'an fenzhi, xueshu jianzhi, tuxiang xuanchuan yu zuqun zhengzhi (1945–2000) (Political Separation of the Two Sides of the Strait: The Organization of Learning, Visual Propaganda, and Ethnic Policies)*, Taipei: Academia Sinica, 2012, pp. 395–427.

Changde Huijiao Jiaoyu Puzhuhui, *Huiwen duben (Arabic Language Textbook)* [1925], reprinted in Wang Jianping (ed.), *Zhongguo Yisilan jingdian jixuan (Compiled Islamic Texts from China)*, vol. 4, Shanghai: Guji chubanshe, 2007, pp. 2367–79.

Chao Chiu-ti, *Linxia zongpai: Zhongguo Musilin de zongjiao minzuxue (Religious Solidarities in Linxia: Religious Ethnology of Muslims in China)*, Taipei: Zhengda Chubanshe, 2012.

Chao Chiu-ti, 'Shei shi Huizu? Lishi yu xiandai yiti jiaohui xia de lunshu' ('Who are the *Huizu*? A proposition at the juncture of historical and contemporary issues'), *Guoli Zhengzhi Daxue minzu xuebao*, 30 (September 2012): 37–57.

Chen Guangyuan, 'Zenyang danghao yiming ahong: Laoxiaoyou Chen Guangyuan zai xiaoqing dahuishang de jianghua' ('How to act as a good *ahong*: old schoolmate Chen Guangyuan's discourse at the [China Islamic] Institute's Anniversary Conference'), *Zhongguo Musilin*, Special issue (1995): 28–9.

Chen Guangyuan. *Xin shiqi ahong shiyong shouce* (*An Ahong's Manual for the New Age*), Beijing: Dongfang Chubanshe, 2005.

Chen Guangyuan (ed.), *Zhongguo Yisilanjiao lishi wenxian* (*Historical Materials on Islam in China*), Beijing: Dongfang Chubanshe, 2009.

Chen Keli, 'Sumiao wode jingtang shengya' ('Outline of my life at the madrasa'), *Huisheng Yuekan*, 1(7/8) (1946).

Cheng, D. Chang, 'Democracy is in its details: the 1909 Provincial Assembly elections and the print media', in Sherman Cochran and Paul Pickowicz (eds), *China on the Margins*, Ithaca, NY: Cornell University Press, 2010, pp. 195–220.

Chérif-Chebbi, Leila, 'Brothers and comrades: Muslim fundamentalists and Communists allied for the transmission of Islamic knowledge in China', in Stéphane A. Dudoignon (ed.), *Devout Societies vs. Impious States? Transmitting Islamic Learning in Russia, Central Asia and China, through the Twentieth Century*, Berlin: Klaus Schwarz, 2004, pp. 61–90.

Chérif-Chebbi, Leila, 'Chen Keli', in Kate Fleet, Gudrun Kramer, Denis Matringe, John Nawas and Everett Ronson (eds), *Encyclopedia of Islam*, 3rd edn, Leiden and Boston, MA: Brill, 2011, pp. 119–22.

Cotter, Francis J. M. and Karl L. Reichelt, 'The three character classic for Moslems', *The Chinese Recorder*, 18 (October 1917): 645–52.

Crossley, Pamela Kyle, 'Thinking about ethnicity in early modern China', *Late Imperial China*, 11(1) (June 1990): 1–34.

Da Xinwu, 'Zhongguo Yisilanjiao shuairuo zhi yuanyin ji wanjiu de wo jian' ('My views on the causes of and remedies for Chinese Islam's weakness'), *Mumin*, 1(10) (1931).

DeBary, Theodore and Irene Bloom (eds). *Sources of Chinese Tradition*, 2nd edn, vol. 1, New York: Columbia University Press, 2000.

Di Jingxiu, 'Gaishan halifa jiaoyu fangshi ji ahong shenghuo huanjing' ('Improvement of madrasa students' pedagogy and ahongs' living environment'), *Huijiao zhoubao*, 19 March 1943.

'Di wujie Musilin baokan bianji lianyihui wenji' ('Collection of the fifth symposium of the Muslim Periodical Editors' Unity and Friendship Association'), held at Dali, Yunnan, 21 October 2011, available at: http://www.2muslim.

com/home.php?mod=space&uid=72179&do=blog&id=95958, last accessed 6 August 2015.

Dicks, Anthony R., 'New lamps for old: the evolving legal position of Islam in China, with special reference to family law', in C. Mallat and J. Connors (eds), *Islamic Family Law*, London: Sterling, 1993.

Ding Jun, 'Civilian-operated Arabic language schools and the development of Muslim society: a historical and contemporary review', in *Muslims and a Harmonious Society: Selected Papers from a Three-Conference Series on Muslim Minorities in Northwest China, Gansu Province, 2008, Shaanxi Province, 2009, Xinjiang Autonomous Region, 2009*, trans. Christine Sun, Beijing: Ethnic Minority Group Development Research Institute, Development Research Center of China's State Council and the Religion and Security Research Project, Center on Faith & International Affairs, Institute for Global Engagement, 2011, pp. 17–29, available at: https://www.globalengage.org/attachments/1209_IGE_MuslimSociety_singlePage.pdf, last accessed 18 September 2015.

Ding Kejia and Yu Ting, 'Shilun Sufei zhuyi yu jingtang jiaoyu de guanxi ji qi liubian' ('The relationship between Sufism and madrasa education and its changes'), *Xibei Minzu Yanjiu*, No. 3 (2001).

Ding Rong, 'Ma Dexin *Chaojin tuji* yanjiu' (*Research on Ma Dexin's* Record of the Pilgrimage Journey), *Zhongshan daxue yanjiusheng xuekan*, 28(3) (2008): 60–9.

Ding Shiren, '20 shiji Hezhou jingtang jiaoyu de liangci zhongda tupo' ('Two 20th century breakthroughs in mosque education in Hezhou'), *Huizu yanjiu*, No. 64 (2006): 51–5.

Ding Shiren, 'Yisilan wenhua bentuhua de tantu yu Yisilanjiao bentuhua de juejing' ('A smooth path for indigenization of Islamic culture and the impasse of indigenization of Islam'), *Yisilan wenhua*, 3 (2010): 40–50.

Ding Shiren, Ding Jun and Hu Long (eds), *Yisilan wenhua* (*Islamic Culture*), Lanzhou: Gansu Renmin Chubanshe, vol. 1, 2008; vol. 2, 2009; vol. 3, 2010; vol. 4, 2011; vol. 5, 2012.

Ding Zhuyuan, 'Jinggao Huijiao Jujinhui' ('A warning to the CIPA'), *Zhengzong Aiguobao*, 15 August 1912. Cited in Zhang Juling, 'Zhongguo Huijiao Jujinhui', p. 14.

Du Weiming, 'Wenming duihua de fazhan ji qi shijie yiyi' ('The development of civilizational dialogue and its world significance'), *Huizu yanjiu*, No. 3 (2003).

Du Wenxiu, 'Shuaifu Bugao' ('Announcement from the Commander's headquarters'), in Bai Shouyi (ed.), *Huimin qiyi* (*Righteous Uprisings of the* Hui *People*), vol. II, Beijing: Shenzhou Guoguangshe, 1952, p. 123.

Effenberg, J. H., 'The Moslems of China', *XXth Century*, 1 (1941): 199–200.

Elman, Benjamin, *Philosophy to Philology: Intellectual and Social Aspects of Change in Late Imperial China*, Cambridge, MA: Harvard University Council on East Asian Studies, 1984.

Esenbel, Selçuk, 'Utsunomiya Tarō nikki no Osuman Toruko to Isuramushugi kan' ('Perceptions of the Ottoman Turks and Islamism in Utsunomiya Tarō's diary'), presented at the conference, 'Islamic Area Studies', Waseda University, 15 December 2012.

'Fangtan Hezhou cheng: Jiu Axiao 30 nian qianhou yu Zhang Weizhen xiaozhang de tanhua' ('A visit to the town of Hezhou: talking with Zhang Weizhen about thirty years of the Arabic School'), available at: http://www.2muslim.com/forum.php?mod=viewthread&tid=302854, last accessed 21 April 2012.

Feng Jinyuan, 'Jin Jitang', in *Zhongguo Yisilan baike quanshu* (*Encyclopedia of Islam in China*), Chongqing: Sichuan Chuban Jituan, 2007, p. 259.

Feng Zenglie, *Qingdai tongzhi nianjian Shaanxi Huimin qiyi yanjiu* (*A Study of the Shaanxi Hui Uprising during the Tongzhi Era*), Xi'an: San Qin Chubanshe, 1994.

Feng Zenglie, 'Yisilan zhexue yu Huizu Yisilanjiao qianyi' ('A short survey of Islamic philosophy and Islam among the *Huizu*'), in *Zhongguo Yisilanjiao yanjiu* (*Studies on Islam in China*), Xining: Qinghai Renmin Chubanshe, 1997, pp. 138–47.

Foreign Ministry [of the Republic of China], 'Memo from Ma Jian and Pang Shiqian as an Appendix to Memo No. 664 from Embassy in Cairo to the Foreign Ministry', February 1939, *Guoshiguan* (*Academia Historica*), Xingzhengyuan Documents, vol. 062:529, Taipei, Taiwan.

Frankel, James D., 'Liu Zhi's journey through the ritual law to Allah's Chinese name: conceptual antecedents and theological obstacles to the Confucian–Islamic harmonization of the *Tianfang dianli*', PhD dissertation, Columbia University, 2005.

Frankel, James, *Rectifying God's Name: Liu Zhi's Confucian Translation of Monotheism and Islamic Law*, Honolulu, HI: University of Hawai'i Press, 2011.

Gaimushō (Foreign Ministry of Japan), 'Kakkoku ni okeru shūkyo oyobi fukyō kankei zakken/kaikyō kankei' ('Miscellaneous information on religions and missions in foreign countries'), *Gaimushō gaikō monjo* (Diplomatic archive of Japan), JACAR B04012550200 (1938).

Gao Fayuan, *Musheng houyi* (*Descendant of Prophet Muhammad*), 2nd edn, Kunming: Yunnan Renmin Chubanshe, 2004.

Gao Zhanfu, 'Zhongguo Yisilanjiao Xidaotang yanjiu de huigu yu pingshu

(1935–2002)' ('Review of research on the Chinese Islamic Xidaotang, 1935–2002'), *Shijie zongjiao yanjiu*, 4 (2002): 133–43.

Gardner, Daniel K., *Zhu Xi's Reading of the Analects: Canon, Commentary, and the Classical Tradition*, New York: Columbia University Press, 2003.

Garnaut, Anthony, 'Hui legends of the companions of the Prophet', *China Heritage Newsletter*, No. 5, March 2006, available at: http://www.chinaheritagequarterly.org/articles.php?searchterm=005_legends.inc&issue=005, last accessed 14 September 2015.

Giersch, C. Patterson, *Asian Borderlands: The Transformation of Qing China's Yunnan Frontier*, Cambridge, MA: Harvard University Press, 2006.

Giles, Herbert A., *Elementary Chinese – San Tzu Ching*, Leiden: Brill, 1900.

Gladney, Dru C., *Muslim Chinese: Ethnic Nationalism in the People's Republic*, Cambridge, MA: Harvard University Council on East Asian Studies, 1991.

Gladney, Dru C., 'The Salafiyya movement in northwest China: Islamic fundamentalism among the Muslim Chinese', in Leif Manger (ed.), *Muslim Diversity: Local Islam in Global Contexts*, Richmond: Curzon, 1999, pp. 102–49.

Gongheguomin (pseud.), 'Huijiao Huizu bian' ('Differentiation of *Huijiao* and *Huizu*'), *Zhengzong Aiguobao*, No. 1901, 8 April 1912.

Green, Nile, 'Emerging approaches to the Sufi traditions of South Asia: between text, territories and the transcendent', *South Asia Research*, 24(2) (2000): 123–48.

Guomin zhengfu (Government of the Republic of China), 'Guomin dahui qiaomin daibiao xuanju an (1)' ('Plan for electing overseas Chinese representatives to the National Congress, Part 1'), Guoshiguan (Academia Historica) Archives 001000000230A, 1936/06/10-1937/08/31.

Gwynne, Rosalind, *Logic, Rhetoric and Legal Reasoning in the Qur'an: God's Arguments*, London: Routledge, 2004.

Hai Weiliang, 'Yilang zhi zongjiao' ('The religion of Iran'), Zhongguo dier lishi danganguan (Second historical archive in China), Nanjing, Folder No. 18-1514, 1942.

Hammond, Kelly, 'The conundrum of collaboration: Japanese involvement with Muslims in North China, 1931–1945', PhD dissertation, Georgetown University, 2015.

He Zhiming, 'Qingmo minchu "Wuzu gonghe" sixiang jianlun' ('A short commentary on the idea of "unity of five *minzu*" in the late Qing and early Republican eras'), *Ningxia shehui kexue*, 4 (July 2006): 129–34.

Hedin, Sven, *The Flight of Big Horse: The Trail of War in Central Asia*, New York: E. P. Dutton, 1936.

Hengli, '*Xibei xingji* zhi "Linxia de jiyi"' ('"Souvenirs from Linxia" in *Travels in the Northwest*'), available at: http://www.2muslim.com/forum.php?mod=viewthread&tid=55235, last accessed 4 June 2009.

Ho, Wai-Yip, 'Islamic axis as transborder connectivity: China digital Islam, Middle East and reimagining the *Ummah*', paper presented at the 2009 Biannual International Forum on Asia–Middle East Studies, 'Transcending Borders: Asia, Middle East, and the Global Community', 2009.

Hsia, R. Po-chia, *A Jesuit in the Forbidden City: Matteo Ricci 1552–1610*, reprint Oxford: Oxford University Press, 2012.

Hu Dawud and Li Salih, 'Danbo mingzhi duxue bujuan. Muhanmode Aimin Ma Enxin laoshi fang' ('Selfless and clever minded, untiring in study: a visit to teacher Muhammad Amīn Ma Enxin'), *Gaoyuan*, No. 4 (2004); available at: http://www.xmuslim.net/forum.php?mod=viewthread&tid=179, last accessed 11 November 2011.

Hu Fangquan, 'Zhongguo liuai xueshengbu Hu Enjun laihan' ('Letter from a Chinese student in Egypt, Hu Enjun'), *Rendao*, 1(8–10) (1 March 1935): 32–3.

Hua Tao and Zhai Guiye, 'Minguo shiqi de Huizu jieshuo yu Zhongguo Gongchandang *Huihui Minzu Wenti* de lilun yiyi' ('The definition of *Huizu* in the Repubican period and the theoretical significance of *Huihui minzu wenti*, published by the Chinese Communist Party'), *Minzu yanjiu*, 1 (2012): 12–24.

Huang Chengjun, 'Huanxing Huizhong, gongtu guoqiang: Du Liudong Qingzhen Jiaoyuhui pian *Xinghuipian*' ('To awaken the Muslims and strengthen the country: reading the *Xinghuipian*, published by the Muslim Educational Association of Students in Tokyo'). *Huizu yanjiu*, 2 (2002): 88–91.

Huang Dengwu (ed.), *Zhongguo jingtang jiaoyu yu Shaanxue ahong* (*Madrasa Education in China and Ahongs of the Shaanxi School*), Pingliang: n.p., 2009.

Huang Zhenpan, 'Lun Huimin' ('On the Hui people'), in Bai Shouyi (ed.), *Huizu renwu zhi (jindai)*, Yinchuan: Ningxia Renmin Chubanshe, 1997, pp. 236–7.

'*Huijiao Jidujiao yu xueshu wenhua* xian yi chuban!!!' (*Islam and Christianity in Scholarly Culture* is now published!!!'), *Yuehua*, 8(24) (30 August 1936): 9.

Israeli, Raphael, 'The Muslim revival in 19th-century China', *Studia Islamica*, 43 (1976): 119–38.

Israeli, Raphael, *Muslims in China: A Study in Cultural Confrontation*, London: Curzon, 1980.

Israeli, Raphael, *Islam in China: A Critical Bibliography*, Westport, CT: Greenwood, 1994.

Ivanhoe, Philip J., *Confucian Moral Self Cultivation*, Indianapolis, IN: Hackett, 2000.
Jaschok, Maria and Shui Jingjun, *The History of Women's Mosques in Chinese Islam: A Mosque of their Own*, Richmond: Curzon, 2000.
Ji Yun et al., *Siku quanshu zongmu* [1782], 4 vols., Reprint Shanghai: Dadong Shuju, 1930.
'Jiaoyu jiyao' ('Education abstracts'), *Huijiao zhoubao*, 1 November 1940.
'Jieshao muyin yuekan' ('Introducing the *Voice of Muslims* monthly'), *Rendao*, 2(1) (1 June 1935): 19.
Jin Diangui, 'Huanying Jin Ma erjun fanguo dahui' ('Welcome-home party for Jin and Ma'), *Chengshi xiaokan*, 3(58/59) (15 March 1937): 6.
Jin Ding, 'Liu Jielian xiansheng mubei' ('Master Liu Jielian's tombstone'), in Bai Shouyi (ed.), *Huizu renwu zhi – Qingdai* (*Records of* Huizu *Biographies: Qing Period*), Yinchuan: Ningxia Renmin Chubanshe, 1992, pp. 360–2.
Jin Jitang, 'Huijiao minzu shuo', in *Zhongguo Yisilanjiao shi cankao ziliao* (*Reference Materials for the History of Islam in China*), vol. 1, pp. 247–61.
Jin Jitang, *Zhongguo Huijiao shi yanjiu* (*Research on the History of Islam in China*) [1935], Reprint Yinchuan: Ningxia Renmin Chubanshe, 2000.
'Kalimat al-Sīn' ('Chinese Address'), in *Khutab haflat al-'iftitah al-kubra li-Mu'tamar al-Barlāmani al-'Alami lil-Bilād al-'Arabiyya wa-al-Islāmiyya lil-Difā' 'an Filastīn* (Addresses at the grand inaugural ceremony of the Conference of the World Arab Islamic Congress for the Defense of Palestine), Cairo: Matba'at 'Abbas 'Abd al-Rahman, 1938), reprinted in Gao Fayuan, *Musheng houyi*, p. 107.
Kang Youxi (trans.), *Buhali shengxun shilu quanji* (*Complete Collection of Bukhari's Authentic Sayings of the Prophet*), Hong Kong: Jishi Chuban Youxian Gongsi, 2008.
Kang Youxi, *Wuwei de mengxiang* (*Audacious Dreams*), Hong Kong: Jishi Chuban Youxian Gongsi, 2009.
Khadduri, Majid, *The Law of War and Peace in Islam: A Study in Muslim International Law*, London: Luzac, 1941.
Kurzman, Charles, *Modernist Islam, 1840–1940: A Sourcebook*, Oxford: Oxford University Press, 2002.
Lee, Thomas H. C. (ed.), 'Ideals and major themes in Chinese education', in *Education in Traditional China: A History*, Leiden: Brill, 2000.
Legge, James (trans.), *Confucius: Confucian Analects, the Great Learning, and the Doctrine of the Mean*, New York: Dover, 1971.

Leibold, James, *Reconfiguring Chinese Nationalism: How the Qing Frontier and its Indigenes Became Chinese*, New York: Palgrave Macmillan, 2007.

Leslie, Donald D., *Islamic Literature in Chinese, Late Ming and Early Qing: Books, Authors, and Associates*, Canberra: Canberra College of Advanced Education, 1981.

Leslie, Donald D., *Islam in Traditional China: A Short History*, Canberra: Canberra College of Advanced Education, 1986.

Leslie, Donald D. and Mohamed Wessel, 'Arabic and Persian sources used by Liu Chih', *Central Asiatic Journal*, 26 (1982): 78–104.

Leung, Angela K., 'Elementary education in the Lower Yangtze region in the seventeenth and eighteenth centuries', in Benjamin A. Elman and Alexander Woodside (eds), *Education and Society in Late Imperial China, 1600–1900*, Berkeley, CA: University of California Press, 1994, pp. 381–416.

Li Chenyang, '*Li* as cultural grammar: on the relation between *li* and *ren* in Confucius' *Analects*', *Philosophy East and West*, 57(3) (2007): 311–29.

Li Jingyuan (Fatumai),*Gulanjing yizhu* (*Commentary on the* Qur'ān), Hong Kong, Shijie Huaren Chubanshe, 2005.

Li Shanmu, *Lun hunhe de zongjiao* (*On Mixing up Religion*), n.p., 2010.

Li Xifeng, 'Xidaotang' ('The Xidaotang'), in *Yisilanjiao wenhua*, Changchun: Changchun Chubanshe, 1992, pp. 393–4.

Li Zhenzhong, *Xuezhe de zhuiqiu: Ma Jian zhuan* (*The Scholar's Quest: A Biography of Ma Jian*), Yinchuan: Ningxia Renmin Chubanshe, 2000.

Liang Xiangming, '"Yi Ru quan Jing" yu "fan Jing yi su": Jiantan Huizu xuezhe Liu Zhi congshi hanwen yizhu de shikong beijing' ('Using Confucianism to comment on Scriptures and "Opposing the Scriptures and diverging from customs": talking about the space and time background of Hui scholar Liu Zhi, engaged in writing and translating into Chinese'), *Huizu yanjiu*, 41(1) (2001): 88–91.

Liang Yijun, '*Zhengjiao zhenquan xu*' ('Introduction to *A True Interpretation of the Orthodox Teaching*') [1642], in Wang Daiyu, *Zhengjiao zhenquan, Qingzhen daxue, Xizhen zhengda*, reprint Yinchuan: Ningxia Renmin Chubanshe, 1999, pp. 4–5.

Lin Changxing, 'Shanghai Kailuo jian de liang kanwu' ('Two periodicals between Shanghai and Cairo'), *Rendao*, 1(8–10) (1 March 1935): 21.

Lin Song, 'Cong *Tianfang dianli* kan Liu Zhi "yi Ru shi Yi" de shikong beijing' ('Examining the background in space and time of Liu Zhi's "using Confucianism to comment on Islam" in *Tianfang dianli*'), *Gansu minzu yanjiu*, 2 (1990): 71–6.

Lin Song, *Huihui lishi yu Yisilan wenhua* (*Huihui History and Islamic Culture*), Beijing: Jinri Zhongguo Chubanshe, 1992.

Lin Song, *Gulanjing zai Zhongguo* (*The Holy* Qur'ān *in China*), Yinchuan: Ningxia Renmin Chubanshe, 2007.

'Linxia de ahong (6). Baha ahong' ('Linxia's *ahong*s (Part 6): *Ahong* Baha'), available at: http://www.2muslim.com/home.php?mod=space&uid=53127&do=blog&id=85634, last accessed 21 January 2012.

Lipman, Jonathan N., 'The third wave: establishment and transformation of the Muslim Brotherhood in China', *Études orientales*, 13–14 (1994): 89–105.

Lipman, Jonathan N., 'Hyphenated Chinese: Sino-Muslim identity in modern China', in Gail Hershatter, Emily Honig, Jonathan Lipman and Randall Stross (eds), *Remapping China: Fissures in Historical Terrain*, Stanford, CA: Stanford University Press, 1996.

Lipman, Jonathan N., *Familiar Strangers: A History of Muslims in Northwest China*, Seattle, WA: University of Washington Press, 1997.

Lipman, Jonathan N., 'Living Judaism in Chinese culture: being Jewish and being Chinese', in Lawrence Fine (ed.), *Judaism in Practice: From the Middle Ages through the Early Modern Period*, Princeton, NJ: Princeton University Press, 2001, pp. 265–78.

Lipman, Jonathan N., 'White hats, oil cakes and common blood: the *Huizu* in the contemporary Chinese state', in Morris Rossabi (ed.), *Governing China's Multiethnic Frontiers*, Seattle, WA: University of Washington Press, 2004, pp. 19–52.

Lipman, Jonathan N., '"A fierce and brutal people": On Islam and Muslims in Qing law', in Pamela Crossley, Donald Sutton and Helen Siu (eds), *Empire at the Margins: Culture, Ethnicity and Frontier in Early Modern China*, Berkeley, CA: University of California Press, 2006, pp. 83–101.

Liu, Lydia, *Translingual Practice: Literature, National Culture, and Translated Modernity: China, 1900–1937*, Stanford, CA: Stanford University Press, 1995.

Liu Mengyang, 'Liu Mengyang zhi Wuzu Guomin Hejinhui Beijing Zonghui shu' ('Letter from Liu Mengyang to the Beijing General Assembly of the Association for Common Progress of the Five *Zu*'), *Zhengzong Aiguobao*, No. 1953, 30 May 1912.

Liu Xueqiang, *Yiwei ahong de shinian xinlu* (*One Ahong's Ten Years of Soul-searching*), Hong Kong: Jishi Chuban Youxian Gongsi, 2010.

Liu Yihong, *Huiru duihua: Tianfang zhi jing yu Kongmeng zhi dao* (*Dialogue between*

Islam and Confucianism: Arabic Scriptures and the Way of Confucius and Mencius), Beijing: Zongjiao Wenhua Chubanshe, 2006.

Liu Zhi, 'Yuanjiao pian', in *Tianfang dianli zeyao jie* (*Selective Explanation of the Norms and Rituals of Islam*) [1710], Reprint Hong Kong: Hong Kong Muslim Propagation Society, 1971.

Liu Zhi, *Tianfang xingli* (*Islamic Metaphysics*) [1706], Reprint Shanghai: Shanghai Guji Chubanshe, 1995.

Liu Zhi, *Tianfang dianli* (*Norms and Rituals of Islam*), in *Qingzhen Dadian* (*The Great Canon of Islam*), Hefei: Huangshan Shushe, 2005, vol. 15.

Liu Zhi, *Tianfang dianli* (*Norms and Rituals of Islam*), ed. Ma Baoguang, n.p., 2005.

Liu Zhi, *Tianfang dianli zeyao jie* (*Selective Explanation of the Norms and Rituals of Islam*) [1710], in *Huizu dianzhang quanshu* (*Complete Collection of Huizu Classics*), Yinchuan: Ningxia Renmin Chubanshe, 2008, vol. 20.

Liu Zhi, *Tianfang sanzijing* (*Three Character Classic of Islam*), with commentary by Ma Fuchu (Dexin) [1858], in *Huizu dianzhang quanshu* (*Complete Collection of Huizu Classics*), Yinchuan: Ningxia Renmin Chubanshe, 2008, vol. 26.

Liu Zhi, 'Zhushu Shu' in Bai Shouyi (ed.), *Huizhu renwu zhi – Qingdai* (*Records of Huizu Biographies: Qing Period*), Yinchuan: Ningxia Renmin Chubanshe, 1992.

Ma Anli, 'Xu' ('Preface'), in Ma Dexin, *Sidian yaohui* (*Essence of the Four Canons*), in Ma Jizu (ed.), *Ma Fuchu yizhu xuan* (*Selection of Ma Fuchu's Extant Writings*), Hong Kong: Guoji Huaren Chubanshe, 2003.

Ma Dexin, *Chaojin tuji* (*Record of the Pilgrimage Journey*), in Ma Jizu (ed.), *Ma Fuchu yizhu xuan* (*Selection of Ma Fuchu's Extant Writings*), Hong Kong: Guoji Huaren Chubanshe, 2003.

Ma Dexin, *Sidian yaohui* (*Essence of the Four Canons*), in Ma Jizu (ed.), *Ma Fuchu yizhu xuan* (*Selection of Ma Fuchu's Extant Writings*), Hong Kong: Guoji Huaren Chubanshe, 2003.

Ma Dexin, *Mingde jing* (*Scripture of Bright Virtue*), in Ma Jizu (ed.), *Ma Fuchu yizhu xuan* (*Selection of Ma Fuchu's Extant Writings*), Hong Kong: Guoji Huaren Chubanshe, 2003.

Ma Enxin, *Ma Enxin wenji* (*The Collected Works of Ma Enxin*), Lanzhou: Gansu Minzu Chubanshe, 2012.

Ma Fulong, *Ma Fulong ahong zishu* (*Autobiography of Imam Ma Fulong*), Hong Kong: Jishi Chuban Youxian Gongsi, 2010.

Ma Guibao, *Ahong zhi zhong* (*The Ahong's Burden*), Hong Kong: Tianma Tushu Youxian Gongsi, 2010.

Ma Haiguo and Ma Yan, 'Shilun Yang Du guanyu xiandai minzu guojia de sixiang:

ping Yang Du "Jintie Zhuyi Shuo"' ('Preliminary discussion of Yang Du's thought on the contemporary national state: an evaluation of Yang Du's "On the doctrine of gold and iron"'), *Minzu Luntan*, 5 (2013): 10–13.

Ma Jian, 'Liugan diansheng Ma Jian jun deng zhi benbao zhiyuan Liang Cheng jun shu' ('Letter from Yunnanese students in Gansu, Ma Jian and others, to our staff member Liang Cheng'), *Yunnan qingzhen duobao*, 3 (10 April 1929): 30–1.

Ma Jian, 'Ma Zishi jun zhi laihan' ('Letter from Mr Ma Zishi [Ma Jian]'), *Yuehua*, 4(10–12) (5 April 1932): 34–6.

Ma Jian, 'Aiji tongxin' ('Letter from Egypt'), *Yuehua*, 4(35) (15 December 1932): 11–14.

Ma Jian and Hu Fangquan, 'Zhongguo Huijiao gaiguan (1)' ('Overview of Islam in China, Part 1'), *Rendao*, 1(8–10) (1 March 1935): 8–10.

Ma Jian and Hu Fangquan, 'Zhongguo Huijiao gaiguan (3)' ('Overview of Islam in China, Part 3'), *Rendao*, 2(1) (1 June 1935): 9–10.

Ma Jian and Hu Fangquan, 'Zhongguo Huijiao gaiguan (4)' ('Overview of Islam in China, Part 4'), *Rendao*, 2(2) (July 1935): 3.

Ma Jing, 'Qingdai guanfang wenxian zhong de Liu Zhi' ('Liu Zhi in official Qing documents'), paper delivered at the Fourth Dialogue between Chinese and Islamic Civilizations, Nanjing, 2010.

Ma Jitang, *Chen Keli zhuan* (*Biography of Chen Keli*), Hong Kong: Tianma Tushu Youxian Gongsi, 2003.

Ma Kainan (Yūsuf), '"Foreign relations between the Republic of China and the Kingdom of Saudi Arabia: The process of establishing and sustaining relationships (1936–1986)', PhD dissertation, University of Miami, 1988.

Ma Mingliang, *Yisilan wenhua xinlun (xiudingben)* (*New Discussions on Islamic Culture, Revised*), Yinchuan: Ningxia Renmin Chubanshe, 2006.

Ma Mingliang, 'Dangjin Zhongguo tong Yisilan guojia de wenhua jiaoliu yu wenming duihua' ('Present-day cultural exchanges and civilisational dialogue between China and Islamic countries'), *Xiya feizhou*, 12(4) (2009): 37–41.

Ma Mingliang, 'Yisilanjiao de Zhongguohua yu "yi Ru quan Jing"' ('Sinicization of Islam and "using Confucianism to comment on the Scriptures"'), *Alabo shijie yanjiu*, 5 (2009): 53–61.

Ma Mingliang, '"Yi Ru quan Jing" huodong jiqi dui dangdai wenming duihua de qishi yiyi' ('"Using Confucianism to comment on the Scriptures" and its enlightening significance for contemporary civilizational dialogue'), available at: http://www.china-sufi.com/forum.php?mod=viewthread&tid=14475&page=1, last accessed 5 October 2015.

Ma Qiang, *Minguo shiqi Guangzhou Musilin baokan ziliao jilu (1928–1949)* (*Compilation of Materials from Periodicals of the Guangzhou Muslims during the Republican Era, 1928–1949*), Yinchuan: Ningxia Renmin Chubanshe, 2004.

Ma Qiang, *Liudong de jingshen shequ: Renleixue shiye xia de Guangzhou Musilin zhemati yanjiu* (*Spiritual Communities in Movement: Anthropological Research on the* jama'a *of the Guangzhou Muslims*), Beijing: Zhongguo Shehui Kexue Chubanshe, 2006.

Ma Qiang, *Huifang neiwai: Chengshi xiandaihua jinchengzhong de Xi'an yisilanjiao yanjiu* (*Inside and Outside the Muslim Quarter: Research on Islam in Xi'an in the Process of Urban Modernization*), Beijing: Zhongguo Shehui Kexue Chubanshe, 2011.

Ma Qiang, 'Quanqiuhua beijingxia de Zhongguo Yisilanjiao yanjiu jidai jiaqiang' ('The urgent need to study Islam in China in the context of globalization'), *Zhongguo minzu bao*, 10 January 2012, available at: http://www.mzzjw.cn/zgmzb/html/2012-01/10/content_82073.htm, last accessed 10 May 2012.

Ma Qiang, *Kuayue bianjie: Zhongguo he Malaixiya guixin musilin tianye fangtan* (*Transcending Boundaries: Field Interviews of Muslim Converts in China and Malaysia*), Lanzhou: Gansu Minzu Chubanshe, 2013, 2 vols.

Ma Qiang and Hu Qunqiong, 'Quanqiuhua beijingxia Zhongguo ahong mianlin de tiaozhan yu shiming' ('Challenges and missions confronted by Chinese ahongs in the context of globalization'), *Qinghai minzu yanjiu*, 22(1) (2011):130–6.

Ma Songting, 'Zhongguo Huijiao de xianzhuang' ('The current state of Islam in China'), *Yuehua*, 5(16–18) (May–June 1933).

Ma Songting, 'Zhongguo Huijiao yu Chengda Shifan Xuexiao' ('Islam in China and the Chengda Teachers' College'), *Yugong*, 5(11) (1936).

Ma Tong, 'Jibuci yu Xidaotang' ('The kibbutz and the Xidaotang'), *Xibei minzu yanjiu*, No. 2 (1994).

Ma Tong, *Zhongguo Yisilan jiaopai yu menhuan zhidu shilüe* (*The History of China's Islamic System of Religious Solidarities and* Menhuan)[1983], Reprint Yinchuan: Ningxia Renmin Chubanshe, 1995.

Ma Tong, *Zhongguo Yisilan jiaopai yu menhuan suyuan* (*The Origins of China's Muslim Solidarities and* Menhuan)[1986], Reprint Yinchuan: Ningxia Renmin Chubanshe, 2000.

Ma Xian, *Bihai tanzhu: Nu'erman Ma Xian cungao* (*Searching for Pearls in the Ocean: Writings of Nu'man Ma Xian*), Yinchuan: Ningxia Renmin Chubanshe, 2011, 2 vols.

Ma Yan, 'Huizu jingtang jiaoyu jiaocai yanjiu' ('On the education and textbooks of Sino-Muslim madrasas'), MA thesis, Ningxia University, 2005.

Ma Zhixin (Bahā' al-Dīn), 'Jiaoyu yu zongjiao cishan: Cong geren congshi banxue sanshi nian kan Linxia Musilin canyu jiaoyu shiye guannian de chuanbian yu lishi jingyan' ('Benevolence in education and religion: from my own experience of running a school for thirty years, considering historical experience and change in Linxia Muslims' opinion of educational activities'), available at: http://www.qhhsjzh.com/LYZZ/GZJL/201003/10.html, last accessed 16 August 2012.

Ma Zhu, *Qingzhen zhinan (The Guide to Islam)* [1868], in *Huizu he Zhongguo Yisilanjiao guji ziliao huibian*, Yinchuan: Ningxia Renmin Chubanshe, n.d., Collection 1, box 7, reproducing an 1868 woodblock edition.

Ma Zhu, *Qingzhen zhinan (The Guide to Islam)* [c. 1710], Reprint Tianjin: Huizu Zhongguo Yisilanjiao chubanshe, 1987.

'Ma Zishi zuijin xin chuangzuo' ('Recent new works of Ma Zishi [Ma Jian]'), *Rendao*, 1(8–10) (1 March 1935): 37.

Makeham, John, *Transmitters and Creators: Chinese Commentators and Commentaries on the Analects*, Cambridge, MA: Harvard University Asia Center, 2003.

Mann, Susan, 'The education of daughters in the mid-Qing period', in Benjamin A. Elman and Alexander Woodside (eds), *Education and Society in Late Imperial China, 1600–1900*, Berkeley, CA: University of California Press, 1994.

Matsumoto Akirō, 'Ba Rengen cho "Tianfang xingli Awen zhujie" no kenkyū' ('A study of Ma Lianyuan's *Arabic Commentary on [Liu Zhi's] Islamic Metaphysics*'), *Tōyōshi kenkyū*, 58(1) (1999).

Matsumoto Akirō, 'Chūgoku Isurāmu no seishin sekai: Ryū Chi no "Wu geng yue" ni tsuite' ('The spiritual world of Islam in China: on Liu Zhi's "Wu geng yue"'), *Shisō*, 941 (2002).

Matsumoto Akirō, 'Chūgoku Isurāmu sonzai issei ron no "tai-itsu" ni tsuite' ('On the "Embodied One" in the unity of existence discourse of Chinese Islam'), *Kiyo ningen bunka*, 6 (2003): 1–23.

Matsumoto Akirō, 'Ba Tokushin to Isurāmu shisō no Jugakuteki tenkai' ('Ma Dexin and the Confucian evolution of Islamic thought'), *Sapiencha: Eichi daigaku ronsō*, 40 (2006): 141–60.

Matsumoto Akirō, 'Chūgoku Isurāmu tetsugaku shisō ni okeru "zentai taiyō" ni kansuru kosaku' ('An investigation of *quanti dayong* in Chinese Islamic philosophical thought'), *Sapiencha: Eichi daigaku ronsō*, 41 (2007): 269–87.

Matsumoto Akirō, 'The Sufi intellectual tradition among Sino-Muslims', in Lloyd

Ridgeon (ed.), *Sufism: Critical Concepts in Islamic Studies*, vol. 2, London: Routledge, 2008.

Matsumoto Akirō, *Chūgoku Isurāmu shisō no kenkyū* (*Research on Chinese Islamic Thought*), Tokyo: Rakudasha, 2010.

Matsumoto Akirō, 'Ba Tokushin no *Hanyi daoxing jiujing* to Ajīzu Nasafī no *'Maqsad-e Aqsa* (Saien no mokuteki chi) ni kansuru ichiosatsu' ('A study of Ma Dexin's *Hanyi daoxing jiujing* and Azīz Nasafī's *'Maqsad-e Aqsa'*), *Sapiencha: Eichi daigaku ronsō*, 46 (2012): 1–26.

Matsumoto Masumi, 'Esunishiti to nashonaru aidentitī: Chūgoku Isurāmu shin bunka undō to Chūgoku kokka' ('Ethnicity and national identity: the new culture movement in Chinese Islam and the Chinese nation-state'), in Nishimura Shigeo (ed.), *Gendai Chūgoku no kōzō hendō: Nashonarizumu – rekishi kara no setten* (*Structural Evolution of Contemporary China: Nationalism – Historical Points of Contact*), Tokyo: University of Tokyo Press, 2000, pp. 99–125.

Matsumoto Masumi, 'Chūgoku no Isurāmu shin bunka undō' ('The Islamic new culture movement in China'), in Komatsu Hisao and Kosugi Yasushi (eds.), *Gendai Isurāmu shisō to seiji undō* (*Thought and Political Movements in Contemporary Islam*), Tokyo: University of Tokyo Press, 2003.

Matsumoto Masumi, *Zhongguo minzu zhengce zhi yanjiu: Yi Qingmo zhi 1945 nian de 'minzulun' wei zhongxin* (*Research on China's Minzu Policies: Minzu Discourses from the Late Qing to 1945*), trans. Lu Zhonghui, Beijing: Minzu Chubanshe, 2003.

Matsumoto Masumi, 'Protestant Christian missions to Muslims in China and the Islamic reformist movement', *Annual Report of JAMES*, 21(1) (2005): 147–71.

Matsumoto Masumi, 'Rationalizing patriotism among Muslim Chinese: the impact of the Middle East on the *Yuehua* journal', in Stéphane Dudoignon, Hisao Komatsu and Yasushi Kosugi (eds), *Intellectuals in the Modern Islamic World: Transmission, Transformation, Communication*, London: Routledge, 2006, pp. 117–42.

Matsumoto Masumi, 'Sakuma Teijirō no tai Chūgoku Isurāmu kōsaku to Shanghai Musurimu: Aru Ajiashugisha o meguru kosaku' ('Sakuma Teijirō's maneuvers toward Islam in China and the Muslims in Shanghai: an introductory discussion of a Pan-Asianist'), *Jōchi Ajia gaku*, 27 (2009): 115–34.

Matsumoto Masumi, *Isurāmu e no kaiki: Chūgoku no musurima tachi* (*Returning to Islam: Muslim Women in China*), Tokyo: Yamakawa Shuppansha, 2010.

Matsumoto Masumi and Shimbo Atsuko, 'Islamic education in China: triple discrimination and the challenge of Hui women's madrasas', in Sakurai Keiko,

Fariba Adelkhah and Dale Eickelman (eds), *The Moral Economy of the Madrasa: Islam and Education Today*, London: Routledge, 2010, pp. 86–103.

Meijer, Roel (ed.), 'Introduction', in *Global Salafism: Islam's New Religious Movement*, London: Hurst, 2009, pp. 1–32.

Millward, James, *Beyond the Pass: Economy, Ethnicity and Empire in Qing Central Asia, 1759–1864*, Stanford, CA: Stanford University Press, 1998.

Min Junqing and Ding Kejia, 'Wuben hengyi lishen, wei xue yijin tianming: Fang Huizu Musilin xuezhe Nu'erman Ma Xian xiansheng' ('Establishing himself through devotion to the Constant, pursuing knowledge to fulfil the will of Heaven: a visit to the *Huizu* Muslim scholar Nu'man Ma Xian'), *Huizu yanjiu*, 69(1) (2008): 123–31.

Min Shengguang (Hajji Muhammad Nur al-Dīn), *Ma Qixi shilian shangshi* (*Appreciation of Ma Qixi's Poems and Couplets*), Beijing: Zhonghua Shuju, 2004.

Min Shengguang (Hajji Muhammad Nur al-Dīn), *Zhongguo yisilanjiao Xidaotang yanjiu wenji* (*Texts for Research on the Islamic Xidaotang of China*), Lanzhou: Gansu Renmin Chubanshe, 2010, 3 vols.

Mote, Frederick, *Intellectual Foundations of China*, 2nd edn, New York: McGraw-Hill, 1988.

Mouline, Nabil, *Les clercs de l'islam: autorité religieuse et pouvoir politique en Arabie Saoudite, XVIIIe–XXIe siècle*, Paris: PUF, 2011.

Mu Chengzhu and Mu Chengren, 'Mujiazhuang' ('Mu family village'), *Zhenzongbao yuekan*, 6(1/2) (1940).

Mu Zhi (pseud.), 'Zhongguo yisilan jiaoyu mantan' ('Musings on Islamic education in China'), *Yuedu yinqing*, No. 2 (2004), available at: http://islambook.net/xueshu/list.asp?id=2526, last accessed 21 November 2007.

Muhammad Fuad 'Abd al-Baqi, *Shengxun zhuji* (*Pearls of the Ḥadīth*), trans. Ma Xian, Beijing: Zongjiao Wenhua Chubanshe, 2002.

Muhammad Fuad 'Abd al-Baqi, *Shengxun zhuji* (*Pearls of the Ḥadīth*), trans. Muhammad 'Uthman, n.p., 1985.

Muhammad Makin (Ma Jian) (trans.). *Kitāb al-Hiwār li-Konfushius* (*The Dialogues [Analects] of Confucius*), Cairo: Al-Matba'a al-Salafiyya, 1935.

Murata, Sachiko, *Chinese Gleams of Sufi Light: Wang Tai-yü's Great Learning of the Pure and Real and Liu Chih's Displaying the Concealment of the Real Realm, with a New Translation of Jāmī's Lawā'ih from the Persian by William C. Chittick*, Albany, NY: State University of New York Press, 2000.

Murata, Sachiko, 'The unity of being in Liu Chih's "Islamic Neoconfucianism"', *Journal of the Muhyiddin Ibn 'Arabi Society*, 36 (2004), available at: http://

www.ibnarabisociety.org/articles/islamicneoconfucianism.html, last accessed 18 September 2015.

Murata, Sachiko, William C. Chittick and Wei-ming Tu, *The Sage Learning of Liu Zhi: Islamic Thought in Confucian Terms*, Cambridge, MA: Harvard University Press, 2009.

Na Guochang, 'Qimeng duwu *Tianfang sanzijing*' ('The educational primer *Three Character Classic of Islam*'), *Zhongguo Musilin*, 6 (1996): 11–15.

Na Lanzhen, 'Huainian "shiji" laoren Lin Xinghua' ('Remembering an "old man of the century", Lin Xinghua'), *Kaituo*, 2 (2001): 22–3.

Na Zhong, 'Na Zijia jun zhi laihan' ('Letter from Mr Na Zijia [Na Zhong]'), *Yuehua*, 4(10–12) (5 April 1932): 36–9.

Na Zhong, 'Shizijun zhanzheng zhong zhi Huijiaoren yu xifangren' ('Muslims and Westerners in the Crusades'), *Yuehua*, 8(26) (20 September 1936): 4–5.

Na Zhong, 'Jinian Ma Jian jiaoshou guizhen shizhounian' ('Remembering Professor Ma Jian on the tenth anniversary of his passing'), *Zhongguo Musilin*, 1 (1989): 17–19.

Na Zhong, Audio Interview by Xue Qingguo, Arabic Department, Beijing Foreign Studies University. Audio interviews between Na and Xue are on cassettes and are in the author's personal library.

Nakanishi Tatsuya, 'Ryū Chi no *Tianfang xingli* ni okeru *Mirsād al-ibād* no kaishaku ni tsuite' ('On the interpretation of *Mirsād al-ibād* in Liu Zhi's *Tianfang xingli*'), *Seinan Ajia kenkyū*, 60 (2004): 46–61.

Nakanishi Tatsuya, *Chūka to taiwa suru Isurāmu: 17–19 seiki Chūgoku Musurimu no shisōteki eii* (*Islam in Dialogue with Zhonghua: The 17th–19th Century Chinese Muslim Intellectual Profession*), Kyoto: Kyoto University Press, 2013.

Pang Shiqian, 'Faluke liuai xueshengtuan guiguo riji' ('Diaries of Faruk students in Egypt returning to China'), *Yuehua* (November 1947), pp. 26–7.

Pang Shiqian, *Aiji jiunian*, reprinted in Zhou Xiefan (ed.), *Qingzhen dadian* (*Great Compendium of Islam*), vol. 20, Hefei: Huangshan Shushe, 2005, pp. 365–476.

Pang Shiqian, 'Zhongguo Huijiao siyuan jiaoyu zhi yange ji keben' ('The evolution and textbooks of China's Islamic mosque education'), *Yugong*, 7(4) (1937).

Papas, Alexandre, *Mystiques et vagabonds en Islam: portraits de trois soufis qalandar*, Paris: Éditions du CERF, 2000.

Park, Hyunhee, *Mapping the Chinese and Islamic Worlds: Cross-Cultural Exchange in Premodern Asia*, Cambridge: Cambridge University Press, 2012.

Petersen, Kristian, 'Reconstructing Islam: Muslim education and literature in Ming–Qing China', *American Journal of Islamic Social Sciences*, 23(3) (2006): 24–53.

Pillsbury, Barbara, '"No pigs for the ancestors": pigs, mothers, and filial piety among the Taiwanese Muslims', paper presented at the Symposium on Chinese Folk Religions, University of California at Riverside, 1974.

Qi Xueyi, 'Zhongguo de shengxun yijie yu yanjiu' ('Ḥadīth translations and studies in China'), *Beifang minzu daxue xuebao*, 91(1) (2010): 113–16.

Rawsky, Evelyn S., *Education and Popular Literacy in Ch'ing China*, Ann Arbor, MI: University of Michigan Press, 1979.

Rosati, Francesca, 'Musilin funü zongjiao yishi de zijue yu shehui hudong: Yi dangdai Linxia de zongjiao nüxiao weilie' ('Self-consciousness of religious awareness and social interactivity of Muslim women: the case of contemporary Linxia female religious schools'), MA thesis, National Chengchi University, Taipei, Taiwan, 2009.

Roussillon, Alain. *Identité et modernité: les voyageurs égyptiens au Japon (XIXe–XXe siècle)*, Paris and Arles: Sindbad-Actes Sud, 2005.

Rowe, William T., 'Ancestral rites and political authority in late imperial China: Chen Hongmou in Jiangxi', *Modern China*, 24(4) (October 1998): 378–407.

'*Ruhua haishi huaru: Cong Yisilan wenming kan Hui-Ru duihua*' ('Confucianizing or changing Confucianism: observing the Islamic–Confucian dialogue from within Islamic civilization'), *Yuedu yinqing*, 6 (2007).

Rudelson, Justin Jon, *Oasis Identities: Uyghur Nationalism along China's Silk Road*, New York: Columbia University Press, 1997.

Sai Shengbao, 'Aiguo zhuyizhe, Yisilan jingxue jiaoyujia Ma Songting da ahong' ('Patriot and teacher of Islamic scriptures, the great *Ahong* Ma Songting'), *Huizu yanjiu*, 6(2) (1992): 98–100.

Sakamoto Tsutomu (ed.), *Nitchū sensō to Isurāmu: Manmō-Ajia chiiki ni okeru tōchi kaijū seisaku* (*The Sino-Japanese War and Islam: Control and Persuasion Policies in Manchuria, Mongolia, and Asia*), Tokyo: Keio University Press, 2008.

Sato Minoru, *Ryū Chi no shizengaku: Chūgoku Isurāmu shisō kenkyū josetsu* (*Liu Zhi's Study of Nature: An Introduction to Research on Islamic Thought in China*), Tokyo: Kyuko Shoin, 2008.

Schneider, Lawrence, *Ku Chieh-kang and China's New History: Nationalism and the Quest for Alternative Traditions*, Berkeley, CA: University of California Press, 1971.

Schwarcz, Vera, *The Chinese Enlightenment: Intellectuals and the Legacy of the May Fourth Movement of 1919*, Berkeley, CA: University of California Press, 1990.

Sha Zongping, *Zhongguo de Tianfang xue: Liu Zhi zhexue yanjiu* (*Chinese Islamica: Research on Liu Zhi's Philosophy*), Beijing: Beijing Daxue Chubanshe, 2004.

Shami, Salih Ahmad, *Al-Ghazali's Revival of the Religious Sciences: An Abridgement*, trans. Zhang Weizhen and Ma Yulong, *Shengxue fusu jingyi* (*Revival of Religious Sciences*), Hong Kong: Shangwu Yinshuguan, 2001, 2 vols.

Shan Guoqing, 'Guayanzhe de'an' ('Silence is golden'), *Muyin yuekan*, 1(3) (1933).

Shan Guoqing, 'Wo jiao dangju de benlai mianmu' ('The original features of our religion's power'), *Muyin yuekan*, 2(1–6) (1934).

Shi Zizhou, 'Huijiao jiaozhang yu Huimin zhanshi jiaoyu' ('Imams and Muslims' education during the Anti-Japanese War'), *Yiguang*, No. 98 (November 1938).

Shimbo Atsuko, 'Nitchū sensōki ni okeru Nihon to Chūgoku Isuramu kyōto: Chūgoku Kaikyō Sōrengokai o chūshin to shite' ('Japan and Muslims in China during the Sino-Japanese War: focus on the All-China Islamic Union'), *Ajia kyōikushi kenkyū*, No. 7 (1998).

Shimbo Atsuko, 'Mōkyō seiken ni okeru Isuramu kyōto kōsaku to kyōiku: Zenrin kaimin jojuku o chūshin to shite' ('Japan's efforts toward and education of Muslims under the Inner Mongolian puppet regime'), *Chūgoku kenkyū geppō*, 53(5) (1999): 1–13.

Shimbo Atsuko, 'Nihon senryōka no kahoku ni okeru Isuramu seinen kōsaku: Chūgoku Kaikyō Seinendan o megutte' ('Japan's efforts towards Muslim youth in occupied North China: on the Chinese Muslim Youth Corps'), *Waseda kyōiku hyōron*, No. 14 (2000).

Shimbo Atsuko, 'Nihon senryōka no Pekin ni okeru kaimin kyōiku' ('Muslim education in occupied Beijing'), in Watabe Sōsuke and Takenaka Ken'ichi (eds), *Kyōiku ni okeru minzokuteki sokoku* (*Ethnic Antagonism in Education*), Tokyo: Tōhō Shoten, 2000, pp. 231–62

Shimbo Atsuko, 'Nihongun senryōka ni okeru shūkyo seisaku: Chūgoku kahoku no Isurāmu kyōto o megutte' ('Japan's religion policy in military-occupied areas: on Muslims in North China'), *Gakujutsu kenkyū: Kyōiku/Shakai kyōiku hen*, No. 52 (2003).

Shou Jin, 'Huijiao Huizu zhi qubie (1)' ('Differentiating *Huijiao* and *Huizu*, Part 1'), *Zhengzong Aiguobao*, No. 1945 (1912).

Shou Jin, 'Huijiao Huizu zhi qubie (2)' ('Differentiating *Huijiao* and *Huizu*, Part 2'), *Zhengzong Aiguobao*, No. 1946 (1912).

Shun, Kwong-loi, 'Ren 仁 and Li 禮 in the *Analects*', in Bryan W. Van Norden (ed.), *Confucius and the* Analects: *New Essays*, Oxford: Oxford University Press, 2002, pp. 53–72.

Simpfendorfer, Ben, *The New Silk Road: How a Rising Arab World is Turning Away from the West and Rediscovering China*, New York: Macmillan, 2009.

Skaovgaard-Peterson, Jakob and Bettina Graf, *Global Mufti: The Phenomenon of Yusuf al-Qaradawi*, London: Hurst, 2009.

Slingerland, Edward, *Confucius Analects: With Selections from Traditional Commentaries*, Indianapolis, IN: Hackett, 2006.

Stalin, Joseph, 'The nationality question and Leninism: reply to Comrades Meshkov, Kovalchuk and others', in Joseph Stalin, *Works, vol. 11: 1928–March 1929*, Moscow: Foreign Languages Publishing House, 1954, pp. 348–72.

Stoecker-Parnian, Barbara, *Jingtang Jiaoyu: Die Buecherhallen Erziehung (Jingtang Jiaoyu: Education in the Scripture Hall)*, Frankfurt am Main: Peter Lang, 2003.

Sun Shengwu, *Huijiao luncong (Collected Writings on Islam)*, Taipei: Zhonghua Wenhua Chubanshiyeshe, 1963.

Sun Zhenyu, *Wang Daiyu, Liu Zhi pingzhuan (Critical Biographies of Wang Daiyu and Liu Zhi)*, Nanjing: Nanjing Daxue Chubanshe, 2006.

Tian Pu and Feng Wu, 'Zhongguo guomin waijiao zai Aiji' ('Chinese citizen diplomacy in Egypt'), *Yuehua*, 13(28–30) (25 October 1941): 24.

Tianjin qu benbu, 'Fenhui zhangcheng zhaiyao shuoming' ('Explaining the branch's regulations and abstracts'), *Huijiao*, 1(3) (1939).

Tillman, Hoyt, 'Chen Liang on statecraft: reflections from examination essays preserved in a Song rare book', *Harvard Journal of Asiatic Studies*, 48(2) (1988): 403–31.

Ting, Dawood C. M., 'Islamic culture in China', in Kenneth W. Morgan (ed.), *Islam – the Straight Path: Islam interpreted by Muslims*, New York: Ronald Press, 1958, pp. 344–74.

Tontini, Roberta, '*Tianfang dianli*: a Chinese perspective on Islamic law and its legal reasoning', *Ming–Qing Studies*, Milan, 2011.

Tontini, Roberta, *Muslim Sanzijing: Shifts and Continuities in the Definition of Islam in China*, Leiden: Brill, forthcoming.

Tsafrir, Nurit, *The History of an Islamic School of Law: The Early Spread of Hanafism*, Cambridge, MA: Harvard University Press, 2004.

Uno Nobuhiro, Matsuoka Hitoshi and Matsuda Koichi, 'Genchō kōki Karakorumu jōshi hānkā kensetu kinen Perushago hibun no kenkyū' ('A Persian inscription commemorating the establishment of a *khānqāh* at Qaraqorum in the late Yuan'), *Nairiku Ajia gengo no kenkyū*, 14 (1999): 1–64.

Voll, John, *Islam: Continuity and Change in the Modern World*, Syracuse, NY: Syracuse University Press, 1994.

Waley, Arthur (trans.), *The Analects of Confucius*, New York: Vintage, 1989.

Wang Daiyu, *Zhengjiao zhenquan, Qingzhen daxue, Xizhen zhengda (True Explanation of the Orthodox Teaching, Great Learning of Islam, Orthodox Responses on the Rare Truth*), ed. Yu Zhengui, Reprint Yinchuan: Ningxia Renmin Chubanshe, 1987.

Wang Huanchen, *Liuxue jiaoyu: Zhongguo liuxue jiaoyu shiliao* (*Education Abroad: Historical Materials on Chinese Education Abroad*), Taipei: Taiwan Guoli Bianyi Guan, 1980.

Wang Jingzhai. 'Wushi nian qiuxue zishu' ('Memoir of fifty years spent seeking knowledge'), *Yugong*, 7(4) (1937).

Wang Jingzhai, 'Fayang Yisilan wenhua zhi biyao' ('The necessity to enhance Islamic culture'), *Huijiao luntan banyuekan*, 2(2–5) (1939).

Wang Shiming, 'Jiaqiang zhongai wenhua jingji zhengzhi guanxi gangyao' ('Outline for strengthening Sino-Egyptian cultural, economic, and political relations'), Zhongguo Dier Lishi Dang'anguan (Second Historical Archive of China), Nanjing, Folder No. 18-1594.

Wang Yingqi, 'Fasheng zai qingzhensili Rijun da tusha' ('The Japanese Army's massacre at a mosque'), *Zhongguo Musilin*, No. 2 (2005).

Wang Zengshan, Cable to Jiang Jieshi [Chiang Kai-shek], 14 May 1938, in 'Jiang Jieshi chaofa zhongguo Huijiao jindong fangwentuan zai Aiji xuanchuan jingguo baogao dian' ('Jiang Jieshi's copy of a cable from the Chinese Islamic Delegation to the Near East on propaganda efforts in Egypt'), in Zhongguo dier lishi dang'anguan (Second Historical Archive of China) (ed.), *Zhonghua minguo shi dang'an ziliao huibian* (*Collection of Archival Material on Republican History*), Nanjing: Jiangsu Guji Chubanshe, 1997, pp. 701–3.

Wiktorowicz, Quintan, 'Anatomy of the Salafi movement', *Studies in Conflict and Terrorism*, 29(3) (April/May 2006): 207–39.

Wilson, Thomas A., 'Genealogy and history in Neo-Confucian sectarian uses of the Confucian past', *Modern China*, 20(1) (January 1994): 3–33.

Wo'erzi yanjiang ji (*Anthology of* wa'z [*sermon*] *Discourses*), Beijing: Zhongguo Yisilanjiao Xiehui, 1999.

Wobang (pseud.), 'Wei "Gaishang Awen jiaoyu de xianyi" hou' ('Response to the essay, "Doubts about the reform of Arabic education"'), *Huijiao zhoubao*, 4 April 1941.

Wu Yandong, *Zhongguo Huizu sixiangjia pingshu* (*Critical Study of Chinese Huizu Thinkers*), Beijing: Zongjiao Wenhua Chubanshe, 2004.

Wu Zixian, *Guizhen yaodao*, n.p., 1891.

Wuhuaguo (pseud.), *Musilin xiwang zhi lu: Zhonghua Musilin de xiankuang yu zhanwang* (*The Road of Hope for Muslims: The Current Situation and Future Prospects of China's Muslims*), n.p., 2004.

Wuhuaguo (pseud.), 'Yisilan zai Zhongguo chuanbo de zhuyao zhang'ai' ('The main obstacles to propagation of Islam in China'), available at: http://www.2muslim.com/forum.php?mod=viewthread&tid=409116, last accessed 15 October 2012.
Wuhuaguo (pseud.), *Yu yige Jidutu de bianlun* (*Debate with a Christian*), available at: http://www.xaislam.com/mktb/list.asp?id=1952.
'Xiao Ma A-ge: Wangluo jiu shi shenghuo, shenghuo jiu shi wangluo' ('Xiao Ma A-ge: internet is life, life is internet'), *Wangyou*, No. 2 (2005), available at: http://www.2muslim.com/forum.php?mod=viewthread&tid=15658&extra=page%3D1, last accessed 23 October 2006.
'Xingzhengyuan ni tongling: Quanguo gaizheng Huiren chengwei zhineng chengwei Huijiaotu buneng chengwei Huizu' ('A general order of the Executive Yuan: Muslims may only be referred to as *Huijiaotu*, not as *Huizu*'), *Dagongbao*, 16 September 1940.
Xue Wenbo (Dawude), 'Zhongguo Huizu yundong' ('The Chinese *Huizu* movement'), *Huijiao qingnian*, 7 January 1933, p. 7.
Xue Wenbo (Dawude), 'Guanyu Huizu yu Hanren xinyang Huijiao wenti' ('On the question of *Huizu* and Han believers in Islam'), *Huizu qingnian*, 30 October 1933, pp. 9–14.
Xue Wenbo, 'Guanyu Wuru Huizu an' ('On cases of offence against the *Huizu*'), *Yuehua*, 4(28–30) (1932).
Xue Wenbo, 'Fakanci' ('On initiating this publication'), *Huizu qingnian*, 7 January 1933.
Yajima Yoichi, 'Genchōki higashi Ajia no Sūfizumu' ('Sufism in Yuan period East Asia'), in *Chūgoku no Isurāmu shisō to bunka* (*China's Islamic Thought and Culture*), *Ajia yūgaku*, No. 129, Tokyo: Bensei Shuppan, 2009.
Yamazaki Noriko, 'Nitchū sensōki no Chūgoku Isuramu shakai ni okeru "qin Ri pai" Musurimu ni kansuru ikkosatsu: Chūgoku kaikyō sōrengokai no Tang Yichen o chūshin ni' ('Pro-Japanese Muslims in Chinese Islamic society during the Sino-Japanese War: focus on Tang Yichen of the All-China Islamic Union'), *Chūgoku kenkyū geppō*, 65(9) (2011): 1–19.
Yamazaki Noriko, 'Kindai Chūgoku ni okeru "Kanjin Kaikyōto" setsu no tenkai: 1930 nendai no Musurimu erīto ni yoru gensetsu o tegakari ni' ('Development of the "Han-Muslims" in modern China: with a clue to Muslim elite discourses of the 1930s'), *Komaba Journal of Area Studies*, 17 (2014): 136–56.
Yang Guiping, 'Ming–Qing shiqi Zhongguo Yisilanjian Hanwen yizhu zhong de Huizu zhexue sixiang' ('*Huizu* philosophical thought in the Ming–Qing period

Chinese Islamic translations and commentaries in Chinese'), *Huizu yanjiu*, 17 (1995): 25–34.

Yang Huaizhong and Yu Zhengui, *Yisilan yu Zhongguo wenhua* (*Islam and Chinese Culture*), Yinchuan: Ningxia Renmin Chubanshe, 1982.

Yang Huaizhong and Yu Zhengui, *Zhongguo Yisilan wenxian zhuyi tiyao* (*Summaries of Works and Translations of Chinese Islamic Documents*), Yinchuan: Ningxia Renmin Chubanshe, 1993.

Yang Huiyun (ed.), *Huizu dacidian* (*Dictionary of the* Huizu), Shanghai: Shanghai Cishu Chubanshe, 1993.

Yang Sishi, 'Duiyu Aiji Huiguang yuekan de pingyu' ('Comments on the Egyptian monthly journal *Nur al-Islām*'), *Yuehua*, 4(33) (25 November 1932): 11–13.

Yang Wenjiong, 'Wenhua zijue yu jingshen hewang dushi zuqun yanjiu: *Kaituo*, yizhong wenhua xianxiang' ('Cultural self consciousness and thirst for spirituality in studying urban ethnic communities: *Kaituo*, a cultural phenomenon'), *Huizu yanjiu*, 41(1) (2001): 70–5.

Yang Zhanwu, *Huihui yuyan wenhua* (*The Language Culture of the Huihui*), Yinchuan: Ningxia Renmin Chubanshe, 1996.

Yao Jide, 'Wenming duihua shiyexia de Yisilan henuo linian: Yizhong guoji de guancha he sikao' ('Islamic harmonious perspectives in civilizational dialogue: an international observation and reflection'), *Yisilan wenhua*, 3 (2010): 1–11.

Yin Boqing, 'Huijiao yu Huizu bian' ('Differentiation between *Huijiao* and *Huizu*'), in Li Xinghua and Feng Jinyuan (eds), *Zhongguo Yisilanjiao shi sankao ziliao xuanpian* (*Selected Sources on the History of Islam in China*), Yinchuan: Ningxia Renmin Chubanshe, 1985, pp. 262–5.

'Yiwei meiti jizhe yu Jin Biao ahong de duihua' ('Dialogue between a media journalist and *ahong* Jin Biao'), available at: http://www.noorislam.org/forum.php?mod=viewthread&tid=66673&highlight=%D2%BB%CE%BB%C3%BD%CC%E5%BC%C7%D5%DF%D3%EB%BD%F0%EF%DA, last accessed 25 September 2010.

'Yu Jinbiao ahong de zongjiao jiaoliu' ('Religious exchange with *ahong* Jinbiao'), 18 September 2010, available online at a Buddhist blog, as well as the Muslim site *Yiguang*: http://blog.sina.com.cn/s/blog_5cf4c0070100lh0i.html, last accessed 9 March 2011.

Yu Ke, 'Wo suo gongxian yu liuxue Aiji zhujun de jige yijian' ('A few suggestions to the gentlemen studying in Egypt'), *Yuehua*, 4(16–18) (1932): 11–18.

Yuan Guozuo, *Tianfang sanzijing zhujie qianshuo* (*Commentary and Introduction to*

the Three Character Classic of Islam) [1870], Reprint Taipei: Huijiao Jingshu Zhengyinhui, 1989.
Yusuf al-Qaradawi, *Khutab al-shaykh al-Qardhawi* (*The Middle Way* [edited version]: *Speeches of Yusuf al-Qaradawi*), ed. Yuan Taiping (Luqman), trans. Cheng Yongsheng (Yunus), Hong Kong: Tianma Chuban Youxian Gongsi, 2011.
Zai Wei (pseud.), 'Nüzi jiaoyu yingzou de tujing: Jiazheng jiaoyu' ('The preferred path for women's education: domestic science'), *Huijiao zhoubao*, 27 March 1942.
Zeghal, Malika (ed.), 'Intellectuels de l'islam contemporain. Nouvelles générations, nouveaux débats', *Revue des mondes musulmans et de la méditerranée*, 123(1) (2008).
Zhang Chengqian (Yisima'er), *Yisilan de zhaohuan* (*The Call of Islam*), n.p., 1992.
Zhang Chengqian, *Heping xinyang yu renlei zhongji zhuiqiu* (*Peaceful Belief and Humankind's Final Goal*), Hong Kong: Tianma Chuban Youxian Gongsi, 2012, 2 vols.
Zhang Juling, 'Zhongguo Huijiao Jujinhui chuchuang jiping, zhong' ('Evaluation of the establishment phase of the Chinese Islamic Progressive Association, Part 2'), *Huizu yanjiu*, 1 (1998): 16–18.
Zhang Juling, *Lüyuan gouchen: Zhang Juling Huizu shi lunxuan* (*Quest in the Green Garden: Selections from Zhang Juling's Writings on* Huizu *History*), Beijing: Renmin Chubanshe, 2001.
Zhang Juling, 'Qingmo minchu de Huizu baokan yu Ding Baochen deng wu da baoren' ('The *Huizu* press in the late Qing and early Republic: Ding Baochen and the five great journalists'), *Yunmeng xuekan*, 5 (2006): 25–37.
Zhang Weizhen (Hange), *Huanyuan Yisilan zhen jingshen* (*Restore the True Spirit of Islam*), n.p., 1993.
Zhang Weizhen (Hange), 'Zenyang duidai shengxun?' ('How shall we deal with Sunna/Hadith?'), *Gaoyuan*, No. 4 (2008), available at: http://yigelan2007.blog.163.com/blog/static/557836512009717114519672, last accessed 25 September 2015.
Zhang Weizhen, *Gaoyuan*, available at: http://www.yslzc.com/zazhi/gy/dishibaqi/200806/26184.html, last accessed 5 August 2008.
Zhang Weizhen, 'Shilun Yiben Taimiye dui Yalishiduode zhexue de pipan' ('On Ibn Taymiyah's critique of Aristotle's philosophy'), *Yisilan wenhua*, 3 (2010): 30–9.
Zhang Zaili, *Zhida linghun: Yige Hanzu Musilin de sixiang liji* (*Going Straight to Spirit: A Han Muslim's Thinking Notes*), Hong Kong: Tianma Chuban Youxian Gongsi, 2010.

Zhao Can, *Jingxue xichuan pu* (*Genealogy of the Transmission and Lineage of Classical Learning*), [1714], Reprint Xining: Qinghai Renmin Chubanshe, 1989.

Zhao Guojun and Ma Guifen, 'Ershi shiji bashi niandai yilai Zhongguo Musilin minjian kanwu de xianzhuang yu tedian' ('The situation and specifics of Chinese Muslim popular publications since the 1980s'), *Huizu yanjiu*, 50(2) (2003): 86–90.

Zhao Haixia, 'Guanyu "Chan Hui" zhengshi gengming "Weiwu'er" de shijian wenti' ('The question of timing of the formal change of *Chanhui* to *Weiwuer*'), *Huaxia wenhua*, 4 (2010): 37–8.

Zhao Zhenwu, *Xixing riji* (*Diary of a Trip to the West*), Beijing: Chengda Shifan Chubanbu, 1933.

Zhao Zhenwu, 'Sanshinian lai Zhongguo Huijiao wenhua gaikuang' ('Status of Chinese Islamic culture in the past thirty years'), *Yuehua*, 8(22) (10 August 1936): 2–7.

Zhao Zhongqi, 'Lun Zhongguo Huijiao zhi guomin jiaoyu' ('On Chinese Islamic citizens' education'), *Xinghuipian* (1908), pp. 64–9.

Zhongguo Huijiao Zong Lianhehui (All-China Islamic Union), 'Zhongguo Huijiao Zong Lianhehui zuigao zhidao ji weiyuan mingxibiao' ('High-ranking leaders and committee members of the All-China Islamic Union'), in *Zhongguo Huijiao Zong Lianhehui chengli yizhounian jinian nianbao* (*Yearbook Commemorating the First Anniversary of the All-China Islamic Union*)(1939), pp. 37–8.

Zhongguo Musilin (*China Muslim*), 191(3) (2003): 4–7.

'Zhongguo Musilin you yige xuezhe qunti ma?' ('Is there a community of Chinese Muslim scholars?'), available at: http://www.2muslim.com/forum.php?mod=viewthread&tid=67020, last accessed 18 September 2015.

'Zhongguo xuesheng ruxue wenti yi jiejue' ('Chinese students' enrollment issue resolved'), *Yuehua*, 5(15) (1933): 14.

'Zhongguo xueshengbu tushuguan shoudao shubao minxie' ('Thanks from the Chinese student library for book and newspaper donations'), *Rendao*, 2(2) (1 July 1935), inside cover page.

Zhongguo Yisilanjiao Jiaowu Zhidao Weiyuanhui (Directorial Committee for Chinese Muslim Educational Administration) (ed.), *Xin wo'erzi yanjiang ji [shixing ben]* (*New Selected* wa'z [*sermon*] *Discourses: Text Book*), Beijing: Zongjiao Wenhua Chubanshe, vol. 1, 2001; vol. 2, 2003.

Zhou Chuanbin, *Xinhuo xiangchuan de Huizu jiaoyu* (*Huizu Education and its Generational Transmission*), Yinchuan: Ningxia Renmin Chubanshe, 2008.

Zwemer, S. M., 'Islam a missionary problem', *China's Millions*, LXIV (1938, Special Moslem Number).

Websites

http://baike.baidu.com/view/316670.htm, last accessed 18 November 2011.
http://blog.sina.com.cn/s/blog_5ef66f4b0100oksd.html, last accessed 28 October 2012.
http://dev.gansudaily.com.cn/system/2012/03/01/012391850.shtml, last accessed 6 September 2012.
http://hi.baidu.com/mushafuer/item/40f6dab2cced9570254b0949.
http://news.xinhuanet.com/zgjx/2007-06/19/content_6261912.htm.
http://www.2muslim.com/forum.php?mod=viewthread&tid=104937, last accessed 26 May 2011.
http://www.2muslim.com/forum.php?mod=viewthread&tid=3523, last accessed 10 May 2012.
http://www.2muslim.com/forum.php?mod=viewthread&tid=38484&extra=page%3D1, last accessed 24 March 2011.
http://www.iiu.edu.pk, last accessed 5 October 2015.
http://www.islambook.net/shop/sort_book.asp?productno=6826, last accessed 5 October 2015.
http://www.islamcn.net/ask, last accessed 9 September 2012.
http://www.islamcn.net/sv/list/list3_2.html, last accessed 24 March 2011.
http://www.jxmzj.gov.cn/llyd_1/shmwz/201110/t20111007_176438.htm, last accessed 27 August 2012.
http://www.mslwhyp.com/news_view.asp?id=81, last accessed 24 March 2011.
http://www.muslem.net.cn/bbs/article-7411-1.html, last accessed 10 September 2012.
http://www.slate.com/articles/life/faithbased/2007/07/what_to_expect_when_youre_expecting_a_cowife.2.html, last accessed 19 July 2013.
http://www.yslzc.com/rw/Class124/rw1/201201/37735.html, last accessed 5 October 2011.

Index

Abduh, Muhammad, 154–5
acculturation, 1–3, 7, 29, 118, 221
Adam, 83–4, 86, 123
al-Afghānī, Jamāl al-Dīn, 154, 224
Ahmadis, 219
ahong Alif, 204
ahong zaixian ('online' *ahongs*) 204
ahongs (Imams/religious leaders), 199, 201–5
  education, 171, 175–91
  female (*nü ahong*), 210
  new generation, 203–5
  political (*zhengzhi*), 202–3
Aisin Gioro, house of, 114
al-Azhar Mosque, 98
al-Azhar University, 147–67, 186
  motivations for sending students to, 148–52
  students' relations with the Chinese state, 162–6
  students' backgrounds, 152–6
  students' experience, 156–62
Alexander the Great, 113
'Ali, Muhammad Kurd, 156
All-China Islamic Union (*Zhongguo Huijiao Zong Lian hehui*), 187–8, 191
Amin, Ahmad, 156
Analects, 153, 157

Anti-Japanese War, 178, 192
Anti-Religion Campaign, 172
Anti-Rightist Campaign, 172
Arabi, Ibn, 171
Arabic, 215, 219
  ahongs' knowledge of, 178, 182
  learning, 172–3, 175, 183, 188
  status, 181
Arabic literacy, 171, 173, 174, 177–80, 182, 184, 186, 190
  texts, 155, 171, 174, 177, 182–4
  translation of works into, 157
  translation of Arabic works to Chinese, 154, 217
Arabic Bible, 183
Arafat, 90
Ashi'āt al -Lama'āt (Sufi textbook, Jāmī), 47, 192
assimilation (*tonghua*), 1–3, 4, 108, 122, 131, 133, 136, 138, 175–6, 210
Association for Common Progress of the Five *Zu* (*Wuzu Guomin Hejinhui*), 121
Atwill, David, 110
Aubin, Françoise, 2

Baha'is, 219
bai (worship), 83
Bai Shouyi, 2, 199, 212

al-Banna, Hasan, 166, 224
Bao Tingliang, 111, 177
Bao'an *minzu*, 212
Battuta, Ibn, 2
bilingual literacy, 147, 178, 179–81
Beijing, 17–18, 110, 112, 117, 119–20, 157
   Elites, 125
   Japanese occupied, 163, 187
Beiping, 127
Beiping Islamic Students' Association (*Beiping Yisilan Xueyouhui*), 128
Beiping Muslims Association (*Beiping Huimin Gonghui*), 187
Benite, Zvi Ben-Dor, 2, 5, 9, 15, 21, 150, 166, 209–10
Bodde, Derk, 163
bu (cultural spheres of the Qing empire), 114
Buddhism, 4, 44, 58, 87, 118, 125, 135, 154, 212, 222
al-Būṣīrī, Muhammad 98

Cai Dayu, 177
Catholic priests, 5
Chang Zhimei, 173
Chaojin tuji (*Record of the Pilgrimage Journey*, Ma Dexin), 93–101
Chen Guangyuan, 202–3
Chen Keli, 199
Chen Si, 17
Chengda Teachers' College (*Chengda Shifan Xuex,iao*), 122, 123, 136, 147, 148–9, 179–80, 183, 186
Chiang Kai-shek, 122, 126–7, 139
Chinese Association for People-to-People Diplomacy, 163
Chinese Communist Party (CCP), 6–7, 114
   and education, 180, 200
   founding of the Islamic Association of China, 202
   headquarters, 185
   Huizu policy, 107, 128–9, 137, 139–40, 193, 212, 213
   policy on intellectual discourse, 198, 225
   policy on women, 224
   and the *Salafiyya*, 217
   war with Japan, 189, 191

Chinese Islamic Association (*Zhongguo Huijiao Xiehui*), 165–6, 191
Chinese Islamic culture, 43, 45, 198, 222–3
Chinese Islamic modernist programme, 149–52
Chinese Islamic Progressive Association (CIPA, *Zhongguo Huijiao Jujinhui*), 120, 126
   Yunnan branch, 148
Chinese Jews, 5
Chinese language
   learning, 183
   literacy, 57–8, 172–82, 186, 189
Chinese Youth Association (*Zhongguo Huizu Qingnianhui*), 128
Christian writings, 46–7
Christianity, 24, 125, 135, 152, 212, 222
Cieciura, Wlodzimierz, 6, 9, 212
Communists *see* Chinese Communist Party
Confederation of Islam (Egypt), 165
Conference of the World Arab and Islamic Congress for the Defence of Palestine (1938), 160
Confucianism, 4, 6, 15, 17–29, 125, 135, 154, 173, 213
   Dao school, 71–2
   ethical values, 64, 82–3, 87
   Five Meritorious Acts, 85
   integration with Islam, 35–7, 40–51, 57–60, 63–4, 83, 132, 174
   Liu Zhi and, 34–51
   Ma Zhu and, 17–29
   textual studies movement (*kaozheng*), 47
   Wang Daiyu and, 45
   see also Neo-Confucianism
Confucius, 35, 40, 42, 71, 73, 83, 102n
cosmogenesis/cosmology, 16–17, 21–8, 45–6
cosmography, 88–9, 93, 101
   the covenant and, 83–6
Creation, 17, 21–9, 45–6, 63–4, 82, 83–6, 88–9
Cultural Revolution, 199, 201, 202–3, 212, 224
   effect on Islamic education, 172, 185–6, 191, 193

Da Pusheng, 180
Dazan, Muhammad, 148
Da'ud (*Dawude*, Xue Wenbo), 129
dao (the Way), 3, 4, 21, 27, 35, 38, 39, 61, 65–76, 85, 99
Daoism, 4, 44, 58, 87, 118, 125, 135, 154, 222
daotong (filiative transmission of the way), 71–2, 76
daoxu (study of the Way), 190
Daxue (Great Learning), 46
al-Dīn, Bahā, Ma Zhixin (*Baha Ahong*), 206, 209, 217–18, 224
al-Din, Rashid, 2
al-Din, Sayyid Ajjal Shams (Sai Dianchi), 18, 173
Ding Baochen, 115, 120–2
Ding Shiren, 200–1
Ding Zhuyuan, 116–19, 120
Dongxiang *minzu*, 212
Du Wenxiu, 110–11, 116

education
  Japanese modernisation, 188–9
  Salafi, 215–16
  see also madrasa (*jingtang*) education; Persian learning
Effenberg, J. H., 108
Egypt
  Ma Dexin in, 98
  study in *see* al-Azhar University
Egyptian Muslim Brotherhood, 218, 224

Fadli, Captain Ahmad, 177
Faruk, King, 149, 165
Fei Xiaotong, 212
Feng Zenglie, 199
Five Constant Virtues, 82–3
Five Pillars of Islam, 64, 82–3, 85, 87–8, 93, 100
Frankel, James, 21, 211
Fu Tongxian, 2
Fuad I, King, 148

gedimu (traditional non-Sufi Islam), 215
geyi ('concept matching'), 29n

al-Ghāzālī, 224
globalisation, 219–20
God, 35, 171, 174–5, 190, 192
  covenant of, 83–6
  creation of the cosmos, 16–17, 21–9, 43, 46, 63–4, 174
  Muslim's relationship to, 19, 92
  oneness/singularity (Ar. *tawhid*), 184, 188, 215, 218
  revelation to Muhammad, 65–6, 72–5
  union with, 87–8
gong (meritorious acts), 87
Gongheguomin (pseud.), 119
Great Leap Forward, 199, 201
Guangdong, 112
guerbang (*Qurbān*), 91–2
Guomindang (GMD) *see* Nationalist Party

Ha Decheng, 180
hadīth, 17, 26, 71, 93, 180, 193, 202, 203, 207, 208, 216, 223, 225
Hai Weiliang, 148, 162, 163
hajj, 81–102
  al-Azhar students', 163
  effects of, 99–101
  journey, 96–8
  Liu Zhi and, 86–93, 101–2
  Ma Dexin and, 93–101
  practices and rituals, 89–90, 94–6
  substitution of/justification for not completing, 90–1, 96
  Wang Daiyu and, 82–6
Han believers in Islam theory (*Hanren Huijiao shuo*), 109–10, 122–3, 127, 131–8, 193
Han Haichao, 208
Han kitāb (Ch. *Han ketabu*), 3–5, 7, 16, 135, 140, 166, 174, 192, 222
  approach to Creation, 22, 27, 28
  pilgrimage, 82
  see also individual works; Liu Zhi; Ma Zhu; Wang Diayu; Yuan Guozuo;
Han Studies faction (*Hanxuepai*), 214–15
Han, 113–14, 133, 164, 187, 211–13
Hanbal, Ibn, 67
Hanifa, Abu, 65, 67, 69–70; *see also* Hanafi school of jurisprudence

Hanafi school of jurisprudence, 69–70, 73–5, 97, 216
Hanzu, 113
He Yaozu, 164
Hedin, Sven, 108
Hu Dengzhou, 47, 173
Hu Fangquan, 159
Hu Songshan (Imam), 152, 203
Huaishengsi mosque, 112
Huang Wanjun, 205
Huang Zhenpan, 112–14, 124, 136
Hui/*Huizu*, 3, 9
  customs, 124
  definitions, 107–8
  geographical groupings, 130–1
  government policy, 107, 122–3, 127–9, 137, 139–40, 193, 212, 213
  history of terminology, 110–22
  intellectuals' discussions on, 108–9, 199–200, 211–13, 225
  offences againt (*wuru Huizu'an*), 128
  as a pan-Muslim ethnicity, 126–35
  Sinophone Muslim ethnicity, 135–9
  theories, 109–10, 112, 122–3, 126–7, 131–9
  Yin Boqing's view on the concept of, 122–6
Huihe (*Huihu*), 112, 117, 120, 132, 135, 137, 138
Huihui, 37, 113, 124, 133, 137
Huihui minzu shuo (*Huizu shuo*, Hui ethnicity theory), 109
Huihui shuo (*Explaining Huihui*, Liu Zhi), 37
Huihuihua, 11n, 137
Huihuiying mosque, 185
Huijiao, 117–22, 123, 132, 212
Huijiao minzu shuo (Islamic nationality theory), 109, 122, 136–9
Huiru (Sino-Muslim literati), 4, 176–8, 180, 182, 211
Huizu see Hui/*Huizu*
Huizu Association (*Huizuhui*), 120
Huizu Yanjiu (*Journal of Hui Muslim [Minority] Studies*), 200, 213
Huizu Youth (*Huizu Qingnian*) magazine, 128–9, 130, 132

'ibadat, 64
Ikhwan (Brothers) 184, 193, 216, 217, 218–19
Indian Muslims, 159
indiginisation, 221
Internet
  advice, 204
  bookstores, 207
  Muslim websites, 208–9, 212, 225
Islamic Association (*Qingzhenhui*), 120
Islamic Association of Beijing (*Beijing Huijiao Hui*), 187
Islamic Association of China (*Zhongguo Yisilanjiao Xiehui/Yixie*), 7, 200, 202–3, 208, 214
Islamic bookstore (*Qingzhen shuju*), 207
Islamic Culture (journal), 221, 223 225
Islamic culture, secularised accounts, 211–15
Islamic law (Ar. *sharī'a*), 19, 124, 133, 154, 178, 215; *see also Tianfang sanzijing*
Islamic Neo-Confucians, 211
Islamic schools (*Yisilan xuexiao*), 172–3
Islamic Study City (*Yisilan xueshu cheng*), 207
isnad (authentication device), 71–2

Jāmī, 47
Japan, 162–4
  occupation by (1937–45), 127–8, 162, 171–93
  policies towards Islam, 186–91, 193
  study in, 111, 117
Japanese Army, 187–8, 190
Jesus, 34
Jiang Jieshi, 164
jiangjing (discussing/disputing the scriptures), 202
jie (fasting), 83
jiejing (explaining the scriptures), 202
Jin Diangui, 161–2
Jin Jitang, 2, 6, 109, 136–9
Jin Yijiu, 2
Jing Rizhen, 41
jingtang jiaoyu (scripture hall education), 36
Jining East and West Mosques, 190
Jinnah, Muhammad Ali, 129–30

Jintie zhuyi shuo (*On the Doctrine of Gold and Iron*, Yang, Du), 114–15
Judaism, 4–5

Ka'aba, 84–6, 88–9, 93, 98, 101
Kaituo magazine, 208
Kang Youxi, 207–8
karma, 87
Kawamura Kyōdō, 187
Koreans, 187

Laifu stone inscription, 17, 22
Lanzhou University, 223
law
 Qing statute, 19
 to protect Islam, 127, 193
 teaching of, 172
 see also Islamic Law (Ar. *sharī'a*)
Lawā'iḥ fī bayān maʿānī ʿirfāniyya (Jāmī), 47
Leslie, Donald D., 2
Li ahong (Li Xizhen), 190–1
Li Weihan, 139
Li Wenhan, 190
Li Zhenzhong, 154
Liang Yijun, 23
Lin Changxin, 157
Lin Song, 200, 213
Lin Zhongming, 163
Linxia Foreign Language Institute, 223, 225
Linxia Sino-Arabic School, 220, 223–4
Linxia, 205–7, 216–17
literacy, 57–8, 172–82, 186, 189
Liu Mengyang, 121–2, 132–4
Liu Sanjie, 19, 36
Liu Zhi, 5, 7, 22, 26, 34–51, 140
 education, 36–7
 and the hajj, 81–2, 86–93, 101–2
 influences/sources 42–8
 integration of Islam and Confucianism, 35–7, 40–51, 64, 124
 intellectual followers, 42, 197, 210–15
 Islamic law see *Tianfang sanzijing*
 legacy, 42–4
 the Three Teachings, 44, 58
 use of the term *Huihui* 124

works, 37; see also *Tianfang dianli*; *Tianfang sanzijing*; *Tianfang xingli*; *Tianfang zhisheng shilu*
Lu Jiuyuan (Xiangshan), 35
Lu You, 41, 45

Ma Anli, 94, 100
Ma Anliang, 214
Ma Dexin (Ma Fuchu), 5, 81–2, 184
 and the hajj, 93–101, 102
Ma Enxin, 205–6, 209, 218, 223
Ma Fuxiang, 153, 176
Ma Jian, 152–5, 157, 158–9, 162, 166, 199
Ma Lianyuan, 184
Ma Linyi, 120
Ma Minglian, 200
Ma Qiang, 201, 219
Ma Qixi, 50, 214
Ma Songting (Imam), 148–9, 180, 186, 187, 201–2
Ma Tong, 199
Ma Wanfu, 184, 216
Ma Xian, 203
Ma Xiulan, 206, 210
Ma Yulong, 224
Ma Yuming, 208–9
Ma Zhixin (Bahā al-Dīn, Baha Ahong), 206, 209, 217–18, 224
Ma Zhu, 5, 15–29, 37, 45–6, 197, 205
madrasa (*jingtang*) education, 191
 contemporary, 172–3
 curriculum, 171, 173, 185–6
 Japanese influence, 188–91
 modernisation, 182
 pre-modern, 178–9
 schools, 174
Malik, 67
Manchu dynasty, expulsion, 125
Manchu Qing, 111
Manchukuo, 187
Manchuria, Japanese invasion (1931), 127
Manchus, 36, 111, 113–14, 187
Manzu, 124–5
 ruling classes, 130
Mao Zedong, 139
Maqṣad-e Aqṣā (al-Nasafī), 47
Marco Polo Bridge Incident (1937), 149

Matsumoto Akirō, 2
al-Mawdudi, Abu al-'Ala', 218
Mecca, 5, 86, 88, 93, 101–2, 181, 186, 216
 journey to, 96–8
 see also hajj
Medina, 216
Mencius, 26, 35, 42, 83
metaphysics, 41, 43, 45, 100, 200
Metaphysics of Islam, 37, 48
Miao, 113
Min Shengguang, 214
Mina, 90
Ming dynasty, 15, 36, 44, 107, 171, 173–4
Mingde High School (Mingde Zhongxue), 148, 179
Mingde jing (*Scripture of Bright Virtue*, Ma Dexin), 93–101
minzu paradigm, 107, 109–10, 121, 124, 126–40, 212, 226
minzu, shaoshu (national minorities), 7, 212; see also Hui/*Huizu*
Mirsād al-ʿIbād min al-mabdā ilaʾlmaʿād (al-Razi), 22, 47, 175
Mongolia, 125
Mongols, 113–14, 139, 173, 187
Mengzu, 124–5
mu'amalat, 64
Muhammad, Prophet, 20, 22, 34, 184
 the *dao* of, 65–6, 68, 72–5
 integration with Confucius, 35, 42, 51
 position of the descendants of, 18
 tomb of, 90, 98
Mukden Incident (1931), 187
Murata, Sachiko, 2, 5, 9, 26
al-Mursī, Abu'l-'Abbas, 98
Muslim Awakening (*Xinghuipian*), 111, 117, 177
Muslim Brotherhood, 166
Muslim Educational Association of Students (*Liudong Qingzhen Jiaoyuhui*), 111–12, 177
Muslim intellectuals
 academics, 199–201
 and Chinese Islamic tradition, 215
 Laoshis (scholars without positions), 205–10, 217
 followers of Abd al-Wahhab, 215–20, 225
 followers of Liu Zhi, 197, 211–15
 middle way/reconciliatory, 220–5
 religious scholars, 201–5
 scholars (*xuezhe*), 209
 women 210
Muslim Scholarly Association Monthly (*Zhongghuo Huijiao Xuehui Yuekan*), 122
Muslim uprisings, 184, 199

Na Zhong, 152, 155–6, 160, 162–3
Nakada Yoshinobu, 2
Nanjing, 35–7, 42, 46, 50, 58, 61, 86
al-Nasafi, 47
Nasser, Gamal Abdel 224
nationalism, 6, 108, 114, 123, 138, 162, 163, 164, 220–1
Nationalist Party (Guomindang, GMD), 6, 149, 180, 185–6
 Huizu policy, 122–3, 127–8, 133, 139, 193
 Northern Expedition, 122
 retreat, 178, 179, 187, 189, 191
 support for overseas students, 163–6
Neo-Confucianism, 17–29, 45, 47, 185, 197, 211, 213
 cosmogony, 23
 daotong, 71–2, 76
 de-canonisation, 6
 Ma Zhu and, 17, 20–9
 metaphysics, 41, 43
 normative culture, 57
 texts, 17, 47
nian (remembrance), 83
9/11, 220
Norms and Rituals of Islam see *Tianfang dianli*

Old Testament, 16
Opening Love for Ritual and Law (*Lifa Qi'ai*, Ma Anli), 94

Pang Shiqian, 158–9, 160–1, 165–6, 199
People's Republic of China (PRC)
 education in, 179, 185, 191, 193
 Huizu in, 9, 50, 107, 140
 recognition of Islam, 7, 211
 and the Xidaotang, 214

Persian learning, 171–93
  ahongs' knowledge of, 178
  contemporary, 172–3
  maintenance of, 185–6
  exclusion of from curriculum, 183
  history of, 173–5
  pre-modern era, 175–9
  and reformist schooling, 179–84
pilgrimage *see* hajj
Polo, Marco, 2
Protestantism (*Yesujiao*), 118, 222

Qalanders, 19
al-Qaradawi, Yusuf, 218–19, 224
Qi Xueyi, 209
Qianheyan mosque, 217
Qing dynasty
  Education, 6, 58, 61, 176
  establishment of, 35–6, 71
  Huizu, 110–11, 114–15, 128, 131, 140
  legal culture, 55–7, 70, 76
  open door policy, 181
  suppression of Muslim uprisings, 175–6
  texts, 213
Qingzhen zhinan (guide to Islam, Ma Zhu), 16–21, 29
Qingzhenjiao (Islam), 118, 121
Qur'ān, 17, 23, 36, 43, 146, 184, 193, 203, 208, 220, 223
  cosmogenesis, 16, 45
  explaining, 202
  interpretations, 179, 225
  Islamic law, 60, 62, 70, 72, 75, 83–4, 136
  knowledge, of 177, 182
  learning, 171, 173, 215–16
  pilgrimage, 92–3
  translation of, 8, 148, 154, 178, 180, 183, 186, 200
Qurbān (*guerbang*), 91–2
Qutb, Sayyid, 224

Ramadān, 86, 124
Rāzī, Najm al-Din, 22, 47
Religious Affairs Office (*Zongjiao Ju*), 7
renmin, 111
Rāzī, Najim al-Din, 47

Republic of China
  benefit of Islamic teaching for and support for students, 151, 162–6
  establishment of, 114
  Huizu in, 3, 50, 120, 140
  see also Nationalist Party
Revolution of 1911, 114, 125
Revolutionary Alliance *see* Tongmenghui
Ricci, Matteo, 2, 5, 21
Roman Catholicism (*Tianzhujiao*), 4–5, 24, 118, 222
Russian Revolution, 181

Saguchi Tōru, 2
Sailaifeiye see Salafis/Salafism
Sakuma Teijirō, 187
Salafis/Salafism, 198, 203, 215–17, 220–1, 223
  historical *Salafiyya*, 193, 215–17, 219
  Neo-Salafis, 217–20, 224–5
Salar *minzu*, 212
Santai (Three Elevations), 216
Saudi Arabia, 163
  influence on intellectuals, 203, 215–18, 223
  scholars (*xuezhe*), 209
  Japanese, 2
Scripture of Bright Virtue see *Mingde jing*
Sha Shanyu (Shou Yu), 122
Shaanxi, 112
Shafi, 67
al-Shāfi'ī, 98
Shan Guoqing, 179
Shandong school (of Islamic education), 185
Shanghai, 127, 147, 180
Shanghai Islamic Normal School (*Shanghai Yisilan Shifan xuexiao*), 179
Shanghai Islamic Teachers' College, 123, 148–9, 179
sharī'a see Islamic law
sheng (sage), 35
shi (alms giving), 83
Shi Zhizhou, 187, 189
Shi'ites, 219
Shigekawa, Major Hidekazu, 187
Shigekawa Agency (J. *Shigekawa kikan*), 187
Shijiacun mosque, 186

Shou Jin, 119–20, 125
Sidian Yaohui (*Essence of the Four Canons*, Ma Dexin), 99–101
Sidike, 120
Siku quanshu (Compendium of the Four Treasures), 48–50, 211
  Annotated Catalogue, 48–50
Sino-Muslims
  conservatism, 38
  genetic history, 36, 137–8
  religious and national identities, 161–2
  see also Hui/Huizu
Sino-Arabic *pinyin* (*xiaoerjing*), 181
Sino-Arabic schools (*Zhong-A xuexiao*), 172–3, 216
Sino-Egyptian relations, 164–5
Sino-Japanese War (1937), 111, 149, 162–4, 189
Song dynasty, 35
Stalin, Joseph, 137, 139
Sufis/Sufism, 5, 100, 178, 215, 220
  anti-Sufi ideology, 186
  influence on *Han kitāb* scholars, 7, 19, 44–5, 47
  influence on learning, 173, 182, 184
  master (*shaykh/murshid*), 175
  in northwest China, 175, 214
  orders (Ar. *turuq*), 175, 216
  spiritual concepts, 45, 173, 177, 181–2, 184–5, 190–2
  texts, 192, 193, 207
Sun Yat-sen, 111, 115, 126, 137
Sunna, 215, 220
Sunni Islam 36, 56, 218, 219; *see also* Hanafi school of jurisprudence
surnames, 131

Tabligh movement, 220
Taliban, 220
Tanaka Ippei, 187
Tang Yichen, 188
Taoism *see* Daoism
Tatar Muslims, 187
tawhīd (oneness of God), 184, 188, 215
Tazaka Kōdō, 2
Thirteen Classics curriculum (*shisan-ben jing*), 171, 177, 179, 185, 191, 193

Three Teachings (*sanjiao*), 4, 44, 46, 58
Tianfang chunqiu (*Islamic Spring and Autumn Annals*, Liu Zhi), 37
Tianfang dianli (*Norms and Rituals of Islam*, Liu Zhi), 37–8, 40, 41, 44, 48–50
  Islamic law, 56–8, 64
  pilgrimage, 86, 88
  pilgrimage rituals, 89–90
Tianfang sanzijing (*The Three Character Classic of Islam*, Liu Zhi), 4, 37, 55–76
  audience, 55–62
  interpretation of Islamic Law, 62–76
  reception of, 61–2, 74
Tianfang xingli (*Metaphysics of Islam*, Liu Zhi), 37–9, 41, 43, 47
Tianfang zhisheng shilu (*True Record of the Ultimate Sage of Islam*, Liu Zhi), 37–8, 43–4, 48
Tianfang zimu jieyi (*Explaining the Meaning of Arabic Letters*, Liu Zhi), 37
Tianjin, 110, 185, 186, 189–91
Tianmucun, 172, 191, 192
Tibetans, 113–14, 124–5, 214
Tong Jili, 61
tongbao (compatriots), 111
Tongmenghui (Revolutionary Alliance), 111, 120, 176–7
True Record of the Ultimate Sage of Islam *see* Tianfang zhisheng shilu
Tunisia, 225
Turkic Muslims
  far western, 136
  of Xinjiang, 109, 114–15, 121, 124, 160, 198, 201
Turks (Tujue/Tu'erqi), 124, 130, 135

umma (transnational Islamic congregation), 8, 67, 81, 87, 92–3, 101–2, 151, 156, 157
Utsunomiya Tarō, General, 186
Uyghurs, 117, 136–7, 212; *see also* Huihe

Voll, John, 157

wahdat al-wujud (unity of being), 173, 181–2, 185, 190–2

al-Wahhab, Abd, 7–8
    intellectual followers of, 197–8, 203, 210, 215–20
Wahhabi-Salafi movement, 217–21, 224
Wahhabism, 215–25
Wahhabiyya, 198
Wang Daiyu, 4, 5, 16, 124, 140, 197
    God metaphor, 22
    and the hajj, 81–6, 101
    worldview and influence on Liu Zhi, 45–6
Wang Enrong, 190
Wang Jingzhai, 6, 122, 136, 147, 178, 180, 181, 186, 187, 189, 208
Wang Jixian, 61
Wang Kuan (Imam), 119–21, 125, 147
Wang Mengyang, 122
Wang Ruilang, 187
Wang Shiming, 162, 163
Wang Yingqi, 190
Wang Yousan, 120
women
    education of, 188, 214, 218
    intellectuals, 210
    Islamic law and, 59–60
    place in society, 224–5
World Islamic Conference (Palestine, 1932), 158, 160
Wu Sangui, 18
Wu Zixian, 16, 21, 22
wudian (five social norms), 64
wugong (five ritual endeavours/Five Meritorious Acts), 64, 82–7, 99–100
Wuhuaguo, 212–13, 222, 225
Wuxueyuan (Garden of Military Studies), 36
wuzu gonghe (republic of five nations/peoples), 114, 119, 132

xian (famous/learned worthies), 99–100
xiaoerjin(g)
    Arabic-script transliteration, 5
    see also Sino-Arabic pinyin
xiaosheng/xiaozi (young student), 59
Xidaotang ('Hall of the Western Way'), 50, 214–15

Xing Fengsu, 208
Xinjiang, 112, 114, 117, 120
Xinwangsi mosque, 217
Xu Xiake, 17
Xu Yuanzheng, 40
Xue Wenbo (Da'ud), 128–38

Yang Du, 114–15
Yang Guiping, 28
Yang Huaizhong, 2, 200, 211
Yang Feilu, 41, 47, 56–7
Yang, Sishi, 167
Yin Boqing, 6, 122–6, 136, 137
Yisima'er (Ismā'īl) *see* Zhang Chengqian
Yu Ke, 150–2
Yu Zhengui, 2, 200, 211
Yuan Guozuo, 5, 39, 42–4, 48, 61–3, 66–7, 70, 72
Yuan Ruqi, 39–40, 61
Yuan Shikai, 114, 121–2, 125
Yugong (journal), 136
Yunnan, 17–21, 43 110–12, 117, 148, 152, 164, 173–5, 179, 182, 184, 200, 203, 205, 218, 223
Yunnanese Muslims, 111

Zangzu (*Tubote*), 124–5; *see also* Tibetans
Zhang Bingduo, 162
Zhang Chengqian (Yisima'er/Ismā'īl), 208, 225
Zhang Weizhen (Hange), 209, 223–5
Zhang Zai, 16
Zhao Zhongqi, 177
Zhengjiao zhenquan (*True Commentary on the Orthodox Teaching*, Wang Daiyu), 4, 16
Zhengzong Aiguobao (*The [Orthodox] Patriotic Daily*), 115–21
Zhenjing zhaowei (*The Subtleties of Illumination in the True Classic*, Liu Zhi), 37
Zhonghua minzu, 123, 127, 135
Zhou Dunyi, 17, 22, 23–4
Zwemer, Samuel, 184

EU representative:
Easy Access System Europe
Mustamäe tee 50, 10621 Tallinn, Estonia
Gpsr.requests@easproject.com